THE ART OF COMPILATION

Before you start to read this book, take this moment to think about making a donation to punctum books, an independent non-profit press,

@ https://punctumbooks.com/support/

If you're reading the e-book, you can click on the image below to go directly to our donations site. Any amount, no matter the size, is appreciated and will help us to keep our ship of fools afloat. Contributions from dedicated readers will also help us to keep our commons open and to cultivate new work that can't find a welcoming port elsewhere. Our adventure is not possible without your support.

Vive la Open Access.

Fig. 1. Detail from Hieronymus Bosch, *Ship of Fools* (1490–1500)

THE ART OF COMPILATION: MANUSCRIPTS AND NETWORKS IN THE EARLY MEDIEVAL LATIN WEST. Copyright © 2025 by the authors and editors. This work carries a Creative Commons BY-NC-SA 4.0 International license, which means that you are free to copy and redistribute the material in any medium or format, and you may also remix, transform, and build upon the material, as long as you clearly attribute the work to the authors (but not in a way that suggests the authors or punctum books endorses you and your work), you do not use this work for commercial gain in any form whatsoever, and that for any remixing and transformation, you distribute your rebuild under the same license. http://creativecommons.org/licenses/by-nc-sa/4.0/

First published in 2024 by Gracchi Books, Binghamton, NY,
an imprint of punctum books, Earth, Milky Way.
https://punctumbooks.com

ISBN-13: 978-1-68571-158-0 (print)
ISBN-13: 978-1-68571-159-7 (ePDF)

DOI: 10.53288/494.1.00

LCCN: 2024945178
Library of Congress Cataloging Data is available from the Library of Congress

Editing: SAJ & Eileen A. Fradenburg Joy
Book design: Hatim Eujayl
Cover design: Vincent W.J. van Gerven Oei
Cover photograph: Michael J. Kelly, Reccopolis, Spain

spontaneous acts of scholarly combustion

"Too many echoes, not enough voices."
— Cornel West

Anna Dorofeeva &
Michael J. Kelly (eds.)

The Art of Compilation

Manuscripts and Networks in the
Early Medieval Latin West

Contents

Preface
Medieval Manuscript as Antihistorical Object?   19
Michael J. Kelly

Introduction   29
Anna Dorofeeva

KNOWLEDGE SELECTION

Historische Ordnung or Just a Mess? Tracking Dossiers
in Early Medieval Canon Law Collections   45
Michael Eber

Carolingian Collections of Gregory the Great's Letters
and the So-Called *Collectio Pauli*   81
Lucia Castaldi and Laura Pani

Creating the Past in the Carolingian Book of Virgil   119
Sinéad O'Sullivan

MATERIAL REPRESENTATION

The Materiality of Innovation: Formats and Dimensions of
the *Etymologiae* of Isidore of Seville in the Early
Middle Ages   157
Evina Stein

Commented Editions of the Bible in Carolingian Europe:
Otfrid's Approach to the Book of Isaiah 209
Cinzia Grifoni

Rechtsblöcke, Scribes, and Layout Strategies in a
Ninth-Century Legal Collection: Modena, Biblioteca
Capitolare MS O. I. 2 251
Thom Gobbitt

SCRIBAL AGENCY

Sammelhandschriften and the *Breuiarium librorum*
in Sankt Gallen 728 295
Mark Stansbury

Sharing Alphabets: Early Medieval Grammatical
Miscellanies and Their Networks 343
Elizabeth P. Archibald

What Is a Vademecum? The Social Logic of
Early Medieval Compilation 369
Anna Dorofeeva

Afterword
Manuscripts as Layered and Entangled Objects.
New Ways to Explore the Manuscript Book 427
Mariken Teeuwen

Contributors 445

Editors' Acknowledgments

This volume is the product of years of collaborative work. I'm very grateful to the participants of the original small workshop in late 2018 which first developed the concept of compilation with regard to early medieval manuscript culture: Georgios Boudalis, Lucia Castaldi, Sinéad O'Sullivan, Laura Pani, Mark Stansbury, and Mariken Teeuwen. The impulse for the workshop came from conversations in Leiden with Erik Kwakkel, which inspired and set the course of my research for years to come. My grateful thanks go to him and his family.

The 2019 conference hosted papers by Elizabeth P. Archibald, Lucia Castaldi, Michael Eber, Thom Gobbitt, Cinzia Grifoni, Julia Aguilar Miquel, Erik Niblaeus, Irene O'Daly, Sinéad O'Sullivan, Laura Pani, Irene van Renswoude, Mark Stansbury, Evina Stein, Mariken Teeuwen, and Arthur Westwell. This volume is the result of the innovative ideas of these scholars, all of whom helped to shape the research strands presented here, though not all were able to contribute a paper for publication.

The Practices of Knowledge Selection workshop and succeeding conference could not have taken place without the generous funding of the Gladys Krieble Delmas Foundation, Networks & Neighbours, and the UCD College of Arts and Humanities; and without the support of Roy Flechner, Emma Lyons, University College Dublin, and the Irish Research Council, who provided the assistance, space, and freedom to work on challenging ideas. My thanks, finally, to the anonymous peer reviewers for their constructive criticism and useful comments and the editorial team of punctum books for their assiduous care.

—Anna Dorofeeva

I exist because of the early Middle Ages. They are an ontological method and their appearance grounds the infinite into the finite and provides meaning. The contributors to this volume, the team at punctum books, my fellow editor and conference organizer, and all of the funders and space providers mentioned by her have with this method spliced the infinite and made it manifest on the page, as manuscripts unite, and as being and soul, mind and love illuminate the Aleph into which we gaze at the past and find meaning in the universal present.

—Michael J. Kelly

Figures

Figure 4.1: The distribution of page tailles of the surviving early medieval manuscripts transmitting the encyclopedic *Etymologiae* and other manuscripts.

Figure 4.2: The distribution of page tailles of the surviving early medieval manuscripts transmitting the encyclopedic *Etymologiae,* the non encyclopedic *Etymologiae* in grammatical compendia, and the non-encyclopedic *Etymologiae* in pastoral collections.

Figure 5.1: Wolfenbüttel, Herzog August Bibliothek, MS Guelf. 33. Weiss., fol. 5r.

Figure 5.2: Wolfenbüttel, Herzog August Bibliothek, MS Guelf. 49. Weiss., fol. 4r.

Figure 5.3: Wolfenbüttel, Herzog August Bibliothek, MS Guelf. 33 Weiss., fol. 18v.

Figure 5.4: Wolfenbüttel, Herzog August Bibliothek, MS Guelf. 33 Weiss., fol. 38r.

Figure 6.1: Comparison of main contributing hands in Modena, Biblioteca Capitolare, O. I. 2, fol. 53v [51v]: hand 1 (main scribal hand); hand 3 (rubrics); and hand 2 (running heading).

Figure 6.2: Comparison of main contributing hands in Modena, Biblioteca Capitolare, O. I. 2, fol. 54r [52r]: hand 3 (main scribal hand, rubrics) and hand 2 (running heading).

Figure 6.3: Transition from *Lex Baiuvariorum* to Charlemagne's capitularies, Modena, Biblioteca Capitolare, MS O. I. 2, fol. 154r [152r].

Abbreviations

The names of manuscript-holding institutions are generally abbreviated in classmarks throughout the volume for ease of reading. These abbreviations are provided here as a reference aid.

BAV: Biblioteca Apostolica Vaticana
Bb: Burgerbibliothek
BC: Biblioteca Capitolare
BdB: Biblioteca della Badia
BiSM: Bibliothèque interuniversitaire, Section Médecine
BLb: Badische Landesbibliothek
BnF: Bibliothèque nationale de France
BmSM: Bibliothèque municipale Suzanne Martinet
BodL: Bodleian Library
BSb: Bayerische Staatsbibliothek
EDD: Erzbischöfliche Diözesan- und Dombibliothek
Fb: Forschungsbibliothek
HAB: Herzog August Bibliothek
Sb: Staatsbibliothek
Stb: Stiftsbibliothek
Ub: Universiteitsbibliotheek

Dates

Manuscript dates have been represented using the following shorthand throughout the volume. These date ranges appear very precise but are to be taken as indicative only: they standardize the representation of very diverse usage across a variety of catalogues and other scholarly works produced across large geographical and chronological distances. Readers are advised to consult these original works in cases of doubt.

8th century, ¾	751–775
8th century, 4/4	776–800
8th century, 2/2	751–800
8th century, ex.	785–800
8th/9th century, c. 800	790–810
9th century, in.	801–815
9th century, ¼	801–825
9th century, ⅓	801–833
9th century, ½	801–850
9th century, 2/4	826–850
9th century, med.	840–860
9th century, ⅔	834–865
9th century, ¾	851–875
9th century, 4/4	876–900
9th century, 2/2	851–900
9th century, 3/3	867–900
9th century, ex.	885–900

9th/10th century, c. 900	890–910
10th century, in.	901–915
10th century	901–1000

PREFACE

Medieval Manuscript as Antihistorical Object?

Michael J. Kelly

History creates objects of investigation, that is, we historians establish pasts as our objects of study: pasts and facts do not simply exist out there for us to find. Historians form the category "history" and ascribe to it contents: past, facts, events, and objects. We manifest objects: we present items as historical objects, as relics, as proof, as truths, as evidence of a real item for our category "history," and within that a subcategory: object. Further classification categorizes our objects: for example, texts, aqueducts, psyches, landscapes, ceramics, tropes, fossilized vegetation, ideas, and manuscripts. Each type of object works to prove, firstly, that the primary object of the category "history," past, is real, but also that the category "history" itself is real.

The next stage in the progress of historical research should be a reaching beyond simply this—beyond proving that our category is real and that its contents had meaning at various moments: the next stage is to answer the "so what?" In that way, the historical object, such as the medieval manuscript, can satiate the old-school historian who sees their job as an archaeologist digging up pre-existing, ready-made facts; can satiate the neo-Rankean/neo-Objectivist object-oriented ontologist and speculist who, not wanting to be either the former or a postmodern-

19

ist, says there must be universal truths, must be objective facts whose status as such transcends my consciousness; and it also can satiate what I call the antihistorian.[1] The antihistorian sees genuine History as a necessarily radical act that embraces the emancipatory Event as the starting point of historical discourse: that is, History begins with the shattering of history (the imagined "natural" order of things, of time, of space-time, of "human nature," etc.). In other words, the category "history" is a repository of the (once) revolutionary.

As such, as its core, the historical act is post-Eventual; it happens after a historical situation has been shattered or has been shown to be no longer sustainable as reigning ideology, that is, the prevailing truth of a society, for example, capitalism in the US today,[2] or at a much more local scale: a personal relationship, a family situation, a community dynamic, an environmental state of being, a political party's status quo, or any other established historical situation. After the new Idea has emerged and has found traction in disrupting a historical situation, the antihistorian historian, acting as faithful subject to the Event — that

---

[1] For more on my concept of the antihistorian, see Michael J. Kelly, "Preface: Truth & Anti-History," in *Vera Lex Historiae: Constructions of Truth in Medieval Historical Narrative,* ed. Catalin Taranu and Michael J. Kelly (Earth: punctum books, 2022), 13–33, and Michael J. Kelly, "Approaching a Non-Modern Historical Theory: Catholic Theology, Alain Badiou, and Antihistory," in *Understanding Badiou, Understanding Modernism,* ed. Arka Chattopadhyay and Arthur Rose (London: Bloomsbury, 2024), 153–67. On the concept of the "Event," see Michael J. Kelly, *Introducing Alain Badiou: A Graphic Guide,* illus. Piero (London: Icon Books, 2014); Alain Badiou, *Theory of the Subject,* trans. Bruno Bosteels (New York: Bloomsbury, 2013); and Alain Badiou, *The Rebirth of History: Times of Riots and Uprisings,* trans. Gregory Elliot (New York: Verso, 2012).

[2] For further reading on this point, I recommend Branko Milanović's *Capitalism, Alone: The Future of the System that Rules the World* (Cambridge: Belknap Press, 2019), which, although critical of capitalism, ultimately cannot see a world past it. As Slavoj Žižek is fond of saying, Americans can imagine the end of the entire planet and of humanity itself via nuclear disaster, God, or environmental catastrophe, but cannot imagine the end of capitalism: this is ideology at its finest. You can find this sentiment across Žižek's writings and talks, but see, for example, Slavoj Žižek, *First as Tragedy, Then as Farce* (New York: Verso, 2009).

is, believing it to be a real event that has affected change (in thought, in materiality, in logos, etc.) — interrogates and ultimately curates a narrative of the shattering of the objective, that is, the systemic, ways of being in a present, via the antihistorical non-object's becoming a historical object.

In complement to this — and without which the antihistorian would be impossible — the historian typically works to present the non-Eventual object to elicit the existing, whether that existing was recent or in the chronologically distant past. The historian as such thinks not ontologically but epistemologically. The aim is to reconstruct an imagined objectivity of the past, that is, a historical situation, an ideological moment with its peculiar objects and other items. The contributions of this volume in a surrealistically elucidative way interrogate, with eyes toward the reconstruction of an "a" or of a "the," several examples of antihistorical acts, of scribes and others finding a truth (in a narrative) and employing it for reasons other than to confirm (although examples of the opposite are shown below as well), even to shatter. A result of this is that those once antihistorians with their actions and their products have become historical objects, objects in the historian's category of history. And yet, in some cases, as per the emancipatory activity of historians of this volume, these antihistorical acts, with their entangled and miscellaneous manuscript compilations have their radical antihistoricalness re-actualized, that is, the universal potential of the singularity of these compilers' actions, their manuscripts, their Idea, revived.

If these medieval manuscripts are examples of antihistorical moments, if they served as post- and then pre-historical objects — that is, challenges to an existing objectivity that were then, in a different flash in space, subsumed into a new commonsense by the historian — could they also have had (and have?) represented a generic appeal, could they have been (or are?) hedonistic objects, objects which encapsulate desire? Karl Marx argued that

> The mania for possessions is possible without money; but greed itself a product of a definite social development, not natural, as opposed to historical. [...] Hedonism in its general form and miserliness are the two particular forms of monetary greed. Hedonism in the abstract presupposes an object which possesses all pleasures in potentiality. Abstract hedonism realizes that function of money in which it is the material representative of wealth [...]. In order to maintain it as such, it must sacrifice all relationship to the objects of particular needs, must abstain, in order to satisfy the need of greed for money as such.[3]

Was the "art" of compilation ever a hedonistic impulse manifested in the manuscript? I think we could read some instances of the manuscripts discussed in this volume as such, as objects with unlimited hedonistic potential, a sort of alchemy in a period long before capitalism and the singularization of money as *the* hedonistic object: the Gospels compilation, for example, which, if possessed and consumed properly, afforded the fullness of human potential, free will, even if its anti-hero protagonist, Jesus, had been turned by the Catholic Church into a fetish, a what *could* be but never *should* be in "this" world.[4] The repeated creation of entangled manuscripts speaks to a desire for pleasure that found fruition in these objects, whether this desire was for the object to serve as a confirmation of the imagined "natural order," that is, the present situation, the "universal" history, or whether it served to upset a local situation.

In his contribution, Michael Eber, in exploring the relationship between manuscripts, canonical collections, and historiography, shows how each of the three manuscripts that he

---

3 Karl Marx, *Grundrisse* (New York: Penguin, 1993), 222–23.
4 See Mark Stansbury's contribution in this volume for discussion of the Gospels as early *Sammelhandschriften*. On Jesus as a fetish, see Michael J. Kelly, "The Logic of Control: Postulating a Visigothic Ontology of Human Being," in *Leadership, Cohesion and Identity in the Visigothic Kingdom,* ed. Dolores Castro and Fernando Ruchesi (Amsterdam: Amsterdam University Press, 2023), 63–101.

studies represents, I would say, a not-yet fully realized Heideggerian "in itself," each reacting to a localized historical situation and potential caesura in it. The manuscripts demonstrate the importance of authorities to narrate a schism, a potential real historical Event. The papal letters of Vatican City, Biblioteca Apostolica Vaticana, MS Reg. lat. 1997, of Leo I, in particular demonstrate this, serving as warnings against clerics who refused to denounce Pelagianism, one of the most potent threats to the ancient logics of wealth, private property, and plutocracy.[5]

Complementing Eber's demonstration of how early medieval compilers were sometimes historians in the form of anti-antihistorians intervening in the trajectory of the Church and its history, which included the fetishization of Jesus, Laura Pani and Lucia Castaldi effectively reveal Gregory the Great's becoming an iconic fetish, an image frozen in time, made to perpetually repeat itself, and therefore displaced from (political) agency in any present. The authority endowed to the figure ironically deflated its own potential as its Idea but opened it up to being an Idea that could find different manifestations in entangled manuscripts.

In examining the Carolingian book of Virgil, Sinéad O'Sullivan says that "the materials in the book lavish attention on Troy, Rome, and Christ," that is, a Trinitarian Event. And, in using Caelius Sedulius's *Carmen Paschale,* O'Sullivan shows the centrality of the Christ Event in their human history, but, and here I think is the key, the Event is distorted, sublimated into the logics of kingship, Virgil being used to link Christianity (supposed as its real, former self as religion, not, I would say, itself as Catholic ideology) and emperorship. In the manuscript collection that O'Sullivan explores, we see ultimately, again, the sublimation of a once radical Idea, the Christ Event, into the "natural" flow of "universal" history.

Moving the volume from its section on knowledge to materiality, Evina Stein shows the separation of a text, the Visigothic

---

5   On the radicality of the Jesus Event, see again Kelly, "The Logic of Control," and Kelly, "Visigothic Catholicism as Secular Ideology."

etymologies, from its context, effectively becoming a nostalgic icon of the Visigothic past in medieval Spain versus its recontextualization elsewhere. That is, the former manuscripts operated, I would say, to occult the past and the latter to re-actualize etymologies as source Ideas for alternative historical situations: the scribes and compilers, the historians, in the former as fetishists and in the latter as faithful or reactionary subjects, that is, ones who recognized the truths as such and either embraced or denied them.

Cinzia Grifoni narrates a real Event: Biblical exegesis via the first recognized German author, Otfrid. In her essay, Grifoni explores, though, not the originality of the language of Otfrid but rather his imaginative exegetical activities through established language, new ideas safely encased within the existing historical situation so as not to suggest a break from that logical set, that world. But does Otfrid act to subvert the historical language and so situation, or reaffirm them as the natural course? Does the manuscript of Otfrid's commentaries on Isaiah act as confirmation of the historical situation, as a sort of *objet petit a* there to confirm the ideals of the existing situation without their attainability, or does it act as historical object in the radical sense? In contrast, the manuscript collection of early medieval law codes of the West, *sans* the Visigothic material, that Thom Gobbitt analyzes seems to suggest that such a law collection was used to confirm and perhaps apply, that is, re-affirm, established regulations, as opposed to narrate alternative ones.

So far, whether viewed from an epistemological or archival-material perspective, the entangled manuscripts of the earlier Middle Ages demonstrate antihistorical and historical commitments. The final set of essays stare directly into the evental and historical void, with Mark Stansbury, Elizabeth Archibald, and Anna Dorofeeva splicing the volume at scribal agency. Stansbury examines a list of books from the ninth century now in a St. Gallen manuscript to reveal the phenomenon of *Sammelhandschriften*, manuscripts that are unique in content and form and therefore narrative, and so potentially historical as non-object(ive) objects, or, that is, antihistorical historical objects.

Archibald interrogates medieval *grammatica* and miscellaneous manuscripts. The compilers of these manuscripts were free and willing to upset stable texts in order to create new meaning, and they did so in ways that preserved the universality of the Idea of the core material: "Variety and independent approaches to compilation, rather than a drive for standardization and deference to authority, characterize early medieval *grammatica* manuscripts," Archibald notes, adding that "the *grammatica* manuscripts also reveal the complex contours of a robust and enduring intellectual network *transcending* institution and place." Anna Dorofeeva enriches the thesis by eliciting the communality of production beyond the Idea and the individual or select few, with the "vademecum" as proof of coordination, entanglement, and the communal as central to the personal.

This volume is the outcome of the collective activity of colleagues collaborating in the spirit of true communality. The journey to this point began in earnest — but okay, yes, when an experience really "starts" is one of those endless philosophical conundrums — during two research events at University College Dublin titled "Practices of Knowledge Selection in the Early Middle Ages." The first event was a workshop there on October 20, 2018 with almost thirty presenters and discussants, and the second was a conference that ran for two days, May 24–25, 2019, and had around twenty speakers. The workshop introduced the research that would eventually become the contributions to this volume, while the conference presented that research as it had progressed since the suggestions of the workshop discussants and further along the road to this publication.

Anna Dorofeeva and I organized this research series with the help of a generous grant from The Gladys Krieble Delmas Foundation, funding from Networks and Neighbours (N&N), and the wider financial and in-house assistance of Anna's then institution, the College of Arts and the Humanities at UCD, as well as my home institution, Binghamton University, SUNY. As we did with the volume, we ran the events with a commitment to democratizing academia, and the humanities in particular. As such, all of the events were completely free to attend and all of its outcomes are free to access. This volume is being published by Gracchi Books, which is an imprint of punctum books. As an imprint of punctum books, Gracchi is a registered non-profit organization and a no-fees, Open Access publisher in which authors maintain equal rights to their work. Moreover, authors do not pay to publish, and all publications are freely accessible in digital format immediately and permanently. Print books are available at low cost.

Bibliography

Badiou, Alain. *Theory of the Subject*. Translated by Bruno Bosteels. New York: Bloomsbury, 2013.
———. *The Rebirth of History: Times of Riots and Uprisings*. Translated by Gregory Elliot. London: Verso, 2012.
Kelly, Michael J. "Approaching a Non-Modern Historical Theory: Catholic Theology, Alain Badiou, and Antihistory." In *Understanding Badiou, Understanding Modernism,* edited by Arka Chattopadhyay and Arthur Rose, 153–67. London: Bloomsbury, 2024.
———. *Introducing Alain Badiou: A Graphic Guide*. Illustrated by Piero. London: Icon Books, 2014.
———. "Preface: Truth & Anti-History." In *Vera Lex Historiae: Constructions of Truth in Medieval Historical Narrative,* edited by Catalin Taranu and Michael J. Kelly, 1–15. Earth: punctum books, 2022.
———. "The Logic of Control: Postulating a Visigothic Ontology of Human Being." In *Leadership, Social Cohesion, and Identity in Late Antique Spain and Gaul (500–700),* edited by Dolores Castro and Fernando Ruchesi, 63–101. Amsterdam: Amsterdam University Press, 2023.
Marx, Karl. *Grundrisse*. Translated by Martin Nicolaus. London: Penguin, 1993.
Milanović, Branko. *Capitalism, Alone: The Future of the System that Rules the World*. Cambridge: Belknap Press, 2019. DOI: 10.4159/9780674242852.
Žižek, Slavoj, *First as Tragedy, Then as Farce*. New York: Verso, 2009.

Introduction

Anna Dorofeeva

A significant outcome of the past seventy years of research in early medieval manuscript studies, which have changed our view of codices as simple containers of texts to living archaeological artifacts, is the impact on our understanding of compilation.[1] Scholarship in fields as diverse as diplomatic and liturgi-

---

1 To name only a few: John J. Contreni, "The Carolingian Renaissance: Education and Literary Culture," in *The New Cambridge Medieval History 2: c. 700–c. 900*, ed. Rosamond McKitterick (Cambridge; Cambridge University Press, 1995); Rosamond McKitterick, *The Carolingians and the Written Word* (Cambridge: Cambridge University Press, 1989); François Dolbeau, "'La miscellanea informale e le comunità intellettuali nel medioevo latino': Introduction au colloque," *Filologia mediolatina. Rivista della Fondazione Ezio Franceschini* 19 (2012): 1–7; Claudio Leonardi, *Letteratura latina medievale (secoli VI–XV). Un manuale*, Millennio medievale 31 (Florence: SISMEL Edizioni del Galluzzo, 2002); and Mary Garrison, "The *Collectanea* and Medieval Florilegia," in *Collectanea Pseudo-Bedae*, ed. Martha Bayless and Michael Lapidge, Scriptores Latini Hiberniae 14 (Dublin: Dublin Institute for Advanced Studies, 1998), 42–83. Of particular note is the Dutch and Italian project "Storehouses of Wholesome Learning: Accumulation and Dissemination of Encyclopedic Knowledge in the Early Middle Ages," which resulted in four volumes: Rolf H. Bremmer and Kees Dekker, eds., *Foundations of Learning: The Transfer of Encyclopaedic Knowledge in the Early Middle Ages*, Mediaevalia Groningana New Series 9 (Leuven: Peeters, 2007); Rolf H. Bremmer and Kees Dekker, eds., *Fruits of Learning: The Transfer of Encyclopaedic Knowledge in the Early Middle Ages*, Mediaevalia Groningana New Series 21 (Leuven: Peeters, 2016); Concetta Giliberto and

cal, monastic, and musical history has shown conclusively that compilation was not the relatively mechanical work of semi-literate scribes, but rather a complex and creative process that required both authorial and editorial intervention.[2] At the same time, significant advances have been made in both structural and quantitative codicology, which have transformed the way we think about the materiality of the medieval codex.[3] This includes emphasis upon its inherent modularity and fluidity, as well as observations about the precision of medieval production methods. The cumulative weight of this evidence has demonstrated that compilation was a major phenomenon in the history of the early medieval book.

Early medieval compilations — miscellanies — are notoriously difficult to define. They rarely contained exactly the same content, but they often followed similar principles. A non-exhaustive list of representative material might include compu-

---

Loredana Teresi, eds., *Limits to Learning: The Transfer of Encyclopaedic Knowledge in the Early Middle Ages,* Mediaevalia Groningana New Series 19 (Leuven: Peeters, 2013); and Rolf H. Bremmer and Kees Dekker, eds., *Practice in Learning: The Transfer of Encyclopaedic Knowledge in the Early Middle Ages,* Mediaevalia Groningana New Series 16 (Leuven: Peeters, 2010).

2 See, for example, Max Diesenberger, Yitzhak Hen, and Marianne Pollheimer, eds., *Sermo Doctorum: Compilers, Preachers, and Their Audiences in the Early Medieval West,* Sermo 9 (Turnhout: Brepols, 2013).

3 Ezio Ornato, "The Application of Quantitative Methods to the History of the Book," in *The Oxford Handbook of Latin Palaeography,* ed. Frank T. Coulson and Robert G. Babcock (Oxford: Oxford University Press, 2020), 650–68; Ryan Perry, "The Sum of the Book: Structural Codicology and Medieval Manuscript Culture," in *The Cambridge Companion to Medieval British Manuscripts,* ed. Orietta Da Rold and Elaine Treharne (Cambridge: Cambridge University Press, 2020), 106–26; Patrick Andrist, Paul Canart, and Marilena Maniaci, *La syntaxe du codex: essai de codicologie structurale,* Bibliologia 34 (Turnhout: Brepols, 2013); Patrick Andrist, Paul Canart, and Marilena Maniaci, "L'analyse structurelle du codex, clef de sa genèse et de son histoire," in *The Legacy of Bernard de Montfaucon: Three Hunderd Years of Studies on Greek Handwriting. Proceedings of the Seventh International Colloquium of Greek Palaeography (Madrid-Salamanca, 15–20 September 2008),* ed. Antonio Bravo García and Inmaculada Pérez Martín (Turnhout: Brepols, 2010), 289–99.

tus, epigrams, glosses, glossaries, liturgical directions, medical recipes, prognostics and bloodletting instructions, scholia, sermons, and partial texts of all kinds. The specific outlook of the contents often appears to have been determined by the purpose for which the miscellany was intended. Some known categories are baptismal manuals and manuals for rural priests.[4] Through glossing, compilation was also associated closely with the memory-based compositional practice known as *collectio*.[5] Although it was collection or gathering in the sense of listening, rumination, and even invention — an internal, imaginative, and intellectual process — *collectio* is nevertheless inseparable from written texts because they are frequently its product and because they are the only evidence through which we can witness the process. Glosses are the most obvious example, since they were fundamental for the collection and retrieval of knowledge within the memory.[6] They and other texts associated with the

---

4 Susan A. Keefe, *Water and the Word: Baptism and the Education of the Clergy in the Carolingian Empire*, 2 vols., Publications in Medieval Studies (Notre Dame: University of Notre Dame Press, 2002); Steffen Patzold and Carine van Rhijn, eds., *Men in the Middle: Local Priests in Early Medieval Europe* (Berlin: De Gruyter, 2016); and Carine van Rhijn, *Leading the Way to Heaven. Pastoral Care and Salvation in the Carolingian Period* (London: Routledge, 2022).

5 Mary J. Carruthers, *The Book of Memory: A Study of Memory in Medieval Culture*, Cambridge Studies in Medieval Literature 10 (Cambridge: Cambridge University Press, 1990), 245. See also Frances A. Yates, *The Art of Memory* (Chicago: University of Chicago Press, 1966).

6 Sinéad O'Sullivan, "Text, Gloss, and Tradition in the Early Medieval West: Expanding into a World of Learning," in *Teaching and Learning in Medieval Europe: Essays in Honour of Gernot R. Wieland*, ed. Greti Dinkova-Bruun and Tristan Major, The Journal of Medieval Latin Publications 11 (Turnhout: Brepols, 2017), 3–24. See also Mariken Teeuwen and Irene van Renswoude, eds., *The Annotated Book in the Early Middle Ages: Practices of Reading and Writing*, Utrecht Studies in Medieval Literacy 38 (Turnhout: Brepols, 2017); Mariken Teeuwen and Sinéad O'Sullivan, eds., *Carolingian Scholarship and Martianus Capella: Ninth-Century Commentary Traditions on De nuptiis in Context*, Cultural Encounters in Late Antiquity and the Middle Ages 12 (Turnhout: Brepols, 2011); and Franck Cinato, *Priscien glosé: l'Ars grammatica de Priscien vu à travers les gloses carolingiennes*, Studia Artistarum 41 (Turnhout: Brepols, 2015).

practice of *collectio* were also used in early medieval learning environments, which might have been diverse: within the classroom as well as outside it, for adults as well as children, both secular and monastic.

This is a very broad outline of the kind of contents that one might expect to find within a compilation. In the later Middle Ages in Britain, clumps of particular texts, or nodes, begin to appear, and these can have their own set places within manuscripts or booklets.[7] In early medieval Continental manuscripts, however, this is not the case, although, as Michael Eber discusses in his contribution, comparable small clusters of texts (dossiers) can appear in some closely related sub-groups of miscellanies. This question would benefit from further research in these and other categories of compilation manuscripts. But on the whole, the heterogeneity of miscellanies has, in the past, obscured their value, and it still tends to make them difficult to categorize, classify, or otherwise distinguish from one another, although this situation has been rapidly improving in recent years.

The implication of this heterogeneity, which has rarely been fully articulated, is that it reflected a deliberate practice, which we call the "art of compilation" in this volume. This art was centered on creating booklets, and whole manuscripts, which would fulfill specific practical functions, from teaching, to recording a locally relevant ritual, to the multitude of other small tasks for which texts might have been needed. In such a context, it was more important to fit the text or text extract being copied within the new compilation, than it was to maintain the authority of its author or the accuracy of the exemplar. That is not to say that there was no room for correction or emendation, but that there was significant scope for creative combination and even alteration of texts, at either the textual or codicological level, particularly for those booklets or manuscripts which were compiled over years or decades. The art of compilation was therefore directed by the needs, connections, and networks

---

7   Perry, "The Sum of the Book," 119.

of those who made books and ordered books to be made in the early Middle Ages.

This focus on compilation as a process underpins the methodology of the chapters in this volume. It helps to decentralize the focus on the "author-centered study of standard, stable, textually unproblematic texts, to which all have easy access": the issue that New Philology addressed for medieval texts, and which Joseph Dane saw as problematic in the work of those studying Caxton.[8] Such stable texts are modern constructions. A search for patterns and coherence among handwritten text production that ignores, subsumes, or corrects variance is also, unavoidably, artificial. Compilation refocuses our attention on this variance and legitimizes it as an area of study, permitting us to explore it as a key feature of the manuscripts rather than as a fragmenting or destabilizing attribute.

This volume therefore interrogates the medieval manuscript book as a dynamic, constantly changing object, enmeshed in intellectual and cultural networks, constructed and deconstructed by different people, and transmuting in both form and meaning over time. By considering manuscripts not as static, permanently bound and delimited, but rather as bodies of evidence for the layered relationships between texts and their material supports, we gain a clearer view of medieval manuscript culture as driven by the agency and intellectual exchange of the people behind it. This volume looks at early medieval Western European manuscripts as layered objects, focusing on the connections between knowledge selection, material representation, and scribal agency. The contributions look at both the codicological layers and the networks of manuscripts, collectively asking: "How were the different textual and material layers of medieval books brought together over time, and what can we say about the people who were involved?"

The complex road from selecting a text in the early Middle Ages to producing a copy of it in a book is still not well un-

---

8   Joseph A. Dane, *Abstractions of Evidence in the Study of Manuscripts and Early Printed Books* (Farnham: Ashgate, 2009), 137.

derstood, yet it is the key to the historical context of medieval books. The practice of knowledge selection consisted of three key stages: the intellectual selection of the textual content of manuscript collections; the pragmatic action of arranging the textual content in a draft form by authors or editors; and the material representation and aesthetic exposition of texts in manuscripts. These stages were part of a linear development, but also exercised reciprocal influence upon one another. By tracing this process in surviving manuscript collections, we can better understand in what practical ways knowledge was encoded and how these often innovative and experimental practices contributed to the emergence and consolidation of intellectual and scribal traditions.

In particular, the contributions to the volume focus on the people behind the manuscripts. Who made the choices and why? How did compilers, (eventual) users, and scribes work together? These questions matter because manuscript production was almost always a collective endeavor. As a result, the contributions to the volume also consider, through their different approaches, how it might be possible to glimpse the earliest stages of a book through the final product. What can we know about the relationship between manuscript collections and their draft forms, for example? What influence did these draft forms have on practices of knowledge selection? What were the practices behind the selection of texts and text extracts? What role did paratext play in the development or use of the book as a whole?

The Art of Compilation: Manuscripts and Networks in the Early Medieval Latin West therefore looks at how early medieval makers put together their multi-layered manuscripts, and how these manuscripts were then embedded in networks of people. The chapters in this volume are loosely grouped by the core topics raised by these twin ideas — rooted in the innovative historical and codicological research of recent years — of manuscript archaeology and connections between people. As outlined above, these topics are knowledge selection, material representation, and scribal agency.

Knowledge Selection

The first three chapters shine a light on the early medieval strategies for selecting texts for inclusion in a compilation. In *"Historische Ordnung* or Just a Mess? Tracking Dossiers in Early Medieval Canon Law Collections," Michael Eber discusses the organization of early medieval canon law texts into groups or dossiers, exploring the evidence that early medieval compilers understood these texts to belong together, and what this meant for the reception of canon law as well as for the fluidity with which canon law collection circulated in general. To do so, he examines a case study of three synods revolving around Pope Symmachus (498–514) and the Laurentian schism which occurred early in his pontificate. The different transmission strands of these acts in eight separate canonical collections highlight the agency and confidence of early medieval compilers in the selection and — most importantly — re-selection of texts. As Michael Eber demonstrates, collections were made and un-made deliberately, with an eye to new recontextualizations, rather than mechanically.

In "Carolingian Collections of Gregory the Great's Letters and the So-Called *Collectio Pauli*," Laura Pani and Lucia Castaldi take a wholly different methodological approach to knowledge selection. They conduct a meticulous philological study of the *Collectio Pauli*, a collection of letters of Gregory the Great whose compilation has been attributed to Paul the Deacon, and one of the oldest known collections of medieval epistles. The most famous witness of the *Collectio Pauli*, a manuscript now kept in the Russian National Library in St. Petersburg, has been assumed to be its archetype. Yet, as Laura Pani and Lucia Castaldi point out, no philological reconstruction of the manuscript transmission of the *Collectio Pauli* has ever been made. In their study, they demonstrate that another manuscript in Munich descends from an antigraph occupying a higher position in the *stemma codicum,* which means that the St. Petersburg manuscript, despite being the oldest surviving witness, was not the antigraph of the whole *Collectio.* This also points to the conclusion that the *Collectio Pauli* was not compiled by Paul the Deacon. Their contribution highlights that an individual's choices and responsibilities when it comes to collecting and excerpting knowledge determine what then circulates, but that the absorption of both corrections and mistakes into the main text can then also become part of the canon.

Both canon law dossiers and the transmission of Gregory's letters also make it very clear that the selection of knowledge was not merely restricted to choosing and collecting. Instead, knowledge was actively adapted and assimilated. This is demonstrated by Sinéad O'Sullivan's contribution, "Creating the Past in the Carolingian Book of Virgil," which examines a collection now split across two libraries to investigate how Carolingian scholars created the past. This collection highlights a highly prized antique ideal, but also reveals the Carolingian project to calibrate a balance between the sacred and the profane. This was done by creating a compilation whose contents were a deliberate tapestry of exegetical, historiographical, and political material, and whose pagan and Christian origins or connotations were manipulated through strategies such as textual linkage, and marginal and interlinear glossing.

Material Representation

The section of the volume dedicated to material representation focuses on the ways in which the physicality of texts and manuscripts affected the reception of their contents. As with knowledge selection, this is possible in a variety of different ways, and one of these is size, both in terms of length and in terms of dimensions. In "The Materiality of Innovation: Formats and Dimensions of the *Etymologiae* of Isidore of Seville in the Early Middle Ages," Evina Stein investigates these features in a corpus of 434 manuscripts. Quantitative codicological studies open new research pathways because they require us to ask new questions: What happens when the volume of "excerpts" goes above a certain level — are they still excerpts or do they then alter what the text means? How does the fragmentation of a work affect user perspective? Perhaps most importantly, as Stein's contribution notes, medieval users "thought with their hands": they did not think of texts as abstract objects that could be separated from their material embodiments. Further research on these features of the materiality of compilations has the potential to alter our perspective of the medieval codex, perhaps even radically.

No less important than size in the materiality of compilations is their layout. That medieval users were perfectly aware of this is evident from the complex codicological layout of commented biblical editions, which were deliberately selected by Otfrid of Wissembourg to help his audience understand the Bible over other, simpler layouts. This is the subject of Cinzia Grifoni's contribution, "Commented Editions of the Bible in Carolingian Europe: Otfrid's Approach to the Book of Isaiah." Otfrid was the designer of at least five commented editions of several biblical books, which he personally glossed, as well as a rhymed Gospel harmony in Old High German. This work, which took many years, and which involved privileged use of abridgments of authoritative texts, is an example of the extent to which manuscript materiality could be manipulated to fulfill the needs of a target audience, and of the agency an individual could have in creating such a compilation.

The layout of early medieval codices and its associated materiality was rarely directed so closely by a single individual such as Otfrid, however. A collection of early medieval legal texts whose layout was controlled by their scribes is investigated by Thom Gobbitt in the final contribution to this section on materiality, "Rechtsblöcke, Scribes and Layout Strategies in a Ninth-Century Legal Collection: Modena, Biblioteca Capitolare MS O. I .2." Although past scholarship has viewed the "barbarian" laws and imperial capitularies in these collections as separate groups of texts — *Rechtsblöcke* — the paleographical and codicological evidence demonstrates that the scribes in fact viewed the contents as unitary, and that there was a large community around these compilations which was invested in their production and dissemination as homogeneous books.

Scribal Agency

Moving the focus beyond the textuality and materiality of early medieval compilations, the final section of the volume turns to the people who were their copyists, users, and audiences. In *"Sammelhandschriften* and the *Breuiarium librorum* in Sankt Gallen 728," Mark Stansbury uses a ninth-century booklist to examine the different forms of the book in the early Middle Ages. In the booklist, these include *codex, codicillum, libellulus, mappa, quaternio, rotulus, sceda, scedula,* and *volumen.* These terms highlight the diversity of codicological formats available in the early Middle Ages. Mark Stansbury engages closely with the definition of a *Sammelhandschrift* — the core concept of this volume, a compilation or miscellany — and the ultimate fluidity of this object, which is dependent on how it is received by its audience, whether modern or medieval. Certainly at St. Gall there is a demonstrable link between the way texts were kept and assembled into *Sammelhandschriften* and the requirements of the people who lived there. This connection between texts, books, and people is the basis of the art of compilation.

Miscellany codices can also be gateways to wide-ranging early medieval networks. One of the most prominent categories of surviving early medieval miscellanies is grammatical and other elementary didactic manuscripts. There seems to have been no coordinated effort at a curriculum-based corpus, for no two grammatical miscellanies are alike. Nevertheless, they have shared preoccupations and interests, as Elizabeth P. Archibald shows in "Sharing Alphabets: Early Medieval Grammatical Miscellanies and Their Networks." By tracing the history of a short exposition of the letters of the alphabet, her study reveals that *grammatica* was a pervasive discipline whose scraps filled the available manuscript space, resulting in a "fuzzy" but shared curriculum. The relationships between the different texts were complex: scribes expanded and rearranged, motivated by utility more than authority (that is, less concerned about the integrity and authority of the exemplar than interested in what it can give and how it can be supplemented). This was not a curriculum in a way that we would understand it today; it was more expansive, and more long-lived, involving multiple strands of education and compilation over many years. In this narrative of integration over fragmentation, the binding agent is early medieval scribes.

In the last paper of this section and the final paper of this volume, "What is a Vademecum? The Social Logic of Early Medieval Compilation," I turn to the role of individuals in the compilation of multi-text books. Is there such a thing as a personal book in the early Middle Ages and, if so, what makes it personal? A useful concept in this regard is the idea of "social logic": that texts are embedded within local systems of communication and power. Individuals, their texts, and their books can be seen as active agents in the creation of their own social logics. Instead of a focus on solitary, brilliant personalities, this approach enables a more fruitful investigation into the precise connection between individual intellectuals, their manuscript books, and the communities in which both operated. Exploring the layered nature of manuscripts and their entanglement in terms of texts, practices and people thus opens up new paths of research, as Mariken Teeuwen argues and illustrates in an Afterword: "Manuscripts as Layered and Entangled Objects: New Ways to Explore the Manuscript Book." In this final contribution threads from discussions that sprang from our meetings are drawn together, and Mariken Teeuwen explores the new approach with a single case study.

The Art of Compilation

Although the nine contributions to this volume are divided up into three different thematic strands, none of them belong exclusively to their sections. There is significant overlap between them, and rightly so: as the chapters show, there is no room between the texts, manuscripts, and networks themselves. They are inextricably connected. By studying the codicology and textual contents of their compilations in an integral manner, each of the papers in this volume reveals the webs of communication that shaped early medieval textual culture. This fits within the new paradigms developed by structural codicology, biocodicology and digital humanities, fields which continue to push the boundaries of what is knowable about the extent to which manuscripts are related to each other, the ways in which codicological units can be linked within individual codices, and the complex interconnectedness of quires and parchment sheets.

The contributions to the volume also highlight the centrality of the physical codex to the very idea of compilation. They join up in a range of sometimes surprising ways. The material at the edges of the book — flyleaves, margins, open spaces of various kinds — which is discarded by traditional editions, is useful for assessing the ways in which manuscripts and communities are entangled. Precarious formats (loose leaves, unbound quires, *schedulae*) are part and parcel of what was a rich codicological background, and, as some of the contributions show, require to be ranked equal to their texts in terms of importance, in order to understand either at all. At the same time, practices of medieval textual scholarship — critical reading, textual annotation, authorial involvement in the shaping of texts (as well as its absence), and the addition of later layers of texts — speak for a historical community. But they never do so in the abstract: there is always a real codex, a physical set of leaves with which scribes had to contend and whose materiality shaped what it was possible to do.

The dynamic life of medieval manuscript compilations investigated in this volume did not come to an end in the Middle Ages: it continues into the modern day, with all the rich implications and complications offered by the gathering and breaking-up of books in both public and private collections, as well as by digitization. Elaine Treharne has described this long life-process of the medieval codex as "dynamic architextuality."[9] As we actively develop new digital and hybrid modes of working

---

9   Elaine Treharne, *Perceptions of Medieval Manuscripts: The Phenomenal Book* (Oxford: Oxford University Press, 2021).

with and preserving codicological heritage, the medieval art of compilation grows increasingly more relevant for understanding and adapting to this dynamic architextuality, both past and future.

Bibliography

Andrist, Patrick, Paul Canart, and Marilena Maniaci. "L'analyse structurelle du codex, clef de sa genèse et de son histoire." In *The Legacy of Bernard de Montfaucon: Three Hunderd Years of Studies on Greek Handwriting. Proceedings of the Seventh International Colloquium of Greek Palaeography (Madrid-Salamanca, 15–20 September 2008)*, edited by Antonio Bravo García and Inmaculada Pérez Martín, 289–99. Turnhout: Brepols, 2010. DOI: 10.1484/M.BIB-EB.3.4533.

———. *La syntaxe du codex: essai de codicologie structurale*. Bibliologia 34. Turnhout: Brepols, 2013.

Bremmer, Rolf H., and Kees Dekker, eds. *Foundations of Learning: The Transfer of Encyclopaedic Knowledge in the Early Middle Ages*. Mediaevalia Groningana New Series 9. Leuven: Peeters, 2007.

———, eds. *Fruits of Learning: The Transfer of Encyclopaedic Knowledge in the Early Middle Ages*. Mediaevalia Groningana New Series 21. Leuven: Peeters, 2016.

———, eds. *Practice in Learning: The Transfer of Encyclopaedic Knowledge in the Early Middle Ages*. Mediaevalia Groningana New Series 16. Leuven: Peeters, 2010.

Carruthers, Mary J. *The Book of Memory: A Study of Memory in Medieval Culture*. Cambridge Studies in Medieval Literature 10. Cambridge: Cambridge University Press, 1990.

Cinato, Franck. *Priscien glosé: l'Ars grammatica de Priscien vue à travers les gloses carolingiennes*. Studia Artistarum 41. Turnhout: Brepols, 2015. DOI: 10.1484/M.SA-EB.5.109560.

Contreni, John J. "The Carolingian Renaissance: Education and Literary Culture." In *The New Cambridge Medieval History, Volume 2: c. 700–c. 900*, edited by Rosamond McKitterick, 709–57. Cambridge: Cambridge University Press, 1995. DOI: 10.1017/CHOL9780521362924.030.

Dane, Joseph A. *Abstractions of Evidence in the Study of Manuscripts and Early Printed Books*. Farnham: Ashgate, 2009.

Diesenberger, Max, Yitzhak Hen, and Marianne Pollheimer, eds. *Sermo Doctorum: Compilers, Preachers, and Their Audiences in the Early Medieval West.* Sermo 9. Turnhout: Brepols, 2013. DOI: 10.1484/M.SERMO-EB.6.09070802050003050305010509.

Dolbeau, François. "'La miscellanea informale e le comunità intellettuali nel medioevo latino.' Introduction au colloque." *Filologia mediolatina. Rivista della Fondazione Ezio Franceschini* 19 (2012): 1–7.

Garrison, Mary. "The *Collectanea* and Medieval Florilegia." In *Collectanea Pseudo-Bedae,* edited by Martha Bayless and Michael Lapidge, 42–83. Scriptores Latini Hiberniae 14. Dublin: Dublin Institute for Advanced Studies, 1998.

Giliberto, Concetta, and Loredana Teresi, eds. *Limits to Learning: The Transfer of Encyclopaedic Knowledge in the Early Middle Ages.* Mediaevalia Groningana New Series 19. Leuven: Peeters, 2013.

Keefe, Susan A. *Water and the Word: Baptism and the Education of the Clergy in the Carolingian Empire.* 2 volumes. Publications in Medieval Studies. Notre Dame: University of Notre Dame Press, 2002.

Leonardi, Claudio. *Letteratura latina medievale (secoli VI–XV). Un manuale.* Millennio medievale 31. Florence: SISMEL Edizioni del Galluzzo, 2002.

McKitterick, Rosamond. *The Carolingians and the Written Word.* Cambridge: Cambridge University Press, 1989. DOI: 10.1017/CBO9780511583599.

Ornato, Ezio. "The Application of Quantitative Methods to the History of the Book." In *The Oxford Handbook of Latin Palaeography,* edited by Frank T. Coulson and Robert G. Babcock, 650–68. New York: Oxford University Press, 2020. DOI: 10.1093/oxfordhb/9780195336948.013.

O'Sullivan, Sinéad. "Text, Gloss, and Tradition in the Early Medieval West: Expanding into a World of Learning." In *Teaching and Learning in Medieval Europe: Essays in Honour of Gernot R. Wieland,* edited by Greti Dinkova-Bruun and Tristan Major, 3–24. Turnhout: Brepols, 2017. DOI: 10.1484/M.PJML-EB.5.113251.

Perry, Ryan. "The Sum of the Book: Structural Codicology and Medieval Manuscript Culture." In *The Cambridge Companion to Medieval British Manuscripts,* edited by Orietta Da Rold and Elaine Treharne, 106–26. Cambridge: Cambridge University Press, 2020. DOI: 10.1017/9781316182659.006.

Patzold, Steffen, and Carine van Rhijn, eds. *Men in the Middle: Local Priests in Early Medieval Europe.* Berlin: De Gruyter, 2016. DOI: 10.1515/9783110444483.

Rhijn, Carine van. *Leading the Way to Heaven: Pastoral Care and Salvation in the Carolingian Period.* London: Routledge, 2022. DOI: 10.4324/9781315149981.

Teeuwen, Mariken, and Sinéad O'Sullivan, eds. *Carolingian Scholarship and Martianus Capella: Ninth-Century Commentary Traditions on 'De nuptiis' in Context.* Cultural Encounters in Late Antiquity and the Middle Ages 12. Turnhout: Brepols, 2011. DOI: 10.1484/M.CELAMA-EB.6.09070802050003050301070806.

Teeuwen, Mariken, and Irene van Renswoude, eds. *The Annotated Book in the Early Middle Ages: Practices of Reading and Writing.* Utrecht Studies in Medieval Literacy 38. Turnhout: Brepols, 2017. DOI: 10.1484/M.USML-EB.5.111620.

Treharne, Elaine. *Perceptions of Medieval Manuscripts: The Phenomenal Book.* Oxford: Oxford University Press, 2021. DOI: 10.1093/oso/9780192843814.001.0001.

Yates, Frances A. *The Art of Memory.* Chicago: University of Chicago Press, 1966.

1

Historische Ordnung or Just a Mess? Tracking Dossiers in Early Medieval Canon Law Collections

Michael Eber

Introduction[1]

In his seminal work on early medieval canon law collections, Friedrich Maassen distinguished between collections of *systematische Ordnung* (systematic arrangement) — collections where individual canons of different councils and decretals on the same topic were grouped together — and *historische Ordnung* (historical arrangement), in which councils and decretals were usually transmitted as complete texts.[2] However, this second category served mostly as a catch-all for collections that were not systematically arranged: Some compilers arranged their texts

---

1 This paper resulted from the DFG project "Der *Codex Remensis* der Staatsbibliothek zu Berlin (Ms. Phill. 1743): Der gallische Episkopat als Mittler antiken Rechtswissens und Mitgestalter merowingischer Politik."
2 Friedrich Maassen, *Geschichte der Quellen und der Literatur des Canonischen Rechts im Abendlande bis zum Ausgange des Mittelalters*, vol. 1: *Die Rechtssammlungen bis zur Mitte des 9. Jahrhunderts* (Graz: Leuschner & Lubensky, 1870), 3–4. "Decretal" refers to a genre of papal letter, in which popes would, usually as an answer to an inquiry by an individual bishop, set norms that, at least in principle, were to be applied all through the universal Church.

geographically, chronologically, or by genre; some switched between or combined organizing principles, and others seem to have produced "*un*structured collections."[3] Since consensus on which texts were to be considered "canonical" only gradually developed over the course of the early Middle Ages, not only the order, but also the content of these collections vary wildly, and the decisions behind the inclusion or exclusion of certain texts sometimes seem just as mysterious as their arrangement.

Still, making as much sense as possible of the content and order of these collections is not a task to be abandoned lightly. These ostensibly legal collections could also, as Rosamond McKitterick has argued, be read as historiography, offering "a progression of ideas and decisions of the church."[4] Seen through this lens, the inclusion, exclusion, and juxtaposition of certain texts can reveal specific visions of the history of the Church underlying individual *libri canonum* — and the visions *are* specific, often allowing us to recover local preferences or demonstrating which issues were particularly salient at the time they were produced.[5]

---

3   Lotte Kéry, *Canonical Collections of the Early Middle Ages (ca. 400–1140): A Bibliographical Guide to the Manuscripts and Literature,* History of Medieval Canon Law 1 (Washington, DC: Catholic University of America Press, 1999), 24, 26, 31, 46, 88. My emphasis. It is not entirely clear, however, which criteria she applied to decide which collections are "unstructured."

4   Rosamond McKitterick, *History and Memory in the Carolingian World* (Cambridge: Cambridge University Press, 2004), 255.

5   See for example Hubert Mordek, "Bischofsabsetzungen in Spätmerowingischer Zeit. Justelliana, Bernensis und das Konzil von Mâlay (677)," in *Papsttum, Kirche und Recht im Mittelalter: Festschrift für Horst Fuhrmann zum 65. Geburtstag,* ed. Hubert Mordek (Tübingen: Niemeyer, 1991), 31–53, who identified a specific synod for which a collection was written. More generally, see Ralph W. Mathisen, "Between Arles, Rome, and Toledo: Gallic Collections of Canon Law in Late Antiquity," *'Ilu. Revista de Ciencias de las Religiones* 2 (1999): 33–46, and Ralph W. Mathisen, "Church Councils and Local Authority: The Development of Gallic *Libri Canonum* During Late Antiquity," in *Being Christian in Late Antiquity: A Festschrift for Gillian Clark,* ed. Carol Harrison, Caroline Humfress, and Isabella Sandwell (Oxford: Oxford University Press, 2014), 175–95.

One way to get a sense of that vision in the case of collections without an apparent overarching organizing principle is to identify dossiers, that is, smaller sequences of texts whose order seems less arbitrary than the order of the collection as a whole.[6] There is, however, no clear definition of what constitutes a dossier: the texts might be related by topic, by region, or by relevant persons; and their relatedness may or may not be indicated in the finished codex. One possible criterion to identify texts as belonging to a dossier could be their independent circulation or transmission. Eckhard Wirbelauer, for example, defined dossiers as *separat archivierte Hefte* (separately archived booklets).[7] Booklets, in turn, have been defined by Pamela Robinson as a "self-sufficient unit," "the beginning and end [of which] always coincides with the beginning and end of a text or a group of texts."[8] Her definition was qualified by Ralph Hanna who rightly insisted that the perspective of the person producing the booklet was the relevant one: *they* needed to be aware of the self-

---

[6] See, for example, Antoine Chavasse, "Les lettres de Saint Léon le Grand dans le supplément de la Dionysiana et de l'Hadriana et dans la collection du manuscrit du Vatican," *Revue des Sciences Religieuses* 38, no. 2 (1964): 157–58, who refers (among others) to an anti-Pelagian, an anti-Nestorian, and an anti-Eutychian dossier in the *collectiones Vaticana, Dionysiana,* and *Dionysio-Hadriana,* or Ralph W. Mathisen, "The 'Codex Sangallensis' 190 and the Transmission of the Classical Tradition during Late Antiquity and the Early Middle Ages," *International Journal of the Classical Tradition* 5, no. 2 (1998): 178–9, who mentions a "Faustus dossier" in the *collectiones Corbeiensis* and *Pithouensis.*

[7] Eckhard Wirbelauer, *Zwei Päpste in Rom. Der Konflikt zwischen Laurentius und Symmachus (498–514): Studien und Texte,* Quellen und Forschungen zur antiken Welt 16 (Munich: Tuduv, 1993), 68. He cited Chavasse, "Les lettres," for this definition. Chavasse, however, never gave a clear definition of what he meant by *dossier* and used it interchangeably to refer to a) consecutive texts on similar topics transmitted in the same order in different collections (157–58), b) non-consecutive texts on the same topic or taken from the same source (166), and c) as a synonym for "small collection" (169).

[8] Pamela R. Robinson, "The 'Booklet': A Self-Contained Unit in Composite Manuscripts," in *Codicologica 3: Essais Typologiques,* ed. Albert Gruys and Johann P. Gumbert, Litterae Textuales (Leiden: Brill, 1980), 47.

sufficiency of a textual unit if it was to be qualified as a booklet.[9] In their purest form, then, we might think of dossiers as a small number of quires containing texts that were understood to be related and that were intended to form independently circulating units.

However, since most, especially pre-Carolingian, *libri canonum* are only transmitted in copies made substantially after the collections were initially compiled, it is often very challenging to find evidence that the original compilers used "separately archived booklets" or thought of some of their sources as a "self-sufficient unit." Almost none of the possible indications for booklets that Robinson and Hanna came up with — like differences in handwriting or decoration, in size or material of the pages, in quire structure or signatures — are applicable to copies of collections.[10] In some cases, there may be other evidence, such as a shift in the way the individual canons are numbered, or in the kinds of incipits, explicits, or dating clauses used. But none of these are conclusive either. They may simply indicate that the compiler switched sources, without telling us anything about whether they thought that the texts they took from one source were more closely related to one another than to the rest of the collection. If the texts of a putative dossier are included in the same order in collections that otherwise share little or no similarities, this might be taken as a sign that they circulated independently of either collection. But, again, it could also just mean that the compiler of one collection found only one part of the other particularly interesting. In general, the compil-

---

9   Ralph Hanna, "Booklets in Medieval Manuscripts: Further Considerations," *Studies in Bibliography* 39 (1986): 101–2. See also Gumbert's critique of Muzerelle's term *recueil organisé*: Johann P. Gumbert, "Codicological Units: Towards a Terminology for the Stratigraphy of the Non-Homogeneous Codex," in *Il codice miscellaneo: Tipologie e funzioni. Atti del Convegno internazionale, Cassino, 14–17 maggio 2003*, ed. Edoardo Crisci and Oronzo Pecere, Segno e testo 2 (Turnhout: Brepols, 2004), 19–20.

10 Robinson, "The 'Booklet,'" 47–48; Hanna, "Booklets in medieval manuscripts," 108.

ers of early medieval *libri canonum* tended to deal rather freely with their source material, rearranging, adding to, and cutting from the dossiers at their disposal.[11] So, what seemed like a self-sufficient textual unit to one compiler may not have done so to another.

In light of these difficulties, what I propose is not a change in the technical definition of the term "dossier," but rather more of a general approach. If making sense of the sequence of texts in these manuscripts is supposed to help us make sense of the compilers' view of the history of the Church, then we need to look for indications that successive texts seemed related to their early medieval compilers wherever we may find them. To demonstrate this approach, I will focus on one group of texts, intended to bolster the legitimacy of Pope Symmachus (498–514) and initially assembled shortly after the end of the Laurentian schism that had beset the early years of his pontificate. These texts were included in several early *libri canonum* but were treated very differently by individual compilers. In some collections, they appear in chronological order, or reverse-chronological in others; some compilers supplemented them by other, often only vaguely connected texts; other compilers arranged them using formal criteria which, applied somewhat haphazardly, obscured their coherence. Thus, these texts make an ideal test case to see when and how we can recover evidence that they were understood to belong together. This will not only reveal the ability of early medieval canonists to properly contextualize the Laurentian Schism in the "progression of ideas of the Church," but also the fluidity of canon law collections in general, demonstrating the facility with which dossiers were integrated into larger collections and parts of larger collections were made into dossiers to be circulated independently.

---

11 Mathisen, "Church Councils," 183–84.

The Laurentian Schism

The Laurentian schism, the conflict that brought about the composition of the texts under consideration here, was essentially a schism within a schism.[12] The churches of Rome and Constantinople had not been in communion since 484, when Pope Felix III had excommunicated Patriarch Akakios of Constantinople due to a dispute over the heritage of the council of Chalcedon (451). After Akakios's death, successive popes insisted that his name be struck from the diptychs in Constantinople, though some made that demand more aggressively than others.[13] In particular, Anastasius II (496–498) had struck a somewhat more conciliatory tone than his predecessor Gelasius I (492–496), which seems to have been controversial even among his contemporaries.[14]

After Anastasius's death, the deacon Symmachus and the archpresbyter Laurentius were elected as pope on the same day. While several fault lines ran through the Roman clergy at the time — conflicts between deacons and presbyters, a generational divide, and factionalism of the Roman (lay) elites[15] — it has long been the standard interpretation that Laurentius was the candidate of those who favored Anastasius's approach to the Acacian schism, Symmachus of those who preferred Gelasian severity. The sources that arose directly from the Laurentian schism, though, are rather silent on Chalcedon and the Acacian

---

12 For a more detailed discussion, see Erich Caspar, *Das Papsttum unter Byzantinischer Herrschaft*, Geschichte des Papsttums von den Anfängen bis zur Höhe der Weltherrschaft 2 (Tübingen: Mohr, 1933), 87–118; John Moorhead, "The Laurentian Schism: East and West in the Roman Church," *Church History* 47, no. 2 (1978): 125–36; Wirbelauer, *Zwei Päpste*, esp. 9–65.

13 For an overview of the Acacian Schism, see Jan-Markus Kötter, *Zwischen Kaisern und Aposteln. Das Akakianische Schisma (484–519) als Kirchlicher Ordnungskonflikt der Spätantike*, Roma Aeterna. Beiträge zu Spätantike und Frühmittelalter 2 (Stuttgart: Franz Steiner, 2013).

14 His death is portrayed as divine punishment in the *Liber Pontificalis:* Louis Duchesne, ed., *Le Liber Pontificalis: Texte, introduction, et commentaire* 1 (Paris: E. Thorin, 1886), 258.

15 Kötter, *Zwischen Kaisern*, 114–22.

schism,[16] so much so that Kristina Sessa has questioned whether they played any role at all.[17] As will be shown later, at least some compilers of canon law collections drew a connection between this inner-Roman dispute and the wider Mediterranean conflicts that the Roman Church had to contend with at the time.

After the schismatic election, both parties called on Theoderic to decide. He found in favor of Symmachus, a decision that Laurentius seems to have accepted at first. In 499, Symmachus held a synod in Rome, trying to prevent future contested papal elections by establishing appointment by the outgoing pope as the norm.[18] Laurentius subscribed to the acts of that synod, using his old title of archpresbyter.[19] Shortly after that, Symmachus promoted him to the see of Nocera, presumably to remove his rival from the city. Soon, however, tensions began to rise again. In the winter of 500/501, Laurentian clerics brought charges against Symmachus, accusing him of alienation of church property, sexual impropriety, and liturgical error. More synods were held in Rome to deal with these accusations.[20] At a synod in 501, an edict of the praetorian prefect Basilius prohibiting alienation of church property — doubtless the legal basis for the accusations against Symmachus — was rejected on the grounds that, as a layman, Basilius had not had the authority to make such a decision.[21] This synod also decreed that *a praesenti die* (from this day forward) no church property was allowed to pass into the hands of laypeople,[22] which could be interpreted as a grandfather clause tacitly legalizing the sales to laypeople that

---

16 John Moorhead, *Theoderic in Italy* (Oxford: Clarendon Press, 1992), 135.
17 Kristina Sessa, *The Formation of Papal Authority in Late Antique Italy: Roman Bishops and the Domestic Sphere* (Cambridge: Cambridge University Press, 2012), 212–46.
18 *Acta synhodorum habitarum Romae*, in *Monumenta Germaniae Historica, Auctores antiquissimi 12*, ed. Theodor Mommsen (Berlin: Weidmann, 1894), 403–4.
19 *Acta synhodorum*, 410.
20 For the dating of these synods, see Wirbelauer, *Zwei Päpste*, 21–23.
21 *Acta synhodorum*, 444–48.
22 *Acta synhodorum*, 449–51; quote on 449.

had already occurred under Symmachus.[23] A synod held in 502 essentially declared itself not competent: judgement of the occupant of the Apostolic See was left to God. In the meantime, all churches and properties pertaining to that see were to be returned to Symmachus, though clerics who had been in opposition to Symmachus could remain in office as long as they were penitent.[24] Neither of the synods was successful in ending the schism, however. In fact, support for Symmachus among the Roman clergy seems to have been dwindling. By this point, Laurentius had returned to Rome and acted as de-facto bishop for his supporters. The schism festered until late 506 or early 507, when Laurentius finally backed down just before his death.

The rest of this chapter is concerned with the transmission of the synods of 499, 501, and 502. Their acts, transmitted in eight separate canonical collections, were identified as a potential dossier in 1993 by Eckhard Wirbelauer.[25] Using his work as a launching point, I will analyze the disparate traditions of these synodal acts, asking how they were understood as connected to different texts by different compilers and what this can tell us about their vision of the recent, for them, history of the Church.

The Roman Synods of 499–502 in the Dionysian Tradition

The most straightforward case of the acts of these synods being transmitted as a dossier comes from the work of Dionysius Exiguus, the great canonist of the early sixth century. He published three separate recensions of his collection of canons of Greek and African church councils, the former of which he also re-translated into Latin each time; only the first two versions, the so-called *collectio Dionysiana I* and *II*, have come down to us. At some point after he had finished the second version, that is, probably during Symmachus's pontificate, Dionysius also added a number of letters by fourth- and fifth-century popes to

---

23 Wirbelauer, *Zwei Päpste*, 24.
24 *Acta synhodorum*, 430–32.
25 Wirbelauer, *Zwei Päpste*, 117–22.

it, ending with one by Symmachus's predecessor Anastasius II to emperor Anastasios.[26] This letter was Anastasius's clearest articulation of a conciliatory approach to the Acacian schism.[27] By contrast, there is no Symmachan material, which has been interpreted by some as Dionysius taking a stance against Symmachus and his hardline policies toward Constantinople,[28] though others have insisted that there is no proof he ever belonged to the Laurentian faction.[29] Recently, Conrad Leyser has argued that Dionysius was stridently non-partisan, offering a vision of the history of the Church that would "remind all parties of the wider whole to which they belonged."[30]

This latter reading would seem to fit better with Dionysius's subsequent treatment of his collection of papal letters. In the manuscript Vatican City, Biblioteca Apostolica Vaticana, MS Vat. lat. 5845, the *Dionysiana II* (with papal letters) is supplemented by a large number of texts, the first of which are the acts of the three Roman synods under consideration here (fols. 135vb–146ra). While this manuscript was produced only in the tenth century, it is commonly assumed that at least part of the supplemental material, including the three synods, was added

---

26 Maassen, *Geschichte der Quellen*, 431; in the *praefatio* to his collection of papal letters, Dionysius refers to the Greek canons as having been translated recently (*dudum*): Dionysius Exiguus, *Praefatio* in *collectione decretorum pontificum ad Iulianum presbyterum*, in Corpus Christianorum Series Latina 85, ed. Salvatore Gennaro and François Glorie (Turnhout: Brepols, 1972), 45. There is only one manuscript that contains the original form of the papal letter collection: Paris, Bibliothèque nationale de France, lat. 3837, fols. 93vb–169va, directly following the second recension of the collection of conciliar canons.

27 Anastasius II, *Exordium pontificatus mei* (J³ 1403), in *Epistolae Romanorum pontificum genuinae*, ed. Andreas Thiel (Brunsberg: E. Peter, 1886), 615–23.

28 Eduard Schwartz, "Die Kanonessammlungen der alten Reichskirche," *Zeitschrift der Savigny-Stiftung für Rechtsgeschichte; Kanonistische Abteilung* 25 (1936): 109–10; Wirbelauer, *Zwei Päpste*, 120–22, 129–34.

29 Hubert Wurm, *Studien und Texte zur Dekretalensammlung des Dionysius Exiguus*, Kanonistische Studien und Texte 16 (Bonn: L. Röhrscheid, 1939), 16–20, and Hubert Mordek, "Dionysius Exiguus," in *Lexikon des Mittelaltars*, vol. 3 (Munich: Artemis, 1986), 1091–92.

30 Conrad Leyser, "Law, Memory, and Priestly Office in Rome, c. 500," *Early Medieval Europe* 27, no. 1 (2019): 82.

to the collection already by Dionysius Exiguus himself.[31] The Symmachan synods are transmitted in reverse chronological order, starting with the synod of 502, here entitled the *Constitutum synodale de papae symmachi absolutione* (*Synodal Constitution on Pope Symmachus's Absolution*). We know of a Laurentian polemic against the proceedings of this very synod called *Adversus synodum absolutionis incongruae (Against the Synod of Incongruous Absolution).*[32] For Dionysius, starting his new supplement with the last, most controversial synod may therefore have been meant to convince the former supporters of Laurentius. At the very least, the echo of the title of the Laurentian polemic suggests that the memory of the controversy was still fresh when the acts of these synods were added to the collection.[33]

While the tenth-century copyist left no traces of the codicological make-up of the manuscript that Dionysius worked with in the sixth century, there is still evidence that the acts of the three synods came into his possession as a self-sufficient tex-

---

31 Maassen, *Geschichte der Quellen*, 449–50, and Wirbelauer, *Zwei Päpste*, 121, and 219–20.

32 The text itself is lost, but the title and some of the arguments can be reconstructed through the reply written by Ennodius, later bishop of Pavia, deacon of the church of Milan at the time and one of Symmachus's most prominent supporters. See Wirbelauer, *Zwei Päpste*, 147–49; Stefanie A.H. Kennell, *Magnus Felix Ennodius: A Gentleman of the Church*, Recentiores (Ann Arbor: University of Michigan Press, 2000), 186–201; Stéphane Gioanni, "La contribution épistolaire d'Ennode de Pavie à la primauté pontificale sous le règne des papes Symmaque et Hormisdas," *Mélanges de l'école française de Rome: Moyen Âge* 113, no. 1 (2001): 246–50.

33 The acts of synods of 499–502 were also included in later collections dependent on the *Dionysiana*—the *Dionysiana Bobiensis*, the *Dionysio-Hadriana*, and the *Dionysiana adaucta*. Since the *Dionysiana Bobiensis* was probably already assembled in the seventh century, this is another piece of evidence that they had been included in the *collectio Dionysiana* at an early date. In the latter two collections, the chronological order of the synods of 499–502 was re-established and the possibly controversial heading of the synod of 502 was changed. See Friedrich Maassen, "Bibliotheca Latina Iuris Canonici Manuscripta 1.1," *Sitzungsberichte der Kaiserlichen Akademie der Wissenschaften, Philosophisch-Historische Classe* 53 (1866–1867): 417; Maassen, *Geschichte der Quellen*, 448–50; Kéry, *Canonical Collections*, 13–21.

tual unit. Both the original papal letter collection ending with Anastasius II and the next part of the supplemental material after the Symmachan synods — letters by the fifth-century popes Hilarius, Simplicius, and Felix III that were missing from the original collection, also commonly held to have been added by Dionysius himself — have a collective table of contents listing the titles of the following texts and the content of their individual chapters (see fols. 70vb–75va and 146rb). The synods of 499, 501, and 502 appear in neither; they have their own, collective, heading — *constituta papae Symmachi (Constitutions by Pope Symmachus)*[34] — and are numbered consecutively. These three texts are therefore obviously related by content, absent in an earlier recension of the collection and actively marked as related to one another, but separate from the rest of the collection. Not only is this an ideal type of dossier in many ways, it also provides more evidence that Dionysius Exiguus had a largely non-partisan view of the Laurentian schism.

A "Symmachus Dossier" in Vatican City, Biblioteca Apostolica Vaticana, MS Reg. lat. 1997?

The transmission of the three Roman synods in the so-called *collectio Teatina* presents more difficulties in this regard. This collection was originally compiled in Italy shortly after the death of Pope Hormisdas (523) and is singularly transmitted in the manuscript Vatican City, Biblioteca Apostolica Vaticana, MS Reg. lat. 1997, produced in the mid-ninth century.[35] According to a colophon on fol. 153ra–b, this manuscript was written by a certain Sicipertus in Chieti (ancient *Teate*), from which the collection gets its name. It is also sometimes referred to as *col-*

---

34 Dionysius — as well as the other canonists dealing with these texts, as we shall see later — seems to have conceived of these synods as papal rather than synodal decrees, even though their decisions were technically reached by consent of all the bishops assembled in Rome; Symmachus himself was not even present at the synod of 502.
35 Digitized at https://digi.vatlib.it/view/MSS_Reg.lat.1997.

lectio Ingilramni, after the bishop Ingilramnus who, according to Sicipertus, ordered him to produce this copy.[36]

The material related to the Roman synods runs from fol. 116va to fol. 137ra. The *acta* themselves are supplemented by several related texts. Integrated directly into the subscriptions of the synod of 499 is a short text by John, a deacon of the Roman Church, dated to September 18, 506, in which he submitted to Symmachus after previously having been part of the Laurentian faction (fol. 121v). This is followed by a list of popes and the lengths of their pontificates, ending with Symmachus's successor Hormisdas (fols. 121v–122r). While John's submission may have served as a general model for reconciliation for Laurentian clerics, it also has been suggested that he is to be identified with Pope John I, Hormisdas's successor, and that this collection was drafted upon his accession to the papal throne. There would have been increased scrutiny of his "schismatic" past, so the submission and the papal list might have served to illustrate his affiliation with the legitimate papal line of succession.[37]

Between the acts of the synods of 501 and 502, the compiler inserted a short letter of Pope Zosimus (†418) to clerics in Ravenna, warning them not to enter communion with some other clerics who had recently accused him of an unspecified crime at emperor Honorius's court (fols. 127rb–vb).[38] This was presumably meant to set a precedent for the rejection of the charges brought against Symmachus at Theoderic's court. Zosimus's letter is followed by five pieces of correspondence between

---

[36] Kéry, *Canonical Collections,* 24, with references; see Wirbelauer, *Zwei Päpste,* 211–13 for a detailed table of contents. Up to this colophon, the ninth-century copyists seem to have reproduced the sixth-century collection faithfully; after this, a second, though probably also ninth-century, scribe added some texts that fill the rest of the remaining quaternio plus an added binio. The additions are not of interest here.

[37] Wirbelauer, *Zwei Päpste,* 117–18, with references. For a somewhat more cautious interpretation, Charles Piétri and Luce Piétri, *Prosopographie chrétienne du Bas-Empire 2,1: Prosopographie de l'Italie chrétienne (313–604), A-K* (Rome: École Française de Rome, 1999), 1072, 1074, and 1080 (IOHANNES 22, 26, and 28).

[38] Zosimus, *Ex relatione fratris* (J³ 750), in Patrologia Latina 56, cols. 573–74.

Theoderic and leading Italian bishops in Rome at the time (fols. 127vb–132vb), illustrating the way the synod in late 502 came about. The bishops, unable to come to an agreement, kept pushing king Theoderic to make a ruling. The king, however, kept insisting that he would not interfere in ecclesiastical matters and would wait to accept whatever outcome restored peace to the Church.[39] There seems to have been some anxiety to avoid the accusation that the synod — and, by inference, the decision in favor of Symmachus — had occurred on Theoderic's secular authority alone, even as the synod began.[40] Combatting this idea may have been even more pressing after 506/507, when, at least according to the Laurentian tradition, the schism was finally ended by royal decree.[41] Adding the correspondence to the synodal *acta* could prove that the decision had been the bishops' to make.

While the inclusion of the texts that are interspersed with the synodal *acta* in Vatican City, BAV, MS Reg. lat. 1997 does not in itself need explanation, it is less clear if the compiler of the collection thought of them as a "self-sufficient textual unit." Here, unlike in the Dionysian tradition, the acts of the Roman synods and the supplemental materials are not marked as separate in any way. If they became available to the compiler of the collection as a self-sufficient unit, the ninth-century copyist left no traces of that. Additionally, many more texts in Vatican City, BAV, MS Reg. lat. 1997 are as germane to the Laurentian schism as the ones just mentioned. Wirbelauer, for instance, believed that a letter by Pope Boniface I to emperor Honorius (fols. 110va–111va) and his reply (fols. 111va–112rb), an edict by emperor Glycerius (fols. 112rb–114rb) and letters by Leo the Great to the bishops of Aquileia (fols. 114rb–116ra) and Altinum (fols. 116ra–va), all could be considered part of the dossier. It would certainly make sense to include the correspondence between Boniface and Honorius in a dossier on the Laurentian schism,

---

39 *Acta synhodorum*, 419–26.
40 Ibid., 426–27.
41 *Fragment Laurentien,* in *Le Liber Pontificalis,* 46.

since they set a relevant precedent on how to deal with contested papal elections.[42] Glycerius's edict against simony may have been relevant because both sides seem to have accused each other of this offense. Leo's letters are harder to integrate, however. Wirbelauer suggested that they were meant to serve as *exempla* of submission to papal authority to the successors of their addressees in the sees of Aquileia and Altinum, both of whom had sided with Laurentius,[43] but both letters are concerned quite specifically with the issue of clerics in Aquileia who had refused explicitly to condemn Pelagianism.[44]

Two other texts in Vatican City, BAV, MS Reg. lat. 1997 also seem more directly connected to the Laurentian schism by content but are separated even from the correspondence between Boniface and Honorius by several, definitely unrelated, texts: Leo's Tome to Flavian of Constantinople (fols. 65rb–70vb)[45] — which, at least for some Westerners, was a more important formulation of Chalcedonian orthodoxy than even the acts of Chalcedon themselves[46] — and the *Gesta de nomine Acaci* (fols. 96ra–99va),[47] a short account of how the Acacian schism came to be (from a distinctly Roman perspective; often attribut-

---

42 Honorius, *Ad Bonifatium Episcopum Romanum*, in *Collectio Avellana*, ed. Otto Günther, Corpus Scriptorum Ecclesiasticorum Latinorum 35 (Vienna: Tempsky, 1895–1898), vol. 1, 84; Wirbelauer, *Zwei Päpste*, 11–13, and Eckhard Wirbelauer, "Die Nachfolgerbestimmung im römischen Bistum (3.-6. Jahrhundert): Doppelwahlen und Absetzungen in ihrer Herrschafts soziologischen Bedeutung," *Klio* 76 (1994): 414–16.

43 Wirbelauer, *Zwei Päpste*, 117.

44 Leo I, *Relatione sancti fratris* (J³ 897), in Patrologia Latina 54, cols. 593–97, and Leo I, *Lectis fraternitatis tuae* (J³ 898), in Patrologia Latina 54, cols. 597–98.

45 Eduard Schwartz, ed., *Acta Conciliorum Oecumenicorum* (hereafter, *ACO*) 2.2.1 (Berlin: De Gruyter, 1932), 24–33.

46 Richard Price, "The Three Chapters Controversy and the Council of Chalcedon," in *The Crisis of the Oikoumene: The Three Chapters and the Failed Quest for Unity in the Sixth-Century Mediterranean*, ed. Celia Chazelle and Catherine Cubitt, Studies in the Early Middle Ages 14 (Turnhout: Brepols, 2007), 34.

47 *Gesta de nomine Acaci*, in *Collectio Avellana*, ed. Otto Günther, Corpus Scriptorum Ecclesiasticorum Latinorum 35 (Vienna: Tempsky, 1895–1898), vol. 1, 440–52.

ed to Gelasius).[48] They serve as a reminder that the compiler of the *collectio Teatina* acquired material on the Laurentian schism from different sources. Thus, in the absence of paleographical or codicological evidence that survived the copying process, the relatedness of the content of these texts is not on its own sufficient to prove that any of them were part of a dossier.

A Gallic "Symmachus Dossier" in Paris, Bibliothèque nationale de France, MS lat. 1564, Munich, Bayerische Staatsbibliothek, MS Clm 5508 and Berlin, Staatsbibliothek, MS Phill. 1743

However, the primary reason to suppose that the texts related to the Laurentian schism in the collection of Vatican City, BAV, MS Reg. lat. 1997 formed a dossier lies not in this manuscript itself, but rather in the evidence that they may have circulated independently of that collection. Three canon law collections from Merovingian Gaul — the *collectio Pithouensis* (Paris, Bibliothèque nationale de France, MS lat. 1564), the *collectio Diessensis* (Munich, Bayerische Staatsbibliothek, MS Clm 5508) and the *collectio Remensis* (Berlin, Staatsbibliothek, MS Phill. 1743) — transmit the synodal acts with the same interspersed material (deacon John's submission, Zosimus's letter, correspondence with Theoderic) as the *collectio Teatina*, save for the list of popes; the first two also in the same order. However, as a more detailed comparison of these collections will demonstrate, this shows not that these texts circulated as a dossier before being integrated into the *collectio Teatina*, but rather that part of a collection dependent on the *collectio Teatina* was made into a dossier in Merovingian Gaul.

The *collectio Teatina* shares more than the above-mentioned texts with all three Gallic collections (see t. 1.1), though it has the least amount of overlap with the *collectio Pithouensis*. This

---

48 Walter Ullmann, *Gelasius I. (492–496): Das Papsttum an der Wende der Spätantike zum Mittelalter,* Päpste und Papsttum 18 (Stuttgart: Hiersemann, 1981), 245–46.

	Vatican City, BAV, MS Reg. lat. 1997	Paris, BnF, MS lat. 1564	Munich, BSb, MS Clm 5508	Berlin, Sb, MS Phill. 1743
Siricius to Himerius of Tarragona (J³ 605)	fols. 52rb–57rb	fols. 114r–118v	fols. 40va–44rb	fols. 79vb–85rs
Leo I to Rusticus of Narbonne (J³ 1098)	fols. 57vb–62ra	x	x (fols. 88ara–91ra)	x (fols. 234va–238vb)
Leo I to bishops of *Mauretania Caesariensis* (J³ 916)	fols. 62ra–65rb	x	fols. 65vb–68ra	fols. 261va–265ra and 208va–vb
Leo I to Flavian of Constantinople (*Tomus Leonis*) (J³ 934)	fols. 65rb–70vb	x (fols. 84r–87v)	x	fols. 208vb–215ra
Leo I to Thoribius of Astorga (J³ 919)	fols. 70vb–78rb	x (fols. 43r–48v)	fols. 55rb–60rb	fols. 215ra–224vb
Leo I to Sicilian bishops (J³ 922)	fols. 78rb–82ra	x	fols. 60rb–63ra	fols. 224vb–229vb
Leo I to Nicetas of Aquileia (J³ 1086)	fols. 82ra–83va	x	fols. 63ra–64ra	fols. 229vb–231va
Innocent I to Victricius of Rouen (J³ 665)	fols. 83va–86va	x (fols. 31r–34r)	x (fols. 46va–47vb [frag.])	fols. 173rb–176vb

Table 1.1. The collection of papal letters in Vatican City, Biblioteca Apostolica Vaticana, MS Reg. lat. 1997 and its transmission in Gaul. Brackets indicate that the manuscript does contain the same text, but in a form that suggests transmission independently of MS Reg. lat. 1997.

	Vatican City, BAV, MS Reg. lat. 1997	Paris, BnF, MS lat. 1564	Munich, BSb, MS Clm 5508	Berlin, Sb, MS Phill. 1743
Celestine I to bishops of *Viennensis* + *Narbonensis* (J³ 821)	fols. 86va–89rb	x (fols. 39r–40v)	x (fols. 50ra–51vb)	fols. 205vb–208va and 255va–256ra
Gelasius I to southern Italian and Sicilian bishops (J³ 1270)	fols. 89rb–96ra	x	x (fols. 68ra–73ra)	fols. 239ra–246rb
Gesta de nomine Acaci	fols. 96ra–99va	x	fols. 52rb–55ra	fols. 287va–291va
Jerome to Evangelus (*Ep.* 146)	fols. 99va–100vb	x	x	x
Innocent I to Exsuperius of Toulouse (J³ 675)	fols. 100vb–103rb	x (fols. 34r–35v)	x (fols. 96va–97vb [frag.])	x (fols. 179vb–181vb)
Innocent I to Macedonian bishops (J³ 691)	fols. 103va–108rb	x (fols. 35r–39r)	fol. 48ra (frag.)	fols. 181vb–185rb
Zosimus to Hesychius of Salona (J³ 745)	fols. 108rb–109vb	x (fols. 30r–31r)	fols. 48ra–49ra	fols. 202ra–203va
Celestine I to Apulian and Calabrian bishops (J³ 823)	fols. 109vb–110va	x (fols. 40v–41r)	fols. 51vb–52rb	fols. 256ra–257ra
Boniface I to emperor Honorius (J³ 787)	fols. 110va–111va	x	fol. 49ra–va	fols. 204ra–205ra
Emperor Honorius to Boniface I	fols. 111va–112rb	x	fols. 49va–50ra	fols. 205ra–vb

	Vatican City, BAV, MS Reg. lat. 1997	Paris, BnF, MS lat. 1564	Munich, BSb, MS Clm 5508	Berlin, Sb, MS Phill. 1743
Edict of emperor Glycerius + promulgation letter	fols. 112rb–114rb	x	fols. 87vb–88ara	x
Leo I to the bishop of Aquileia (J³ 897)	fols. 114rb–116ra	x	fols. 64ra–65rb	fols. 231va–233rb
Leo I to Septimus of Altinum (J³ 898)	fols. 116ra–va	x	fols. 65rb–vb	fols. 234ra–234va
Roman synod of 499	fols. 116va–121va	fols. 118v–121v	fols. 74ra–75vb (frag.)	fols. 246rb–252rb
Submission of the deacon John to Symmachus	fol. 121v	fols. 121v–122r	fols. 75vb–76ra	fols. 252rb–va
List of popes ending with Hormisdas	fols. 121v–122rb	x	x	x (fols. 293vb–294vb)
Roman synod of 501	fols. 122rb–127rb	fols. 122r–125v	fols 76ra–79rb	fols. 252va–255va and 265ra–266va
Zosimus to clerics in Ravenna (J³ 750)	fols. 127rb–vb	fols. 125v–126r	fol. 79rb–va	fols. 203va–204ra
Correspondence between Theoderic and bishops in Rome	fols. 127vb–132vb	fols. 126r–129r	fols. 79va–82vb	fols. 85rb–90rb
Roman synod of 502	fols. 132vb–137ra	fols. 129r–132v	fols. 82vb–85va	fols. 90rb–95vb

canon law collection was probably assembled circa 600 around Sens or Auxerre. It is named after the humanist Pierre Pithou, the early modern possessor of its only manuscript witness, Paris, BnF, MS lat. 1564, which was produced in the late eighth or ninth century at a nunnery in northern France — probably Chelles.[49] Before the material connected to the Roman synods (fols. 118v–132v), it transmits a decretal by Pope Siricius (fols. 114r–118v) in a form closely related to its transmission in Vatican City, BAV, MS Reg. lat. 1127.[50] The content of the decretal bears no obvious relation to the Laurentian schism, and it is separated by some 60 folia from the *acta* of the synod of 499 in the latter codex, making it unlikely that it was part of a dossier on the Laurentian schism that the compiler of the *collectio Teatina* used for their collection.

Additionally, Paris, BnF, MS lat. 1564 shares some texts with the other two Gallic collections under consideration that do not appear in Vatican City, BAV, MS Reg. lat. 1997. Before the Siricius decretal, it transmits the canons of the council of Chalcedon in 451 (fols. 111v–114r). While the text of these canons varies somewhat between the three Gallic *libri canonum*,[51] it is still al-

---

49 Kéry, *Canonical Collections,* 48–49, with references. For the contents of this collection, see Maassen, *Geschichte der Quellen,* 604–10, and Geoffrey Dunn, "*Collectio Corbeiensis, Collectio Pithouensis,* and the Earliest Collections of Papal Letters," in *Collecting Early Christian Letters: From the Apostle Paul to Late Antiquity,* ed. Bronwen Neil and Pauline Allen (Cambridge: Cambridge University Press, 2016), 200–5. Eight quires at the beginning and an indefinite number at the end of the manuscript have been lost; these probably transmitted both the table of contents and the final *Explicit liber canonum* found in most sixth-century canon law collections from Gaul. Without these quires, it is difficult to determine whether the Carolingian nuns only reproduced a Merovingian collection or made their own additions and changes to it.

50 On the transmission of this text in the *collectio Teatina* and the three Gallic collections under consideration, see Klaus Zechiel-Eckes and Detlev Jasper, eds., *Die erste Dekretale: Der Brief Papst Siricius' an Bischof Himerius von Tarragona vom Jahr 385* (JK 255), Monumenta Germaniae Historica, Studien und Texte 55 (Hanover: Hahn, 2013), 46–49, 62–64.

51 Berlin, Staatsbibliothek, MS Phill. 1743 adds a table of contents written, according to Schwartz, by a "barbaric and uneducated man" (*homo barbarus et indoctus*) (Schwartz, *ACO* 2.2.2, Berlin: Walter de Gruyter, 1936, 53),

ways recognizably dependent on the earlier Latin translation by Dionysius Exiguus, and it directly precedes the Siricius decretal in all three.[52] Likewise, a letter from 513 by Symmachus to Caesarius of Arles (fols. 132v–133r)[53] follows some parts of the synodal acts of 499–502 in all three.[54] The compiler of the *collectio Pithouensis* also quite clearly switched from one source to another on (what is now) fol. 111v. From fol. 23r to fol. 111v, the collection depends on the same source as the *collectio Corbeiensis*,[55]

---

and transmits the last canon twice; Munich, BSb, MS Clm 5508 omits all but the last seven canons due to a missing quaternio; Paris, BnF, MS lat. 1564 omits some parts and adds a canon on church asylum, possibly taken from an otherwise unknown Gallic synod; see Emil Seckel, "Studien zu Benedictus Levita VI," *Neues Archiv der Gesellschaft für ältere deutsche Geschichtskunde* 31 (1906): 238–39.

52 Schwartz, *ACO* 2.2.1, 53–60. Berlin, Staatsbibliothek, MS Phill. 1743 is Schwartz's siglum *n*; he used neither Paris, BnF MS lat. 1564 nor Munich, BSb, Clm 5508 for his edition, though Maassen had already identified them as belonging to the Dionysian tradition: Maassen, *Geschichte der Quellen*, 609, 626. The *collectio Teatina* does contain the canons of Chalcedon, but in the so-called *versio Prisca*. See Cuthbert H. Turner, "Chapters in the History of Latin MSs of Canons: VI. The Version Called Prisca: (B) The Chieti MS (= I), now Vatic. Regin. 1997," *The Journal of Theological Studies* os 31, no. 1 (1929): 9–20.

53 Symmachus, *Hortatur nos aequitas* (J³ 1460) in *Monumenta Germaniae Historica, Epistulae* 3, ed. Wilhelm Gundlach (Berlin: Weidmann, 1892), 37–40 (=*Epistolae Arelatenses* 26).

54 Duchesne suggested that the acts of the Roman synods were sent to Gaul together with this letter: Louis Duchesne, "Les schismes romains au VIᵉ siècle," *Mélanges d'archéologie et d'histoire* 35, no. 1 (1915): 224; cf. Wirbelauer, *Zwei Päpste*, 119–20. This of course makes it impossible that the combination of the acts and the supplemental material was drawn up on the occasion of John's accession to the papacy (see above), though this could still be the reason it was *copied* in the *collectio Teatina*, since the list of popes up to Hormisdas was inserted where it was. If Duchesne was correct, it seems likely that the entire collection of papal letters in Vatican City, BAV, MS Reg. lat 1997 was sent to Gaul in 513, given the amount of overlap between that collection; Munich, BSb, Clm 5508; and Berlin, Sb, MS Phill. 1743 (see t. 1).

55 Maassen, *Geschichte der Quellen*, 610–11; Wurm, *Studien und Texte*, 96; see also the table of contents of both collections in Dunn, "*Collectio Corbeiensis, Collectio Pithouensis*," 190–205. The *collectio Corbeiensis* is transmitted in Paris, Bibliothèque nationale de France, MS lat. 12097.

and the texts it shares with the *collectiones Diessensis* and *Remensis* follow *en bloc* from fol. 111v. Given that these two collections share most of their papal letters with the *collectio Teatina* (see t. 1.1), and even more texts between each other, it seems more plausible that there was a common source for the three Gallic collections that was in turn dependent on the *Teatina*, rather than a dossier that the compilers of both the *Teatina* and the *Pithouensis* used independently.

Since Symmachus's letter to Caesarius was copied into the *collectio Pithouensis* twice (fols. 69v–70r and 132v–133r), the first time from the previously mentioned source shared by this collection and the *collectio Corbeiensis*, the compiler of the *collectio Pithouensis* apparently did not simply take what was missing from their collection from the source that the *Pithouensis, Remensis*, and *Diessensis* share. Thus, it is worth asking if they were reaching for a dossier when they switched from one source to the other[56] — whether, in other words, the shared texts could have circulated independently as a dossier before they found their way into the *collectio Pithouensis*. The transmission of the canons of Chalcedon, Siricius's letter, the acts of the Roman synods of 499–502 with supplemental material and Symmachus's letter to Caesarius in the *Diessensis* and *Remensis* will therefore be investigated for evidence that the compilers of these collections thought of these texts as a self-sufficient unit.

In Munich, BSb, MS Clm 5508, however, Siricius's letter and the canons of Chalcedon, while directly following one another (fols. 40ra–44rb), are separate from the material relating to the Roman synods of 499–502 and Symmachus's letter to Caesarius (fols. 74ra–86rb). This manuscript, written in Salzburg in the late eighth century, contains two canon law collections, only the first of which, the so-called *collectio Diessensis*,[57] is of note here. It was probably originally assembled around the mid-seventh

---

56 A switch in sources is one of the possible indicators for the use of a booklet according to Hanna, "Booklets in medieval manuscripts," 108–9.
57 The collection was named after this manuscript, which belonged to the monastery of Diessen by the fifteenth century.

century and ends, at fol. 130va–b, with "Here end the canons compiled from three books."[58] There is some debate over which three books the compiler used, but one of them seems to have been the aforementioned common source of the three Gallic *collectiones* dependent on the *Teatina*.[59] The grouping in Munich, BSb, MS Clm 5508 makes a certain amount of sense, insofar as Chalcedon is the last piece of a collection of Greek and African councils, with Siricius at the beginning of a collection of papal letters closely related to the one in *collectio Teatina*.

Unlike the *collectio Teatina*, the papal letters were ordered by successive popes.[60] The section devoted to Symmachus contains the acts of the Roman synods with the same supplemental material in the same order as Paris, BnF, MS lat. 1564 — that is to say, even Zosimus's letter to clerics in Ravenna stayed with the rest of the putative dossier (fol. 79rb–va) instead of being sorted with his letter to Hesychius of Salona some 30 folios earlier (fols. 48ra–49ra). However, the compiler may not have been aware that a separate text had begun. For the synod of 501, the attendance list in the beginning records bishops, presbyters, and deacons, but only the subscriptions of the bishops are transmitted at the end, with some version of *item subscriptiones presbyterorum* (likewise the presbyters' subscriptions) or *omnes similiter subscripserunt* (everyone [else] signed similarly) after the last episcopal subscription.[61] Already in Vatican City, BAV, MS Reg. lat. 1997 — which generally offers the most reliable text of the four collections under consideration — the separation of these two texts begins to deteriorate, with "item subscriptio presbyterorum" looking more like the title to Zosimus's letter, though a

---

58 "Expliciunt canones ex tribus libris edita."
59 Wurm, *Studien und Texte*, 100.
60 Siricius's decretal is followed by the canons of Epao (517) (fols. 44va–46rb), which may be a later addition; but other than that, the *Gesta de nomine Acaci* (fols. 52rb–55ra) is the only text that is not a papal letter in this part of the manuscript. They were sorted between the letters of Celestine I (422–432) and Leo the Great (440–461). Since they begin with the exile of Nestorius in 435, this could be seen as a continuation of the principle of chronology, though the last event they record took place in 485.
61 *Acta synhodorum*, 455.

decorated initial "Z" at least clearly marks the beginning of that text.[62] In Paris, BnF, MS lat. 1564 (fols. 125v–126r) and Munich, BSb, MS Clm 5508 (fol. 79rb), the distinction was lost completely. Without a number and display script to mark the beginning, it reads as a continuous text: "They similarly subscribed to Zosimus's letter of instruction to presbyters and deacons who are in Ravenna."[63] Thus, there is reason to doubt that the inclusion of Zosimus's letter in the supplemental material to the Roman synods was intentional. The compiler of the *collectio Diessensis*, then, seems to have seen no connection between Chalcedon and the Siricius letter on the one hand, and the acts of the Roman synods (including John's submission and the correspondence with Theoderic) on the other. Additionally, it is unclear whether the compiler considered Zosimus's letter a separate text connected to the acts in terms of content, or simply as the last part of the acts themselves.

An analysis of the last *liber canonum* to transmit the Roman material (Berlin, Sb, MS Phill. 1743), however, corroborates that the combination of Chalcedon, Siricius, and the acts of the Roman synods in Paris, BnF, MS lat. 1564 was, in fact, perceived as a self-sufficient textual unit. Written probably in Bourges around the mid-eighth century, Berlin, Sb, MS Phill. 1743 belonged to the monastery of St. Remi in Reims by the ninth century. This monastery gave the *Collectio Remensis* its name. The collection was initially assembled in the second half of the sixth century, rearranged some decades later, and then further amended in the seventh century.[64] The relevant texts appear in the following order in the eight-century manuscript:

---

62 Vatican City, BAV, MS Reg. lat. 1997, fol. 127rb; compare, for example, the beginning of Theoderic's *praeceptio* on fol. 127vb.

63 "Similiter subscripserunt zosimus communitorium presbyteris et diaconis qui ravenna sunt."

64 Valentin Rose, *Verzeichnis der lateinischen Handschriften der königlichen Bibliothek zu Berlin 1*, Die Handschriften-Verzeichnisse der königlichen Bibliothek zu Berlin 12 (Berlin: Asher, 1893), 171–79; Bernhard Bischoff, "Panorama der Handschriftenüberlieferung aus der Zeit Karls des Großen," in *Karl der Grosse. Lebenswerk und Nachleben 2: Das geistige Leben*, ed. Helmut Beumann et al. (Düsseldorf: L. Schwann, 1965), 241, and

fols. 74rb–79va:	Canons of the council of Chalcedon (451)
fols. 79vb–85ra:	Siricius to Himerius of Tarragona (J³ 605)
fols. 85rb–90rb:	Correspondence between Theoderic and bishops in Rome
fols. 90rb–95vb:	Roman synod of 502
…	
fols. 203va–204ra:	Zosimus to clerics in Ravenna (J³ 750)
…	
fols. 246rb–252rb:	Roman synod of 499
fols. 252rb–252va:	Submission of the deacon John
fols. 252va–255va:	Roman synod of 501 – first half
…	
fols. 265ra–267vb:	Roman synod of 501 – second half
fols. 267vb–268va:	Symmachus to Caesarius of Arles (J³ 1460)

Covering almost 200 folios, these texts seem neither self-sufficient nor connected. The break in the acts of the synod of 501 is relatively easy to explain, at least. Apparently unnoticed by the eighth-century copyists, some of the quires in their exemplar had been bound out of order, resulting in several mid-sentence switches between texts. However, in the sixth-century collec-

---

Hubert Mordek, *Bibliotheca capitularium regum Francorum manuscripta. Überlieferung und Traditionszusammenhang der Fränkischen Herrschererlasse,* Monumenta Germaniae Historica, Hilfsmittel 15 (Munich: Hahn, 1995), 59–60. See also Michael Eber, Stefan Esders, David Ganz, and Till Stüber, "Selection and Presentation of Texts in Early Medieval Canon Law Collections: Approaching the *Codex Remensis* (Berlin, Staatsbibliothek, Phill. 1743)," in *Creative Selection between Emending and Forming Medieval Memory,* ed. Sebastian Scholz et al., Millennium-Studies 96 (Berlin: De Gruyter, 2021), 105–36 and Till Stüber, *Die sogenannte Collectio canonum Remensis. Entstehung und Rezeption einer frühmittelalterlichen Kirchenrechtssammlung* (in preparation).

tion, the synodal *acta* were still cohesive.[65] Zosimus's letter was removed from the Symmachus material and placed after his letter to Hesychius of Salona (fols. 202ra–203va) already during the rearrangement of the sixth century, when, as in the *collectio Diessensis,* the papal letters in this collection were arranged by successive popes.[66] As mentioned, the other two Gallic collections treat this letter as if it were part of the synodal acts themselves, instead of an inserted text offering an historical precedent for one particular issue at stake during the Laurentian Schism. Since the break between the acts of 501 and Zosimus's letter was apparently still recognizable to the redactor of the *Remensis,* we can tell that this precedent seemed less relevant to them as the schism became more distant, both in time and space.

However, the sixth-century redactor of the *collectio Remensis* also split up the acts of the Roman synods, taking a somewhat formalistic approach. They seem to have only included texts that explicitly refer to Symmachus in the incipit in the section of their collection that contained chronologically arranged papal letters. The incipits of the synod of 499,[67] the submission of the deacon John,[68] the synod of 501,[69] and Symmachus's letter to

---

65 There are roughly 38 columns of text between the two halves of the synod of 501. Taking this as the approximate length of one quire in the exemplar, we would expect there to be some multiple of 38 columns of text between the point where the texts interrupting the *acta* belong (fol. 208v) and where they ended up (fol. 255v). There are, in fact, about 188 columns, or almost exactly 5 × 38.

66 The only extraneous text in the part of the manuscript that contains the chronologically arranged papal letters are some extracts from the acts of the council of Ephesus c. 431 (fols. 186ra–201vb) between the letters of Innocent I and Zosimus. They fill exactly two quires, and the next quire begins with "expliciunt epistulas innocenti" ("Here end the letters of Innocent"), fol. 202ra. Thus, the Ephesus material was not part of the exemplar, but rather an addition made by the eighth-century copyists.

67 "Incipiunt canoni symmachi pape" ("Here begin the canons of Pope Symmachus"), fol. 246rb.

68 "Item lebellus quem obtulit papae symacho caelius Iohannis diaconus ecclesiae romanae" ("Likewise a petition which Caelius Iohannes, deacon of the Roman church, sent to Pope Symmachus"), fol. 252rb.

69 "Constitutio facta ad [*sic*] domno symmacho papa de rebus eclesiae conservandis" ("A constitution made by Pope Symmachus on the conservation

Caesarius[70] all mention him by name, whereas the incipits of the correspondence between Theoderic and the bishops at the synod in 502,[71] and the acts of that synod, do not.[72] Having sorted all texts that mentioned Symmachus in the title with his section in the chronologically ordered collection of papal letters, the redactor seems to have been left with the canons of Chalcedon, the Siricius decretal, and the 502 material. Had they consistently applied their own (apparent) principles, they would, of course, also have had to move the decretal to (what is now) fol. 173r, before the decretals of Innocent I, but they chose not to. And unlike the Zosimus letter in Paris, BnF, MS lat. 1564 and Munich, BSb, MS Clm 5508, the Siricius decretal seems to have been recognizable as a decretal by Pope Siricius, at least judging by the eighth-century copy of the collection. Written in a neat uncial with lines alternating between red and black ink, at fol. 79vb the title reads "Here begin the chapters of a constitution by the Holy Siricius, bishop of the city of Rome."[73] We should therefore assume a conscious decision to let the decretal retain its position with the rest of the putative dossier.

Like the compiler of *collectio Diessensis,* then, the redactor of *collectio Remensis* had a version of the collection of papal letters in Vatican City, BAV, MS Reg. lat. 1997 at their disposal that had already been supplemented by Symmachus's letter to Caesarius and combined with a collection of African and Greek

---

of church property"), fol. 252va.

70 "Dilectissmo fratri caesario Symachus" ("Symmachus to his beloved brother Caesarius"), fol. 267va.

71 "Incipit praeceptio quae missa est per germanum et carosum episcopis" ("Here begins a royal precept, delivered by the bishops Germanus and Carosus"), fol. 85rb; "incipit preceptio regis IIII missa ad synodum" ("Here begins the 4th royal precept sent to the synod"), fol. 86ra–b; "relacio episcoporum ad regem" ("Report by the bishops to the king"), fol. 87va (title not in a display script); "praeceptio regia fl. Theudericus rex" ("Royal precept of King Flavius Theudericus"), fol. 88vb (explicit and incipit not clearly separated); and "agnanusticum regis" ("Declaration by the king"), fol. 89rb (not in a display script, and the explicit of the previous text follows only *after* the title of the next).

72 "Constitucio episcoporum" ("Constitution by the bishops"), fol. 90ra.

73 "Incipiunt capitula de constitutione sancti sirici episcopi urbis romae."

councils — that is to say, the original version of the *collectio Remensis*, which was a common source for both the *Diessensis* and *Pithouensis*.⁷⁴ Unlike the compiler of the *Diessensis*, however, the *Remensis* redactor left traces in his collection that the original *collectio Remensis* was arranged in a way that marked out the texts that later ended up in the *collectio Pithouensis* as an independent textual unit in some way. They seem to have tried to combine two incompatible principles — the connectedness of the dossier, and the chronological order of the papal letters — and while the solution they found may not have been the most elegant one, it does provide evidence that they not only found these texts in the same order as they appear in Paris, BnF, MS lat. 1564, but that both they and the compiler of the *collectio Pithouensis* (who only integrated these texts into their collection) also understood that they belonged together.

While the connection of the synodal acts that proved the legitimacy of Symmachus's papal authority with his letter to Caesarius, in which he made normative decisions based on this authority, is clear, the combination with the Siricius decretal is less immediately intelligible. As one focus of this text is chastity for different clerical grades (ch. 6, 7, 11, 12),⁷⁵ it may have had something to do with the accusations of sexual impropriety leveled against Symmachus.⁷⁶ Given how broad its transmission was,⁷⁷ there might also have been some awareness of the historical importance of the text that its most recent editor has called "the first decretal."⁷⁸ It may, then, have been included as *pars pro*

---

74 A more complete articulation of the arguments in favor of the interdependence of these three collections and analysis of their respective treatments of the Symmachus dossier can be found in Michael Eber, *Christologie und Kanonistik. Der Dreikapitelstreit in merowingischen libri canonum*. Monumenta Germaniae Historica, Schriften 82 (Wiesbaden: Harrassowitz, 2023), 108–17 and 127–34.

75 Zechiel-Eckes and Jasper, *Die erste Dekretale*, 7.

76 Wirbelauer, *Zwei Päpste*, 28.

77 Zechiel-Eckes and Jasper, *Die erste Dekretale*, 19.

78 Some stress the influence of Siricius's predecessor Damasus on the development of this genre of papal decision-making. For a recent overview of the debate, see David L. d'Avray, "Half a Century of Research on the First

toto for papal authority in general, which some canonists may have viewed as threatened during the schism. Neither of these explanations might be particularly satisfying, but the manuscript evidence does demonstrate that these texts were thought to belong together.

The council of Chalcedon bears more obvious relevance to the Laurentian schism. It was, after all, the dispute over its heritage that had led to the Acacian, then the Laurentian schism. Admittedly, the canons of Chalcedon, as opposed to the acts or the creed, were not particularly important in that dispute, so "Chalcedon" may mainly have served as a catchword, but as the first full Latin translation of the acts was probably not produced until the mid-sixth century[79] perhaps there was simply not much alternative Chalcedonian material available.[80] At any rate, the conscious inclusion of the canons of Chalcedon in the Symmachus dossier suggests that at least some contemporaries — even in Gaul, certainly at the periphery of the Christological debates of the fifth and sixth centuries — would have agreed with modern historians on the underlying causes and stakes of the Laurentian schism.

Papal Decretals (to c. 440)," *Bulletin of Medieval Canon Law* 35 (2018): 331–74; since Damasus's purported decretals are nowhere near as ubiquitous in canon law collections as the one by Siricius, early medieval canonists may have agreed with Zechiel-Eckes.

79 Eduard Schwartz, ed., *ACO* 2.3.1 (Berlin: Walter de Gruyter, 1935), vii, and Michael Gaddis and Richard Price, trans., *The Acts of the Council of Chalcedon 1: General Introduction, Documents Before the Council, Session I,* Translated Texts for Historians 45 (Liverpool: Liverpool University Press, 2005), 85.

80 In fact, the only other Chalcedonian text that was definitely available in Gaul in the first half of the sixth century is a short excerpt from the third session in which the papal delegates confirm the sentences against Dioscuros and Eutyches, also transmitted in Paris, BnF, MS lat. 1564 (fols. 87v–88v), as well as Paris, BnF, MS lat. 12097 (fols. 103r-104v), and Cologne, EDD, MS 212 (fols. 143r-144r).

Conclusions

The acts of the synods of 499–502 were a self-sufficient textual unit to Dionysius Exiguus when he included them in the second recension of his collection of decretals, thus signaling his neutrality in the Laurentian schism, but less clearly so to the compiler of the *collectio Teatina*. This compiler collected, among other things, many different texts related to the Laurentian schism, but did not use that relatedness as an organizing principle in their collection of papal letters. Once that collection came to Gaul, however, it became one of the sources for a canon law collection in which the acts of the Roman synods were combined with the canons of Chalcedon, the Siricius decretal, and Symmachus's letter to Caesarius, and then singled out for independent transmission as a dossier on the Laurentian schism. In the eyes of the Gallic canonist that made this decision, texts that the compiler of the *collectio Teatina* had included for their immediate legal precedents—like the Glycerius edict or the correspondence between Boniface and Honorius, but also Zosimus's letter to clerics in Ravenna—seem to have receded in importance, just as texts that provided a hint of the larger Church historical context, like the council of Chalcedon, came to the fore.

Beyond the immediate lessons on different compilers' varied ways of contextualizing the Laurentian Schism, the Gallic collections in particular also provided evidence that dossiers did not simply form the building blocks of what, through almost mechanical agglomeration, would eventually become fully-fledged historically arranged canon law collections. Rather, dossiers could be made and un-made repeatedly. Every step of the way, early medieval canonists had the confidence to make their own decisions about which texts did or did not belong together. Even after a dossier had been integrated into a larger collection, the compilers and users of these collections were often aware of the textual self-sufficiency of the erstwhile dossiers, and there was always the possibility that they might be singled out for independent transmission again.

Bibliography

Manuscripts

Berlin, Staatsbibliothek, MS Phill. 1743.

Cologne, Erzbischöfliche Diözesan- und Dombibliothek, MS 212. https://nbn-resolving.de/urn:nbn:de:hbz:kn28-3-937-p0009-8.

Munich, Bayerische Staatsbibliothek, MS Clm 5508. https://api.digitale-sammlungen.de/iiif/presentation/v2/bsb00036890/canvas/1/view.

Paris, Bibliothèque nationale de France, MS lat. 1564. http://archivesetmanuscrits.bnf.fr/ark:/12148/cc59512f.

Paris, Bibliothèque nationale de France, MS lat. 3837. http://archivesetmanuscrits.bnf.fr/ark:/12148/cc61802r.

Paris, Bibliothèque nationale de France, MS lat. 12097. http://archivesetmanuscrits.bnf.fr/ark:/12148/cc73447g.

Vatican City, Biblioteca Apostolica Vaticana, MS Reg. lat. 1997. https://digi.vatlib.it/view/MSS_Reg.lat.1997.

Vatican City, Biblioteca Apostolica Vaticana, MS Vat. lat. 5845. https://digi.vatlib.it/view/MSS_Vat.lat.5845.

Primary

Acta synhodorum habitarum Romae. In Monumenta Germaniae Historica, Auctores Antiquissimi 12, edited by Theodor Mommsen, 393–455. Berlin: Weidmann, 1894.

Anastasius II. *Exordium pontificatus mei* (J³ 1403). In *Epistolae Romanorum pontificum genuinae,* edited by Andreas Thiel, 615–23. Brunsberg: E. Peter, 1886.

Dionysius Exiguus. In *Praefatio in collectione decretorum pontificum ad Iulianum presbyterum.* Corpus Christianorum Series Latina 85, edited by Salvatore Gennaro and François Glorie, 43–47. Turnhout: Brepols, 1972.

Duchesne, Louis, ed. *Le Liber Pontificalis: Texte, Introduction, et Commentaire* 1. Paris: E. Thorin, 1886.

Fragment Laurentien. In Le *Liber Pontificalis: Texte, Introduction, et Commentaire 1,* edited by Louis Duchesne, 43–46. Paris: E. Thorin, 1886.

Gesta de nomine Acaci. In *Collectio Avellana,* Corpus Scriptorum Ecclesiasticorum Latinorum 35, edited by Otto Günther, Volume 1, 440–52. Vienna: Tempsky, 1895–1898.

Honorius. *Ad Bonifatium episcopum Romanum.* In *Collectio Avellana,* Volume 1: *Prolegomena. Epistulae I-CIV*, edited by Otto Günther, 1, 83–84. Corpus Scriptorum Ecclesiasticorum Latinorum 35. Vienna, Leipzig, Prague: Tempsky, 1895–1898.

Leo I. *Relatione sancti fratris* (J³ 897). Patrologia Latina 54, cols. 593–97.

———. *Lectis fraternitatis tuae* (J³ 898). Patrologia Latina 54, cols. 597–98.

Schwartz, Eduard, ed. *Acta conciliorum oecumenicorum* 2.2.1. Berlin: Walter de Gruyter, 1932.

———, ed. *Acta conciliorum oecumenicorum* 2.3.1. Berlin: Walter de Gruyter, 1935.

———, ed. *Acta conciliorum oecumenicorum* 2.2.2. Berlin: Walter de Gruyter, 1936.

Symmachus, *Hortatur nos aequitas* (J³ 1460). In *Monumenta Germaniae Historica, Epistulae* 3, edited by Wilhelm Gundlach, 37–40. Berlin: Weidmann, 1892.

Zechiel-Eckes, Klaus, and Detlev Jasper, eds. *Die erste Dekretale: Der Brief Papst Siricius' an Bischof Himerius von Tarragona vom Jahr 385 (JK 255).* Monumenta Germaniae Historica, Studien und Texte 55. Hanover: Hahn, 2013.

Zosimus. *Ex relatione fratris* (J3 750). Patrologia Latina 56, cols. 573–4.

Secondary

Bischoff, Bernhard. "Panorama der Handschriftenüberlieferung aus der Zeit Karls des Großen." In *Karl der Grosse. Lebenswerk und Nachleben 2: Das geistige Leben,* edited by Helmut Beumann, Bernhard Bischoff, Wolfgang Braunfels and Percy E. Schramm, 233–54. Düsseldorf: L. Schwann, 1965.

Caspar, Erich. *Das Papsttum Unter Byzantinischer Herrschaft.* Geschichte des Papsttums von den Anfängen bis zur Höhe der Weltherrschaft 2. Tübingen: Mohr, 1933.

Chavasse, Antoine. "Les lettres de Saint Léon le Grand dans le supplément de la Dionysiana et de l'Hadriana et dans la collection du manuscrit du Vatican." *Revue des Sciences Religieuses* 38, no. 2 (1964): 154–76. DOI: 10.3406/rscir.1964.2381.

D'Avray, David L., "Half a Century of Research on the First Papal Decretals (to c. 440)." *Bulletin of Medieval Canon Law* no. 35 (2018): 331–74. DOI: 10.1353/bmc.2018.0007.

Duchesne, Louis. "Les schismes romains au VIe siècle." *Mélanges d'archéologie et d'histoire* 35, no. 1 (1915): 221–56. DOI: 10.3406/mefr.1915.7124.

Dunn, Geoffrey. "*Collectio Corbeiensis, Collectio Pithouensis*, and the Earliest Collections of Papal Letters." In *Collecting Early Christian Letters: From the Apostle Paul to Late Antiquity,* edited by Bronwen Neil and Pauline Allen, 175–205. Cambridge: Cambridge University Press, 2015.

Eber, Michael. *Christologie und Kanonistik. Der Dreikapitelstreit in merowingischen libri canonum.* Monumenta Germaniae Historica, Schriften 82. Wiesbaden: Harrassowitz, 2023.

Eber, Michael, Stefan Esders, David Ganz, and Till Stüber. "Selection and Presentation of Texts in Early Medieval Canon Law Collections: Approaching the Codex Remensis (Berlin, Staatsbibliothek, Phill. 1743)*." In *Creative Selection between Emending and Forming Medieval Memory,* edited by Sebastian Scholz and Gerald Schwedler, 105–36. Millennium-Studies 96. Berlin: De Gruyter, 2021.

Gaddis, Michael, and Richard Price, trans. *The Acts of the Council of Chalcedon 1: General Introduction. Documents Before the Council, Session I.* Translated Texts for Historians 45. Liverpool: Liverpool University Press, 2005.

Gioanni, Stéphane. "La contribution épistolaire d'Ennode de Pavie à la primauté pontificale sous le règne des papes Symmaque et Hormisdas." *Mélanges de l'école française de*

Rome. Moyen Âge 113, no. 1 (2001): 245–68. DOI: 10.3406/mefr.2001.11106.

Gumbert, Johann Peter. "Codicological Units: Towards a Terminology for the Stratigraphy of the Non-Homogeneous Codex." In *Il codice miscellaneo: Tipologie e funzioni. Atti del Convegno internazionale, Cassino, 14–17 maggio 2003*, edited by Edoardo Crisci and Oronzo Pecere, 17–42. Segno e testo 2. Turnhout: Brepols, 2004.

Hanna, Ralph. "Booklets in Medieval Manuscripts: Further Considerations." *Studies in Bibliography* 39 (1986): 100–11. https://www.jstor.org/stable/40371835.

Kennell, Stefanie A.H. *Magnus Felix Ennodius: A Gentleman of the Church*. Recentiores: Later Latin Texts and Contexts. Ann Arbor: University of Michigan Press, 2000.

Kéry, Lotte. *Canonical Collections of the Early Middle Ages (ca. 400–1140): A Bibliographical Guide to the Manuscripts and Literature*. History of Medieval Canon Law 1. Washington, DC: Catholic University of America Press, 1999.

Kötter, Jan-Markus. *Zwischen Kaisern und Aposteln. Das Akakianische Schisma (484–519) als kirchlicher Ordnungskonflikt der Spätantike*. Roma Æterna 2. Stuttgart: Franz Steiner, 2013.

Leyser, Conrad. "Law, Memory, and Priestly Office in Rome, c. 500." *Early Medieval Europe* 27, no. 1 (2019): 61–84. DOI: 10.1111/emed.12314.

Maassen, Friedrich. "Bibliotheca latina iuris canonici manuscripta 1.1." *Sitzungsberichte der Kaiserlichen Akademie der Wissenschaften, Philosophisch-Historische Classe* 53 (1866–1867): 373–427.

———. *Geschichte der Quellen und der Literatur des canonischen Rechts im Abendlande bis zum Ausgange des Mittelalters,* Volume 1: *Die Rechtssammlungen bis zur Mitte des 9. Jahrhunderts*. Graz: Leuschner & Lubensky, 1870.

Mathisen, Ralph W. "Between Arles, Rome, and Toledo: Gallic Collections of Canon Law in Late Antiquity." *'Ilu. Revista de Ciencias de las Religiones* 2 (1999): 33–46. https://revistas.ucm.es/index.php/ILUR/article/view/ILUR9999440033A.

———. "Church Councils and Local Authority: The Development of Gallic *Libri Canonum* during Late Antiquity." In *Being Christian in Late Antiquity: A Festschrift for Gillian Clark,* edited by Carol Harrison, Caroline Humfress, and Isabella Sandwell, 175–93. Oxford: Oxford University Press, 2014.

———. "The 'Codex Sangallensis' 190 and the Transmission of the Classical Tradition during Late Antiquity and the Early Middle Ages." *International Journal of the Classical Tradition* 5, no. 2 (1998): 163–94. DOI: 10.1007/BF02688421.

McKitterick, Rosamond. *History and Memory in the Carolingian World.* Cambridge: Cambridge University Press, 2004. DOI: 10.1017/CBO9780511617003.

Moorhead, John. "The Laurentian Schism: East and West in the Roman Church." *Church History* 47, no. 2 (1978): 125–36. DOI: 10.2307/3164729.

———. *Theoderic in Italy.* Oxford: Clarendon Press, 1992.

Mordek, Hubert. *Bibliotheca capitularium regum Francorum manuscripta. Überlieferung und Traditionszusammenhang der fränkischen Herrschererlasse.* Monumenta Germaniae Historica, Hilfsmittel 15. Munich: Hahn, 1995.

———. "Bischofsabsetzungen in Spätmerowingischer Zeit. Justelliana, Bernensis und das Konzil von Mâlay (677)." In *Papsttum, Kirche und Recht im Mittelalter: Festschrift für Horst Fuhrmann zum 65. Geburtstag,* edited by Hubert Mordek, 31–53. Tübingen: Niemeyer, 1991.

———. "Dionysius Exiguus." In *Lexikon des Mittelalters,* Volume 3, edited by Norbert Angermann, Robert Auty and Robert-Henri Bautier, 1088–1092. Munich: Artemis, 1986.

Piétri, Charles, and Luce Piétri. *Prosopographie chrétienne du Bas-Empire 2, Volume 1: Prosopographie de l'Italie chrétienne (313-604), A-K.* Rome: École française de Rome, 1999.

Price, Richard. "The Three Chapters Controversy and the Council of Chalcedon." In *The Crisis of the Oikoumene: The Three Chapters and the Failed Quest for Unity in the Sixth-Century Mediterranean,* edited by Celia Chazelle and

Catherine Cubitt, 17–37. Studies in the Early Middle Ages 14. Turnhout: Brepols, 2007.

Robinson, Pamela R. "The 'Booklet': A Self-Contained Unit in Composite Manuscripts." In *Codicologica 3: Essais Typologiques,* edited by Albert Gruys and Johann P. Gumbert, 46–69. Litterae Textuales. Leiden: Brill, 1980.

Rose, Valentin. *Verzeichnis der lateinischen Handschriften der königlichen Bibliothek zu Berlin 1.* Die Handschriften-Verzeichnisse der königlichen Bibliothek zu Berlin 12. Berlin: Asher, 1893.

Schwartz, Eduard. "Die Kanonessammlungen der alten Reichskirche." *Zeitschrift der Savigny-Stiftung für Rechtsgeschichte; Kanonistische Abteilung* 25 (1936): 1–114. DOI: 10.7767/zrgka.1936.25.1.1.

Seckel, Emil. "Studien zu Benedictus Levita VI." *Neues Archiv der Gesellschaft für ältere deutsche Geschichtskunde* 31 (1906): 59–139, 238–39.

Sessa, Kristina. *The Formation of Papal Authority in Late Antique Italy: Roman Bishops and the Domestic Sphere.* Cambridge: Cambridge University Press, 2012.

Stüber, Till. *Die sogenannte Collectio canonum Remensis. Entstehung und Rezeption einer frühmittelalterlichen Kirchenrechtssammlung* (in preparation).

Turner, Cuthbert H. "Chapters in the History of Latin MSs of Canons: VI. The Version Called Prisca: (B) The Chieti MS (= I), Now Vatic. Regin. 1997." *The Journal of Theological Studies* os-31, no. 1 (1929): 9–20. DOI: 10.1093/jts/os-XXXI.1.9.

Ullmann, Walter. *Gelasius I. (492–496): Das Papsttum an der Wende der Spätantike zum Mittelalter.* Päpste und Papsttum 18. Stuttgart: Hiersemann, 1981.

Wirbelauer, Eckhard. *Zwei Päpste in Rom. Der Konflikt zwischen Laurentius und Symmachus (498 – 514): Studien und Texte.* Quellen und Forschungen zur antiken Welt 16. Munich: Tuduv, 1993.

———. "Die Nachfolgerbestimmung im Römischen Bistum (3.–6. Jahrhundert): Doppelwahlen und Absetzungen in ihrer herrschaftssoziologischen Bedeutung." *Klio* 76 (1994): 388–437. DOI: 10.1524/klio.1994.76.76.388.

Wurm, Hubert. *Studien und Texte zur Dekretalensammlung des Dionysius Exiguus.* Kanonistische Studien und Texte 16. Bonn: L. Röhrscheid, 1939.

2

Carolingian Collections of Gregory the Great's Letters and the So-Called *Collectio Pauli*

Lucia Castaldi and Laura Pani

This chapter deals with the structure and manuscript transmission of the so-called *Collectio Pauli*, one of the most ancient collections of epistles made in the early Middle Ages. Although it owes its name to Paul the Deacon (c. 720–799), it can now be established that this attribution to him as its compiler is a scholarly mistake. Moreover, philological interrogation has proven that this collection was formed before the Carolingian renaissance, although its oldest surviving witness (St. Petersburg, Rossiyskaya Natsional'naya Biblioteka, MS lat. F.v.I.7) has been made by Paul the Deacon. In the following pages, we present this old witness of the *Collectio Pauli* and the many questions it raises, followed by our initial philological observations on the transmission of the *Collectio*. In addition, we demonstrate in an analysis of the manuscript München, Bayerische Staatsbibliothek, MS Clm 14641 that the whole *Collectio* seems to descend from a common antigraph, which was probably scattered in different sheets.[1]

---

1 In the run-up to publication, an article by Antonio A. Verardi was published which deals with the same topic, albeit in greater depth on the

Gregory the Great and the Eighth-Century Collections of His Letters[2]

The papacy of Gregory the Great (r. 590–604) was a turning point for late-Latin culture and the Catholic Church, and, as such, he has with some justification been called "the inventor of the Middle Ages."[3] He was able to convert the Lombards from Arianism to Catholicism and proposed a new model of humanity and spirituality in his *Dialogues*. Gregory's model of sanctity was no more an intellectual one, as in the past, but the more achievable of a monk, saint Benedict, *sapienter indoctus,* an illitterate learned.[4]

---

  historical and content aspects. See Antonio A. Verardi, "Letters of Gregory the Great, Paul the Deacon and Carolingian Debate," *Nuovi annali della Scuola speciale per Archivisti e Bibliotecari* 36 (2022): 7–41.
2 Sections 1, 3, and 5 were written by Lucia Castaldi, 2 and 4 by Laura Pani, and 6 by both. All translations are our own.
3 Cf. Luigi G.G. Ricci, ed., *Gregorio Magno e l'invenzione del Medioevo* (Florence: SISMEL Edizioni del Galluzzo, 2006).
4 For an essential bibliography see Robert A. Markus, *Gregory the Great and his World* (Cambridge: Cambridge University Press, 1997); *Convegno internazionale: Gregorio Magno nel XIV centenario della morte (Roma, 22–25 ottobre 2003)* (Rome: Accademia nazionale dei Lincei, 2004); Philippe Henne, *Grégoire le Grand* (Paris: Éditions du Cerf, 2007); Giuseppe Cremascoli and Antonella Degl'Innocenti, eds., *Enciclopedia gregoriana. La vita, l'opera e la fortuna di Gregorio Magno* (Florence: SISMEL Edizioni del Galluzzo, 2008); Bronwen Neil and Matthew Dal Santo, eds., *A Companion to Gregory the Great* (Leiden: Brill, 2013); Lucia Castaldi, *La trasmissione dei testi latini del Medioevo / Mediaeval Latin Texts and Their Transmission. Te.Tra 5. Gregorius I papa* (Florence: SISMEL Edizioni del Galluzzo, 2013); Claudio Leonardi, ed., *Gregorio Magno e le origini dell'Europa* (Florence: SISMEL Edizioni del Galluzzo, 2014); and George E. Demacopoulos, *Gregory the Great: Ascetic, Pastor, and First Man of Rome* (Notre Dame: University of Notre Dame Press, 2015). For a complete and exhaustive bibliography, see Robert Godding, *Bibliografia di Gregorio Magno, 1890–1989* (Rome: Città Nuova Editrice, 1990), and Francesca S. D'Imperio, *Gregorio Magno. Bibliografia per gli anni 1980–2003* (Florence: SISMEL Edizioni del Galluzzo, 2005). The problem of the authorship of the *Dialogorum libri IV* will not be addressed here. For the debate on this topic, see the aforementioned bibliography.

During Gregory's pontificate, numerous political events compelled him to write letters to kings, bishops, abbots, noblemen, and clerics from the sixth century, in both western and Byzantine worlds. Most of his letters were on administrative subjects: land reform; *decimae* (tax reform); preventing episcopal abuses of power; and the military defense of the city of Rome.[5] Unfortunately, not all these letters have survived and neither have the fourteen *libri* — one for every year of Gregory's pontificate — that, according to written sources, particularly Gregory's ninth-century biographer John the Deacon, were kept in the Lateran archive, the *scrinium Lateranense:* "he left in the archives as many books of his letters as the years of his pontificate."[6] These *libri* were the chancery registers in which the letters were copied before being sent to their recipients, in order to keep a record of the political correspondence and administrative activity of the pope.[7]

As Gregory emerged, in the eighth century, as both an *auctoritas* and a source for Roman history, his letters were extracted from the registers of the Lateran archive, used for historical works, and organized into collections so that today 800 of his

---

5 Gregory's epistles are quoted according to the numbering in the most recent critical edition: Dag Norberg, ed., *Sancti Gregorii Magni Opera. Registrum epistolarum,* Corpus Christianorum Series Latina 140–140A (Turnhout: Brepols, 1982). This numbering sometimes differs from that of nineteenth-century edition: Paul Ewald and Ludwig M. Hartmann, eds., *Gregorii I papae Registrum epistolarum,* 2 vols., Monumenta Germaniae Historica, Epistolae 1–2 (Berlin: Weidmann, 1887–1899). For the sake of convenience, the letters from this edition are listed as "MGH" in the tables below.

6 "Quarum [i.e., epistolarum] tot libros in scrinio dereliquit, quot annos advixit." "Sancti Gregorii Magni Vita a Joanne diacono scripta libris quatuor," in *Sancti Gregorii Papae I cognomento Magni Opera Omnia, ad manuscriptos codices Romanos, Gallicanos, Anglicanos emendata, aucta et illustrata notis, studio et labore Monachorum Ordinis Sancti Benedicti e Congregatione Sancti Mauri* (Paris: Claudii Rigaud, 1705), vol. 4, 19–188 = "Sancti Gregorii Magni Vita a Joanne diacono scripta libris quatuor," Patrologia Latina 75, col. 223A (4.71).

7 Dag Norberg, In *"Registrum Gregorii Magni" studia critica,* 2 vols. (Uppsala: Lundequist, 1937–1939).

letters survive, thanks to different selections made over the centuries by various people with varying purposes. Some historical data can help to reconstruct the circumstances in which these selections were made, and by whom. The oldest information about a selection of Gregorian letters drawn from the Roman *scrinium,* including seven letters on the mission led by Augustine of Canterbury to Britain,[8] is found in the preface to Bede's (c. 673–735) *Historia ecclesiastica gentis Anglorum:* "Nothelmus, after going to Rome and scanning the Roman ecclesiastical archive, with permission of Pope Gregory II, found some of Gregory the Great's letters and brought them to me so that I could insert them in my work."[9]

Furthermore, at least four collections of Gregory's letters were made in the second half of the eighth century:

---

8 The seven epistles are the following: 6.52–53 (MGH 6.50–50a), 11.36–37, 11.39, 11.45, and 11.56. Another Gregorian letter, the so-called *Libellus responsionum* (11.56a), has to be excluded: Paul Meyvaert's studies and the new critical edition by Valeria Mattaloni have clarified that the text came to Bede from an independent — not Roman — transmission. On this, see Paul Meyvaert, "Les *Responsiones* de S. Grégoire le Grand à S. Augustin de Canterbury. À propos d'un article récent," *Revue d'histoire ecclésiastique* 54 (1959): 879–94; Paul Meyvaert, "Bede's Text of the *Libellus Responsionum* of Gregory the Great to Augustine of Canterbury," in *England before the Conquest: Studies in Primary Sources Presented to Dorothy Whitelock,* ed. Peter Clemoes and Kathleen Hughes (Cambridge: Cambridge University Press, 1971), 15–33; Paul Meyvaert, *Benedict, Gregory, Bede and Others* (London: Variorum Reprints, 1983), x; Paul Meyvaert, *"Libellus responsionum* à Augustin de Cantorbéry: une oeuvre authentique de saint Grégoire le Grand," in *Grégoire le Grand* (Paris: Éditions du Centre national de la recherche scientifique, 1986), 543–50; and Valeria Mattaloni, ed., *Rescriptum beati Gregorii papae ad Augustinum episcopum quem in Saxoniam in praedicatione direxerat (seu Libellus responsionum)* (Florence: SISMEL Edizioni del Galluzzo, 2017).

9 Bertram Colgrave and Roger A.B. Mynors, eds., *Bede's Ecclesiastical History of the English People* (Oxford: Clarendon Press, 1969), *praefatio,* 4: "Qui videlicet Nothelmus postea Romam veniens, nonnullas ibi beati Gregorii papae simul et aliorum pontificum epistolas, perscrutato eiusdem sanctae ecclesiae Romanae scrinio, permissu eius, qui nunc ipsi ecclesiae preest, Gregorii *(scilicet* II) pontificis, invenit reversusque nobis nostrae historiae inserendas cum consilio praefati Albini reverentissimi patris adtulit."

a) The one made by Winfrid (c. 675–754, also known as saint Boniface): He not only repeatedly asked his Roman correspondents for copies of some letters, but also went to Rome and had many Gregorian letters copied and sent to the archbishop of York, Ecbert (d. 766), with these words: "I have sent you some copies of the letters I pulled out of the ecclesiastical archive in Rome, that in my opinion have never come to Britain: and if you ask me, I will send you many others, as I took many from the archive."[10] This collection seems no longer extant.

b) (R) The most important collection was the *Registrum Hadriani,* listed in editions under the siglum R. At the time of Hadrian I (pope from 772 to 795), a large selection of 680 Gregorian letters was made. In the ninth century, John the Deacon wrote in his *Vita Gregorii:* "In the time of Pope Hadrian I, some letters *decretales* were chosen, for each indiction, for each year, and gathered in two volumes."[11] The letters were organized in chronological order, being extracted from each of the fourteen registers, and circulated in two books. This collection survives in a number of manuscripts from the ninth century onwards, either in two volumes or, from the tenth century, in just one.

c) (P) The *Collectio Pauli,* listed under the siglum P. This contains fifty-three or fifty-four of Gregory's letters,[12] thirty-three of which are shared with the *Registrum Hadriani* (R).

---

10 Ernst Dümmler, *Epistolae Merovingici et Karolini aevi,* vol. 1, Monumenta Germaniae Historica, Epistolae 3 (Berlin: Weidmann, 1892), 347, ll. 29–31 (ep. 75): "Interea ad iudicium caritatis fraternitati tuae direxi exemplaria epistolarum sancti Gregorii, quas de scrinio Romanae Ecclesiae excepi; quae non rebar ad Britanniam venisse; et plura iterum, si mandaveris, remittam, quia multas inde excepi."

11 "Sancti Gregorii Magni Vita a Joanne diacono scripta libris quatuor," Patrologia Latina 75, col. 223B (4.71): "Ex quorum multitudine primi Hadriani papae temporibus quaedam epistolae decretales per singulas indictiones excerptae sunt et in duobus voluminibus, sicut modo cernitur, congregatae."

12 The reasons for this double number are explained below.

d) (C) The *Collectio ducentarum epistolarum,* under the siglum C: 200 letters from the ninth book (2nd indiction), fifty-four of which are shared with R. There is no evidence of when it was made other than the fact that it is always found in the same manuscripts as P.[13]

2. The *Collectio Pauli* and the Manuscript St. Petersburg, Rossiyskaya Natsional'naya Biblioteka, MS lat. F.v.I.7

The *Collectio Pauli* "P" owes its name to the presumed compiler of its most famous witness, St. Petersburg, Rossiyskaya Natsional'naya Biblioteka, MS lat. F.v.I.7. The manuscript has belonged to the National Library of Russia (formerly Public Imperial Library, and then Library Saltykov-Ščedrin of Leningrad) since 1805, having arrived in Russia some unknown years before.

The *collectio* is preserved in the first codicological unit (fols. 1–40) of a composite volume. The second unit, fols. 41 to 104, contains the slightly later *Ecloga in Moralia* by Lathcen (d. 661, also known as Laidcenn mac Buith Bannaig). Significantly, the two units share some codicological features: not only their general size, but also the way in which some of the quires were assembled, the position of prickings, the *mise-en-page* on 39 lines, the ruling pattern, and the ruling techniques.[14] It is still unclear whether the two units have a shared origin, but they certainly

---

[13] The manuscript Vatican City, Biblioteca Apostolica Vaticana, MS Pal. lat. 266, from the ninth century (C2), is the only exception: https://digi.vatlib.it/view/bav_pal_lat_266. Although today it contains only *collectio* C, in the beginning it must have had P as well, as shown by an index with 221 items (also attested by the manuscript Pb1-C1, on which see below).

[14] Unit 1: 306 × 192 mm (12.05 × 7.56 in.) = 21 [255] 30 × 7 / 8 [138] 8 / 31 (fol. 10r); Unit 2: 310 × 208 mm (12.20 × 8.19 in.) = 24 [243] 33 × 7 / 7 [145] 8 / 31 (fol. 49r). Unit 1 consists of five quaternions, flesh side out; both the third and fifth quires are made partly of bifolia, partly of single sheets. Gregory's Rule is broken in the first and fifth quire. Unit 2 consists of eight quaternions, all but the second with hair side out; in this second quire Gregory's Rule is not applied. In both units prickings are located on the ruling of the outer margin.

come from the abbey of Corbie and were bound together at the latest in the fourteenth or fifteenth century, when "De Iob" (referring to the second unit) was written in cursive handwriting on fol. 1r. The codicological unit containing Gregory's letters is listed in two of the three inventories of Corbie: one from the twelfth century and another from c. 1200, which may also mention Lathcen's *Ecloga*.[15]

In 1638, the whole manuscript became the property of the Parisian library of Saint-Germain-des-Prés, along with about 400 manuscripts from Corbie.[16] The *ex libris* "Sancti Germani a Pratis" can be read on fol. 1r together with the number "858." From Saint-Germain, it made its way into the collection of Pietr Dubrovsky (1754–1816), a Russian diplomat and book collector based in France before and during the French Revolution, who took advantage of the dissolution of ecclesiastical institutions and the fluid market of manuscripts and rare books of that time.[17] During its long preservation in this library, the manuscript was difficult to access, due both to the geographical distance for some researchers and the closure of the Soviet Union in the middle decades of the twentieth century.[18] Nevertheless, by virtue of its antiquity and the presumed autograph of Paul the Deacon, it has been described in catalogues, including the *Codices Latini Antiquiores*,[19] and is the subject of three paleographical

---

15 Gustav Becker, *Catalogi bibliothecarum antiqui* (Bonn, 1885), 188, no. 163 ("Gregorii epistolae"), and 279, no. 82 ("Epistolae de registro cum exceptione").

16 Léopold Delisle, *Le cabinet des manuscrits de la Bibliothèque nationale*, vol. 2 (Paris: Imprimerie nationale, 1874), 44, 136–39.

17 Patricia Z. Thompson, "Biography of a Library: The Western European Manuscript Collection of Peter P. Dubrovskii in Leningrad," *The Journal of Library History* 19, no. 4 (1984): 479–82.

18 Tamara P. Voronova, "Western Manuscripts in the Saltykov-Shchedrin Library, Leningrad," in *The Book Collector* 5 (1956): 12–18, was a rare attempt to make the most remarkable Western manuscripts of the library known.

19 Antonio Staerk, *Les manuscrits latins du Ve au XIIIe siècle conservés à la Bibliothèque Imperiale de Saint-Pétersbourg. Description, textes inédits, reproductions autotypiques* (Saint-Pétersbourg: Imprimerie artistique Franz Krois, 1910), 39–41; Olga Dobiaš-Roždestvenskaja and Wsevolod W. Bakhtine, *Les anciens manuscrits latins de la Bibliothèque publique*

essays, one of which is in Russian, published between 1929 and 1937 by the Russian scholar Olga Dobiash-Rozhdestvenskaya.[20]

The manuscript looks rather rough. The parchment is of poor quality and the last quire was made by assembling waste or scrap pieces of writing material, with big holes and obvious natural edges. The ornamentation is quite simple, consisting of plain or outline initials drawn using ordinary writing ink and occasionally completed by simple decorative motifs (e.g., a bird on fol. 6v).

This P copy raises a number of questions that will be discussed here. They concern the dedicatory epistle, the corrections and interventions to the text made in the margins and between the lines, the selection of Gregory's letters, their sequence, the compiler who assembled them, and the relations with the other witnesses of the *Collectio Pauli*.

On fol. 1r the manuscript is opened by a dedicatory epistle sent "to the dearest Adalhard, man of God" by a *Paulus supplex* (supplicating/humble Paul).[21] On fols. 1v–2r there is a *tabula* (index) of the letters, from I to LIIIII, introduced by the title "Here begin the chapters of different letters by Gregory, pope in Rome."[22] The series of Gregory's letters begins on fol. 2r and ends on fol. 40r on a sheet that was cut down the middle, after copying was completed.

Saltykov-Ščedrin de Leningrad, trans. Xenia Grichine (Paris: Éditions du Centre national de la recherche scientifique, 1991), 47–51; and Elias A. Lowe, *Codices Latini Antiquiores* (Oxford: Oxford University Press, 1966), vol. 11, nos. 1603 and 1604.

20 Olga Dobiash-Rozhdestvenskaya, "La main de Paul Diacre sur un codex du VIIIᵉ siècle envoyé à Adalhard," *Memorie storiche forogiuliesi* 25 (1929): 129–43; Olga Dobiash-Rozhdestvenskaya, "Itinéraire de Paul, fils de Warnefride l'an 787–788 et les premiers pas de la minuscule de Cividale en Frioul," *Memorie storiche forogiuliesi* 27–29 (1931–33): 55–72; and Olga Dobiash-Rozhdestvenskaya, "Ranniy friul'skij minuskul i odna iz problem zhizni i tvorcchestva langobardskogo istorika VIII v. (s 4 tabl. i rezyume na franc. yaz.)," *AN SSSR: Vspomogatel'nye istoricceskie discipliny. Sbornik stat'ey* (1937): 109–41.

21 "Carissimo fratri et domino Adalardo viro Dei."

22 "Incipiunt capitula diversarum epistularum beati Gregorii papae urbis Romae."

The dedicatory epistle is transmitted only by this manuscript.[23] At the start, Paul says that he had wished to visit Adalhard during the previous summer, when he was *in illis partibus* (not far from him), but that the horses were tired.[24] In the following lines he adds that he wished to obey Adalhard's orders, but could not do it before because he is poor and lacks *librarii* (scribes); moreover, he was ill and stayed in bed from September to Christmas, and the young cleric that somehow wrote *haec eadem* (these very things) could not put his hand to the inkpot.[25]

The most important part of the dedicatory epistle starts from line 11 of the edition. At this point, Paul says that with this book, Adalhard is getting the letters he had asked for, even though he, Paul, being busy, could not re-read them all, despite having corrected thirty-four of them (with the exception of some passages which he found lacking, "minus inveni"). Nevertheless, Paul did not want to change the meaning of Gregory's words, so he put a Z sign on the margins as a *signum vitii,* indicating textual

---

23 Ernst Dümmler, ed., *Epistolae Karolini aevi,* vol. 2, Monumenta Germaniae Historica, Epistolae 4 (Berlin: Weidmann, 1895), 508–9. A recent account and interpretation of the letter can be found in Alberto Ricciardi, "Gli inganni della tradizione. Una silloge del Registrum di Gregorio Magno nei rapporti fra Carolini e papato e nel dibattito sulle immagini sacre," *Studi medievali* 56 (2015): 81–83.

24 Dümmler, ed., *Epistolae Karolini aevi,* vol. 2, 509: "Cupieram, dilecte mi, aestate praeterita videre faciem tuam, quando in illis partibus fui, sed, praepeditus lassitudine sonipedum, ad te venire non potui. Interioribus tamen oculis, quibus solis valeo, tuae fraternitatis dulcedinem frequenter aspicio." ("My beloved, I wished to see you last summer, when I was not far from there, but I could not come to you as the horses were tired. Nevertheless, I often see the sweetness of your brotherhood with my inner eyes.")

25 Dümmler, ed., *Epistolae Karolini aevi,* vol. 2, 509: "Volueram equidem tuis imperiis iam ante parere; sed, utpote pauper et cui desunt librarii, prius hoc facere nequivi, maxime cum me tam prolixa valitudo contriverit, ut a mense Septembrio pene usque ad diem nativitatis Domini lectulo detentus sim nec licuerit clericulo illi, qui haec eadem utcumque scripsit, manum ad atramentarium mittere." ("I had wanted to obey your orders before; but, being poor and lacking scribes, I could not do it so far, especially because a long illness detained me, so that I was in bed from September until Christmas, and the young cleric who somehow wrote all of this could not put his hand to the inkpot.")

corruption.[26] Immediately after this, Paul encourages Adalhard to correct the letters himself *ad emendatiorem codicem,* which could be translated either as "with the help of a more corrected manuscript" or "in order to obtain a more corrected manuscript," and to complete the passages affected by the lacunas.[27] But Paul also advises his correspondent against publishing, that is, disseminating, the letters, because there are topics in them that are better not known by incompetent people.[28] He closes the letter with greetings and some verses in which the Rhine and the Moselle are mentioned.[29]

---

26 Dümmler, ed., *Epistolae Karolini aevi,* vol. 2, 509: "Suscipe tamen quamvis sero epistolas quas desiderasti, et quia mihi eas ante relegere prae occupatione totas non licuit, XXXIIII ex eis scito relectas et prout potui emendatas esse, praeter pauca loca, in quibus minus inveni, et tamen meo ea sensu supplere nolui, ne viderer tanti doctoris verba inmutare; quibus in locis et forinsecus ad aurem zetam, quod est vitii signum, apposui." ("Here you have, though late, the letters you wished, and as I, being busy, could not re-read them all, be aware that I re-read and corrected as I could thirty-four of them, except for some passages in which I found some lacunas and yet could not complete them, in order not to change such a master's words; in those passages and in the margins I put a Z, which is a sign of corruption of the text.")

27 Dümmler, ed., *Epistolae Karolini aevi,* vol. 2, 509: "Tua itaque fraternitas, si se facultas dederit, reliquas epistolas ad emendatiorem relegere studeat codicem, sed et loca, in quibus minus habetur, nihilominus supplere." ("May your brotherhood, if it can, re-read the remaining letters in order to obtain [*or* with the help of] a more correct manuscript, but also complete the passages with the lacunas.")

28 Dümmler, ed., *Epistolae Karolini aevi,* vol. 2, 509: "Hoc tamen sanctitati tuae suadeo, ne passim propter aliqua, quae in eis minus idoneos latere magis quam scire convenit, puplicentur." ("I only beg your holiness not to publish them, due to some topics of which incompetent people should remain ignorant rather than know.")

29 Dümmler, ed., *Epistolae Karolini aevi,* vol. 2, 509: "Vale, frater amabilis, semper in bonis gliscens; et cum mentem ad superna tetenderis, memento mei. Ante suos refluus Rhenum repedabit ad ortus, / Ante petet fontem clara Mosella suum, / Quam tuus e nostro carum ac memorabile semper / Dulce, Adalard, nomen, pectore cedat amor. / Tu quoque, si felix vigeas de munere Christi, / Esto memor Pauli tempus in omne tui." ("Take care, lovable brother, always shining in good, and when you put your mind to God, remember me. The Rhine will go back to its starting point, and the Moselle to its source, before the love for your dear name could leave our hearth,

The letter itself raises a wide range of issues:

a) The identity of the sender and the recipient. There does not seem to be any doubt that Adalardus was Adalhard, abbot of Corbie from 781 to his death in 828. As for the "supplicating" Paul, many details point to Paul the Deacon, the historian of the Lombards, in France as a member of the court and the Carolingian establishment during the 780s. The final verses of the letter very much recall another short poem by Paul the Deacon for an unnamed friend, possibly Charlemagne, in which the river Rhine is mentioned.[30] Furthermore, Paul the Deacon calls himself "Paulus supplex" in another dedicatory epistle, written for Adalperga, at the beginning of his *Historia Romana*.[31] Paul the Deacon and Adalhard frequented the same milieux, had met at Charlemagne's court and possibly even earlier in Montecassino, and they might have called each other "brother." So, who else could this Paul be?[32]

b) The dating and localization of the manuscript. The letter is not dated; we can only infer that it was written after Christmas, when Paul recovered from an illness, so probably at the beginning of the year after his summer attempt to visit Adalhard, but the year remains undetermined. Paul is supposed to have been in France from 782 to 787, but neither the date of his departure nor the chronology of many of the stages of his life are certain.[33] This also applies to Adalhard: at the time

---

sweet Adalhard. And you, if you by God's gift can live happily, do always remember your Paul.")

30 Karl Neff, *Die Gedichte des Paulus Diaconus. Kritische und erklärende Ausgabe* (Munich: Beck'sche Verlagsbuchhandlung, 1908), 40: "Ante potest flavos Rhenus repedare Suavos / Ad fontem et versis pergere Tibris aquis, / Quam tuus e nostro labatur pectore vultus, / Ore colende mihi tempus in omne pater."

31 Neff, *Die Gedichte des Paulus Diaconus*, 12.

32 Hartmut Hoffmann, "Autographa des früheren Mittelalters," *Deutsches Archiv für Erforschung des Mittelalters* 57 (2001): 1–62, at 18.

33 The most recent biography of Paul the Deacon is by Lidia Capo, "Paolo Diacono," in *Dizionario biografico degli Italiani*, vol. 81 (Rome: Istituto per l'Enciclopedia italiana, 2014), 151–62.

when Paul wanted to see him, he could have been in Corbie, in Italy,[34] or somewhere else. A clue to the place where the manuscript was made may come from its paleographical analysis.

c) The script. Paul mentions both the lack of scribes and a young cleric who wrote "all these very things," but there are four hands identifiable in the manuscript, two of which are in the dedicatory letter itself. The *tabula* and text of the *Collectio* are copied by three different scribes, one of which, "A," is more prominent than the other two (maybe this is the *clericulus?*): he copied fols. 1v–8r (line 20), 8r (line 30)–10v (line 26), 11v–13r (line 28), 13r (line 30)–14v (line 5), 15r (lines 16–20), 15v–16r, 17r–23r (line 4), 23r (line 9)–39r, and 40r. A second hand, "B," shortly intervened in A's work on fols. 8r (lines 21–29), 10v (line 26)–11r, 13r (lines 28–29), 14v (line 5)–15r (line 15), 15r (from line 20), 16v, and 23r (lines 5–9). The third hand, "C," copied fol. 39v but appeared again on fol. 1r for the first 12 lines of the letter to Adalhard, which means that the epistle was written once the rest of the manuscript had been copied, its first sheet having been left blank on purpose. This is not at all surprising, because the letter refers to the rest of the manuscript as already copied and corrected. The lines from 13 onwards were copied by yet another scribe, "D," who made some spelling mistakes (e.g., "ad aurem" instead of "ad oram"; "puplicentur"). The four hands share a common graphic culture. They know Caroline minuscule and therefore belong to a milieu in which it is already used or has begun its spread, although it is still very far from reaching canonization.[35] They all use cursive ligatures to a greater or lesser extent, and each hand can be distinguished from the others not only by its general aspect, but also by the frequency with which it em-

---

34 Ricciardi, "Gli inganni della tradizione," 85.

35 Scribe A only uses the Caroline *a* (with a back angled at 45°) until fol. 22r, but then alternates it with the *cc*-shaped cursive form, also regularly used by hands B and C. Scribe A also uses the half-uncial *g*, whereas the other hands make an effort to trace it with a closed upper bowl. All the scribes use cursive ligatures with *e, l (li),* and *r*.

ploys pre-Caroline features. It is a rough script, as the manuscript itself is rough, but it is also mature or advanced, which particularly applies for hand D.

d) Paul's hand. Olga Dobiash-Rozhdestvenskaya was the first to identify two hands in the dedicatory epistle, hypothesizing that the scribe of the first twelve lines was Paul the Deacon, who then dictated the rest of the letter.[36] In addition, Paul declares that he has re-read and corrected the first thirty-four letters, putting a Z where he could not complete the lacunas. The manuscript is full of corrections both in the margins and between the lines, and some of them are associated with a Z, the correction sign ζήτει used until the sixth century or later in Byzantium and in Italy until the ninth century.[37] But, most importantly, they end on fol. 26r with letter no. 35, which has not actually been thoroughly revised. A complete census of these corrections is a work in progress, but it is very possible that most of them, starting with the ones marked with Z, were made by Paul the Deacon himself, so that we are seeing Paul's autograph. These notes allow us to point out the features of Paul's handwriting, and so to distinguish it from that of the other hands that copied the manuscript. It does not seem to have anything to do either with scribe C, the copyist of the first twelve lines of the letter (and the penultimate page of the manuscript), nor with any of the others.[38] On the other hand, the analysis of what is presumably Paul's handwriting, a Caroline minuscule with very few signs of pre-Caroline script, opens up the question of Paul's graphic education, already raised by Bernhard Bischoff.[39]

e) Adalhard's role. Despite Paul urging him to complete his emendation work, and although Adalhard, according to Paul, had long wished for a collection of Gregory's letters, he does not seem to intervene in the manuscript, most of the

---

36 Dobiash-Rozhdestvenskaya, "La main de Paul Diacre," 134–6.

37 Evina Steinová, *"Notam superponere studui": The Use of Annotation Symbols in the Early Middle Ages* (Turnhout: Brepols, 2019), 161, 223.

38 Hoffmann, "Autographa," 19, appears uncertain on this point.

39 Ibid., 20.

corrections being in the same hand (that of Paul). Moreover, it is doubtful why, in Paul's opinion, Adalhard should not disseminate the content of the manuscript: what was in it that could be dangerous for non-experts? Does it have anything to do with the political meaning of the collection as a whole?

To answer this last question, an analysis of the structure of the *Collectio Pauli* is required. As previously noted, the collection includes fifty-four letters. The first twenty-one are taken from the fifth book of Gregory's letters (corresponding to the years 594–595, the thirteenth indiction) and are in chronological order. Letters 22 to 37 come from Book 11 and the years 600–601, the fourth indiction. Fourteen more letters are from Book 2 (years 592–593, the tenth indiction) and, unlike the others, have a title (e.g., at fol. 31v, *Gregorius Felici episcopo Mensanensi de aecclesia construenda*). These second and third blocks of letters are not in chronological order, but the chronology of letters and books is notoriously complicated, at least in the second block of Gregory's letters.[40] The last three letters are even more problematic: one is from Book 9 (9.148) and concerns iconoclasm, while also presenting itself in an interpolated form which is transmitted only by the *Collectio Pauli*; another one, the famous letter 11.10 on the worship of images, is from Book 11 but not present in the second block of letters; the last one, letter 11.1, is a duplicate from the second block. Both the letters 9.148 and 11.10 are quoted in an epistle sent in 791 by Pope Hadrian I to Charlemagne against the iconoclastic ideas expressed in the *Libri Carolini* that the king had sent to Rome.[41] This could represent a *terminus ante quem* for the dating of the St. Petersburg manuscript, but only if the interpolation of ep. 9.148, as well as the whole selection of Gregorian letters, were Paul's work.[42] Yet this is highly suspect, as will be shown below. It must also be pointed out that in some

---

40 See the discussion in Norberg, *"In Registrum Gregorii Magni."*
41 Ernst Dümmler, ed., *Epistolae Karolini aevi*, Monumenta Germaniae Historica, Epistolae 5 (Berlin: Weidmann, 1899), vol. 3, 5–57.
42 This is still Ricciardi's opinion: Ricciardi, "Gli inganni," 100–1.

manuscripts of the *Collectio* these three letters (here nos. 52–54) are the nos. 1–3 of the series. Furthermore, there is a significant discrepancy between the list of letters in the index and the subsequent text of the collection. As a matter of fact, letter no. 41 to the Gallic bishops Syagrius, Etherius, Virgil, and Desiderius is announced in the index but not present in the manuscript. So, the sequence of numbers in the index goes up to 55, but the text encompasses numbers 1 to 54, and all the witnesses of the *Collectio* notoriously consist of fifty-four letters. Moreover, the letter in question is no. 218 from Book 9 and therefore has nothing to do with the block of letters in which it was inserted.

Letter	Book/no.
1	5.6
2	5.8
3	5.24
4	5.29
5	5.30
6	5.31
7	5.32
8	5.38
9	5.39
10	5.40
11	5.41
12	5.42
13	5.43
14	5.44
15	5.49
16	5.50
17	5.58
18	5.59

Table 2.1. Sequence of letters in P.

Letter	Book/no.
19	5.60
20	5.62
21	5.63
22	11.36
23	11.37
24	11.38
25	11.39
26	11.40
27	11.1
28	11.2
29	11.9
30	11.43
31	11.46
32	11.47
33	11.48
34	11.49
35	11.52
36	11.53
37	11.27
38	2.45 (MGH 2.8)
39	2.6 (MGH 2.9)
40	2.46 (MGH 2.10)
<41 (index)>	<9.218>
41	2.30 (MGH 2.31)
42	2.29 (MGH 2.30)
43	2.4 (MGH 2.7)
44	2.27 (MGH 2.32)
45	2.26 (MGH 2.29)
46	2.28 (MGH 2.33)

Letter	Book/no.
47	2.47 (MGH 2.34)
48	2.48 (MGH 2.35
49	2.49 (MGH 2.36)
50	2.31 (MGH 2.37)
51	2.50 (MGH 2.38)
52	9.148 (MGH 9.147)
53	11.10
54	11.1

It is therefore worth asking: was Paul the Deacon the compiler of this collection of Gregory's letters? If so, did he personally choose and extract them from the Lateran archive, in order to have them copied by his scribes and sent to Adalhard? Or was the St. Petersburg manuscript copied from a pre-existing selection of letters? How did this presumed antigraph look? Why could neither Paul nor his scribes complete and correct the corrupted passages of the text? And finally, can the St. Petersburg manuscript really be considered the ancestor of the *Collectio Pauli*?

The Transmission of P: Initial Philological Observations

The presence of Paul the Deacon's letter to Adalhard of Corbie in the oldest manuscript of the *Collectio* made scholars believe that Paul the Deacon himself selected the fifty-three or fifty-four letters and sent them to Adalhard. Indeed, Ernst Dümmler wrote at the end of the nineteenth century that the *Collectio* was "a Paulo parata," made by Paul the Deacon;[43] even in recent years scholars have shown no hesitation in attributing it to him.[44] Gregory the Great's letters always have had political value and so have often been interpolated: Gregory was an au-

---
43 Ernst Dümmler, ed., *Epistolae Karolini aevi*, vol. 2, 509.
44 E.g., Ricciardi, "Gli inganni."

thority and the use of his works and epistles created *auctoritas*. So, if Paul the Deacon was the compiler of *Collectio Pauli*, the political value of this selection should be ascribed to him, for he would have decided which Gregorian letters to select and why. Our understanding of the role played by Paul the Deacon in the Carolingian renaissance could change completely. But if Paul the Deacon was the author of the collection, and the corrections and *marginalia* in the St. Petersburg manuscript could be attributed to him, some indication of this should be evident from the manuscript transmission.

That the St. Petersburg manuscript is the archetype of the *Collectio Pauli*, and all the other manuscripts of the collection were copied from it, is a very appealing hypothesis that nevertheless needs philological evidence. But no philological reconstruction of the manuscript transmission of the *Collectio Pauli* has ever been made. No scholar has ever checked the place of the St. Petersburg manuscript in the transmission of the *Collectio Pauli*: neither Paul Ewald and Ludwig Moritz Hartmann in their critical editions of Gregory the Great's *Registrum* in 1899 for the *Monumenta Germaniae Historica* series, nor Dag Norberg in his more recent edition in 1982 for the *Corpus Christianorum* series. In Norberg's edition there is one *stemma codicum* for the *Registrum Hadriani* (R) and one for the *Collectio ducentarum epistularum* (C) but not one for the *Collectio Pauli*.[45] Thus, some philological considerations will be presented below, not in order to provide a complete reconstruction of the transmission or the final conclusions of the investigation on this collection, but rather to present preliminary observations and a crucial new discovery.[46]

Paul Ewald classified the manuscripts of the *Collectio Pauli* into two groups: the families Pa (the oldest witness of which is the St. Petersburg manuscript, Pa1) and Pb. The manuscripts of

---

45 *Registrum epistolarum*, ed. Norberg, x–xi.
46 The manuscripts considered for this chapter are only the ones in which the *Collectio Pauli* is transmitted alone or together with the *Collectio ducentarum epistularum*. Later composite collections including a portion of the collection R (such as C+P+r, or r+P) are not taken into account.

the Pb family share what, at first glance, would seem a common error: the date that is normally present at the end of a letter is moved forward, into the title of the following epistle, thereby assigning the date of one letter to the following one.[47]

For example, in the Pa family, the end of the third epistle and the beginning of the fourth one (the Gregorian epistles 5.24 and 5.29) are as follows:

(ep. 5.24)
De clericis vero praeter eos qui venire deliberant, si quos alios praesentes esse necessarios aestimas, ad nos sine mora transmitte, ut ad ordinandam Dei ecclesiam nec excusatio nec aliqua possit provenire dilatio.
Data die X mensis Februarii indictione XIII.

(ep. 5.29)
Gregorius Iuliano scriboni
Si saecularibus officiis ordo suus et tradita a maioribus disciplina servanda est […][48]

In the Pb family the date slides down, after (or sometimes before) the name of the recipient:

(ep. 5.24)
De clericis vero praeter eos qui venire deliberant, si quos alios praesentes esse necessarios aestimas, ad nos sine mora transmitte, ut ad ordinandam Dei ecclesiam nec excusatio nec aliqua possit provenire dilatio.

---

47 As a matter of fact, the actual position of the date of the Gregorian letters in the *Registrum* of the Lateran archive seems to be a more complex issue than Ewald and Hartmann supposed or conceded. The epistles transmitted by *collectio R* have no date at all, and in some manuscripts of the *Collectio Pauli* the dates are in the margin of the leaves.

48 *Registrum epistolarum,* ed. Norberg, 291 and 295, and *Registrum epistolarum,* ed. Ewald and Hartmann, vol. 1, 305 and 309.

(ep. 5.29)

GREGORIUS IULIANO SCRIBONI. **Data die X mensis Februarii indictione XIII**. Si saecularibus officiis ordo suus et tradita a maioribus disciplina servanda est [...].

Paul the Deacon wrote in the dedicatory letter to Adalhard that he put a *Z* sign on the margins of the epistle when an omission occurred. The tenth letter of the collection (5.40) has a significant example of this. It is transmitted from both the *Registrum Hadriani* and the *Collectio Pauli*. In the *Registrum Hadriani* the text is complete until the end:

Sunt enim in Sicilia insula ecclesiae **vacantes** episcopis, et si vobis placet auctore Deo ecclesiam regere, iuxta beati Petri apostoli limina cum eius adiutorio melius potestis. Sin vero non placet, feliciter state, et pro nobis infelicibus exorate. Omnipotens autem Deus, in quocumque loco vos esse voluerit, sua protectione custodiat et ad caelestia vos dona perducat...[49]

In Pa1 (fol. 7r), this letter *ends* with the word "vacantes" and in the margin are the *Z* and the note, most probably by Paul's hand, "Ista epistula finita non est." In all the other manuscripts of the *Collectio Pauli,* as in Pa1, the letter is cut short and ends with the word "vacantes":

- Pa1bis = Paris, Bibliothèque nationale de France, MS lat. 6638 (10th century), fol. 39v
- Pa2 = Bamberg, Staatsbibliothek, MS Patr. 23 (10th century), fol. 119r
- Pb1-C1 = Cologne, Erzbischöfliche Diözesan- und Dombibliothek, MS 92 (8th century), fol. 113va
- Pb1bis-C1bis = Cologne, Erzbischöfliche Diözesan- und Dombibliothek, MS 93 (10th century), fol. 115rb

---

49 *Registrum epistolarum,* ed. Norberg, 331, ll. 5–9, and *Registrum epistolarum,* ed. Ewald and Hartmann, vol. 1, 331, ll. 5–9.

- Pb1ter-C4 = Paris, Bibliothèque nationale de France, MS lat. 14500 (10th century), fol. 69v
- Pb2 = Vienna, Österreichische Nationalbibliothek, MS 934 (9th century), fol. 63v
- Pb2bis = Einsiedeln, Stiftsbibliothek, MS 179 (10th century), p. 16
- Pb3-C3 = Düsseldorf, Universitätsbibliothek, MS B. 79 (9th century), fol. 13v

Two observations can be inferred from this situation:

a) The compiler, whoever they were, does not seem to have had the complete epistle 5.40 at their disposal when they organized the *Collectio* (were they not in Rome? Did they not have time to check the letter held in its complete form in the Lateran archive?); the epistle was complete in the original collection, but the antigraph — on which the manuscript transmission of P depends — lost the final sentences.
b) Nobody, neither Adalhard nor anyone else, found an "emendatior codex," a more correct manuscript, to complete the letter.[50]

In some cases, the evidence of manuscript transmission leads to the assumption that the St. Petersburg manuscript is the antigraph of the *Collectio Pauli*. For example, in epistle 5.29, transmitted only by the *Collectio Pauli*, there is the sentence:

> Nam si, quod absit, ecclesiasticam sollicitudinem vigoremque neglegimus, perdit **desidia** disciplinam et animabus

---

50 One exception is the manuscript Munich, Bayerische Staatsbibliothek, MS Clm 2648 (Pb2ter, 13th century), fol. 123vb, in which epistle 5.40 ends with the words "infelicibus orate," thus adding some passages but still not reaching the end of the letter. It is probably interpolated, as the variant "orate" instead of "exorate" seems to suggest.

fidelium profecto nocebitur, dum talia a suis pastoribus exempla suscipiunt.[51]

In Pa1 fol. 3r the word "desidia" is added in the margin, while in all the other manuscripts it is part of the textblock:

- Pa1bis, fol. 35v
- Pa2, fol. 114r–v
- Pb1–C1, fol. 107ra
- Pb1bis–C1bis, fol. 108vb
- Pb1ter–C4, fol. 65v
- Pb2, fol. 60v
- Pb2bis, p. 8
- Pb2ter = Munich, Bayerische Staatsbibliothek, MS Clm 2648 (13th century), fol. 122ra
- Pb3–C3, fol. 8r

The question is then, is "desidia" Gregory's word or a correction made by Paul the Deacon? In this case, a comparison with the *Registrum Hadriani* is not possible, as this letter is not present in R and only Gregory's *usus scribendi* could help. But for now, the most remarkable fact is that all the manuscripts of the *Collectio Pauli* agree with the correction in Pa1.

Letter 5.41, transmitted from both the *Registrum Hadriani* and the *Collectio Pauli*, offers a more intriguing example:

> Sed quemadmodum illius gubernante gratia **petendum est ut** nulla nos superveniens exterius unda conturbet, ita ex totis orandum est visceribus, frater carissime, ut suae providentiae dextera cumulum sentinae nobis interioris exhauriat.

In Pa1, fol. 8v "petendum est ut" is a correction: "petendum est" is added in the line-spacing and "ut" on the line. The other man-

---

51 *Registrum epistolarum*, ed. Norberg, 296, ll. 13–15, and *Registrum epistolarum*, ed. Ewald and Hartmann, vol. 1, 309, ll. 16–18.

uscripts of the Pa family and Paris, BnF, MS lat. 14500 (Pb1ter-C4) have incorporated the correction into the text:

- Pa1bis, fol. 40v
- Pa2, fol. 120v
- Pb1ter-C4, fol. 70v

All the manuscripts of the Pb family, on the other hand, have "petendum est" and omit "ut," apparently misunderstanding the correction in Pa1:

- Pb1-C1, fol. 115va
- Pb1bis-C1bis, fol. 117rb
- Pb2, fol. 64v
- Pb2bis, p. 18
- Pb2ter, fol. 124vb
- Pb3-C3, fol. 15r

The text of the letter in the *Registrum Hadriani* is even more surprising and interesting: it does not have "petendum est ut" and the grammatical and logical sense is stronger. In this case the editors have made different choices: Ewald and Hartmann accepted "petendum est," while Norberg did not.[52]

From these examples it could be assumed that Pa1 is the antigraph of the *Collectio Pauli*, but actually it is not, at least not on the basis of a synchronic philological reconstruction and a static *stemma codicum*. A sentence in letter 11.27, transmitted from both the *Registrum Hadriani* and the *Collectio Pauli*, is crucial:

> Sed in heremo alios hostes invenimus, **quia dum in hac vita vivimus,** priusquam ad promissionis patriam pertingamus,

---

[52] *Registrum epistolarum,* ed. Norberg, 323, ll. 86–89, and *Registrum epistolarum,* ed. Ewald and Hartmann, vol. 1, 334, ll. 1–3.

multae nos temptationes fatigant et ad terram viventium tendentibus iter intercludere festinant.[53]

In this case, in Pa1, fol. 30r, the sentence "quia dum in hac vita vivimus" is omitted by homoioteleuton, without compromising the sense of the passage. The other manuscripts of the Pa family and, once again, Paris, BnF, MS lat. 14500 (Pb1ter-C4) omit it:[54]

- Pa1bis, fol. 63v
- Pa2, fol. 147r
- Pb1ter-C4, fol. 93r.

By contrast, the sentence is present in the Pb family:

- Pb1-C1, fol. 153ra
- Pb1bis-C1bis, fol. 152ra
- Pb2, fol. 86r
- Pb2bis, pp. 68–69
- Pb2ter, fol. 143vb
- Pb3-C3, fol. 44r

So, on the basis of this error and the different behavior of the two families Pa and Pb, Pa1 cannot be the antigraph of the *Collectio Pauli*.

A Strange Witness of P: Munich, Bayerische Staatsbibliothek, MS Clm 14641

The manuscript Clm 14641 from the Bavarian State Library in Munich was included by the German editors in the Pb family as Pb7, but the manuscript evidence suggests that its position in the text transmission was misunderstood. This Munich manu-

---

[53] *Registrum epistolarum,* ed. Norberg, 910, ll. 240–44, and *Registrum epistolarum,* ed. Ewald and Hartmann, vol. 2, 295, ll. 22–25.

[54] This omission (as the aforementioned correction "petendum est ut") suggests that Paris, BnF, MS lat. 14500 does not belong to the Pb family, deriving instead from Pa.

script is a medium-sized, almost square (215 × 180 mm [8.46 × 7.09 in.]) composite volume, consisting of three codicological units.[55] The first contains a part of the *Collectio Pauli*, but begins with two letters by Jerome (or pseudo-Jerome) to Oceanus, on the hierarchy of bishops and monogamy, respectively.[56] The most famous part of the manuscript is probably the second unit, which contains an Easter table with annalistic notes.[57] The third unit is a copy of Ambrose's *De officiis* from the second half of the ninth century.

This manuscript belonged to the library of the Bavarian abbey of St. Emmeram before coming to the Bavarian Royal Library in the nineteenth century, but, as far as the first two codicological units are concerned, it was copied in Fulda at the beginning of the ninth century. The first part of the manuscript, fols. 1–31, was copied by three different hands (A, B, and C), taking over from each other at the start of a new letter. They belong to the first phase of Caroline minuscule in Fulda and share many common features, such as long and thick ascenders, long-shouldered *a* and majuscule *i* at the beginning of words, the 3-shaped *g* with a very small, often open upper bowl, and the insular symbols ÷ for *est* and *h* for *autem*. According to Herrad Spilling, at least one of

---

55 Bernhard Bischoff, *Die südostdeutschen Schreibschulen und Bibliotheken in der Karolingerzeit*, vol. 1: *Die bayrischen Diözesen* (Wiesbaden: Harrassowitz, 1974), 252, and Bernhard Bischoff, *Die südostdeutschen Schreibschulen und Bibliotheken in der Karolingerzeit*, vol. 2: *Die vorwiegend österreichischen Diözesen* (Wiesbaden: Harrassowitz, 1980), 243. The manuscript is fully digitized and available online: https://daten.digitale-sammlungen.de/db/0006/bsb00065770/images/.

56 Bernard Lambert, *Bibliotheca Hieronymiana manuscripta. La tradition manuscrite des oeuvres de saint Jérôme*, vol. 1B (Steenbrugge: Nijhoff, 1969), 729–34, no. 69; vol. 3A (Steenbrugge: Martin Nijhoff, 1972), 166–76, no. 342.

57 Paul Lehmann, *Fuldaer Studien* (Munich: Bayerische Akademie der Wissenschaften, 1925), 28–33, and Richard Corradini, "The Rhetoric of Crisis: *Computus* and *Liber annalis* in Early Ninth-Century Fulda," in *The Construction of Communities in the Early Middle Ages: Texts, Resources and Artefacts*, ed. Richard Corradini, Max Diesenberger, and Helmut Reimitz (Leiden: Brill, 2003), 286–91.

		hand
fols. 1r–4r	*Hieronimus ad Oceanum de gradu episcoporum*	A
fols. 4r–12r	*Hieronimus ad Oceanum de unius uxoris viro*	
fols. 12v–31v	*Collectio Pauli:*	
fols. 12v–18v	37 (11.27)	
fols. 18v–20r	18 (5.59)	
fols. 20r–22r	<41 *(tabula)*> (9.218)	
fol. 22r	38 (2.45; MGH 2.6)	
fols. 22v–23r	39 (2.6; MGH 2.9)	
fol. 23r	40 (2.46; MGH 2.10)	B
fol. 23r–v	15 (5.49)	
fols. 23v–24r	16 (5.50)	
fols. 24r–26r	17 (5.58)	
fol. 26r–v	41 (2.30; MGH 2.31)	C
fols. 26v–27r	42 (2.29; MGH 2.30)	
fols. 27r–31v	52 (9.148; MGH 9.147)	
fol. 31v	*Epitaphium Caroli*	Insular

Table 2.2. Munich, BSb, MS Clm 14641.

these hands is found in another Fulda manuscript.[58] Some marginal corrections and the addition of Charlemagne's epitaph in Insular minuscule at the very end of this codicological unit,[59] as well as the script and notes in the second one, confirm the origin of this manuscript.[60]

---

58 Herrad Spilling, "Die frühe Phase karolingischer Minuskel in Fulda," in *Kloster Fulda in der Welt der Karolinger und Ottonen,* ed. Gangolf Schrimpf (Frankfurt am Main: Josef Knecht, 1996), 249–84, at 257n31.
59 Matthias Tischler, *Einharts "Vita Karoli": Studien zur Entstehung. Überlieferung und Rezeption* (Hanover: Hahnsche Buchhandlung, 2001), 53.
60 Herrad Spilling, "Angelsächsische Schrift in Fulda," in *Von der Klosterbibliothek zur Landesbibliothek. Beiträge zum zweihundertjährigen Bestehen*

Munich, BSb, MS Clm 14641 contains just twelve of Gregory's letters, as shown in table 2.2.

These letters are only one part of the *Collectio* as transmitted by the St. Petersburg manuscript, but have some interesting features:

- A number of them are taken from coherent blocks of letters and form coherent sequences themselves.
- The last letter in the Munich manuscript is the problematic, interpolated, iconoclasm-related letter 9.148, the third to last in the St. Petersburg manuscript.
- The letter to the four Gallic bishops, listed as number 41 in the index but not present in the St. Petersburg manuscript, is found in the Munich manuscript.
- This letter is incomplete, lacking more than half, ending with "et bene adquisitis impenditur."[61]

The Place of the Munich Manuscript in the Transmission of P: Preliminary Hypotheses

The place of Munich, BSB, MS Clm 14641 in the manuscript transmission of the *Collectio Pauli* remains to be determined, as does its relationship to the Pb family, to which Ewald and Hartmann believed it belonged. It is clear that eleven of the twelve Gregorian letters in the Munich manuscript are also in the *Collectio Pauli*. More interestingly, the philological evidence proves that the text of the Gregorian epistles of the Munich manuscript comes from the *Collectio Pauli* itself, because it shares some conjunctive errors with the other witnesses of the *Collectio*.

Epistle 5.58, transmitted by both the *Registrum Hadriani* and the *Collectio Pauli,* has the following passage: "Nam ipse quoque qui ad sacrum **honorem** perducitur, iam in ipsa provectus

---

der Hessischen Landesbibliothek Fulda, ed. Artur Brall (Stuttgart: Anton Hiersemann, 1978), 86.

61 *Registrum epistolarum,* ed. Ewald and Hartmann, vol. 2, 207, l. 11.

sui radice vitiatus, paratior est aliis venundare quod emit."[62] The word "honorem" is transmitted by the manuscripts of *Registrum Hadriani* only, while all the manuscripts of the *Collectio Pauli* have "ordinem," as does the Munich witness[63]:

- Pa1, fol. 14v
- Pa1bis, fol. 46v
- Pa2, fol. 127v
- Pb1-C1, fol. 125vb
- Pb1bis-C1bis, fol. 127ra
- Pb2, fol. 69r
- Pb2bis, p. 30
- Pb2ter, fol. 129va
- Pb3-C3, fol. 23v
- Pb7, fol. 25r

Similarly, epistle 11.27 is transmitted by both the *Registrum Hadriani* and the *Collectio Pauli* and there is a textual difference between the two collections. Consider the following passage: "[…] in quo principaliter ad caelestis munditiae mysterium anima ligatur, ut absoluta radicitus a peccatis omnibus soli illi inhaereat, **de quo propheta ait**: 'Mihi autem adhaerere Deo bonum est.'"[64] The phrase "de quo propheta ait" is present in the manuscripts of the *Registrum Hadriani*, whereas the *Collectio Pauli* and Pb7 have "de quo scriptum est" (the only exception are Pa1bis and Pa2, which share the variant "de quo dicitur"):

- Pa1, fol. 30r
- Pa1bis, fol. 63v ("de quo dicitur")
- Pa2, fol. 147r ("de quo dicitur")
- Pb1-C1, fol. 153ra
- Pb1bis-C1bis, fol. 152ra

---

62 *Registrum epistolarum*, ed. Norberg, 355, l.41–356, l.44, and *Registrum epistolarum*, ed. Ewald and Hartmann, vol. 1, 369, ll. 20–22.
63 Paris, BnF, MS lat. 14500 does not have this epistle.
64 *Registrum epistolarum*, ed. Norberg, 910, ll. 233–36, and *Registrum epistolarum*, ed. Ewald and Hartmann, vol. 2, 295, ll. 16–19.

- Pb1ter-C4, fol. 93r
- Pb2, fol. 86r
- Pb2bis, p. 68
- Pb2ter, fol. 143vb
- Pb3-C3, fol. 44r
- Pb7, fol. 17r

Moreover, in the sentence "Sed ita **suprascripto** vos episcopo devotissime oportet in omnibus adherere" (ep. 2.29, present in both the *Registrum Hadriani* and the *Collectio Pauli*), the word "suprascripto" is omitted in the *Collectio Pauli* and therefore also in Pb7:[65]

- Pa1, fol. 32v
- Pa1bis, fol. 65v
- Pa2, fol. 149v
- Pb1-C1, fol. 156va–b
- Pb1ter-C4, fol. 95r
- Pb2, fol. 87v
- Pb2bis, p. 73
- Pb2ter, fol. 145vb
- Pb3-C3, fol. 46v
- Pb7, fol. 26v

On the other hand, the Munich manuscript sometimes does not share errors with the *Collectio Pauli,* appearing to be independent from it. In epistle 5.59 (transmitted by both the *Registrum Hadriani* and the *Collectio Pauli*) we find the sentence: "[…] quis hominum abnuat huic se libenter dispositioni submittere **cui novit etiam angelos oboedire?** Hinc etenim pax et caritas mutua se vice complectuntur."[66] The Munich manuscript has

---

65 *Registrum epistolarum,* ed. Norberg, 116, ll. 17–18, and *Registrum epistolarum,* ed. Ewald and Hartmann, vol. 1, 127, ll. 10–11 (*ep.* 2.30). The manuscript Pb1bis-C1bis omits this epistle.
66 *Registrum epistolarum,* ed. Norberg, 358, ll. 14–16, and *Registrum epistolarum,* ed. Ewald and Hartmann, vol. 1, 371, ll. 20–22.

"cui novit etiam angelos oboedire," but all the manuscripts of the *Collectio Pauli* omit these words:[67]

- Pa1, fol. 15v
- Pa1bis, fol. 47v
- Pa2, fol. 128v
- Pb1-C1, fol. 127rb
- Pb1bis-C1bis, fol. 128va
- Pb2, fol. 69v
- Pb2bis, p. 32
- Pb2ter, fol. 130rb
- Pb3-C3, fol. 24v
- Pb7, fol. 19r

In the decisive epistle 11.27, discussed above, is the sentence: "Aspectu enim et auditu iustus erat, habitans **apud eos,** qui de die in diem animam iusti iniquis operibus cruciabant."[68] But the manuscripts of the *Collectio Pauli* have "cum hiis" instead of "apud eos," while Pb7 has "apud eos," remaining consistent with the transmission of the *Registrum Hadriani*:

- Pa1, fol. 28r
- Pa1bis, fol. 61r
- Pa2, fol. 144v
- Pb1-C1, fol. 149rb
- Pb1bis-C1bis, fol. 148va
- Pb1ter-C4, fol. 90v
- Pb2, fol. 84r
- Pb2bis, p. 63
- Pb2ter, fol. 141vb
- Pb3-C3, fol. 41v
- Pb7, fol. 14r

---

67 Paris, BnF, MS lat. 14500 does not have this epistle.
68 *Registrum epistolarum,* ed. Norberg, 904–5, ll. 75–76, and *Registrum epistolarum,* ed. Ewald and Hartmann, vol. 2, 291, ll. 28–29.

Furthermore, in the aforementioned epistle 5.58, Pb7 (fol. 25v) and the *Registrum Hadriani* have the sentence: "Qui videlicet error in subditis **cum augmento** propagatur,"[69] but all the other witnesses of the *Collectio Pauli* omit the words "cum augmento":

- Pa1, fol. 14v
- Pa1bis, fol. 46v
- Pa2, fol. 127v
- Pb1-C1, fol. 125vb
- Pb1bis-C1bis, fol. 127ra
- Pb2, fol. 69r
- Pb2bis, p. 30
- Pb2ter, fol. 129va
- Pb3-C3, fol. 23v

All of this means that Munich, BSb, MS Clm 14641 not only does not belong to the Pb family, but must also occupy a higher position in the *stemma codicum* of the *Collectio Pauli* than all the other witnesses. However, for chronological reasons and because it only has eleven of the fifty-four Gregorian epistles of the *Collectio Pauli*, it cannot be the antigraph of the *Collectio* itself.

Conclusions

In conclusion, this analysis of the so-called *Collectio Pauli*, its transmission and some of its codices indicates that much must be revised in our understanding both of the circumstances in which it was assembled, and of the relationships between its manuscripts and families of witnesses. As has been demonstrated, the St. Petersburg manuscript, despite being the oldest surviving witness, was not the antigraph of the whole *Collectio*, as the Munich manuscript seems to descend from an antigraph occupying a higher position in the *stemma codicum*. This also

---

69 *Registrum epistolarum*, ed. Norberg, 355, ll. 40–41, and *Registrum epistolarum*, ed. Ewald and Hartmann, vol. 1, 369, ll. 19–20. As already noted, Paris, BnF, MS lat. 14500 omits this epistle.

points to the conclusion that the *Collectio Pauli* was not compiled by Paul the Deacon, who could simply have had a pre-existing selection of Gregorian letters copied and sent to Adalhard instead, that is the St. Petersburg manuscript.

Furthermore, the manuscript evidence suggests that both the St. Petersburg and the Munich manuscripts were copied from a fragmented or damaged exemplar — as proven by the presence of an incomplete letter in both of them — probably consisting of drafts on small sheets of parchment or even papyrus, not organized in proper quires, which could allow both for the loss of some of them and the disarrangement of others. Whether these drafts had been extracted from the Lateran archive and when and by whom, what Paul the Deacon had in front of him when he had the St. Petersburg manuscript copied, and what the scribes of the Fulda-Munich manuscript had, remains to be investigated. Certainly, from what we know so far, both the St. Petersburg and the Fulda-Munich manuscripts testify to an early, strong interest in one of the first collections of letters ever compiled in the early Middle Ages.

Bibliography

Manuscripts

Bamberg, Staatsbibliothek, MS Patr. 23. https://zendsbb.digitale-sammlungen.de/db/0000/sbb00000151/images/.

Cologne, Erzbischöfliche Diözesan- und Dombibliothek, MS 92. https://digital.dombibliothek-koeln.de/hs/handschriften/content/titleinfo/282101.

Cologne, Erzbischöfliche Diözesan- und Dombibliothek, MS 93. https://digital.dombibliothek-koeln.de/hs/handschriften/content/titleinfo/282474.

Düsseldorf, Universitätsbibliothek, MS B. 79.

Einsiedeln, Stiftsbibliothek, MS 179. https://www.e-codices.unifr.ch/de/searchresult/list/one/sbe/0179.

Munich, Bayerische Staatsbibliothek, MS Clm 14641. https://daten.digitale-sammlungen.de/db/0006/bsb00065770/images/.

Munich, Bayerische Staatsbibliothek, MS Clm 2648. https://opacplus.bsb-muenchen.de/title/BV037448950.

Paris, Bibliothèque nationale de France, MS lat. 6638. http://archivesetmanuscrits.bnf.fr/ark:/12148/cc65748d.

Paris, Bibliothèque nationale de France, MS lat. 14500. http://archivesetmanuscrits.bnf.fr/ark:/12148/cc75254w.

St. Petersburg, Rossiyskaya Natsional'naya Biblioteka, MS lat. F.v.I.7.

Vatican City, Biblioteca Apostolica Vaticana, MS Pal. lat. 266. https://digi.vatlib.it/view/bav_pal_lat_266.

Vienna, Österreichische Nationalbibliothek, MS 934. http://data.onb.ac.at/rec/AC13956491.

Primary

Iohannes Diaconus. "Sancti Gregorii Magni Vita a Joanne diacono scripta libris quatuor." In *Sancti Gregorii Papae I cognomento Magni Opera Omnia, ad manuscriptos codices Romanos, Gallicanos, Anglicanos emendata, aucta et illustrata notis, studio et labore Monachorum Ordinis Sancti*

Benedicti e Congregatione Sancti Mauri IV, by Pope Gregory I the Great, 19–188. Paris: Claudii Rigaud, 1705.

Dümmler, Ernst, ed. *Epistolae Karolini aevi.* Volumes 1–3. Monumenta Germaniae Historica, Epistolae 3–5. Berlin: Weidmann, 1892–1899.

Ewald, Paul, and Ludwig M. Hartmann, eds. *Gregorii I papae "Registrum epistolarum."* Monumenta Germaniae Historica, Epistolae 1–2. Berlin: Weidmann 1887–1899.

Norberg, Dag, ed. *Sancti Gregorii Magni Opera. "Registrum epistolarum."* Corpus Christianorum Series Latina 140–140A. Turnhout: Brepols, 1982.

Secondary

Becker, Gustav. *Catalogi bibliothecarum antiqui.* Bonn: Fr. Cohen, 1885.

Bischoff, Bernhard. *Die südostdeutschen Schreibschulen und Bibliotheken in der Karolingerzeit,* Volume 1: *Die bayrischen Diözesen.* Wiesbaden: Harrassowitz, 1974.

———. *Die südostdeutschen Schreibschulen und Bibliotheken in der Karolingerzeit,* Volume 2: *Die vorwiegend Österreichischen Diözesen.* Wiesbaden: Harrassowitz, 1980.

Capo, Lidia. "Paolo Diacono." In *Dizionario biografico degli Italiani,* Volume 81, 151–62. Rome: Istituto per l'Enciclopedia italiana, 2014.

Castaldi, Lucia. *La trasmissione dei testi latini del Medioevo / Mediaeval Latin Texts and Their Transmission. Te.Tra 5. Gregorius I papa, con un saggio conclusivo sulla Regula Pastoralis di Paolo Chiesa.* Florence: SISMEL Edizioni del Galluzzo, 2013.

Colgrave, Bertram, and Roger A.B. Mynors, eds. *Bede's Ecclesiastical History of the English People.* Oxford: Clarendon Press, 1969.

Convegno Internazionale: Gregorio Magno nel XIV centenario della morte (Roma 22–25 ottobre 2003). Rome: Accademia nazionale dei Lincei, 2004.

Corradini, Richard. "The Rhetoric of Crisis: *Computus* and *Liber annalis* in Early Ninth-Century Fulda." In *The Construction of Communities in the Early Middle Ages: Texts, Resources and Artefacts*, edited by Richard Corradini, Max Diesenberger, and Helmut Reimitz, 269–321. Leiden: Brill, 2003. DOI: 10.1163/9789047404064_016.

Cremascoli, Giuseppe, and Antonella Degl'Innoncenti, eds. *Enciclopedia gregoriana. La vita, l'opera e la fortuna di Gregorio Magno*. Florence: SISMEL Edizioni del Galluzzo, 2008.

Delisle, Léopold. *Le cabinet des manuscrits de la Bibliothèque nationale*. Volume 2. Paris: Imprimerie nationale, 1874.

Demacopoulos, George E. *Gregory the Great: Ascetic, Pastor, and First Man of Rome*. Notre Dame: University of Notre Dame Press, 2015. DOI: 10.2307/j.ctvpj75m1.

D'Imperio, Francesca S. *Gregorio Magno. Bibliografia per gli anni 1980–2003*. Archivum Gregorianum 4. Florence: SISMEL Edizioni del Galluzzo, 2005.

Dobiash-Rozhdestvenskaya, Olga. "Itinéraire de Paul, fils de Warnefride l'an 787–788 et les premiers pas de la minuscule de Cividale en Frioul." *Memorie storiche forogiuliesi* 27–29 (1931–1933): 55–72.

———. "La main de Paul Diacre sur un codex du VIIIe siècle envoyé à Adalhard." *Memorie storiche forogiuliesi* 25 (1929): 129–43.

———. "Ranniy friul'skiy minuskul i odna iz problem zhizni i tvorcchestva langobardskogo istorika VIII v. (s 4 tabl. i rezyume na franc. yaz.)." *AN SSSR: Vspomogatel'nye istorichheskie discipliny. Sbornik stat'ey* (1937): 109–41.

Dobiash-Rozhdestvenskaya, Olga, and Wsevolod W. Bakhtine. *Les anciens manuscrits latins de la Bibliothèque publique Saltykov-Shchedrin de Leningrad*. Translated by Xénia Grichine. Paris: Éditions du Centre national de la recherche scientifique, 1991.

Godding, Robert. *Bibliografia di Gregorio Magno, 1890–1989*. Opere di Gregorio Magno, Complementi 1. Rome: Città Nuova Editrice, 1990.

Henne, Philippe. *Grégoire le Grand*. Paris: Éditions du Cerf, 2007.

Hoffmann, Hartmut. "Autographa des früheren Mittelalters." *Deutsches Archiv für Erforschung des Mittelalters* 57 (2001): 1–62.

Lambert, Bernard. *Bibliotheca Hieronymiana manuscripta: La tradition manuscrite des oeuvres de saint Jérôme*. Volumes 1B and 3A. Turnhout: Brepols, 1969 and 1972. DOI: 10.1484/M.IPM-EB.5.112095.

Lehmann, Paul. *Fuldaer Studien*. Munich: Bayerische Akademie der Wissenschaften, 1925.

Leonardi, Claudio, ed. *Gregorio Magno e le origini dell'Europa*. Florence: SISMEL Edizioni del Galluzzo, 2014.

Lowe, Elias A. *Codices Latini Antiquiores*. Volume 11. Oxford: Clarendon Press, 1966.

Markus, Robert A. *Gregory the Great and His World*. Cambridge: Cambridge University Press, 1997. DOI: 10.1017/CBO9781139171236.

Mattaloni, Valeria, ed. *Rescriptum beati Gregorii Papae ad Augustinum Episcopum quem in Saxoniam in praedicatione direxerat (seu Libellus responsionum)*. Florence: SISMEL Edizioni del Galluzzo, 2017.

Meyvaert, Paul. "Bede's Text of the *Libellus Responsionum* of Gregory the Great to Augustine of Canterbury." In *England before the Conquest: Studies in Primary Sources Presented to Dorothy Whitelock,* edited by Peter Clemoes, Kathleen Hughes, and Dorothy Whitelock, 15–33. Cambridge: Cambridge University Press, 1971.

———. "Les Responsiones de S. Grégoire le Grand à S. Augustin de Canterbury. À propos d'un article récent." *Revue d'histoire ecclésiastique* 54 (1959): 879–94.

———. "*Libellus responsionum* à Augustin de Cantorbéry: une oeuvre authentique de saint Grégoire le Grand." In *Grégoire le Grand: Chantilly, Centre culturel Les Fontaines, 15–19 septembre 1982. Actes,* ed. Jacques Fontaine, Robert Gillet, and Stan M. Pellistrandi, Colloques internationaux de Centre national de la recherche scientifique, 543–50. Paris:

Editions du Centre national de la recherche scientifique, 1986.
Neff, Karl. *Die Gedichte des Paulus Diaconus: Kritische und erklärende Ausgabe.* Munich: Beck'sche Verlagsbuchandlung, 1908.
Neil, Bronwen, and Matthew Dal Santo, eds. *A Companion to Gregory the Great.* Leiden: Brill, 2013. DOI: 10.1163/9789004257764.
Norberg, Dag. *"In Registrum Gregorii Magni" studia critica.* 2 Volumes. Uppsala: Lundequist, 1937–1939.
Ricci, Luigi G.G., ed. *Gregorio Magno e l'invenzione del Medioevo.* Florence: SISMEL Edizioni del Galluzzo, 2006.
Ricciardi, Alberto. "Gli inganni della tradizione. Una silloge del *Registrum* di Gregorio Magno nei rapporti fra Carolini e papato e nel dibattito sulle immagini sacre." *Studi medievali* 56 (2015): 79–126.
Spilling, Herrad. "Angelsächsische Schrift in Fulda." In *Von der Klosterbibliothek zur Landesbibliothek. Beiträge zum zweihundertjährigen Bestehen der Hessischen Landesbibliothek Fulda,* edited by Artur Brall, 47–98. Stuttgart: Anton Hiersemann, 1978.
———. "Die frühe Phase karolingischer Minuskel in Fulda." In *Kloster Fulda in der Welt der Karolinger und Ottonen,* edited by Gangolf Schrimpf, 249–84. Frankfurt am Main: Josef Knecht, 1996.
Staerk, Antonio. *Les manuscrits latins du Ve au XIIIe siècle conservés à la Bibliothèque Imperiale de Saint-Pétersbourg. Description, textes inédits, reproductions autotypiques.* St. Petersburg: Imprimerie artistique Franz Krois, 1910.
Steinová, Evina. *"Notam superponere studui": The Use of Annotation Symbols in the Early Middle Ages.* Turnhout: Brepols, 2019.
Thompson, Patricia Z. "Biography of a Library: The Western European Manuscript Collection of Peter P. Dubrovskii in Leningrad." *The Journal of Library History* 19, no. 4 (1984): 477–503.

Tischler, Matthias. *Einharts "Vita Karoli." Studien zur Entstehung, Überlieferung und Rezeption.* 2 Volumes. Monumenta Germaniae Historica, Schriften, 48. Hanover: Hahnsche Buchhandlung, 2001.

Voronova, Tamara P. "Western Manuscripts in the Saltykov-Shchedrin Library, Leningrad." *The Book Collector* 5 (1956): 12–18.

3

Creating the Past in the Carolingian Book of Virgil

Sinéad O'Sullivan

This chapter focuses on compilation in a Carolingian book of Virgil to show that ancient Rome and Christianity sat comfortably side by side.[1] It studies the assembly of texts, commentaries, glosses, and excerpts in a miscellany to throw light on how Carolingian scholars created the past. Once a single book, the collection is extant in a manuscript currently housed in Paris and in two fragments now in the Vatican City. In it, the past, embracing myth and history, stretches from the foundations and rise of Rome to the prophetic and triumphant arrival of Christ. An excerpt from a Carolingian poem by John Scottus Eriugena, references to the Franks, the names of Carolingian scholars, overlap with glossed Carolingian Virgil manuscripts, textual affinities with a specific group of ninth-century Virgil manuscripts, and numerous links with Carolingian Laon give the collection a strong Carolingian flavor.

The principal texts comprise the three major works of Virgil and the biblical epics of Juvencus and Sedulius. Cumulatively, the materials in the book lavish attention on Troy, Rome, and

---

1   I am enormously grateful to Anna Dorofeeva and John Contreni for their many insights and observations.

Christ. From the very beginning, the collection establishes the importance of Christ and the celestial kingdom. It does so through Caelius Sedulius's *Carmen Paschale* ("The Paschal Song"), a five-book Latin poem on Christ, which contains Old Testament miracles often interpreted typologically. In his preface, Sedulius declares that Christ's *regnum* is *sine tempore* ("without end") and Christ's *potestas* is one with that of the Father *arcibus aetheriis* ("in the vaults of heaven").[2] Christ is also the center of attention in Juvencus's *Evangeliorum libri quattuor* ("Four Books of the Gospels"), which opens with a reflection on the transitory nature of all earthly kingdoms, including golden Rome, and avows to concentrate on Christ, the gleaming judge who will descend *flammivoma* [...] *nube* ("in a flame-belching cloud").[3] Power and kingship are key themes in the collection. Cosmology is also a central interest. It features at the start of Juvencus's biblical epic, at the end of the collection in a poem depicting Christ as *mundi saluator* ("savior of the world"), and in an excerpt from Priscian's guide to the *Aeneid* focused on *Oceanus,* a feature of the *orbis terrarum* in the geocentric universe. Christ bookends the collection.

That the celestial or eternal kingdom, the province of Christ, is an important focus is further attested to by another work in the miscellany, that is, by an excerpt from a poem by Eriugena, whose thinking has been characterized as shaped by a Christocentric cosmology.[4] In the excerpt, we read that the celestial realms, a fiery domain experienced in the mind, are associated with the *templa sophiae* ("temples of wisdom").[5] In Eriugena's

---

2   Carl P.E. Springer, trans., *Sedulius: The Paschal Song and Hymns,* Society of Biblical Literature 35 (Atlanta: Society of Biblical Literature, 2013), 4–5.

3   Scott McGill, trans., *Juvencus' Four Books of the Gospels: Evangeliorum Libri Quattuor* (London: Routledge, 2016), 7.

4   T. Alexander Giltner, "*Intimae Theologiae:* The Christocentric Cosmology of John Scottus Eriugena in the *Homilia super "In principio erat verbum,"* *Archives d'histoire doctrinale et littéraire du Moyen Âge* 83, no. 1 (2016): 7–32.

5   For the excerpt, see Ludwig Traube, ed., *Iohannis Scotti carmina,* Monumenta Germaniae Historica, Poetae Latini aevi Carolini 3 (Berlin: Weidmann, 1896), 537, and Michael W. Herren, ed., *Iohannis Scotti Eriugenae*

cosmology, Christ was never far from view. A distich by Eriugena at the end of the collection calls upon the reader to sing praises to the living Christ.[6] Composed in Greek, the couplet is provided with a Latin interlinear gloss. Moreover, the cosmic importance of Christ is celebrated in another poem at the end of the collection, that is in two couplets written upside down by a hand dated to the ninth century. Significantly, the text refers to *pius Augustus Hludowicus,* thus bringing the Franks into the picture.[7] Another text in the collection also mentions the Franks, the *Epitaphium Aelberhti* of Alcuin. The *Epitaphium* relates how Alcuin went to Rome, "a city venerated by all peoples and to the flourishing kingdoms of the Franks."[8] The *regna Francorum* are part of a collection, which, as we shall see, celebrated not only Christ, but also ancient Rome. This collection includes glosses on a Golden Age of regeneration mentioned in the Fourth Eclogue, interpreted by early medieval glossators as referring to Augustus, Christ, and Mary.[9]

Ancient Rome features prominently in the book. The compilers were evidently interested in *Roma antiqua,* as is illustrated by the glosses on pagan antiquity that accompany the works of Virgil, by the commentaries that were placed alongside Virgil's works (Servius's commentaries on Virgil and Pseudo-Dares Phrygius's *The Destruction of Troy* [*De excidio Troiae historia*])

Carmina, Scriptores Latini Hiberniae 12 (Dublin: Dublin School of Celtic Studies, 1993).

6 Claudio Leonardi, "Nuove voci poetiche tra secolo IX e XI," *Studi Medievali* 2 (1961): 139–68, at 146, gives a transcription of the distich and interlinear Latin gloss.

7 For the couplets, see Leonardi, "Nuove," 144, who noted that similar themes appear in the carmina of Alcuin. See Ildar H. Garipzanov, *The Symbolic Language of Authority in the Carolingian World (c. 751–877),* Brill's Series on the Early Middle Ages 16 (Leiden: Brill, 2008), 343–45, for Carolingian titles in diplomas, on bulls, seals, and coins

8 *Dum Romam cunctis venerandam gentibus urbem, vel iam Francorum florida regna petit.* Alcuin, *Epitaphium Aelberhti,* ed. Ernst Dümmler, Monumenta Germaniae Historica, Poetae Latini aevi Carolini 1 (Berlin: Weidmann, 1881), 206–7.

9 Sinéad O'Sullivan, "Glossing Virgil and Pagan Learning in the Carolingian Age," *Speculum* 93, no. 1 (2018): 159.

and by the Trojan genealogy found among the prefatory texts to the *Aeneid*. This genealogy, appearing also in other Carolingian books of Virgil, includes a synopsis of Aeneas's journey from Troy to Italy and his marriage to Lavinia, daughter of Latinus, king of the Latins, an ancient tribe associated with the rise of Rome. The glosses, compiled from Servian and non-Servian sources, comprise ancient and medieval materials. They include information not found in the extant commentaries on Virgil but attested elsewhere in glossed Virgil manuscripts.

The marginal and interlinear glosses in the collection are a prime mechanism for examination of the Carolingian appropriation of Virgil. They not only provide valuable insight into the reception of Virgil, whose works advanced the idea of a Golden Age, promoted the prestige of Rome, and celebrated Rome's foundations and apogee embodied by Aeneas and Augustus respectively. More than that, the glosses furnish a critical apparatus to the works of Virgil. Following Virgil's lead, they build a picture of ancient Rome focused on the empire of Augustus, an empire that harked back to the Trojan hero Aeneas and to the mythical origins of Rome herself. The age of Augustus, celebrated by Virgil, was presented in the Carolingian reception of the poet as a powerful demonstration of Roman might. Glossators noted that during the reign of Augustus Christ was born.[10] In the context of salvation history, this coincidence took on momentous significance. The Carolingian reception of Virgil demonstrates that Augustan Rome carried weight. For the Carolingians, Rome was manifestly a multi-faceted concept simultaneously embracing both a classical and a Christian heritage. Above all, Rome was an imperial concept, a concept embodied by Augustus, and Virgil was a portal to an illustrious past.

---

10 Paris, Bibliothèque nationale de France, MS lat. 10307, fol. 54v: "Hanc Eglogam compositam esse aiunt in honore Asinii Pollionis [...] uel in honorem Octauiani Augusti" ("They say that this Eclogue was composed in honor of Asinius Pollio [...] or Octavianus, Augustus"). Georg Thilo and Hermann Hagen, eds., *Servii grammatici qui feruntur in Virgilii carmina commentarii* (Leipzig: Teubner, 1881–1902), vol. 3.2, 72. O'Sullivan, "Glossing Virgil," 159.

This chapter argues that the picture of the past in the miscellany, a past embracing secular and sacred history, coheres with the Carolingian *Weltbild* and construction of power. Carolingian scholars connected the Frankish dynasty with the Graeco-Roman and Judeo-Christian heritages. A few examples should suffice. Helmut Reimitz has observed that the *Annales regnum Francorum*, a Carolingian product, adopts a Christocentric perspective, integrating the Carolingian view of history into a "Calendar of Triumph, in which the triumph of Christianity is directly linked to the triumph of the Carolingian family and the Frankish people."[11] Rosamond McKitterick noted that the *Annales* deploy the year of the Incarnation as the "organising principle of the narrative on a yearly basis."[12] Christ was at the center of history. In the anonymous ninth-century Latin epic known as *Karolus magnus et Leo papa*, Charlemagne is compared to Aeneas.[13] A fascinating miscellany from Carolingian Lorsch (s. VIII^ex/IX^in) links Trojan, Roman, and Frankish history. It transmits excerpts from the *Aeneid*, together with Dares Phrygius and the eighth-century Frankish chronicle, *Liber historiae Francorum*, which maps the Trojan ancestry of the Franks.[14] The early ninth-century *Egloga ad Karolum* of the Frankish poet

---

[11] Helmut Reimitz, *History, Frankish Identity and the Framing of Western Ethnicity, 550–850* (Cambridge: Cambridge University Press, 2015), 336.

[12] Rosamond McKitterick, "Constructing the Past in the Early Middle Ages: The Case of the Royal Frankish Annals," *Transactions of the Royal Historical Society* 7 (1997): 110.

[13] Otto Zwierlein, "Karolus Magnus — alter Aeneas?," in *Literatur und Sprache im europäischen Mittelalter: Festschrift für Karl Langosch zum 70. Geburtstag,* ed. Alf Önnerfors, Johannes Rathofer, and Fritz Wagner (Darmstadt: Wissenschaftliche Buchgesellschaft, 1973), 44–52; Christine Ratkowitsch, *Karolus Magnus — alter Aeneas, alter Martinus, alter Iustinus: Zu Intention und Datierung des "Aachener Karlsepos,"* Wiener Studien, Beiheft 24 (Vienna: Österreichische Akademie der Wissenschaften, 1999).

[14] Richard A. Gerberding, "Paris, Bibliothèque Nationale Latin 7906: An Unnoticed Very Early Fragment of the *Liber historiae francorum*," *Traditio* 43 (1987): 381–6, and Bernhard Bischoff, *Katalog der festländischen Handschriften des neunten Jahrhunderts (mit Ausnahme der wisigotischen),* vol. 3: *Padua-Zwickau,* ed. Birgit Ebersperger (Wiesbaden: Harrassowitz, 2014), no. 4512, 135.

Modoin, a work modeled on the *Eclogues*, promotes the restoration of Golden Rome in the Carolingian Age.[15] In Carolingian political and intellectual culture, the ruling elite was manifestly connected with Christ and Rome.

Taken as a whole, the classical and Christian materials in the collection cohere with the Carolingian *Weltanschauung*. In the collection, Christian materials abound. We find Christian poems (including acrostic poems), hymns and prayers, Asterius's eight-line epigram regularly copied in Sedulius manuscripts, and Alcuin's epitaph for Ælberht.[16] The typological interpretations in Sedulius's *Carmen Paschale* together with the other Christ-centered works in the collection accord with the ambient Christocentrism of Carolingian exegetical, historiographical, and political culture. The rich tapestry of glosses accompanying the works of Virgil were part of a flourishing Carolingian tradition of glossing *the* poet of antiquity. This tradition emerged in Carolingian centers, especially in northeastern France in the second half of the ninth century.[17] Though copied primarily by a single hand dated to the tenth century, the glosses are part of a rich Carolingian tradition of glossing Virgil. The Trojan and Roman materials in the miscellany complement the wider Carolingian interest in Graeco-Roman antiquity (e.g., its cosmology, geography, history, mythology, and science). Such materials resonate with the Carolingian cultivation of a well-established tradition that explicitly placed the Franks in a continuum with the Trojans. They also accord with the Carolingians' self-perception

---

15 "Aurea Roma iterum renovata renascitur orbi" ("Golden Rome is reborn and restored anew to the world"). Ernst Dümmler, ed., *Modoin, "Ecloga,"* Monumenta Germaniae Historica, Poetae Latini aevi Carolini 1 (Berlin: Weidmann, 1881), 385, and Peter Godman, *Poetry of the Carolingian Renaissance* (London: Duckworth, 1985), 193.

16 Carl P.E. Springer, *The Manuscripts of Sedulius: A Provisional Handlist*, Transactions of the American Philosophical Society 85, no. 5 (Philadelphia: American Philosophical Society, 1995), 18 and 25. Alexander Riese, ed., *Anthologia Latina sive Poesis Latinae Supplementum, pars prior, Carmina in codicibus scripta. Fasc. II,* (Leipzig: Teubner, 1870), no. 491.

17 Silvia Ottaviano, "La tradizione delle opere di Virgilio tra IX e XI sec." (PhD Diss., Scuola Normale Superiore, Pisa, 2014), 42, 69–70.

as inheritors of *aurea Roma*. This self-perception was rooted in Augustan ideology, with its promotion of Trojan descent and Roman hegemony. Adapting the Hellenocentric concept of *oikoumenē* ("the inhabited earth") and its Latin counterpart, *orbis terrarum* ("the circle of lands"), Augustan propaganda positioned Rome in the center of the world.[18] The Carolingians, in turn, appropriated this imperial ideal, fusing it with the biblical notion of Jerusalem as global center point to project a story of power centered on their ruling dynasty.

Building on recent scholarly research on miscellanies, this chapter supports the call to examine the gathering of materials in a single manuscript or a multi-volume collection integrally and to see in the practice of *collectio* "assembly, not disintegration, a centripetal not a centrifugal endeavour."[19] I argue that the materials in the Carolingian book of Virgil under review were not randomly selected. Rather the assembly of classical and Christian materials provides insight into the Carolingian understanding of their place in the world, a place rooted in the heritages of Rome and Christianity.

Una miscellanea scolastica (y)

In many respects, the collection labeled by Claudio Leonardi "a scholastic miscellany" can be seen as the culmination of in-

---

18 Sinéad O'Sullivan, "The *Oikoumenē* and the Carolingian Reception of Virgil," in *The Elements in the Medieval World: Interdisciplinary Perspectives: Earth*, ed. Marilina Cesario, Hugh Magennis, and Elisa Ramazzina (Leiden: Brill, 2024), 121–51.

19 Mary Garrison, "The *Collectanea* and Medieval Florilegia," in *Collectanea Pseudo-Bedae,* ed. Martha Bayless and Michael Lapidge, Scriptores Latini Hiberniae 14 (Dublin: Dublin Institute for Advanced Studies, 1998), 43. See especially the work of Anna Dorofeeva, "Miscellanies, Christian Reform and Early Medieval Encyclopaedism: A Reconsideration of the Pre-Bestiary *Physiologus* Manuscripts," *Historical Research* 90, no. 250 (2017): 665–82, and also Rolf H. Bremmer Jr. and Kees Dekker, "Practice in Learning: An Introduction," in *Practice in Learning: The Transfer of Encyclopaedic Knowledge in the Early Middle Ages,* ed. Rolf H. Bremmer Jr. and Kees Dekker, Mediaevalia Groningana New Series 16 (Leuven: Peeters, 2010), xi.

tense efforts by Carolingian scholars to surround the principal works of Virgil with supplementary elements.[20] Around Virgil, compilers created what Silvia Ottaviano has labeled *il libro altomedievale di Virgilio* ("the early medieval book of Virgil").[21] Like many Carolingian books of Virgil, the works of the poet in this *miscellanea scolastica* were accompanied by commentaries, excerpts, glosses, poems, and prefatory materials. What makes this miscellany so interesting is the appearance of Christian materials. Paris, Bibliothèque nationale de France, MS lat. 10307 + Vatican City, Biblioteca Apostolica Vaticana, MS Reg. lat. 1625 (III) transmit classical, late antique, and medieval texts, commentaries and excerpts, including, but not limited to, Homer, Ennius, Sallust, Virgil, Pseudo-Ovid, Servius, Pseudo-Dares Phrygius, Priscian, Caelius Sedulius, Juvencus, Alcuin, and John Scottus Eriugena. The range of materials is impressive, embracing a literary inheritance from the Greek and Roman epic poets to their Christian counterparts. Following Ottaviano, I use the siglum *y* to denote the collection of materials in what is essentially a Carolingian book of Virgil.[22]

The origin of the collection is unknown. Bernhard Bischoff suggested eastern France (Lorraine), Contreni Auxerre-Rheims, and Ottaviano northeastern France.[23] The text of Virgil, commentary of Servius, and Virgil glosses connect the collection to other manuscripts emanating from northeast, north-central, or east-central France in the ninth century. Though uncertainty remains regarding the precise origin of the collection, many factors link it with Laon and its ninth-century masters. Bischoff suggested that the manuscript was at Laon. Contreni provided detailed evidence for a Laon association.

The connection with Laon is attested to by the additions of a hand dated to the late ninth or early tenth century and charac-

---

20 Leonardi, "Nuove," 140.
21 Ottaviano, "La tradizione," 3.
22 Ibid., 270–79.
23 Bischoff, *Katalog* 3, no. 4627, 160–61; John J. Contreni, "A propos de quelques manuscrits de l'école de Laon au IXe siècle: découvertes et problèmes," *Le Moyen Âge* 78 (1972): 34–38; and Ottaviano, "La tradizione," 270.

terized as exhibiting Irish traits.²⁴ This hand was responsible for copying all kinds of materials in Paris, BnF, MS lat. 10307, fols. 95va and 246v and on the two *membra disiecta* in the Reginensis (now folios 65 and 66 of Reg. lat. 1625). The *membra disiecta* were identified by Contreni as once belonging to the Paris manuscript.²⁵ The additions include prayers, poems, distichs, inscriptions, grammatical notes, a Latin palindrome, and excerpts from Homer, Ennius, Sallust, Servius, and Priscian. In subject matter, they incorporate elements relating to *Roma antiqua*, Mary, and Christ. Time and cosmology are also evoked in the additions, as is illustrated by a poem on the months, an extract on the fiery heavens from an Eriugenian poem, and a hymn to the Virgin in which *omnis creatura* ("all creation") celebrates Mary's role as *dei genitrix* (i.e., the mother of Christ).²⁶

As for possible links with Laon, the additions include inscriptions and *graeca collecta* found in Laon manuscripts closely associated with Martin of Laon, an extract from a poem and a distich by John Scottus Eriugena, verses attributed to a Iohannis (one of which has been characterized as a "Bacchic distich"), and the names of Irishmen associated with Laon or having ties to the school of Laon in the ninth century (Martin of Laon, John Scottus Eriugena, Sedulius Scottus, and Fergus).²⁷ Evidence of a

---

24 John J. Contreni, *The Cathedral School of Laon from 850 to 930: Its Manuscripts and Masters*, Münchener Beiträge zur Mediävistik und Renaissance-Forschung 29 (München: Arbeo-Gesellschaft, 1978), 93, 119–20, and Contreni, "A propos," 37.

25 Contreni, "A propos," 31. See also his letter to Bernhard Bischoff dated June 29, 1970, preserved in the *Nachlass* of Bernhard Bischoff in the Bayerische Staatsbibliothek, in which he writes: "The rulings for the Virgil text and Servius commentary in the Paris ms are also found in the Vatican leaves. Finally, my photos of the Vatican leaves even show that the worm-holes of those leaves match the holes in the Paris ms exactly." See also https://twitter.com/litteracarolina/status/1287705757983682563.

26 Full transcription of the hymn: Contreni, "A propos," 32–33.

27 References are made to a Iohannis, very likely John Scottus Eriugena. An extract from a poem by Eriugena appears in the collection. The reference to Fergus occurs alongside what Michael Herren constructed as a note of Sedulius Scottus to a certain Fergus. Interesting is the inclusion of the names of Irishmen: Michael W. Herren, "Sedulius Scottus and the

Laon connection is further attested to by the Virgil glosses in the collection. Some glosses contain information found in an anonymous Virgilian *Vita* transcribed in the handbook on Virgil and Sedulius produced at Laon in the last quarter of the ninth century: Laon, Bibliothèque municipale Suzanne Martinet, MS 468. Contreni detected that the anonymous *Vita* transmits information that does not appear in other texts in the *Vitae Virgilianae* tradition.[28] Some of this "unique" information occurs in glosses in the collection (see the appendix). A variant in a Virgil gloss provides another link with Laon, BmSM, MS 468.[29] Finally, the

---

Knowledge of Greek," in *Early Medieval Ireland and Europe: Chronology, Contacts, Scholarship. A Festschrift for Dáibhí Ó Cróinín*, ed. Pádraic Moran and Immo Warntjes, Studia Traditionis Theologiae 14 (Turnhout: Brepols, 2015), 520–21. For the "Bacchic distich" attached to his name, see Paul Edward Dutton, "Evidence that Dubthach's Priscian Codex Once Belonged to Eriugena," in *From Athens to Chartres: Neoplatonism and Medieval Thought: Studies in Honour of Edouard Jeauneau*, edited by Haijo Jan Westra, Studien und Texte zur Geistesgeschichte des Mittelalters 35 (Leiden: Brill, 1992), 22. There is overlap between the materials in the collection and two Laon manuscripts, one of which has been described as "Laon's important Greek-Latin glossary and compendium of Greek-Latin *grammatica* [...] copied at Laon under the supervision of Martin Hiberniensis." Contreni, *Cathedral School*, 57.

28 John J. Contreni, "Getting to Know Virgil in the Carolingian Age: The *Vita Publii Virgilii*," in *Rome and Religion in the Medieval World: Studies in Honour of Thomas F.X. Noble*, ed. Valerie L. Garver and Owen M. Phelan (Farnham: Ashgate, 2014), 30–31.

29 See the gloss on Tereus in Paris, BnF, MS 10307, fol. 57v. The lemma is on fol. 58r, l. 10. Silvia Ottaviano, "Reading between the Lines of Virgil's Early Medieval Manuscripts," in *The Annotated Book in the Early Middle Ages: Practices of Reading and Writing*, ed. Mariken Teeuwen and Irene van Renswoude, Utrecht Studies in Medieval Literacy 38 (Turnhout: Brepols, 2017), 407–8, edits the gloss as found in various manuscripts. See also O'Sullivan, "Glossing Virgil," 160–61. The information in the gloss relies heavily on Servius: *Servii grammatici qui feruntur in Virgilii carmina commentarii*, 3.1, 80–81. In the story, Procne, wife of Tereus, kills her son, Itys, in revenge for the rape of her sister, Philomela, by her husband Tereus. In early medieval annotations, there is sometimes confusion between Procne, wife of Tereus, and Procne's sister, Philomela. In Paris, BnF, MS 10307, one reads that the sister gave birth to the boy: *tempus pariendi suae sororis*. In other manuscripts, it is the wife Procne who gives birth: *tempus pariendi suae uxoris*. The same variant (i.e., *sororis*) appears in Paris, BnF, MS 10307

Greek words and *graeca collecta* in the collection cohere with the well-known Hellenism of Laon's masters.

Dated by Bischoff and Contreni to the last quarter of the ninth century, many hands can be identified in the collection.[30] They primarily date to the ninth and tenth centuries. The hand responsible for the Virgil text beginning on fol. 50v copied the Trojan genealogy. Various hands, not much younger than this text hand, copied the commentary of Servius.[31] Following Bischoff and Franck Cinato, I date the hand copying the work of Pseudo-Dares Phrygius to the tenth century.[32] The marginal and interlinear Virgil glosses are primarily entered by one hand, dated by Ottaviano to the tenth century and characterized as *pressoché contemporanei* ("almost contemporary").[33] Birger Munk Olsen described the collection as comprising two contemporary and homogeneous elements: 1–43 and 44–245.[34] Various factors suggest that the different portions of the collection belonged to the same enterprise and were conceived as a unit (the largely two-column format, initials written in uncials and capitals, and the presence of initials decorated with an interlace pattern throughout the collection). According to Bischoff, the collection was written in three stages: 1) fols. 50–245; 2) fols. 1–43 *in demselben Skriptorium, z.T. von den gl. Hden* ("in the same scriptorium partly by the same hands"); and 3) fols. 44–49 *etwa glz. den Kommentaren in den Vergil-Teilen* ("around the same time as the commentaries in the Virgil parts").[35] Thus, according to Bischoff, fols. 1–43 were written in the same scripto-

---

and in Laon, BmSM, MS 468, fol. 8r. In Paris, BnF, MS lat. 7925, fol. 7v, one finds *uxoris* changed to *sororis*.

30 Bischoff, *Katalog* 3, no. 4627, 161; Contreni, "A propos," 34n61.
31 Ottaviano, "La tradizione," 272–73 and 278.
32 Bischoff, *Katalog* 3, no. 4627, 161; Franck Cinato, https://archivesetmanuscrits.bnf.fr/ark:/12148/cc13369k.
33 Ottaviano, "La tradizione," 273.
34 Birger Munk Olsen, *L'étude des auteurs classiques latins aux XIe et XIIe siècles*, vol. 2: *Catalogue des manuscrits classiques latins copiés du IXe au XIIe siècle* (Paris: Éditions du Centre national de la recherche scientifique, 1985), 764–65.
35 Bischoff, *Katalog* 3, no. 4627, 161.

rium as fols. 50–245 and in part by the same hands. As already noted, additions by a late ninth- or early tenth-century hand were identified by Contreni.

Parallels and Interconnections

In the Sedulius-Juvencus section, Ottaviano noted *utili paralleli* ("useful parallels").[36] Parallels and interconnections of all sorts can be observed in the miscellany. For example, just as Virgil and Servius were transmitted side by side, so too Sedulius was flanked by Juvencus. Ottaviano has suggested that Sedulius was accompanied by Juvencus probably because they both deal with the same subject matter. Moreover, in the Sedulius-Juvencus portion, Sedulius was copied first and occupies the interior columns (*ra* and *vb*); Juvencus is found in the outer columns (*rb* and *va*).[37] The result is a kind of mirror effect, with Juvencus on the *verso* facing Juvencus on the *recto* and Sedulius on the *verso* facing Sedulius on the *recto*. According to Franck Cinato, Juvencus was copied after Sedulius by another contemporary hand. He suggested that the space may originally have been intended for a commentary. If so, then the collection may once have been envisaged as a compendium on Virgil and Sedulius. The prefatory materials accompanying Virgil and Sedulius would support such a conclusion. Given the connections between the collection and Laon, it is interesting to recall that a "guide to the works of Virgil and Sedulius" was produced at Laon in the third quarter of the ninth century and that overlap with this guide is evident in the materials entered by the late ninth- or early tenth-century hand in the miscellany.[38]

In the Virgil section, the well-known Homer-Virgil linkage appears in a marginal gloss at the start of the *Georgics*.[39] This linkage has analogues. For instance, the preface of Juvencus re-

---

36 Ottaviano, "La tradizione," 272.
37 Cinato, https://archivesetmanuscrits.bnf.fr/ark:/12148/cc13369k.
38 Contreni, *Cathedral School*, 39; Bischoff, *Katalog* 2, no. 2128, 37.
39 Paris, BnF, MS lat. 10307, fol. 63r. *Servii grammatici qui feruntur in Virgilii carmina commentarii*, 3.1, 128.

fers to both Homer and Virgil, thus situating Juvencus's work in the epic tradition of the Greek and Roman poets.[40] Additionally, the extract from Ennius reminds one of Homer.[41] The foundational importance of Homer binds together Ennius, Virgil, Juvencus, and Sedulius. No surprise, then, that the late ninth- or early tenth-century hand should add a quotation from Homer in Greek with interlinear Latin translation. The quotation was derived from Martianus's *De nuptiis* v.430.[42] And Martianus is also the source of another extract, this time from Ennius on the *dii Consentes,* the twelve major gods of the Roman pantheon, the equivalent of the Dodekatheon, that is, the twelve major deities of the Greek pantheon.[43] The Homeric and Greek world is never far from view, as is further illustrated by the abundance of Greek words in the collection.

Numina falsa

Classical antiquity was greatly valued by the compilers of the collection. It was part of the Carolingian understanding of the past. Though Juvencus proclaimed that the subject of his work was Christ and not the *mendacia* ("lies") of the ancient poets, and though an anonymous poem lamented being led astray by *numina falsa* ("false gods") and Martianus Capella, the collection testifies to the wholesale endorsement of the ancient

---

40 McGill, *Juvencus' Four Books of the Gospels,* 6.
41 Peter Aicher, "Ennius' Dream of Homer," *The American Journal of Philology* 110, no. 2 (1989): 227–32. See also Jackie Elliott, "Ennius as Universal Historian: The Case of the *Annales*," in *Historiae Mundi: Studies in Universal History,* ed. Peter Liddel and Andrew Fear (London: Bloomsbury, 2010), 148, for "Ennius' co-option of the Homeric texts with their undisputed claim to cultural supremacy."
42 Homer, *Iliad* XI.654; Leonardi, "Nuove," 145.
43 Leonardi, "Nuove," 146. In addition, the reference to the empyrean realm in the extract from an Eriugenian poem recalls Martianus's *De nuptiis Philologiae et Mercurii.* In the allegorical books, Philology's celestial journey culminates in an *empyrio* […] *intellectualique mundo* ("empyrean and intellectual realm"). James Willis, ed., *Martianus Capella,* Bibliotheca scriptorum Graecorum et Romanorum Teubneriana (Leipzig: Teubner, 1983), 55.

world.[44] The collection exhibits a dual heritage: classical and Christian. This heritage is prominently attested to by Juvencus's *Evangeliorum libri IV,* which was greatly indebted to Virgil's *Aeneid.* The importance of Juvencus's text has been summarized by Scott McGill as follows: it was "the first classicizing, hexameter poem on a Christian topic to appear in the western tradition."[45] The classical and Christian influences underpinning Juvencus's work shaped the intellectual horizons of late-antique and early medieval thinkers grappling with questions regarding the utility and purpose of the pagan past. Crucial in this regard was the Eusebian historiographical model. Eusebius's *Chronicon,* synthesizing secular and sacred history, promoted a key message — namely that the classical and Christian pasts were part of universal history.

Troy and Rome

The Trojan past features prominently in the collection. This past is central to Virgil's story of the rise of Rome recounted in his *Aeneid.* Virgil's Latin epic contained prophetic visions of Rome's destiny that included the battle of Actium and Augustus's Golden Age. In the miscellany, considerable attention was accorded to the Trojan past (e.g., its legendary kings and figures, the Trojan War and post-war diaspora).[46] The attention paid to Troy emerges in the texts, commentaries, and glosses that accompany the works of Virgil. The summary preceding the *Aeneid* mentions *Excidium Troie* ("the fall of Troy").[47] A good illustration of the prestige of Troy is provided by a Trojan genealogy, which

---

[44] For the preface of Juvencus: Paris, BnF lat. 10307, fol. 2rb–2va. For discussion: Robert W. Carrubba, "The Preface to Juvencus' Biblical Epic: A Structural Study," *American Journal of Philology* 114, no. 2 (1993): 303–12.

[45] See the preface to McGill, *Juvencus' Four Books of the Gospel.*

[46] Attention will be paid to the glosses on Troy and Rome in other works, including my next book, provisionally titled *Poetry of Empire: Psalms, Prophecy and Power in Carolingian Europe.*

[47] Paris, BnF, MS lat. 10307, fol. 97ra. Ralph Hexter, Laura Pfuntner, and Justin Haynes, eds. and trans., *Appendix Ovidiana: Latin Poems Ascribed to Ovid in the Middle Ages* (Cambridge: Harvard University Press, 2020), 3.

furnishes an account of Aeneas's journey to Italy. This genealogy was copied as an independent text before the beginning of the *Aeneid*. It traces Trojan patrilineal descent exclusively through the male royal line from the founding ancestor Dardanus, son of Jupiter and Electra, one of the Pleiades. The Trojan genealogy maps out the ancestors of Aeneas: Erichthonius, Tros, Ilus, Assaracus, Laomedon, Priam, Capys, and Anchises. Circulating in other Carolingian manuscripts, the Trojan genealogy is accorded special prominence. It is written by the same hand that wrote the Virgil works and appears as an *accessus* before the *Aeneid*. The importance of Troy is further attested to by the copying of the text ascribed to Dares Phrygius, a work prefaced with the title *Fabula de Troia*.

In the collection, considerable attention was lavished on Rome of the late republic and early empire. This is demonstrated by glosses on the political and military conflicts of the age of Julius Caesar, as well as by annotations on Virgil's contemporaries, Virgil himself, and Augustus. The additions by a late ninth- or early tenth-century hand continue this interest with an excerpt from the Roman historian Sallust, whose works chronicled events of the late republic. In short, the miscellany demonstrates that the early medieval book of Virgil was a history book.

Conclusion

Cumulatively, the gathering of materials in the collection, entered by anonymous hands dating to the ninth and tenth centuries, is significant. Indebted to Carolingian tradition, the assembled elements present an image of the world rooted in two inheritances — the Graeco-Roman and Judeo-Christian. The complementarity of these two inheritances is attested to by Carolingian book and material culture. For instance, it is vividly illustrated by the flabellum of Tournus, with its Christian and classical imagery.[48] The materials in the collection include pagan and Christian imagery. They range in interest from pagan my-

---

48 Contreni, "Getting to Know Virgil," 21.

thology and ancient history to the story of Christ. Glosses and texts focused on Troy and Rome accord with the well-known Carolingian appropriation of Augustan ideology and perspective. Virgil, the most important poet of antiquity in the Carolingian age, was a pipeline to *aurea Roma*. Through the art of compilation, the compilers painted a picture of the past embracing secular and sacred history, rooted in a Christocentric universe and spanning the *saecula* from Homer to Eriugena.

Appendix

Paris, Bibliothèque nationale de France, MS lat. 10307 + Vatican City, Biblioteca Apostolica Vaticana, MS Reg. lat. 1625 (III)

Paris, Bibliothèque nationale de France, MS lat. 10307 + Vatican City, Biblioteca Apostolica Vaticana, MS Reg. lat. 1625 (III) (fols. 246 + 2, 9th century, ¾ or ⁴⁄₄, 350 × 255 mm [13.78 × 10.04 in.], written space 280 × 210 mm [11.02 x. 8.27 in.]), consists of 32 gatherings, mostly regular quires of eight.[49] The last quire comprises a number of singletons, perhaps the remnants of an original quire of 8 with the Vatican leaves in the following order: Vatican fol. 65 after Paris fol. 245 and Vatican fol. 66 after Paris fol. 246. Collation is as follows: $1-5^8\ 6^4$ (wants 4 after fol. 43) $7^6\ 8^{10}$ (wants 3 after fol. 51 and 7 after fol. 54) $9-31^8\ 32^2$ + five singletons (fols. 242, 244, 245 + the two Vatican folios, fols. 65 and 66) [40 + 3 + 6 + 8+ 184 + 2 + 5 = 248].[50]

Fols. 1r–43r has Sedulian texts together with prefatory and other works: Caelius Sedulius's *Epistula ad Macedonium* on

---

[49] For descriptions: Leonardi, "Nuove," 139–68; Contreni, "A propos," 5–39; Élisabeth Pellegrin, *Les manuscrits classiques latins de la Bibliothèque Vaticane* 2.1 (Paris: Éditions du Centre national de la recherche scientifique, 1978), 325–29; Munk Olsen, *L'étude*, vol. 2, 764–65; Bischoff, *Katalog* 3, no. 4627, 160–1; Cinato, https://archivesetmanuscrits.bnf.fr/ark:/12148/cc13369k; and Ottaviano, "La tradizione," 270–79.

[50] For the final quire: Contreni, "A propos," 31, whose observations are confirmed by the notes of Bernhard Bischoff preserved in the Bayerische Staatsbibliothek. Bischoff observed that folios 242, 244, and 245 are singletons and that folios 243 and 246 are a bifolium.

fols. 1ra–2ra; Asterius's epigram on fol. 2vb;[51] Caelius Sedulius's *Carmen Paschale* on fols. 3vb–31vb; hymns on fols. 31vb–33ra, 33vb–34ra; acrostic poems commonly ascribed to a certain Liberatus scolasticus and to a certain Bellesarius on fols. 33ra–33vb, the initial and final letters of which spell out Sedulius antistes.[52] The Sedulian corpus is flanked by Juvencus's *Evangeliorum libri quattuor*. This is found on fols. 2rb–43rb. It occupies both columns from fol. 34v until fol. 43rb. Juvencus is followed by a short piece (*Epitaphium Aelberhti*, fol. 43rb) attributed to Alcuin.[53] Fols. 50v–245v transmit the works of Virgil together with the commentary of Servius. The latter begins as an independent text on fols. 44r–49v. Servius finishes on fol. 233va and ends with a reference to Homer. The *Eclogues* are preceded on fol. 50r–v by a summary and the poem *Caesari Augusto tributum*.[54] Pseudo-Ovidian *argumenta* precede *Georgics* 1 on fol. 63r, *Georgics* 3 on fol. 79r, *Aeneid* 1 on fol. 97r.[55] Pseudo-Ovidian *argumenta* precede most of the books of the *Aeneid*.[56] They also appear after the *Georgics* on fol. 96r.[57] Fol. 95va transmits an excerpt from a poem by John Scottus Eriugena and a Marian hymn.[58] Fol.

---

51 *Anthologia Latina*, vol. 2, 491.
52 *Anthologia Latina*, vol. 2, 493 and 492. Springer, *Manuscripts*, 16 and 25. Sedulius is referred to by Isidore as a presbyter. However, uncertainty surrounds Sedulius's life and career. In the collection, the initial letters of every other line and most of the final letters in the acrostic poems are omitted. Franck Cinato suggested these were probably intended to be filled in by a rubricator: https://archivesetmanuscrits.bnf.fr/ark:/12148/cc13369k.
53 Ernst Dümmler, ed., *Epitaphium [Aelberhti]*, Monumenta Germaniae Historica, Poetae latini aevi Carolini 1 (Berlin: Weidemann, 1881), 206–7.
54 *Anthologia Latina*, vol. 1, 2, ll. 1–4, and vol. 2, 672.
55 *Anthologia Latina*, vol. 1, 2, ll. 9–12; vol. 1, 2, ll. 17–20; and vol. 1, 1:1.
56 For example, on fols. 108v, 120r, 131r, 141v, 154v–55r, 168v, 181r, 192r, 204r–v, 217v–218r, and 231v.
57 *Anthologia Latina*, vol. 1, 256 and 257. See Ottaviano, "La tradizione," 273–74.
58 For the poem: Monumenta Germaniae Historica, Poetae Latini aevi Carolini 3, 537. For the hymn, Contreni, *Cathedral School*, 70, n21 and Édouard Jeauneau, "Theotokia grecs conservés en version latine," in *Philohistor: Miscellanea in Honorem Caroli Laga Septuagenarii*, ed. Antoon Schoors

96r–v contain a passage titled *Nomina Musarum* and a verse *De XII libris Aeneidos*.[59] On fols. 96vb–97ra there is a Trojan genealogy beginning *Dardanus ex Ioue et Electra filia* (in other manuscripts titled *Origo Troianorum*);[60] on fol. 233va, a grammatical note on *vesper*; on fols. 234rb–239va, *De excidio Troiae historia*, attributed to Dares Phrygius; on fol. 246v, a Greek–Latin glossary that corresponds with the *Graeca collecta*, that is, the Greek entries and Latin pairings, in Laon, Bibliothèque municipale Suzanne Martinet, MS 444, fols. 290r–91r.[61] Fol. 246v transmits an inscription that Michael Herren has reconstructed as a composition by Sedulius Scottus to a certain Fergus, as well as an extract from Priscian's *Partitiones duodecim versuum Aeneidos principalium* copied above the reference to Fergus on the left-hand side.[62] Fol. 65r–v of the Vatican manuscript transmits an anonymous poem which laments being led astray by the *numina falsa* and by Martianus Capella, together with the work *Officia xii mensium*, a text beginning *Obtrectatorum murmurosa garrulitas et rationis laudabile consilium*, a Latin palindrome, and excerpts from a) Homer's *Iliad* XI.654 in Greek with Latin translation, b) Sallust's *Bellum Catilinae*, c) Priscian's *Partitiones*,

---

and Peter Van Deun, Orientalia Lovaniensia Analecta 60 (Leuven: Uitgeverij Peeters en Department Oriëntalstiek, 1994), 399–421.

59 *Anthologia Latina*, vol. 2, 664 and 634.

60 Ottaviano, "La tradizione," 303–4.

61 The *Graeca collecta* in Laon, Bibliothèque municipale Suzanne Martinet, 444, are transcribed by Emmanuel Miller, "Glossaire grec-latin de la Bibliothèque de Laon," *Notices et extraits des manuscrits de la Bibliothèque nationale et autres bibliothèques*, vol. 29.2 (Paris, 1880), 181–85.

62 For the inscription: Bernhard Bischoff, "Das griechische Element in der abendländischen Bildung des Mittelalters," in Bernhard Bischoff, *Mittelalterliche Studien: Ausgewählte Aufsätze zur Schriftkunde und Literaturgeschichte*, 3 vols. (Stuttgart: Hiersemann, 1966–1981), vol. 2, 267n107, and Herren, "Sedulius Scottus and the knowledge of Greek," 520–21. The extract from Priscian begins "Cur singulare in usu non est" and ends "huius armi." See Priscian, *Partitiones duodecim versuum Aeneidos Principalium*, in *Prisciani Caesariensis Opuscula*, ed. Marina Passalacqua, Sussidi Eruditi 48 (Rome: Edizioni di storia e letteratura, 1999), vol. 2, 49. The extracts from Priscian's *Partitiones* in the Reginensis have been catalogued by Pellegrin, "Les manuscrits classiques," 325–29, and discussed by Leonardi, "Nuove," 147.

and d) Servius's commentary on the *Aeneid*.⁶³ Fol. 66r of Reg. lat. 1625 has a) inscriptions of Martin of Laon in Greek (these appear in Laon, Bibliothèque municipale Suzanne Martinet, MS 444, fols. 296v and 297v); b) extracts from Servius's commentary on the *Aeneid* and Ennius's *Annales* (the passage from Ennius is cited in Martianus Capella, *De nuptiis Philologiae et Mercurii*, 1.42);⁶⁴ c) a prayer in Greek; d) a distich of John Scottus Eriugena in Greek with interlinear Latin translation; and e) two distichs discussed by Claudio Leonardi. The distichs are in Latin and contain a Greek word. They are labelled *Versus Iohannis* and *Item Iohannis*; f) a grammatical note on the first two personal pronouns in Greek (also in Laon, Bibliothèque municipale Suzanne Martinet, MS 444, fol. 303v).⁶⁵

This Carolingian book of Virgil has modern foliation at the top right-hand corner of each folio recto and is ruled in hard point for the Virgil text and for the commentary of Servius. Uncials and rustic capitals are used for the first letters of each line. Rustic capitals are deployed for incipits and explicits, captions, titles, and *litterae notabiliores*. Very little decoration appears in this collection (fols. 2r, 14v, 50r–v, 63r, 96v, 181r, and 231v have initials decorated with an interlace pattern in Franco-Saxon or Franco-Insular style;⁶⁶ on fol. 50v glosses enclosed in a box decorated with a leaf design; on fol. 66v a circle with four vertical lines that resembles the *mappae mundi* illustrating *Georgics*

---

63 For the passage from Sallust: Contreni, "A propos," 36. For a translation of the anonymous poem: Mariken Teeuwen, "Seduced by Pagan Poets and Philosophers: Suspicious Learning in the Early Middle Ages," in *Limits to Learning: The Transfer of Encyclopaedic Knowledge in the Early Middle Ages*, ed. Concetta Giliberto and Loredana Teresi (Leuven: Peeters, 2013), 78–79.

64 Ennius is prefaced with the heading *Distichos Ennianus*. The passage is the Ennian dodekatheon (cited in Martianus Capella, *De nuptiis Philologiae et Mercurii*, 1.42).

65 For the Vatican folios, see Leonardi, "Nuove," 145–52; Contreni, "A propos," 29–31; and Pellegrin, *Les manuscrits classiques*, 325–29.

66 On occasion, initials appear to be prepared for decoration but are not decorated or filled in with the interlace pattern found in other initials. This is the case, for instance, for initials found on fols. 2r, 5r–v, 57v, 58r, and 71r.

1.233 circulating in early medieval Virgil manuscripts; on fol. 173r a knot design). Syntactical glosses appear here and there.[67] Rubrication occurs only in the Juvencus/Sedulius section. The following punctuation is supplied for the text: *punctus, punctus versus,* and *punctus elevatus*. Sheets are arranged so that flesh faces flesh and hair faces hair. The collection is carefully laid out with two columns throughout, apart from fols. 44v–49r where the commentary of Servius (*Eclogue* 1–3.105) is written as an independent text. The commentary of Servius continues uninterrupted on fol. 50rb at *Eclogue* 3.105 and accompanies prefatory materials. From fol. 50v onwards, it accompanies the text of Virgil. Occasionally, the collection has three columns (fols. 33v–34r). The text of Virgil is placed in the inner column of the page and the commentary of Servius in the outer column in a well-ordered and neatly arranged fashion.[68] Contemporary quire signatures (i–xxiii) occur on fols. 57v–233v.

Many hands, primarily from the ninth and tenth centuries, are attested to in the collection. The hand responsible for the Virgil text beginning on fol. 50v is also found copying the Pseudo-Ovidian *argumenta* and the text *Dardanus ex Ioue et Electra filia*. Many of the features of this hand have been identified by Ottaviano, who noted that the scribe wrote in a clear Carolingian minuscule with few abbreviations. Characteristic elements of this hand are the three-shaped *g*, *ct* and *st* ligatures, and *x* with long descender to the left. Not much younger than this text hand are the various hands that copied the commentary of Servius, the first of which, identified by Ottaviano, occurs on fols. 44r–55r. Bischoff noted that fols. 44–49 are about contemporary with the commentary of Servius in the Virgil section.[69] The lemmata of the commentary of Servius are sometimes writ-

---

[67] For example, on fols. 88ra, 89vb, 91ra, 92ra, 94vb, 107ra, 122vb, 142vb, and 145vb. I am grateful to John Contreni for this observation.

[68] Regarding the layout of Virgil manuscripts: Louis Holtz, "Les manuscrits latins à gloses et à commentaires de l'antiquité à l'époque carolingienne," in *Atti del convegno internazionale 'Il libro e il testo'*, ed. Cesare Questa and Renato Raffaelli (Urbino: Università degli Studi di Urbino, 1984), 163.

[69] Ottaviano, "La tradizione," 272–73, and Bischoff, *Katalog* 3, no. 4627, 161.

ten in majuscules and the Greek is not transliterated. Fols. 55v–57v do not contain the Servian commentary. Missing sections in Servius are, on occasion, supplied in the margins.[70] Servius is sometimes furnished with additional information: references are found to *fabulae* (e.g., with the characteristic abbreviations *Fa* and *Fab* in the margins on fols. 54v, 58r and 70v); words in Servius are singled out and written in the margins, a feature found in other manuscripts (e.g., *synheresin, Eclogue* 6.78 on fol. 58r; *figurate, Eclogue* 7.16 and *allegoria, Eclogue* 7.21 on fol. 58v; *anapestus, Eclogue* 8.78 on fol. 60r).[71] Sometimes, the comments in Servius are copied like glossary entries with lemma and *interpretamentum* on a single line.[72] The abbreviated forms of the Virgilian lemmata in the commentary of Servius are preserved.[73] Ottaviano observed that the commentary was written after the text and most of the captions.[74] Contreni pointed out that there is a mismatch between the text of Virgil and the commentary.[75] The commentary of the vulgate Servius finishes before the end of the *Aeneid* and the remaining folios are filled with a large portion of the work ascribed to Dares Phrygius.[76] The hand copying the work of Dares Phrygius (fols. 234r–239v) has been variously dated to the tenth and eleventh centuries. Following Bischoff and Franck Cinato, I date this hand to the tenth century, which often resembles other hands working throughout the collection. Features of this hand are the occasional use of uncial *m* and *d*,

---

70 For example, a passage in the commentary of Servius on the *Aeneid* 1, 203 is missing and is written in the margins by a corrector and linked to the text by a *signe de renvoi*. The omitted passage is an instance of haplography. Paris, BnF, MS lat. 10307, fol. 105r; *Servii grammatici qui feruntur in Virgilii carmina commentarii*, vol. 1, 79, ll. 9–12.

71 Sinéad O'Sullivan, "Servius in the Carolingian Age: A Case Study of British Library, Harley 2782," *The Journal of Medieval Latin* 26 (2016): 101.

72 See some of the entries in Paris, BnF lat. 10307, fol. 89r.

73 See the commentary of Servius on *Georgics* 4, 150: Paris, BnF, MS lat. 10307, fol. 90r, line 18. *Servii grammatici qui feruntur in Virgilii carmina commentarii*, vol. 3.1, 331, line 24.

74 Ottaviano, "La tradizione," 272.

75 Contreni, "A propos," 32.

76 *Daretis Phrygii de excidio Troiae historia*, ed. Ferdinand Meister (Leipzig: Teubner, 1873), 1–50.

and an *or* ligature. The Sedulius-Juvencus portion was copied, as Cinato noted, by different but contemporary hands. A few interlinear glosses appear in this portion, for example on fol. 27r. The hand responsible for copying Sedulius often deployed an *or* ligature. The hand that copied the Juvencus portion also wrote the *Epitaphium* on fol. 43rb. Further additions were made to the collection by a late ninth-/early tenth-century hand. Contreni observed that the same hand wrote the two *membra disiecta* now in the Vatican Library.[77]

After the scribes had copied the text, captions, and the commentary of Servius, marginal and interlinear glosses were added and accommodated to the existing space.[78] The glosses were written in very small Caroline script and require a magnifying glass to read. Marginal glosses are found on the *Eclogues* and the beginning of the *Georgics* until fol. 66v. Interlinear glosses continue until fol. 184r. The marginal glosses are linked to their lemmata by *signes de renvoi*. They often have lines drawn around them so that they appear to be neatly enclosed in a box, a feature also found in other ninth- and tenth-century glossed Virgil manuscripts.[79] This feature underscores the attention paid to the layout of information in the collection. The marginal glosses are sometimes cut off in the margins, which have been trimmed.[80] The glosses are primarily entered by one hand, dated by Ottaviano to the tenth century.

The glosses draw heavily upon the well-known commentaries on Virgil, as well as on annotations that are not attested in the extant Virgil commentaries but are found elsewhere in ninth- and tenth-century Virgil manuscripts. The most striking feature of the hand transcribing the glosses is the *ri* ligature,

---

77 Contreni, "A propos," 31 and 37.
78 See, for example, Paris, BnF, MS lat. 10307, fol. 51r, line 16 where the final word in a gloss (*ingenio*) is split, with the last letters *nio* copied in superscript above *inge*. This has been done in order to be able to squeeze in the gloss beside the commentary of Servius.
79 O'Sullivan, "Glossing Virgil," 164.
80 See especially fol. 63v where the marginal glosses at the start of the *Georgics* on the left-hand side of the folio have been trimmed.

the *i* of which curves to the left. Other features are the use of *e caudata*, as well as *st, rt, et,* and *nt* ligatures. Similar or near-identical glosses appear in other ninth-century glossed Virgil manuscripts (see below).

As for the origin and provenance of the collection, these remain uncertain. A later note mentions a certain Bernardus, whose identity also remains uncertain.[81] A tie with Rheims was postulated on the basis that the only other witness for the *Epitaphium Aelberhti* is a Rheims manuscript.[82] Links with Auxerre were observed by Contreni. For instance, the extract from Sallust, transcribed by Contreni, indicates a possible link with Auxerre, where a collection transmitting excerpts from authors such as Sallust and Priscian from the second half of the ninth century was thought to be in circulation (according to Bischoff, this collection originates near Ferrières).[83] And the links with Laon are manifold.

Northeast, north-central, and east-central France is the common link underpinning the text of Virgil, commentary of Servius, and glosses. The commentary of Servius follows the so-called Tours group, a subgroup of Servius manuscripts. Some of the manuscripts in this family are from northeast and north-central France.[84] Ottaviano demonstrated that the text of Virgil belongs to a specific group. She not only refined one of the groups of Virgil manuscripts identified by Robert Kaster, namely the second of three Carolingian groups which he classified on the grounds of textual similarities, but also highlighted, through conjunctive errors, the textual relationship between the collection and two other manuscripts: Hamburg, Staats- und Universitätsbib-

---

81 Contreni, *Cathedral School,* 139n14, and Leonardi, "Nuove," 147.
82 Contreni, "A propos," 35.
83 The excerpt from Sallust occurs in a collection extant in manuscripts in Bern, Leiden, and Paris. The excerpts are in Bern, Burgerbibliothek, MS 357, fol. 32rb. See Contreni, "A propos," 36n69, and Bischoff, *Katalog* 1, no. 579, 123.
84 Charles E. Murgia, *Prolegomena to Servius 5: The Manuscripts,* University of California Publications: Classical Studies 11 (Berkeley: University of California Press, 1975), 37.

liothek, MS 52 in scrinio (9th century, ¾, Saint-Germain-des-Prés?) and Montpellier, Bibliothèque interuniversitaire, Section Médecine, MS H 253 (9th century, ⅔, north-east France?).[85] According to Ottaviano, then, the collection is part of a group. The links between the collection and these two manuscripts are further underscored by their glosses (see below).

Analogues are to be found between the glosses in the collection and entries in a ninth-century Laon manuscript studied by Contreni, namely, Laon, Bibliothèque municipale Suzanne Martinet, MS 468. In addition, there is also overlap between the annotations in the collection and glosses in Virgil manuscripts emanating from northeast, north-central, and east-central France in the ninth century.[86] Below is a list of manuscripts transmitting, at times, similar materials (for most of the *sigla*, I follow Ottaviano):

- e = Bern, Burgerbibliothek, MS 167 (9th century, ¾, northern France, Auxerre, Fleury, Brittany)[87]
- f = Oxford, Bodleian Library, MS Auct. F. 2. 8 (9th century, med., Paris region)[88]
- g = Paris, Bibliothèque nationale de France, MS lat. 7925 (9th century, ex., Limoges, southern France?)[89]

---

85 Ottaviano, "La tradizione," 79, 89, 276, added new witnesses to Kaster's Group 2. Robert A. Kaster, *The Tradition of the Text of the Aeneid in the Ninth Century* (New York: Garland, 1990), 8. For the Hamburg and Montpellier manuscripts: Murgia, *Prolegomena*, 37; Bischoff, *Katalog* 1, no. 1494, 311 and vol. 2, no. 2852, 205; and Ottaviano, "La tradizione," 219–23 and 263–69.

86 There is one notable exception, namely Paris, Bibliothèque nationale de France, MS lat. 7925 (9th century, Limoges, southern France?). Paris, BnF, MS lat. 7925, however, is closely connected with Oxford, Bodleian Library, MS Auct. F. 2. 8 from the Paris region. O'Sullivan, "Glossing Virgil," 139.

87 Bischoff, *Katalog* 1, no. 542, 114. For an overview of the possible origins of Bern, Burgerbibliothek, MS 167: Ottaviano, "La tradizione," 184–95.

88 Bischoff, *Katalog* 2, no. 3771, 358; Ottaviano, "La tradizione," 196; and O'Sullivan, "Glossing Virgil," 132–65.

89 Murgia, *Prolegomena*, 50; Bischoff, *Katalog* 3, no. 4513, 136; Martin Hellmann, *Tironische Noten in der Karolingerzeit am Beispiel eines Persius-Kommentars aus der Schule von Tours*, Monumenta Germaniae Historica,

- *h* = Valenciennes, Bibliothèque municipale, MS lat. 407 (9th century, med., northeastern France)[90]
- *k* = Hamburg, Staats- und Universitätsbibliothek, MS 52 in scrinio (9th century, ²/₄, Saint-Germain-des-Prés?)[91]
- *L* = Laon, Bibliothèque municipale Suzanne Martinet, MS 468 (9th century, ¾, Laon)[92]
- *r* = Paris, Bibliothèque nationale de France, MS lat. 7926 (9th century, med., Auxerre, Fleury?)[93]
- *x* = Montpellier, Bibliothèque interuniversitaire, Section Médecine, MS H 253 (9th century, ⅔, northeastern France?)[94]
- *y* = Paris, Bibliothèque nationale de France, MS lat. 10307 + Vatican City, Biblioteca Apostolica Vaticana, MS Reg. lat. 1625 (III) (9th century, ¾ or ⁴/₄, northeastern France?)
- γ = Wolfenbüttel, Herzog August Bibliothek, MS Guelf. 70 Gud. lat. (c. 9th century, ²/₄, or med., Lyons?)[95]
- *z* = Vatican City, Biblioteca Apostolica Vaticana, MS Reg. lat. 1670 (9th century, Saint-Maur-des-Fossés?)[96]

In its glosses, *y* displays strong affinities with *f*. Not only do we find what appear to be unique glosses in both, but also the same

---

Studien und Texte 27 (Hanover: Hahnsche Buchhandlung, 2000), 246; and Ottaviano, "La tradizione," 196–7.

90 Kaster, *Tradition,* 27, and Bischoff, *Katalog* 3, no. 6394, 400 locate the manuscript in north-east France. Ottaviano, "La tradizione," 198–203.
91 Bischoff, *Katalog* 1, no. 1494, 311, and Ottaviano, "La tradizione," 219–23.
92 John J. Contreni, *Codex Laudunensis 468: A Ninth-Century Guide to Virgil, Sedulius and the Liberal Arts,* Armarium Codicum Insignium 3 (Turnhout: Brepols, 1984), and Bischoff, *Katalog* 2, no. 2128, 37.
93 Bischoff, *Katalog* 3, no. 4514, 136, and Ottaviano, "La tradizione," 233–44.
94 Bischoff, *Katalog* 2, no. 2852, 205, and Ottaviano, "La tradizione," 263–69.
95 Ottaviano, "La tradizione," 288–98; Bischoff, *Katalog* 3, no. 7309, 501–02; and Sinéad O'Sullivan, "Glossing Virgil in the Early Medieval West: A Case Study of Wolfenbüttel, Herzog August Bibliothek, Cod. Guelf. 70 Gud. lat.," in *Studies on Late Antique and Medieval Germanic Glossography and Lexicography in Honour of Patrizia Lendinara,* ed. Claudia Di Sciacca, Concetta Giliberto, Carmela Rizzo, and Loredana Teresi (Pisa: Edizioni ETS, 2018), 547–64.
96 On MS Reg. lat. 1670: Charlotte Denoël, "Un catalogue des manuscrits de Saint-Maur-des-Fossés au XIIe siècle," *Scriptorium* 60, no. 2 (2006): 186–205, and O'Sullivan, "Glossing Virgil," 132–65.

run of glosses.[97] Moreover, very similar glosses occur in *y* and *γ*.[98] There is also overlap between notes in *y*, *f*, and Laon, Bibliothèque municipale Suzanne Martinet, MS 468.[99] And we have already noted a gloss on Tereus shared by *f*, *g*, *y*, and Laon 468.[100] Furthermore, the Trojan genealogy occurs in *k*, *r*, *x*, *y*, *γ*, and Laon 468.[101] Analogues are also to be found between some of the glosses in *y* and those in an eleventh-century codex, namely, *z*, a manuscript that shares a number of glosses with *f*, also from the same region.[102]

In addition, similar glosses appear in *y* and in clusters of Virgil manuscripts identified by Ottaviano. She noted shared annotations in *eghkxyy* and *fgx*.[103] These clusters are important as similar sets of annotations occur in *fgyx*,[104] *gyγ*,[105] and *hyγ*.[106] Particularly striking is the overlap between entries in *y*, manuscripts in the clusters identified by Ottaviano, and Laon 468. To begin with, *y* and Laon 468 sometimes transmit the same information.

---

97 Many of the glosses in Paris, BnF, MS 10307, fol. 57v, ll. 29–32, appear in Oxford, fol. 8v, ll. 7–10. For example, see the same run of glosses on *Eclogue* 6.64–67 in both manuscripts: CANIT *ille Silenus*; ERRANTEM *lustrantem*; PERMESSI *flumen Boeti<a>e*; AONAS *mons nympharum*; VIRO *Gallo*; CHORVS *honorauit eum tot[i]us chorus Phoebi in illo monte*; and LINVS *Teocritus*.

98 Ottaviano, "Reading between the lines," 423.

99 Ottaviano, "Reading between the lines," 407, and O'Sullivan, "Glossing Virgil," 148.

100 See footnote 29.

101 Ottaviano, "La tradizione," 303–4, and O'Sullivan, "Glossing Virgil in the early medieval West," 559–60.

102 For example, the same glosses on *Eclogue* 4.4, *Eclogue* 4.15, and *Eclogue* 4.56 are attested in these two manuscripts. See Hendrikje A. Bakker, "*Totus quidem Virgilius scientia plenus est*: De glossen bij de vierde Ecloga en het zesde boek van de Aeneis (The Glosses on the Fourth Eclogue and the Sixth Book of the Aeneid)" (PhD Diss., Utrecht University, 2007), 113, 118, and 131, and O'Sullivan, "Glossing Virgil," 146.

103 Ottaviano, "Reading between the lines," 421 and "La tradizione," 311.

104 INCONDITA *incomposita uel rustica* (*Eclogue* 2.4; Paris, BnF, MS lat. 10307, fol. 51v, l. 31; Oxford, BodL, MS Auct. F. 2. 8, fol. 1v, l. 4; Paris, BnF, MS lat. 7925, fol. 3r, l. 4; Montpellier, BiSM, MS H 253, fol. 5r, l. 21).

105 Ottaviano, "Reading between the lines," 422.

106 Ibid.

For example, *y* carries elements found in the anonymous Virgilian *Vita* transmitted in Laon 468. In the manuscript, the title of this *Vita* is the *Vita Publii Virgilii*.[107] Contreni demonstrated the links between it and other ancient and medieval Virgilian *Vitae*, including the *Vita Suetonii vulgo Donatiana*.[108] One section of the anonymous *Vita* (lines 13–27) appears as a marginal gloss at the beginning of the *Eclogues* in *y*.[109] Another portion derived

---

107 Contreni highlighted the connection between the Laon *Vita* and *Vita Bernensis I*. See Contreni, "Getting to Know Virgil," 32–34.
108 Ibid., 37–45, provides a transcription, notes, and translation of the Laon *Vita*.
109 Paris, BnF, MS 10307, fol. 50v: "Virgilius dictus uel a patre quasi uerecundus. Ideo Virgilius quia concipiens illum mater sua somniauit se laureum ramum peperisse, uel quia in loco quo cecidit noscens (lege nascens), secundum morem regionis in puerperiis illius uirga populea depacta est quae in breui ita conualuit, ut multo ante satis populis ad<a>equaretur; quae arbor 'Virgilii' ex eo dicta atque consecrata est. Est autem illi ut Virgilius uocetur agnomen; Maro uero cognomen a patre ut dicitur. Qui in scribendis carminibus naturalem ordinem secutus est. Primo enim pastoralem uitam in montibus ex<s>equtus est stilo, secundo agricolendi (lege agricolandi), tertio bellandi. Et pastoralem in Bucolicis, agriculturae in Georgicis, bellorum uero in Aeneidis rationem descripsit. Vnde non solum agros suos et Mantuanorum apud Caesarem optinuit ut redderentur, sed et toga meruit indui quod nulli erat licitum gestare nisi imperatori aut consuli. Fuit autem Mantuanus a Mantua quae est ciuitas primae partis Venetiae. Nam et Cremon<a>e et Mediolani et Neapoli litteris studuit. Vno tantum uitio laborans, nam inpatiens libidinis fuit." (trans. Contreni, "Getting to Know Virgil," 37–38 and 41–42: "He was called Virgil either after his father, Virgil, or on account of his bashfulness. He was also called Virgil because when his mother conceived him she dreamt that she brought forth a laurel bough, or because, according to the custom of the region in which he was born, during delivery a poplar branch was cut [and planted] that in a short time grew as tall as poplars already planted. This tree was called 'Virgil' after the poet and was dedicated to him. He was called by the surname Virgil and by the added name, Maro, from his father. He followed the natural order when he composed his poems: the first one was expressed in the style of mountainous pastoral life, the second, in the style of farming life, and the third, in the style of military life in the *Aeneid*. Then, not only did he obtain the return of his fields and those of the Mantuans from Caesar, but he earned [the right] to put on the toga, which no one except the emperor or consul could legally wear. He was a Mantuan from Mantua, which is a city in the first part of Venetia, though he studied lit-

from the *Vita Suetonii vulgo Donatiana* occurs in *g*, *y*, and *γ*.[110] Significantly, a lengthy marginal gloss in *y* shares some "unique" elements with the *Vita Publii Virgilii*. Contreni observed that the *Vita Publii Virgilii* transmits information drawn from Orosius regarding the economic benefits derived from the defeat of Artavasdes, King of Armenia. According to Orosius, the treasure of Artavasdes was exploited by Antony in his campaign against Octavian. In the *Vita Publii Virgilii*, the account of the treasure

---

erature in Cremona, Milan and Naples. He struggled with only one defect, for his lust was unchecked.") Contreni, "A propos," 23n37.

110 Paris, BnF, MS lat. 10307, fol. 50v: "Numerus Eglogarum manifestus est, nam x sunt, ex quibus proprie Bucolice vii esse creduntur quod ex his excipiantur. <'Pollio'>, 'Silenus' et 'Gallus'. Prima igitur de agro et dicitur 'Tytirus'; secunda amorem pueri, et dicitur 'Alexis'; tertia certamen pastorum et dicitur 'Palemon'; quarta genethlia et dicitur 'Pollio'; quinta epitaphion, et dicitur 'Daphnis'; sexta metamorphosis et dicitur 'Varus' vel 'Silenus'; septima delectatio pastorum et dicitur 'Coridon'; octaua mores diuersorum sexuum et dicitur 'Damos'; nona propriam poetae conquestionem de amisso agro et dicitur 'Moeris'; decima desiderium Galli circa Polim<n>iam et dicitur 'Gallus'. illud tenendum est in bucolicis ut neque nusquam neque ubique figurate aliquid dici existimes ut dicit Seruius." (trans. Contreni, "Getting to Know Virgil," 42: "The number of *Eclogues* is obvious for there are ten, of which seven properly are considered to be *Bucolics* because the 'Pollio', the 'Silenus' and the 'Gallus' are excepted. The first one, then, concerns the land, and is called the 'Tityrus'; the second, the love of a boy and is called the 'Alexis'; the third, rivalry among shepherds and is called 'Palaemon'; the fourth is a *genethlia* [birthday poem] and is called the 'Pollio'; the fifth is an *epitaphium* [funeral oration] and is called the 'Daphnis'; the sixth concerns *metamorphosis* and is called the 'Varus' or the 'Silenus'; the seventh, the pasttimes of shepherds and is called the 'Corydon'; the eighth, the ways of the different sexes and is called the 'Damon'; the ninth, the poet's own complaint about the loss of [his] land and is called the 'Moeris'; the tenth, Gallus' longing for Polimnia and is called the 'Gallus'. This is to be kept in mind: in the *Bucolics* neither nowhere nor everywhere is anything said figuratively. You should form [your own] opinion, as Servius says.") In Paris, Bibliothèque nationale de France, MS 7925, fol. 1v, the manuscript transmits the final line, which is not in Laon, Bibliothèque municipale Suzanne Martinet, MS 468, fol. 1rv or in Wolfenbüttel, Herzog August Bibliothek, MS Guelf. 70, fol. 4v. For the account in the *Vita Suetonii vulgo Donatiana*, see Jacob Brummer, ed., *Vitae Virgilianae* (Leipzig: Teubner, 1912), 17–18, and Jan M. Ziolkowski and Michael C.J. Putnam, eds., *The Virgilian Tradition: The First Fifteen Hundred Years* (New Haven: Yale University Press, 2008), 188–89.

of Artavasdes, ultimately derived from Orosius, does not appear in the other *Vitae Virgilianae*. In the lengthy marginal gloss in *y*, we find details on Antony, Artavasdes, and the treasure, details that appear in lines 65–68 of the anonymous *Vita*.[111] In the gloss, these details are part of a larger picture underscoring the fall of Antony and rise of Octavian, the future Augustus. Once again, imperial Rome comes into focus.

---

[111] "Antonius autem Artabanen Armeniae regem deuincens catena argentea religatum coegit ad perditionem suorum thesaurorum quorum multiplicitate elatus indicere bellum Caesari coepit et Octauiae sororis eius coniugis suae repudium" (Paris, BnF, MS lat. 10307, fol. 55r, l. 12). Orosius, *Hist. adv. Paganos 6.19*, 3–4; Marie-Pierre Arnaud-Lindet, ed. and trans., *Orose: Histoires (Contre les Païens)*, vol. 2 (Paris: Budé, 1990–1991), 223: "Antonius Artabanen Armeniae regem proditione et dolo cepit: quem argentea catena uinctum ad confessionem thesaurorum regiorum coegit, expugnatoque oppido, in quo conditos esse prodiderat, magnam uim auri argentique abstulit. Qua elatus pecunia denuntiari bellum Caesari atque Octauiae, sorori Caesaris, uxori suae, repudium indici iussit." (Andrew T. Fear, trans., *Orosius: Seven Books of History against the Pagans*, Translated Texts for Historians 54 [Liverpool: Liverpool University Press, 2010], 306: "Antony captured Artabanes, the king of Armenia, by treachery and deceit. He was bound with silver chains and forced to reveal the whereabouts of the royal treasury. Antony then stormed the city where the king had be trayed that the treasure was hidden and carried off a great amount of gold and silver. Elated by obtaining this money, he ordered that war be declared on Caesar, and divorce proceedings be begun against his wife, Octavia, who was Caesar's sister.") For discussion of Antony and King Artabanes, called Artavasdes by Livy, see Contreni, "Getting to Know Virgil," 30–31, 43.

Bibliography

Manuscripts

Bern, Burgerbibliothek, MS 167. https://www.e-codices.unifr.ch/en/list/one/bbb/0167.

Bern, Burgerbibliothek, MS 357. https://www.e-codices.unifr.ch/en/list/one/bbb/0357.

Hamburg, Staats- und Universitätsbibliothek, MS 52 in scrinio.

Laon, Bibliothèque municipale Suzanne Martinet, MS 444. https://bibliotheque-numerique.ville-laon.fr/ressources-numerisees/item/1472-redirection.

Laon, Bibliothèque municipale Suzanne Martinet, MS 468. https://bibliotheque-numerique.ville-laon.fr/ressources-numerisees/item/1473-redirection.

Montpellier, Bibliothèque interuniversitaire, Section Médecine, MS H 253.

Oxford, Bodleian Library, MS Auct. F. 2. 8. https://medieval.bodleian.ox.ac.uk/catalog/manuscript_630.

Paris, Bibliothèque nationale de France, MS lat. 10307 + Vatican City, Biblioteca Apostolica Vaticana, MS Reg. lat. 1625 (III). https://archivesetmanuscrits.bnf.fr/ark:/12148/cc13369k and https://digi.vatlib.it/view/MSS_Reg.lat.1625.

Paris, Bibliothèque nationale de France, MS lat. 7925. https://archivesetmanuscrits.bnf.fr/ark:/12148/cc8936z.

Paris, Bibliothèque nationale de France, MS lat. 7926. https://archivesetmanuscrits.bnf.fr/ark:/12148/cc11298h.

Valenciennes, Bibliothèque municipale, MS lat. 407. http://initiale.irht.cnrs.fr/codex/7898.

Vatican City, Biblioteca Apostolica Vaticana, MS Reg. lat. 1670. https://digi.vatlib.it/view/MSS_Reg.lat.1670.

Wolfenbüttel, Herzog August Bibliothek, MS Guelf. 70 Gud. lat. http://diglib.hab.de/?db=mss&list=ms&id=70-gud-lat&lang=en.

Primary

Anthologia Latina sive Poesis Latinae Supplementum, pars prior, Carmina in codicibus scripta. Fasc. I. Libri salmasiani aliorumque carmina. Edited by Alexander Riese. Leipzig: Teubner, 1869.

Anthologia Latina sive Poesis Latinae Supplementum, pars prior, Carmina in codicibus scripta. Fasc. II. Edited by Alexander Riese. Leipzig: Teubner, 1870.

Appendix Ovidiana: Latin Poems Ascribed to Ovid in the Middle Ages. Edited and translated by Ralph Hexter, Laura Pfuntner, and Justin Haynes. Cambridge: Harvard University Press, 2020.

Bischoff, Bernhard. *Katalog der festländischen Handschriften des neunten Jahrhunderts (mit Ausnahme der wisigotischen),* Volume 1: *Aachen-Lambach.* Wiesbaden: Harrassowitz, 1998.

———. *Katalog der festländischen Handschriften des neunten Jahrhunderts,* Volume 2: *Laon-Paderborn,* edited by Birgit Ebersperger. Wiesbaden: Harrassowitz, 2004.

———. *Katalog der festländischen Handschriften des neunten Jahrhunderts (mit Ausnahme der wisigotischen),* Volume 3: *Padua-Zwickau,* edited by Birgit Ebersperger. Wiesbaden: Harrassowitz, 2014.

Daretis Phrygii de excidio Troiae historia. Edited by Ferdinand Meister. Leipzig: Teubner, 1873.

Epitaphium [Aelberhti]. In *Monumenta Germaniae Historica, Poetae latini aevi Carolini* 1. Edited by Ernst Dümmler, 206–7. Berlin: Weidemann, 1881.

Iohannis Scotti Eriugenae Carmina. Scriptores Latini Hiberniae 12. Edited by Michael W. Herren. Dublin: Dublin School of Celtic Studies, 1993.

Martianus Capella. Edited by James Willis. Bibliotheca scriptorum Graecorum et Romanorum Teubneriana. Leipzig: Teubner, 1983.

McGill, Scott, trans. *Juvencus' Four Books of the Gospels: Evangeliorum Libri Quattuor.* London: Routledge, 2016.

Orose: Histoires (Contre les païens). Edited and translated by Marie-Pierre Arnaud-Lindet. 3 Volumes. Paris: Budé, 1990–1991.

Orosius: Seven Books of History against the Pagans. Translated by Andrew T. Fear. Translated Texts for Historians 54. Liverpool: Liverpool University Press, 2010.

Prisciani Caesariensis Opuscula. Volume 2. Edited by Marina Passalacqua. Sussidi Eruditi 48. Rome: Edizioni di storia e letteratura, 1999.

Scholia Bernensia ad Virgili Bucolica atque Georgica. Edited by Hermann Hagen. Jahrbücher für classische Philologie: Supplementband 4. Leipzig: Teubner, 1867; repr. Hildesheim: G. Olms, 1967.

Sedulius. *The Paschal Song and Hymns*. Translated by Carl P.E. Springer. Society of Biblical Literature 35. Atlanta: Society of Biblical Literature, 2013. DOI: 10.2307/j.ctt16xwbx5.

Servii grammatici qui feruntur in Virgilii carmina commentarii. Edited by Georg Thilo and Hermann Hagen. 3 Volumes. Leipzig: Teubner, 1881–1902.

Vitae Vergilianae. Edited by Jacob Brummer. Leipzig: Teubner, 1912.

Secondary

Aicher, Peter. "Ennius' Dream of Homer." *The American Journal of Philology* 110, no. 2 (1989): 227–32. DOI: 10.2307/295173.

Bakker, Hendrikje A. *"Totus quidem Virgilius scientia plenus est:* De glossen bij de vierde Ecloga en het zesde boek van de Aeneis (The Glosses on the Fourth Eclogue and the Sixth Book of the Aeneid)." PhD Diss., Utrecht University, 2007.

Bischoff, Bernhard. "Das griechische Element in der abendländischen Bildung des Mittelalters." In Bernhard Bischoff, *Mittelalterliche Studien: Ausgewählte Aufsätze zur Schriftkunde und Literaturgeschichte,* Volume 2, 246–75. Stuttgart: Hiersemann, 1967.

Bremmer Jr., Rolf H., and Kees Dekker. "Practice in Learning: An Introduction." In *Practice in Learning: The Transfer of Encyclopaedic Knowledge in the Early Middle Ages,* edited by Rolf H. Bremmer Jr. and Kees Dekker, Mediaevalia Groningana New Series 16, xi–xvi. Leuven: Peeters, 2010.

Carrubba, Robert W. "The Preface to Juvencus' Biblical Epic: A Structural Study." *American Journal of Philology* 114, no. 2 (1993): 303–12. DOI: 10.2307/295316.

Contreni, John. J. "A propos de quelques manuscrits de l'école de Laon au IXe siècle: découvertes et problèmes." *Le Moyen Âge* 78 (1972): 5–39.

———. *Codex Laudunensis 468: A Ninth-Century Guide to Virgil, Sedulius and the Liberal Arts.* Armarium Codicum Insignium 3. Turnhout: Brepols, 1984.

———. "Getting to Know Virgil in the Carolingian Age: The *Vita Publii Virgilii*." In *Rome and Religion in the Medieval World: Studies in honour of Thomas F.X. Noble,* edited by Valerie L. Garver and Owen M. Phelan, 21–45. Farnham: Ashgate, 2014.

———. *The Cathedral School of Laon from 850–930: Its Manuscripts and Masters.* Münchener Beiträge zur Mediävistik und Renaissance-Forschung 29. Munich: Arbeo-Gesellschaft, 1978.

Denoël, Charlotte. "Un catalogue des manuscrits de Saint-Maur-des-Fossés au XIIe siècle." *Scriptorium* 60, no. 2 (2006): 186–205. DOI: 10.3406/scrip.2006.3940.

Dorofeeva, Anna. "Miscellanies, Christian Reform and Early Medieval Encyclopaedism: A Reconsideration of the Pre-Bestiary *Physiologus* Manuscripts." *Historical Research* 90, no. 250 (2017): 665–82. DOI: 10.1111/1468-2281.12198.

Dutton, Paul Edward. "Evidence that Dubthach's Priscian Codex Once Belonged to Eriugena." In *From Athens to Chartres: Neoplatonism and Medieval Thought: Studies in Honour of Edouard Jeauneau,* edited by Haijo Jan Westra, Studien und Texte zur Geistesgeschichte des Mittelalters 35, 15–45. Leiden: Brill, 1992. DOI: 10.1163/9789004451902_008.

Elliott, Jackie. "Ennius as Universal Historian: The Case of the *Annales*." In *Historiae Mundi: Studies in Universal History,* ed. Peter Liddel and Andrew Fear, 148–61. London: Bloomsbury, 2010.

Garipzanov, Ildar H. *The Symbolic Language of Authority in the Carolingian World (c. 751–877).* Brill's Series on the

Early Middle Ages 16. Leiden: Brill, 2008. DOI: 10.1163/ej.9789004166691.i-394.

Garrison, Mary. "The *Collectanea* and Medieval Florilegia." In *Collectanea Pseudo-Bedae,* edited by Martha Bayless and Michael Lapidge, Scriptores Latini Hiberniae 14, 42–83. Dublin: Dublin Institute for Advanced Studies, 1998.

Gerberding, Richard A. "Paris, Bibliothèque Nationale Latin 7906: An Unnoticed Very Early Fragment of the *Liber historiae Francorum*." *Traditio* 43 (1987): 381–86. DOI: 10.1017/S0362152900012617.

Giltner, T. Alexander. "*Intimae Theologiae:* The Christocentric Cosmology of John Scottus Eriugena in the *Homilia super "In principio erat verbum."* *Archives d'histoire doctrinale et littéraire du Moyen Âge* 83, no. 1 (2016): 7–32. DOI: 10.3917/ahdlm.083.0007.

Godman, Peter. *Poetry of the Carolingian Renaissance.* London: Duckworth, 1985.

Hellmann, Martin. *Tironische Noten in der Karolingerzeit am Beispiel eines Persius-Kommentars aus der Schule von Tours.* Monumenta Germaniae Historica, Studien und Texte 27. Hanover: Hahnsche Buchhandlung, 2000.

Herren, Michael W. "Sedulius Scottus and the Knowledge of Greek." In *Early Medieval Ireland and Europe: Chronology, Contacts, Scholarship: A Festschrift for Dáibhí Ó Cróinín,* edited by Pádraic Moran and Immo Warntjes, Studia Traditionis Theologiae 14, 513–35. Turnhout: Brepols, 2015. DOI: 10.1484/M.STT-EB.5.103134.

Holtz, Louis. "Les manuscrits latins à gloses et à commentaires de l'antiquité à l'époque carolingienne." In *Atti del convegno internazionale 'Il libro e il testo,'* edited by Cesare Questa and Renato Raffaelli, 139–67. Urbino: Università degli Studi di Urbino, 1984.

Jeauneau, Édouard. "Theotokia grecs conservés en version latine." In *Philohistor: Miscellanea in Honorem Caroli Laga Septuagenarii,* edited by Antoon Schoors and Peter Van Deun, Orientalia Lovaniensia Analecta 60, 399–421. Leuven: Uitgeverij Peeters en Department Oriëntalstiek, 1994.

Kaster, Robert A. *The Tradition of the Text of the Aeneid in the Ninth Century.* New York: Garland, 1990.

Leonardi, Claudio. "Nuove voci poetiche tra secolo IX e XI." *Studi Medievali* 2 (1961): 139–68.

McKitterick, Rosamond. "Constructing the Past in the Early Middle Ages: The Case of the Royal Frankish Annals." *Transactions of the Royal Historical Society* 7 (1997): 101–29. DOI: 10.2307/3679272.

Miller, Emmanuel. "Glossaire grec-latin de la Bibliothèque de Laon." In *Notices et extraits des manuscrits de la Bibliothèque nationale et autres bibliothèques.* Volume 29.2. Paris, 1880.

Munk Olsen, Birger. *L'étude des auteurs classiques latins aux XIe et XIIe siècles,* Volume 2: *Catalogue des manuscrits classiques latins copiés du IXe au XIIe siècle.* Paris: Éditions du Centre national de la recherche scientifique, 1985.

Murgia, Charles E. *Prolegomena to Servius 5: The Manuscripts.* University of California Publications: Classical Studies 11. Berkeley: University of California Press, 1975.

O'Sullivan, Sinéad. "Glossing Virgil and Pagan Learning in the Carolingian Age." *Speculum* 93, no. 1 (2018): 132–65. DOI: 10.1086/695492.

———. "Glossing Virgil in the Early Medieval West: A Case Study of Wolfenbüttel, Herzog August Bibliothek, Cod. Guelf. 70 Gud. lat." In *Studies on Late Antique and Medieval Germanic Glossography and Lexicography in Honour of Patrizia Lendinara,* edited by Claudia Di Sciacca, Concetta Giliberto, Carmela Rizzo, and Loredana Teresi, 547–64. Pisa: Edizioni ETS, 2018.

———. "Servius in the Carolingian Age: A Case Study of British Library, Harley 2782." *The Journal of Medieval Latin* 26 (2016): 77–123. DOI: 10.1484/J.JML.5.112081.

———. "The *Oikoumenē* and the Carolingian Reception of Virgil." In *The Elements in the Medieval World: Interdisciplinary Perspectives: Earth,* edited by Marilina Cesario, Hugh Magennis, and Elisa Ramazzina, 121–51. Leiden: Brill, 2024.

———. "The Sacred and the Obscure: Greek and the Carolingian Reception of Martianus Capella." *Journal of Medieval Latin* 22 (2012): 67–94. DOI: 10.1484/J.JML.1.10252.

Ottaviano, Silvia. "La tradizione delle opere di Virgilio tra IX e XI sec." PhD Diss., Scuola Normale Superiore, Pisa, 2014.

———. "Reading Between the Lines of Virgil's Early Medieval Manuscripts." In *The Annotated Book in the Early Middle Ages: Practices of Reading and Writing,* edited by Mariken Teeuwen and Irene van Renswoude, Utrecht Studies in Medieval Literacy 38, 397–426. Turnhout: Brepols, 2017. DOI: 10.1484/M.USML-EB.5.115029.

Pellegrin, Élisabeth. *Les manuscrits classiques latins de la Bibliothèque Vaticane* 2.1. Paris: Éditions du Centre national de la recherche scientifique, 1978.

Ratkowitsch, Christine. *Karolus Magnus — alter Aeneas, alter Martinus, alter Iustinus: Zu Intention und Datierung des "Aachener Karlsepos."* Wiener Studien: Beiheft 24. Vienna: Österreichische Akademie der Wissenschaften, 1999.

Reimitz, Helmut. *History, Frankish Identity and the Framing of Western Ethnicity, 550–850.* Cambridge: Cambridge University Press, 2015. DOI: 10.1017/CBO9781139505765.

Savage, John J.H. "The Manuscripts of the Commentary of Servius Danielis on Virgil." *Harvard Studies in Classical Philology* 43 (1932): 77–121. DOI: 10.2307/310668.

Springer, Carl P.E. *The Manuscripts of Sedulius: A Provisional Handlist.* Transactions of the American Philosophical Society 85, no. 5. Philadelphia: American Philosophical Society, 1995. DOI: 10.2307/1006648.

Teeuwen, Mariken. "Seduced by Pagan Poets and Philosophers: Suspicious Learning in the Early Middle Ages." In *Limits to Learning: The Transfer of Encyclopaedic Knowledge in the Early Middle Ages,* edited by Concetta Giliberto and Loredana Teresi, 63–80. Leuven: Peeters, 2013.

Teeuwen, Mariken, and Sinéad O'Sullivan. "The Harvest of Ancient Learning: Healthy Fruits or Rotten Apples?" In *Fruits of Learning: The Transfer of Encyclopaedic Knowledge in the Early Middle Ages,* edited by Rolf H. Bremmer Jr.

and Kees Dekker, *Storehouses of Wholesome Learning IV*, 303–20. Leuven: Peeters, 2016.

Ziolkowski, Jan M., and Michael C.J. Putnam, eds. *The Virgilian Tradition: The First Fifteen Hundred Years*. New Haven: Yale University Press, 2008.

Zwierlein, Otto. "Karolus Magnus — alter Aeneas?" In *Literatur und Sprache im europäischen Mittelalter: Festschrift für Karl Langosch zum 70. Geburtstag*, edited by Alf Önnerfors, Johannes Rathofer, and Fritz Wagner, 44–52. Darmstadt: Wissenschaftliche Buchgesellschaft, 1973.

4

The Materiality of Innovation: Formats and Dimensions of the *Etymologiae* of Isidore of Seville in the Early Middle Ages

Evina Stein

Since the advent of the material turn in historical disciplines in the 1990s, the medieval book has become a subject of renewed interest that has propelled it beyond the limited orbit of paleographers, codicologists, and art historians.[1] It is now less common to treat the medieval manuscript as a mere physical vessel for the abstract text, which, once this text is extracted, can be relegated to a footnote. Even historians are becoming attuned to the fact that the manuscript is an object worthy of study in its own right and a valuable source of information about medieval

---

1 Research presented in this article was conducted between September 2018 and August 2021 in the context of the *Innovating Knowledge* project funded by a VENI grant from the Dutch Research Organization (NWO). The dataset referenced in this article is available at: https://innovatingknowledge.nl/?page_id=104. I would like to thank the editors of this volume, and the two reviewers for their comments. A special thanks goes to Prof. Ezio Ornato (Centre national de la recherche scientifique, CNRS) who was kind enough to read a draft of this chapter, re-examine the dataset used for my analysis, and make many valuable suggestions to improve this chapter.

economy, society, and cultural life.[2] Yet there is still much to be done in this line of research, especially in the arena of the quantitative study of the codex, which was masterfully inaugurated in the twentieth century by Eric Turner, Johan Peter Gumbert, Carla Bozzolo, and Ezio Ornato, and continued in recent decades by Marilena Maniaci.[3] This chapter was inspired by the work of these and other scholars, employing the quantitative approach to examining the material properties of the early medieval manuscripts transmitting the *Etymologiae* of Isidore of Seville.

---

2   See, for example, Lars B. Mortensen, "Change of Style and Content as an Aspect of the Copying Process. A Recent Trend in the Study of Medieval Latin Historiography," in *Bilan et perspectives des études médiévales en Europe. Actes du premier Congrès européen d'études médiévales (Spoleto, 27–29 mai 1993),* ed. Jacqueline Hamesse, Textes et Études du Moyen Age 3 (Turnhout: Brepols, 1995), 265–76, and Walter Pohl, "History in Fragments: Montecassino's Politics of Memory," *Early Medieval Europe* 10, no. 3 (2001): 343–74.

3   See Eric Turner, *The Typology of the Early Codex,* Haney Foundation Series 18 (Philadelphia: University of Pennsylvania Press, 1977); Johan P. Gumbert, "The Sizes of Manuscripts. Some Statistics and Notes," in *Festschrift Wytze Hellinga* (Amsterdam: Nico Israel, 1980), 277–88; Carla Bozzolo and Ezio Ornato, *Pour une histoire du livre manuscrit au Moyen Âge: Trois essays de codicologie quantitative,* Equipe de recherche sur l'humanisme français, Textes et études 2 (Paris: CNRS, 1980); Johan P. Gumbert, "Sizes and Formats," in *Ancient and Medieval Book Materials and Techniques,* ed. Marilena Maniaci and Paola F. Munafò, Studi e Testi 357 (Vatican City: Biblioteca Apostolica Vaticana, 1993), vol. 1, 227–63; Ezio Ornato et al., *La face cachée du livre médiéval: l'histoire du livre vue par Ezio Ornato, ses amis et ses collègues* (Rome: Viella, 1997); Marilena Maniaci, "Costruzione e gestione dello spazio scritto fra Oriente e Occidente: principi generali e soluzioni specifiche," in *Scrivere e leggere nell'alto Medioevo,* Settimane di studio del Centro italiano di studi sull'alto Medioevo 59 (Spoleto: Centro Italiano di Studi sull'Alto Medioevo, 2012), 473–512; and Ezio Ornato, "The Application of Quantitative Methods to the History of the Book," in *The Oxford Handbook of Latin Palaeography,* ed. Frank T. Coulson and Robert G. Babcock (Oxford: Oxford University Press, 2020), 651–68. An updated bibliography of quantitative codicology can be found in Marilena Maniaci, *Archeologia del manoscritto: metodi, problemi, bibliografia recente* (Rome: Viella, 2002), 179–266.

The Corpus

Early medieval manuscript corpora are, in general, unsuitable for quantitative analysis due to their limited state of preservation. However, as more than 500 pre-1000 CE codices and fragments containing the text of the *Etymologiae* have been identified in recent years, the corpus presented below has the necessary size for quantitative approach. This being said, it still presents certain challenges due to its limited intrinsic diversity, gaps, and fuzzy data. Certain kinds of quantitative analyses cannot be carried out on this corpus. Some of the conclusions presented below need to be accepted as preliminary and in need of further corroboration by qualitative methods or by a collection of additional quantitative data (e.g., on the thickness of parchment and ruling patterns).

The following analysis is based on a corpus of 434 manuscripts representing all known substantially preserved codices transmitting material from the *Etymologiae* surviving from before the early eleventh century as of 2021.[4] The core central to the analysis performed in this article is a smaller set constituted by a set of 95 manuscripts representing all of the manuscripts transmitting the text of the *Etymologiae* integrally, that is, as an encyclopedia in multiple books (22% of the corpus). As needed, it is supplemented by two other sets of items: a) manuscripts, mostly florilegia and miscellanies, transmitting anonymous

---

[4] This corpus is a subset of the larger corpus of 477 manuscripts representing all known codices transmitting material from the *Etymologiae* predating the early eleventh century that was assembled in the framework of the *Innovating Knowledge* project by October 2021, when the last revisions were made to this article. Since then 30 manuscripts, including substantially preserved codices have been discovered. The corpus used in this article omits 31 significantly cropped fragments of the *Etymologiae*, the material properties of which cannot be reconstructed, and 12 manuscripts, in which material from the *Etymologiae* appears as a secondary addition. It consists of 408 wholly or well-preserved manuscripts and 25 fragments, whose pages are wholly preserved.

excerpts from the *Etymologiae*[5] (142 manuscripts, 33% of the corpus), and b) manuscripts transmitting medium-length selections from the *Etymologiae* that do not represent the encyclopedic text nor can be considered excerpts (189 manuscripts, 44% of the corpus).[6]

---

5   I define an excerpt as those instances of the transmission of material from the *Etymologiae* that a) are relatively short (i.e., at most several consecutive chapters of the *Etymologiae*); b) are clearly derived from the *Etymologiae* (i.e., rather than from a compendium or collection of some sort); c) do not alter the function of the material significantly; and d) appear in a manuscript context that reinforces their status as a selection from a larger source (i.e., in miscellanies, florilegia, compendia, handbooks, etc.). For miscellanies, see George Rigg, "The Manuscript Miscellany," in *The Oxford Handbook of Latin Palaeography*, ed. Frank T. Coulson and Robert G. Babcock (Oxford: Oxford University Press, 2020), 879–83; and Anna Dorofeeva, "Reading Early Medieval Miscellanies," in *Scribes and the Presentation of Texts (from Antiquity to c. 1550)*, ed. Barbara A. Shailor et al. (Turnhout: Brepols, 2021), 334–60.

6   Compare with Carmen Codoñer Merino, "Transmisión y recepción de las Etimologías," in *Estudios de latín medieval hispánico. Actas del V Congreso Internacional de Latín Medieval Hispánico*, ed. José Martínez Gázquez, Óscar Luis de la Cruz Palma, and Cándida Ferrero Hernández (Florence: SISMEL Edizioni del Galluzzo, 2011), 5. This category includes eight manuscripts containing what may be described as an epitome of the *Etymologiae*. Some are discussed in Codoñer Merino, "Transmisión y recepción de las Etimologías," 14–18, and Carmen Cardelle de Hartmann, "Uso y reception de las *Etymologiae* de Isidoro," in *Wisigothica. After M. C. Díaz y Díaz*, ed. Carmen Codoñer Merino and Paulo Farmhouse Alberto, mediEVI 3 (Florence: SISMEL Edizioni del Galluzzo, 2014), 477–502, at 490–92. It also contains fifty-five manuscripts that transmit a selection from the *Etymologiae* that has been reordered and recontextualized into a novel thematic collection. For example, a legalistic collection entitled *De legibus divinis sive humanis* compiled from Books II, V, and XVII of the *Etymologiae* survives in seven manuscripts from the corpus; see Ernest-Joseph Tardif, "Un abrégé juridique des *Étymologies* d'Isidore de Séville," in *Mélanges Julien Havet* (Paris: Ernest Leroux, 1895), 659–81. Whole books or book sections of the *Etymologiae* were transmitted as autonomous anonymous works, for example the first section of Book V, *De legibus* (*On Laws*) in the context of the study of law; see Tardif, "Un abrégé juridique des *Étymologies* d'Isidore de Séville," 660, and Cardelle de Hartmann, "Uso y reception de las *Etymologiae* de Isidoro," 485. Even some of the chapters could have been transmitted separately as self-standing works, as happened to two chapters from Book VIII enumerating various Jewish

For this study, two types of quantified information about the 434 manuscripts in the corpus have been examined: a) metadata about the manuscripts, including the place and date of origin, script, and type;[7] and b) information about their material properties, including the number of folia, page height and width, writing block height and width, and the number of lines and columns per page.[8] The physical measurements of the manuscripts were taken in person when possible and otherwise taken from available catalogues.[9] Since the information about manuscripts provided by manuscript catalogues is sometimes incomplete, the corpus records the number of columns of 99% of manuscripts (430 items), page dimensions of 98.5% of manuscripts (427 items), the number of lines of 96% of manuscripts (417 items), and the writing block dimensions of 81% of manuscripts

---

and Christian heresies that also circulated as an anti-heretical treatise; see Codoñer Merino, "Transmisión y recepción de las *Etimologías*," 7–8.

7   The date and place of origin have been assigned based on manuscript catalogues, especially Elias A. Lowe, *Codices Latini Antiquiores: A Palaeographical Guide to Latin Manuscripts Prior to the Ninth Century*, 12 vols. (Oxford: Clarendon Press, 1934–1966), and Bernhard Bischoff, *Katalog der festländischen Handschriften des neunten Jahrhunderts (mit Ausnahme der wisigotischen)*, Veröffentlichungen der Kommission für die Herausgabe der mittelalterlichen Bibliothekskataloge Deutschlands und der Schweiz, 4 vols. (Wiesbaden: Harrassowitz, 1998–2017). The type is expressed using 18 categories (with the number of assigned items): only *Etymologiae* (95), miscellany (57), grammatical collection (43), collection of canon law (32), collection of secular law (31), pastoral collection (29), computistic collection (27), theological or patristic collection (25), medical collection (16), glossary (13), mathematical collection (13), music collection (7), scientific collection (7), a collection of works on the trivium (7), Bible (6), historiographical collection (5), exegetical collection (4), and classical text (4). Ten items were not assigned to any category because of a lack of information about their content. Detailed information about the sources of the manuscript metadata and the categorization criteria are available at the website of the *Innovating Knowledge* project, https://innovatingknowledge.nl.

8   A manuscript may consist of leaves with variable dimensions and with a variable format (i.e., writing window and number of lines). For the purpose of this study, I used the minimum size of the page dimensions and writing window dimensions and an average number of lines per page.

9   I personally remeasured a little over 120 items, or approximately a quarter of the corpus.

(350 items). Moreover, the place of production of 25 items and the script of 12 manuscripts cannot be determined. Complete information about their material properties is available for 347 items (80% of the corpus), while complete information about all properties is available for 330 items (76% of the corpus).

Since only substantially preserved manuscripts were selected for this corpus, it is assumed that they have not been significantly damaged or materially altered since the time of their production, except for the loss of folia and a certain degree of trimming.[10] We can therefore, use them to examine the decision-making of early medieval manuscript producers as far as the page and writing block dimensions, the number of lines, and page layout are concerned. It is also important to emphasize that the corpus represents material *surviving* from the early Middle Ages, rather than produced and circulated in this period. It is very likely that material properties, which are the subject of this article, affected the survival rate of early medieval manuscripts, distorting some of the observations presented here.[11] It should, for example, be assumed that large-format, high-grade and immobile books tend to survive at higher rates than small, low-grade and portable books, and that the corpus therefore privileges the former over the latter.[12] Due to the uneven patterns of survival of material from different regions, furthermore, the majority of the manuscripts in the corpus examined come from

---

10 At least 54 manuscripts (12%) can be shown to have been trimmed. However, as Bozzolo and Ornato have shown, trimming rarely decreased the page dimensions by more than 1 cm and this can therefore be discounted here; see Bozzolo and Ornato, *Pour une histoire du livre manuscrit au Moyen Âge*, 245–47. At least 52 manuscripts from the corpus are currently missing folia.

11 This can be shown from the comparison of substantially preserved manuscripts of the *Etymologiae* and fragments, see Evina Steinová, "The Oldest Manuscript Tradition of the *Etymologiae*," *Visigothic Symposia* 4 (2020): 114–15.

12 See Bozzolo and Ornato, *Pour une histoire du livre manuscrit au Moyen Âge*, 73–74, and George D. Greenia, "The bigger the book: On oversize medieval manuscripts," *Revue Belge de Philologie et d'Histoire* 83 (2005): 723–46.

the Carolingian environment (314 items).[13] This means that more definitive conclusions can be reached only about Carolingian material, although, as will be shown below, useful observations can also be made about other cultural milieux.

Many of the observations and conclusions about the material properties of the surviving early medieval manuscripts transmitting the *Etymologiae* are not particular to this text but extend to early medieval manuscripts in general. For example, observations about manuscripts transmitting excerpts and non-encyclopedic *Etymologiae* are likely valid for any manuscripts transmitting excerpts and medieval appropriations of notable works, while some of the conclusions about the encyclopedic manuscripts of the *Etymologiae* can be also extended to other long authoritative works circulating one work per codex. When examining the surviving early medieval manuscript witnesses of the *Etymologiae*, then, this chapter often offers insights that go beyond a single textual tradition. Because of the exceptional number of surviving witnesses, the *Etymologiae* represent a useful corpus for the examination of the material properties of the early medieval Western codex. It would be useful to build other text-specific manuscript corpora of similar size to compare and contrast them in order to better discern to what extent particular material properties are general to the early medieval codex, and which may represent developments particular to specific textual traditions.

The *Etymologiae* as a Codex

The *Etymologiae,* a vast encyclopedia covering subjects from grammar, medicine, law, and ecclesiastical hierarchies to pa-

---

13 To be more precise, the items in the corpus are copied in the following scripts (with the number of items assigned): Caroline minuscule (300), late Caroline minuscule, that is, developing towards the Gothic script (34), pre-Caroline minuscules (21), Visigothic minuscule (16), Italian minuscules and cursives (12), Beneventan minuscule (11), various Insular scripts, such as Anglo-Saxon majuscule and minuscule, and Irish minuscule (10), early Caroline minuscule (10), and uncial (1). Three items copied in minuscule have not been assigned to any more specific category.

gan gods, precious stones, human pastimes, and footwear, was Isidore's final and most ambitious work.[14] The Sevillan bishop had been working on his masterwork for several decades when he died in 636 without putting a final version into circulation.[15] Unlike some of the late-antique luminaries, he did not leave behind instructions on how his work was meant to be copied or disseminated.[16] We can, nevertheless, get indirect insight into

---

14 Some of the most important scholarly works on Isidore of Seville and the *Etymologiae* include Jacques Fontaine, *Isidore de Séville et la culture classique dans l'Espagne wisigothique*, 2nd edn. (Paris: Études augustiniennes, 1983); Mark E. Amsler, *Etymology and Grammatical Discourse in Late Antiquity and the Early Middle Ages* (Amsterdam: John Benjamins Publishing, 1989); Carmen Codoñer Merino, *Introducción al Libro X de las "Etymologiae": su lugar dentro de esta obra, su valor como diccionario* (Logroño: Fundación San Millán de la Cogolla, 2002); and Manuel C. Díaz y Díaz, "Introdución," in *San Isidoro de Sevilla. Etimologías: edicion bilingüe*, ed. José Oroz Reta and Manuel-A. Marcos Casquero (Madrid: Biblioteca de Autores Cristianos, 2004), 1–2. Two recently published collected volumes devoted to Isidore are Andrew Fear and Jamie Wood, eds., *Isidore of Seville and His Reception in the Early Middle Ages: Transmitting and Transforming Knowledge*, Late Antique and Early Medieval Iberia 2 (Amsterdam: Amsterdam University Press, 2016), and Andrew Fear and Jamie Wood, eds., *A Companion to Isidore of Seville*, Brill's Companions to the Christian Tradition 87 (Leiden: Brill, 2020).

15 There are many problems with the early transmission of this text. See Walter Porzig, "Die Rezensionen der *Etymologiae*," *Hermes* 72, no. 2 (1937): 162–66; Marc Reydellet, "La diffusion des Origines," *Mélanges d'archéologie et d'histoire* 78, no. 2 (1966): 386–88; and more recently Carmen Codoñer Merino, José Carlos Martín Iglesias, and María Adelaida Andrés Sanz, "Isidorus Hispalensis Ep.," in *La trasmissione dei testi latini del medioevo/ Medieval Texts and Their Transmission*, Mediaeval Latin Texts and Their Transmission, vol. 2, ed. Paulo Chiesa and Lucia Castaldi (Florence: SISMEL Edizioni del Galluzzo, 2005), 281–84; and Díaz y Díaz, "Introdución."

16 Notable examples of authors that provide instruction on how their works should be disseminated include Augustine and Cassiodorus; see Emanuela Colombi, "Assetto librario ed elementi paratestuali nei manoscritti tardoantichi e carolingi del 'De civitate dei'di Agostino: alcune riflessioni," *Segno e testo* 11 (2013): 183–272, and Patrizia Stoppacci, "Cassiodorus Senator. *Expositio Psalmorum*," in *La trasmissione dei testi latini del medioevo*, Mediaeval Latin Texts and Their Transmission, vol. 2, ed. Paolo Chiesa and Lucia Castaldi (Florence: SISMEL Edizioni del Galluzzo, 2005), 143–59. All that remains of Isidore's voice is a short dedication to king Sisebut that is found in most manuscripts of the *Etymologiae*: "En tibi, sicut pol-

his thought through the *Renotatio librorum domini Isidori* of Isidore's junior colleague and friend, Braulio of Zaragoza, in which he refers to the publication of the *Etymologiae* as follows:[17]

[Isidore produced] an enormous codex of the *Etymologies,* structured by him by means of *tituli* rather than books, which, since he wrote it on my request, and although he left it incomplete, I divided into twenty books.[18]

This short description suggests that Isidore intended to publish a work whose main structural feature were *tituli* (of which there are more than 750 in the text) rather than books, as was noted by scholars,[19] that it was physically embodied in a single *volumen* (rather than in multiple *volumina*), and that this codex was exceptionally large. The two latter properties reflect a particular material choice. They suggest a work that could serve as a majestic gift for a king, symbolic in its size and unifying quality, but as a result also confined to a limited readership, impracti-

---

licitus sum, misi opus de origine quarundam rerum ex veteris lectionis recordatione collectum atque ita in quibusdam locis adnotatum, sicut extat conscriptum stilo maiorum"; edited in Wallace M. Lindsay, *Etymologiarum sive Originum libri XX* (Oxford: Clarendon Press, 1911), vol. 1, 10. The problems surrounding this dedication are discussed already in Wallace M. Lindsay, "The Editing of Isidore's *Etymologiae*," *The Classical Quarterly* 5, no. 1 (1911): 51.

17 On Braulio's role as the first editor of the *Etymologiae*, see Jacques Elfassi, "Isidore of Seville and the *Etymologies*," in *A Companion to Isidore of Seville*, ed. Andrew Fear and Jamie Wood (Leiden: Brill, 2020), 245–49.

18 José Carlos Martín Iglesias, ed., *Scripta de vita Isidori Hispalensis episcopi*, Corpus Christianorum Series Latina 113B (Turnhout: Brepols, 2006), 203: "Etymologiarum codicem nimiae magnitudinis distinctum ab eo titulis, non libris, quem, quia rogatu meo fecit, quamuis inperfectum ipse reliquerit, ego in uiginti libros diuisi." The translation is my own.

19 Lindsay, "The Editing of Isidore's *Etymologiae*," 50; more recently Carmen Cardelle de Hartmann, "Wissensorganisation und Wissensvermittlung im ersten Teil von Isidors *Etymologiae* (Bücher I–X)," in *Exzerpieren — Kompilieren — Tradieren: Transformationen des Wissens zwischen Spätantike und Frühmittelalter*, ed. Stephan Dusil, Gerald Schwedler, and Raphael Schwitter, Millennium-Studien 64 (Berlin: De Gruyter, 2017), 89; and Elfassi, "Isidore of Seville and the *Etymologies*," 254.

cal to use, and endowed with low portability.[20] Isidore crafted a grandiose encyclopedia for the learned Visigothic elite, rather than a textbook for schools or a practical aid for the clergy and lay population.[21]

Despite its vagueness, the description of the *Etymologiae* as a codex serves as a useful benchmark for assessing the material properties of the manuscripts of this text in the following centuries. We can dub manuscripts innovative or conservative based on whether they remained large format and single-volume or whether they acquired new traits. Thus, Braulio acted as an innovator when he divided the *Etymologiae* into twenty books and enriched them with a preface in the form of the letter exchange between himself and Isidore, and lists of *capitula* derived from Isidore's *tituli* preceding individual books or book sections. Moreover, we can judge his innovations to be particularly successful, as we find them in all but few surviving early medieval encyclopedic copies of the *Etymologiae*.[22] However, he presumably did not deviate from Isidore's formula of a large format and single volume.

The same formula seems to have been maintained by many Visigothic copyists, who continued to produce copies of the *Etymologiae* notable for their size. The surviving Visigothic manuscripts transmitting Isidore's text tend to be larger than manuscripts surviving from other regions, having an average taille (page height + page width) of 585 mm (23.03 in.), or almost 12 cm (4.72 in.) more than the average of the corpus (466 mm [18.35 in.]).[23] The surviving Visigothic manuscripts transmitting the encyclopedic *Etymologiae* are even larger, with an

---

20 Compare with Cardelle de Hartmann, "Uso y reception de las *Etymologiae* de Isidoro," 482.
21 See Cardelle de Hartmann, "Wissensorganisation und Wissensvermittlung," 99–100.
22 See Porzig, "Die Rezensionen der *Etymologiae*," 166–67.
23 Throughout this chapter, taille is used to represent the page dimensions, because it proved to be more adequate for the purposes of this study than other possible methods of representation (e.g., page surface or diagonal). The taille has been devised in Bozzolo and Ornato, *Pour une histoire du livre manuscrit au Moyen Âge*, 217. For a critique of taille and a comparison

average taille of 630 mm (24.8 in.), or almost 9 cm more than the average of the corpus (542 mm [21.34 in.]). Four of the six codices in the corpus with tailles above 700 mm were likewise copied in Visigothic minuscule.[24] Furthermore, all but one unusual Visigothic manuscript transmitting the entire *Etymologiae* are single-volume copies.[25] It should also be noted that all but this outlier are laid out in two columns, a potential hint that the seventh-century layout of Isidore's encyclopedia was in two or even three columns per page.[26] Overall, it can be said that the *Etymologiae* was treated more conservatively in the Visigothic region than elsewhere, perhaps as a sign of reverence for its author, and that Visigothic manuscripts preserved for a long time archaic features that were disappearing elsewhere.

---

with its alternatives, see Johan Peter Gumbert, "Livre grand, livre petit: un problème de taille," *Gazette du livre médiéval* 38 (2001): 55–58.

24 These are: El Escorial, Monasterio San Lorenzo, MS D.I.1 (c. 994, San Millán de la Cogolla, 755 mm); El Escorial, Monasterio San Lorenzo, MS D.I.2 (c. 974–76, Albelda, 780 mm); El Escorial, Monasterio San Lorenzo, MS P.I.7 (9th c., ex., northern Spain, 710 mm); and El Escorial, Monasterio San Lorenzo, MS &.I.14 (9th century, med., Spain, 880 mm). The dating of the Visigothic manuscripts in this article is based on the work of Ainoa Castro Correa, "Online Catalogue of Visigothic Script Codices," at: http://www.litteravisigothica.com/visigothic-script-topics/codicology.

25 The anomalous El Escorial, Monasterio San Lorenzo, MS &.I.14 (9th century, med., Spain) is divided into two volumes and laid out in three columns per page. It is the only Visigothic codex containing additional texts attached to Isidore's encyclopedia, and due to its truly gigantic dimensions (515 × 365 mm [20.28 × 21.1 in.]), an outlier eluding a comparison. This manuscript is discussed in Bernhard Bischoff, "Die europäische Verbreitung der Werke Isidors von Sevilla," in *Isidoriana: colección de estudios sobre Isidore de Sevilla,* ed. Manuel C. Díaz y Díaz (León: Centro de estudios San Isidoro, 1961), 320.

26 Compare with Bischoff, "Die europäische Verbreitung der Werke Isidors von Sevilla," 326, and Franck Cinato, "Que nous apprennent les écritures des plus anciens témoins du *Liber Glossarum* sur l'archétype?," *Dossiers d'HEL* 10 (2016): 121. The oldest Latin manuscripts tend to be laid out in two or more columns; see Elias A. Lowe, "Some Facts about Our Oldest Latin Manuscripts," in *Palaeographical Papers,* ed. Ludwig Bieler (Oxford: Clarendon, 1972), vol. 1, 201–2. Maniaci shows that long lines gradually came to predominate in Western books in the early Middle Ages. See Maniaci, "Costruzione e gestione dello spazio scritto," 495.

The Material Evolution of the Encyclopedic *Etymologiae*

The 95 surviving manuscripts of encyclopedic *Etymologiae* represent a homogeneous sub-population that can be defined by a set of shared traits: the attribution to Isidore, the title *Etymologiae*, presentation of Isidore's text in a specific order and integrally, division into books, a preface constituted by letters exchanged between Isidore and Braulio, and paratextual elements such as lists of *capitula* preceding individual books or book sections and chapter *tituli* and numbers.[27] It is the only format of the *Etymologiae* that acquired a high-end feel, attracting ornamentation, illuminated initials, and similar decorative features.[28] As they continued to transmit Isidore's work integrally as an encyclopedia, they clearly represented the more conservative line of transmission of his text. Nevertheless, they became an important locus of change, as is evidenced by textual and material variety among the surviving manuscripts. Thus, while Braulio divided the *Etymologiae* into twenty books, we also encounter alternative divisions of the text.[29] Many codices of the encyclopedic text

---

27 At the end of the eighth century, a general list of *libri* was added at the beginning of the text and became absorbed into the encyclopedic format. See Veronika von Büren, "La place du manuscrit Ambr. L 99 sup. dans la transmission des *Étymologies* d'Isidore de Séville," in *Nuove ricerche su codici in scrittura latina dell'Ambrosiana*, ed. Mirella Ferrari and Marco Navoni (Milan: Vita e Pensiero, 2007), 25–44.

28 The surviving luxurious copies of the encyclopedic *Etymologiae* include Berlin, Staatsbibliothek, MS Dep. Breslau 16 (9th century, ⅔, Tuscany or Umbria); Brussels, Koninklijke Bibliotheek, MS II 4856 (8th century, ex., Corbie); Einsiedeln, Stiftsbibliothek, MS 167 (10th century, Einsiedeln); Madrid, Real Academia de la Historia, MS 25 (c. 946, San Millán de la Cogolla); St. Gall, Stiftsbibliothek, Cod. Sang. 231–232 (880–890, St. Gall); and several of the El Escorial manuscripts.

29 Tours, Bibliothèque municipale, MS 844 (9th century, ½, Tours); Chartres, Bibliothèque municipale, MS 16 (11th century, unknown); and Krakow, Biblioteka Jagiellońska, MS 484 (10th/11th century, unknown) are divided into 17 books. Leiden, Universiteitsbibliotheek, MS Voss. Lat. F 74 (9th century, ¾, Fulda and Ferrières) is divided into 21 books; Vatican City, Biblioteca Apostolica Vaticana, MS Vat. lat. 7803 (9th century, med., northern Italy) is divided into 25 books; and Berlin, Staatsbibliothek, MS Ham. 689 (11th century, northern Italy) is divided into 29 books.

remained laid out in two columns, but we also see manuscripts of the encyclopedic *Etymologiae* copied in long lines.[30]

The most significant innovations of the encyclopedic line of transmission concerned its size. The extra-Iberian manuscripts are no longer as large as those copied in Visigothic minuscule but belong for the most part to Bozzolo and Ornato's *moyen-grands* category (491–670 mm [19.33–26.38 in.]).[31] Their average taille is 534 mm (21.02 in.) (t. 4.1), that is, they are on average 5 cm (1.97 in.) smaller than Visigothic manuscripts in the corpus and almost 10 cm (3.94 in.) smaller than a Visigothic codex of the encyclopedic text. Nevertheless, they are still on average more than 5 cm (1.97 in.) larger than the average Western manuscripts copied between the fourth and the tenth centuries recorded by Maniaci (480 mm [18.9 in.]),[32] and more than 3 cm (1.18 in.) larger than the ninth- and tenth-century codices studied by Bozzolo and Ornato (500 mm [19.69 in.]).[33]

---

30 The average number of blocks per page of the manuscripts of encyclopedic *Etymologiae* is approximately 1.5, meaning that the number of manuscripts laid out in two columns and long lines is even. Indeed, among the 94 manuscripts, whose layout is known, there are 47 manuscripts copied in long lines, 46 manuscripts laid out in two columns, and one manuscript copied in three columns. The manuscripts copied in long lines slightly prevail prior to 800 (1.44) and in the tenth century (1.46).

31 To be more precise, 66 manuscripts, or about two-thirds, are *moyen-grands* according to Bozzolo and Ornato's classification, 25 manuscripts are *petit-moyens* (321–490 mm [12.64–19.29 in.]), and two Visigothic copies are *grands* (above 670 mm [26.38 in.]). For two manuscripts, I lack dimensions that would enable me to calculate their taille.

32 Maniaci's average taille for all medieval manuscripts is 492 mm (19.37 in.) or about 4 cm (1.57 in.) less than the average taille of an early medieval non-Visigothic codex of encyclopedic *Etymologiae;* see Maniaci, "Costruzione e gestione dello spazio scritto," 484.

33 See Bozzolo and Ornato, *Pour une histoire du livre manuscrit au Moyen Âge,* 265.

Taille range	No. of manuscripts	No. of manuscripts (excl. Visigothic)
< 400 mm (15.75 in.)	2	2
400–450 mm (15.75–17.72 in.)	9	9
451–500 mm (17.72–19.67 in.)	16	15
501–550 mm (19.67–21.65 in.)	24	22
551–600 mm (21.65–23.62 in.)	23	23
601–650 mm (23.62–25.59 in.)	14	11
651–700 mm (25.59–27.56 in.)	3	3
> 700 mm (27.56 in.)	2	0

Table 4.1. The distribution of the surviving early medieval manuscripts transmitting the encyclopedic *Etymologiae* based on their page tailles. Included are 93 manuscripts whose page dimensions are known.

The manuscripts of the encyclopedic *Etymologiae* are also notably larger than other manuscripts transmitting the text of the *Etymologiae* (i.e., those containing both excerpts and non-encyclopedic *Etymologiae*). The average taille of the latter is only 445 mm (17.52 in.), making them on average almost 9 cm (3.54 in.) smaller than manuscripts transmitting the encyclopedic *Etymologiae*. In fact, if we compare the distribution of the tailles of encyclopedic *Etymologiae* and other manuscripts in the corpus, it emerges that they represent two materially specific populations (fig. 4.1).[34] While these two populations overlap — mostly because other manuscripts appear in all size ranges and not because manuscripts of the encyclopedic *Etymologiae* could be smaller than a certain size — the physical size is such a reliable indicator of the integral versus other transmission pattern that page dimensions often allow for assessing whether a substan-

---

34 At the same time, there are little to no differences in size between manuscripts transmitting non-encyclopedic *Etymologiae* and excerpts of this text.

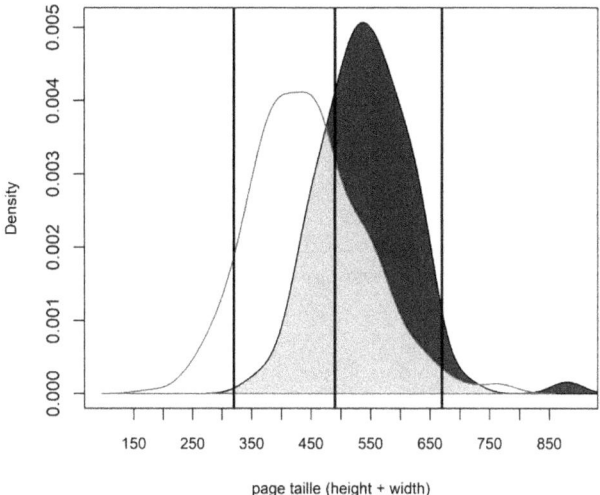

Fig. 4.1. The distribution of page tailles of the surviving early medieval manuscripts transmitting the encyclopedic *Etymologiae* (black, 93 manuscripts) and other manuscripts (white, 330 manuscripts). The y-axis shows the proportion of manuscripts with a given taille in a given sub-population (%). Vertical lines mark Bozzolo and Ornato's typological categories: *petits* (<320 mm [12.6 in.]), *petit-moyens* (320–490 mm [12.6–19.29 in.]), *moyen-grands* (491–670 mm [19.33–26.38 in.]), and *grands* (>670 mm [26.38 in.]). This density graph was plotted with R.

tially damaged fragment of the *Etymologiae* is a remnant of a manuscript of the encyclopedic type or not.[35]

The main reason for chiseling down the *codex nimiae magnitudinis* was surely to make Isidore's voluminous encyclopedia easier to use. As the utility of Isidore's knowledge corpus became obvious, and its fame grew, the demand for copies that had

---

35 In this fashion, 29 of the 59 early medieval fragments containing the text of the *Etymologiae* can be recognized as remnants of manuscripts transmitting the encyclopedic *Etymologiae*, while 15 fragments are due to their small dimensions clearly remnants of other formats.

more manageable dimensions must have increased, especially in areas where the *Etymologiae* may have been a principal source of knowledge on many topics (such as Ireland).[36] Many early medieval *scriptoria,* moreover, may not have been able to afford to produce lavish or large-format books.[37] Before the Carolingian period, in particular, book-copyists may have been keen to make the *Etymologiae* as sober and economic as possible. There is no reason to seek a single location where this material development originated, as it was undoubtedly driven by practical concerns common to a large proportion of early medieval users, such as limited resources.[38]

At more than 1,200,000 characters (give or take few hundred thousand characters depending on the used script and punctuation system), the text of the complete *Etymologiae* has a textual

---

[36] See Michael W. Herren, "Storehouses of Learning: Encyclopaedias and Other Reference Works in Ireland and Pre-Bedan Anglo-Saxon England," in *Practice in Learning: The Transfer of Encyclopaedic Knowledge in the Early Middle Ages,* ed. Rolf Bremmer and Kees Dekker, Mediaevalia Groningana 16 (Paris: Peeters, 2010), 9–10; more recently, Marina Smyth, "Isidorian Texts in Seventh-Century Ireland," in *Isidore of Seville and His Reception in the Early Middle Ages,* ed. Andrew Fear and Jamie Wood (Amsterdam: Amsterdam University Press, 2016), 111–30; and Martin J. Ryan, "Isidore amongst the Islands: The Reception and Use of Isidore of Seville in Britain and Ireland in the Early Middle Ages," in *A Companion to Isidore of Seville,* ed. Andrew Fear and Jamie Wood, Brill's Companions to the Christian Tradition 87 (Leiden: Brill, 2020), 424–56.

[37] See Greenia, "The Bigger the Book," 727–28; David Ganz, "Book Production in the Carolingian Empire and the Spread of Caroline Minuscule," in *The New Cambridge Medieval History,* vol. II. c. 700–900, ed. Rosamond McKitterick (Cambridge: Cambridge University Press, 1995), 801; and Armando Petrucci, "Dal libro unitario al libro miscellaneo," in *Scrivere e leggere nell'Italia medievale/Writers and Readers in Medieval Italy,* trans. Charles M. Radding (New Haven: Yale University Press, 2007), 17.

[38] Nevertheless, even in the absence of surviving complete manuscripts the Insular world, it is tempting to connect some of this development with the reception of the *Etymologiae* in the Insular world and Insular influence on the Continent before the Carolingian period due to the limits of the Insular book production in its earliest phases; see T. Julian Brown, "The Oldest Irish Manuscripts and their Late Antique Background," in *Irland und Europa. Die Kirche im Frühmittelalter,* ed. Próinséas Ní Chatháin and Michael Richter (Stuttgart: Klett-Cotta, 1984), 311–27.

mass that imposed significant constraints on the early medieval scribes who wanted to reproduce this text integrally.[39] Above all, due to the technological limits of early medieval book production, it was not possible to downsize the text beyond a certain limit.[40] Even if the text could be squeezed down somewhat, it could not happen without compromising other aspects of the manuscript. The constraints that the early medieval scribes faced can be expressed as a formula in which the total number of leaves, the size of these leaves, the size and disposition of the writing block, the number of lines per page, the writing module, and additional properties together must accommodate the total textual mass of the copied text. If one variable, such as the page dimensions, was altered, others had to be adjusted to render the book functional. The corpus examined here contains many traces of experimentation with the formatting and layout of Isidore's text that reflect attempts at adjustments of the manuscripts' size.[41]

One avenue that the early medieval copyists explored was to increase the number of lines per page or make the writing module smaller. This seems to have been the strategy of the makers of Cambridge, University Library, MS Add. 5948 (8th century, ex., France), a single leaf remaining of a manuscript with a taille of only 460 mm copied in 45 lines measuring only 4.5 mm, and

---

39 For the discussion of the textual mass and its importance as the "third dimension of the book," see Denis Muzerelle and Ezio Ornato, "The Third Dimension of the Book: Codicological Aspects of Multi-Textuality," in *Trends in Statistical Codicology*, ed. Marilena Maniaci, Studies in Manuscript Cultures 19 (Berlin: De Gruyter, 2021), 377–412.

40 To produce lower-medium-sized manuscripts containing the entire *Etymologiae* was possible only from the thirteenth century onwards thanks to the new technology of parchment production which decreased the thickness of the parchment; see Chiara Ruzzier, "The Miniaturisation of Bible Manuscripts in the 13th Century: A Comparative Study," in *Form and Function in the Late Medieval Bible,* ed. Laura Light and Eyal Poleg, Library of the Written Word 27 (Leiden: Brill, 2013), 105–25. Compare with Johan Peter Gumbert, "The Bearable Lightness of Parchment," *Gazette du livre médiéval* 59 (2012): 70–71.

41 The following overview can be compared with Ruzzier, "The Miniaturisation," 118.

of Berlin, Staatsbibliothek, MS Ham. 689 (11th century, northern Italy) with pages with a taille of 475 mm copied in 46 long lines measuring only 5 mm. By contrast, the average line height of an early medieval encyclopedic copy of the *Etymologiae* is closer to 8 mm,[42] and the average number of lines closer to 33 lines. Yet, to increase the number of lines per page and make the writing module smaller meant to render the manuscript less readable. Perhaps for this reason, only a few scribes followed this path.

Another solution was to sacrifice part of the margin to make the writing block larger. Maniaci estimated that in the manuscripts from the fourth to tenth centuries, the writing window covers on average 57.6% of a manuscript page.[43] This average is similar to the average for the 83 manuscripts of the encyclopedic *Etymologiae* from the corpus whose page dimensions and writing window dimensions are known (58.5%). However, seventeen manuscripts have a writing block covering more than 65% of the page, and in four manuscripts, it covers more than 70% of the page. Among these four manuscripts with an exceptionally large writing block is one with unusually small pages, Milan, Biblioteca Ambrosiana, MS L 99 sup. (8th c., ²/₂, Bobbio), a partial copy containing only Books I–X with a taille of 430 mm (16.93 in.). Another manuscript with a writing block of over 70%, Paris, Bibliothèque nationale de France, MS lat. 17159 (9th century, St. Claude?), is among the largest in the corpus (having a taille of 630 mm [24.8 in.]) but also the thinnest, squeezing the entire *Etymologiae* into only 94 folia.[44] It seems that this strategy was also

---

[42] The corpus does not contain consistent information on the line height. This estimate is based on the measurement of manuscripts I examined in person.

[43] See Maniaci, "Costruzione e gestione dello spazio scritto," 500.

[44] The two remaining manuscripts with small margins, London, British Library, MS Add. 34389 (fol. 20) (9th century, ¼, eastern France), and London, British Library, MS Egerton 267 (fol. 76) (9th century, ⅔, eastern France), are fragments and therefore more cannot be said about the kind of manuscripts they come from.

pursued to some extent, but not too often, perhaps because too large a writing window was not seen as desirable or practical.⁴⁵

Some leeway could have also been gained by using a highly abbreviated, ligature-rich script, as in Wolfenbüttel, Herzog August Bibliothek, MS Guelf. 64 Weiss (8th c., Bobbio?) and Vatican City, Biblioteca Apostolica Vaticana, MS lat. 5763 (mid-8th c., northern Italy), which were copied in a highly abbreviated cursive script.⁴⁶ The taille of the former is 484 mm (19.06 in.), while the taille of the latter is 448 mm (17.64 in.). However, this option was also far from ideal. Too many abbreviations, ligatures, and the use of cursive script often made the text disfigured beyond readability, a problem that is endemic to the early Carolingian copies of the *Etymologiae*.

By far the most successful strategy that enabled the production of smaller copies of the encyclopedic *Etymologiae* was to increase the number of folia. This in turn entailed splitting a manuscript into two or more volumes, as sewing in too many small leaves compromised the binding and made the book difficult to open and use. A peculiar example of how badly a manuscript could be disfigured if not split is Paris, Bibliothèque nationale de France, MS lat. 14085 (third quarter of the 9th c., Corbie), a partial one-volume copy of the *Etymologiae* consisting today of Books II–X and XVI–XX. Its 232 surviving leaves have a taille of only 408 mm [16.06 in.] (245 × 163 mm [9.65 × 6.42 in.]), making it the smallest surviving manuscript of the encyclopedic *Etymologiae* copied in Caroline minuscule, but

---

45 Compare with Ruzzier, "The Miniaturisation," 120. It can be added that manuscripts of the encyclopedic *Etymologiae* copied as a single volume tend to have smaller external margins than other manuscripts, including those of encyclopedic *Etymologiae* in multiple volumes (their writing block covers between 57.5% and 61% of the page on average, depending on the page height, while in other manuscripts, the writing blocks appear in the range of 45.5–58% depending on the page height). This is probably due to the fact that they are more often laid out in two columns than these other manuscripts and the intercolumn takes up some of the white space reserved for the margins.

46 See Lindsay, "The Editing of Isidore *Etymologiae*," 45, and Bischoff, "Die europäische Verbreitung der Werke Isidors von Sevilla," 322.

also a book impossible to keep open because of how tightly it is currently bound. It had presumably originally been a copy in two or more volumes that was bound into one codex in the seventeenth or eighteenth century.

To increase the number of leaves, then, entailed segmenting the twenty books of the encyclopedic *Etymologiae* into multiple volumes. Indeed, partition of the twenty books of the encyclopedic *Etymologiae* into two volumes of ten books became a particularly successful innovation, as is evidenced by the twenty surviving and identifiable two-volume copies of Isidore's encyclopedia.[47] The corpus may also preserve traces of a segmentation sequence constituted by four volumes of five books as certain manuscripts transmit only Books I–V (Munich, Bayerische Staatsbibliothek, MS Clm 6275 and Vatican City, Biblioteca Apostolica Vaticana, MS Vat. lat. 5763), Books VI–X (Würzburg, Universitätsbibliothek, MS M.p.th.f. 143 and Cambridge, Trinity College, MS B.15.33), or Books XVI–XX (Paris, Bibliothèque nationale de France, MS lat. 13028).[48] Two manuscripts transmitting Books I–VI (Paris, Bibliothèque nationale de France, MS lat. 7670 and Vercelli, Biblioteca Capitolare, MS CCII [29]) and Paris, Bibliothèque nationale de France, MS lat. 14085, mentioned earlier, which transmits Books II–X and XVI–XX, are perhaps related to this sequence as well. Three manuscripts represent other selections from the twenty books of the encyclopedic *Etymologiae* that are either not related to any sequence or sole remnants of alternative segmentation sequences.[49]

---

47 In addition, up to seven substantially preserved fragments included in the corpus, which contain only the contents of Books I–X or XI–XX, are perhaps remnants of two-volume copies of the encyclopedic *Etymologiae*.

48 Most of these manuscript date to the second half of the eighth or the first half of the ninth century. They come from all early medieval regions apart from Spain.

49 El Escorial, Monasterio San Lorenzo, MS P.I.6 (9th century, med., southern Spain) contains only Books I–XII, St. Gall, Stiftsbibliothek, Cod. Sang. 233 (c. 800, St. Gall) contains only Books VI–VIII and XII–XV, and Turin, Biblioteca Universitaria, MS D.III.19 (10th/11th century, area of Milan) contains only Books I–XVI.

As shown in table 4.2, the manner of segmentation correlates with the physical dimensions of manuscripts. Single-volume manuscripts are on average larger than manuscripts of two-volume encyclopedic *Etymologiae,* and those are on average larger than manuscripts representing segmentation into smaller parts. In the end, manuscripts belonging to the last category are on average approximately 6.5–10 cm (2.60–3.94 in.) smaller than manuscripts of the single-volume encyclopedic *Etymologiae.* The six smallest manuscripts of the encyclopedic *Etymologiae* in the corpus are all two-volume or multi-volume copies.[50] While these differences in size are not only due to the choice of a segmentation strategy — as they also correlate with the region of production and the choice of script — they suggest that dividing the encyclopedic *Etymologiae* into multiple volumes was the most viable strategy for mitigating problems arising from the textual mass of the *Etymologiae,*[51] even though segmentation also carried its own dangers, most notably loss of one (or more) volumes.[52]

---

50 The smallest copy of the encyclopedic *Etymologiae* is Vercelli, Biblioteca Capitolare, MS CCII (29) (9th century, in., Nonantola), containing only Books I–VI and having a taille of only 355 mm (13.98 in.).

51 Prof. Ornato suggested to me that the splitting of the encyclopedic *Etymologiae* into multiple volumes may have likewise been motivated by the desire to make them more readable, as they are also characterized by having fewer lines per page and smaller "black space" than single-volume copies. However, the number of lines per page is related to the page height (i.e., the smaller the page, the fewer the maximum number of lines that can be fitted on it). By plotting the average number of lines per page against the page height, it can be shown that smaller manuscripts do not have an unusually small number of lines per page (i.e., they are not written in a larger module). Rather, the writing module was kept consistently the same as the pages decreased in size.

52 It is clear that this was a substantial danger from the fact that all but five copies of the two-volume *Etymologiae* are now orphans, as are all copies representing alternative segmentation. The history of Schaffhausen, Stadtbibliothek, MS Min. 42 (9th century, ½, Mainz, Books I–X), is also illustrative. Originally, it had perhaps formed a pair with Paris, Bibliothèque nationale de France, MS lat. 7587 (9th century, ²⁄₄, Mainz, Books XI–XX) or the lost Wiesbaden, Landesbibliothek, MS 242 (9th century, ½, Mainz, Books XI–XX), but already in the second half of the ninth century, the

Manner of segmentation	Average taille	Average taille (excl. Visigothic)
one volume	565 mm (22.24 in., 56 mss.)	562 mm (22.13 in., 50 mss.)
all integral copies	542 mm (21.34 in., 93 mss.)	534 mm (21.02 in., 85 mss.)
two volumes	517 mm (20.35 in., 20 mss.)	498 mm (19.60 in., 19 mss.)
other segmentation	463 mm (18.23 in., 10 mss.)	445 mm (17.52 in., 9 mss.)

Table 4.2. The average page taille of the surviving early medieval copies of the encyclopedic *Etymologiae* based on the manner of their segmentation.

As some of the earliest surviving copies of the encyclopedic *Etymologiae* from the second half of the eighth century are of the multi-volume type, it is clear that this strategy was pursued well before the Carolingian period.[53] Splitting is, in fact, more

---

sequence was broken up and the Schaffhausen codex was sent to St. Gall. St Gall, Stiftsbibliothek, Cod. Sang. 236 (9th century, ¾, St. Gall, Books XI–XX) seems to have been produced to complement it there; see Evina Steinová, "Two Carolingian Redactions of the *Etymologiae* from St. Gallen," *Mittellateinisches Jahrbuch* 56, no. 2 (2021): 322–23. However, this did not prevent the Schaffhausen codex from being separated from its sibling again and sent to the newly founded monastery at Schaffhausen in the early eleventh century, which acquired another manuscript, Schaffhausen, Stadtbibliothek, MS Min. 43 (10th/11th century, Reichenau, Books XI–XX), to complement it.

53 The oldest of them are Vatican City, Biblioteca Apostolica Vaticana, MS Vat. lat. 5763 (8th century, med., northern Italy, Books I–V); and Milan, Biblioteca Ambrosiana, MS L 99 sup. (8th century, ⅔, Bobbio, Books I–X). The latter manuscript shows traces of descending from an insular exemplar and has been seen for a long time as reflecting the insular line of transmission of the encyclopedic *Etymologiae*; see Bischoff, "Die europäische Verbreitung der Werke Isidors von Sevilla," 323; and Reydellet, "La diffusion des *Origines*," 433–36. Other eighth-century copies of the two-volume encyclopedic *Etymologiae* include Brussels, Koninklijke Bibliotheek, MS II 4856 (8th century, ex., Corbie, Books I–X); Karlsruhe, Badische Landesbibliothek, MS Aug. Perg. 57 (8th century, ⅔, northern

Century of production	Average taille, encyclopedic format	Average taille, other formats	Difference between the tailles
8th century	479 mm [18.86 in.] (9 mss.)	413 mm [16.26 in.] (12 mss.)	66 mm [2.6 in.]
9th century	541 mm [21.3 in.] (55 mss.)	435 mm [17.13 in] (209 mss.)	106 mm [4.33 in.]
10th–early 11th century	538 mm [21.18 in] (18 mss.)	461 mm [18.15 in.] (87 mss.)	77 mm [3.03 in.]

Table 4.3. A comparison of the average page tailles of the surviving early medieval manuscripts transmitting the *Etymologiae* by century and format. The averages in column "Average taille, encyclopedic format" do not include manuscripts in Visigothic minuscule due to their abnormally large size. If they were included, the average taille for the eighth century would remain unchanged, but it would increase to 550 mm (21.65 in.) for the ninth century and to 545 mm (21.46 in.) for the tenth and the beginning of the eleventh century.

common among pre-Carolingian copies of the encyclopedic *Etymologiae,* while a single-volume codex is a more typical Carolingian representative. Indeed, the corpus shows that those manuscripts of the encyclopedic *Etymologiae* that survive from the eighth century tend to be on the smaller side and display traces of experimentation that suggest efforts at making them small and economic, including alternative modes of segmentation, a preference for long lines and less ornamentation. The ninth-century manuscripts of the encyclopedic *Etymologiae* seem to break with this earlier trend and revert to being larger, single-volume, laid out in two columns, and embellished with decorative features. The relative growth of the page dimensions of the encyclopedic *Etymologiae* in the ninth century is clear from a comparison with manuscripts from other centuries, and with other manuscripts from the corpus (t. 4.3).

Italy, Books XIII–XX); Modena, Biblioteca Capitolare, MS O.I.17 (760–778, northern Italy, Books I–IX); and Paris, Bibliothèque nationale de France, MS lat. 13028 (8th century, ⅔, northern France, Books XVI–XX + IV).

As table 4.3 shows, the encyclopedic *Etymologiae* grew by almost 6.5 cm (2.56 in.) between the eighth and the ninth centuries only to get somewhat smaller again in the following centuries. No similar pattern of reduction and growth can be observed among other manuscripts transmitting the *Etymologiae*, which grew slightly each century in line with a general trend observed by Maniaci.[54] As a result, the difference between an average manuscript of the encyclopedic and non-encyclopedic *Etymologiae* reached 10.6 cm (4.33 in.) in the ninth century, while both earlier and later it was closer to 7 cm (2.76 in.).

Furthermore, in the eighth century the difference between a one-volume copy of the encyclopedic *Etymologiae* and a copy representing a different pattern of segmentation was minimal — the average taille of the former is 482 mm (18.98 in.) and of the latter 481 mm (18.94 in.). However, in the ninth century, a single-volume copy has an average taille of 541 mm (21.30 in.), while copies reflecting different segmentation patterns have an average taille of 491 mm (19.33 in.).[55] They are, thus, both noticeably smaller than single-volume copies and substantially similar to the surviving eighth-century manuscripts of the encyclopedic *Etymologiae*. The multi-volume copies of encyclopedic *Etymologiae*, it seems, reflect a continuation of the trend that reached its peak before the Carolingian period, while the Carolingian single-volume copies of the encyclopedic *Etymologiae* repre-

---

54 See Maniaci, "Costruzione e gestione dello spazio scritto," 484.

55 These averages exclude Visigothic manuscripts. If included, the average for ninth-century single-volume manuscripts would be 565 mm (22.24 in.) and 515 mm (20.28 in.) for ninth-century manuscripts following other patterns of segmentation. There is no substantial difference in the average tailles of ninth-century single-volume manuscripts copied in Caroline minuscule (524 mm [20.63 in.]) and in scripts other than Caroline and Visigothic minuscules (529 mm [20.83 in.]). However, there is an evident difference in the average tailles of ninth-century multi-volume manuscripts. The ninth-century multi-volume copies of the encyclopedic *Etymologiae* in Caroline minuscule have an average taille of 504 mm (19.84 in.), while the three manuscripts of this type copied in scripts other than the Caroline and the Visigothic minuscules, all produced around 800, have an average taille of 413 mm (16.26 in.).

sent a new stage in the material evolution of the *Etymologiae*. In the end, no surviving single-volume manuscript of the encyclopedic *Etymologiae* copied in Caroline minuscule has a taille smaller than 480 mm (18.9 in.), which represents an increase of 3 cm (1.18 in.) from the minimum of 450 mm reached in the pre-Carolingian period.[56]

After the Visigothic manuscripts with their average taille of 585 mm (23.03 in.), these Carolingian single-volume manuscripts come second as far as their page dimensions are concerned. However, their material similarities are not a consequence of a similar evolution. The Visigothic manuscripts of the encyclopedic *Etymologiae* seem to owe their large dimensions and other physical properties to a high degree of conservativism, stemming presumably from the reverence for tradition, Isidore's status in the Visigothic environment, and other ideological concerns.[57] The size of the Carolingian manuscripts, on the other hand, is a response to novel trends, rather than an indication of a return to older ideas. Perhaps the most important of these was the Caroline minuscule, which allowed fewer ligatures and abbreviations than earlier scripts and thus placed a new constraint on copyists' efforts to keep a codex of the *Etymologiae* small.[58] The growth of the encyclopedic *Etymologiae* should also be situated within broader developments in Carolingian book culture, such as the standardization and refinement of many aspects of book-production and an imposition

---

[56] Interestingly, the Carolingian manuscript with the smallest page taille, Zofingen, Stadtbibliothek, MS Pa 32 (9th century, ⅔, 480 mm [18.90 in.]), is a highly innovative copy of the *Etymologiae* representing a new Carolingian redaction of Isidore's encyclopedia; see Steinová, "Two Carolingian Redactions of the *Etymologiae* from St. Gallen," 306–21.

[57] As Prof. Ornato pointed out to me, if Visigothic manuscripts transmitting the *Etymologiae* are unusually large, this is not because they had to be, as there are manuscripts from the Iberian Peninsula with dimensions similar to the extra-Iberian manuscripts. Madrid, Biblioteca Nacional, MS Vitr. 14-3 (9th century, Spain) has, for example, a taille of only 517 mm (20.35 in.) and El Escorial, Monasterio San Lorenzo, MS T.II.24 (10th century, med., southern Spain) has a taille of only 500 mm (19.67 in.).

[58] Compare with Ganz, "Book Production," 789.

of stricter standards of book-copying. It may also indicate the growth of the wealth of *scriptoria*, which could more easily engage in ambitious book-copying projects and afford to produce even large-format manuscripts. The pressure to make the encyclopedic *Etymologiae* small, portable, and down-to-earth never vanished, as some of the manuscripts from the Carolingian environment continue to demonstrate, but it is overshadowed in the surviving manuscript evidence by a new kind of the encyclopedic *Etymologiae:* large, single-volume, perhaps even luxurious manuscripts that possessed many new features, including running titles that made them more searchable, layouts made cleaner and easier to navigate thanks to a clever deployment of colored initials and white spaces, as well as information sorted as lists, tables, and diagrams.[59] It can be, finally, noted that the return to single-volume and large-format encyclopedic *Etymologiae* coincided with the significant increase in the production of non-encyclopedic formats in the Carolingian period, which is perhaps not incidental.

The Materiality of Non-Canonical Formats of the *Etymologiae*

In contrast to the encyclopedic *Etymologiae,* the non-encyclopedic *Etymologiae* are a heterogeneous category including many different kinds of manuscripts as long as they transmit material from Isidore's encyclopedia otherwise than just as an excerpt. If we exclude the most anomalous and unique codices, such as one or two Visigothic giants and the four Bibles that acquired prefaces taken from the *Etymologiae,* manuscripts belonging to this category, nevertheless, share many traits that distinguish them from the encyclopedic *Etymologiae.* They transmit material from the *Etymologiae* anonymously or attribute it to

---

59 For example, the overview of metrical feet in *Etym.* Bk. I, chap. 17 became a table; the overview of symbols for weights in *Etym.* Bk. XVI, chap. 27 became a list with the symbols inserted, akin to bullet points, in the margin; and a T-O map was added to Book XIV.

someone else other than Isidore; or, if they do attribute it to the Sevillan bishop, they do so under a new title as a separate work. Paratextual elements original to the encyclopedic *Etymologiae*, including the *tituli* and numbering of capitula, are often missing in these manuscripts. Material from the *Etymologiae* is regularly juxtaposed to or combined with material from other texts, presupposing new uses. For the most part, manuscripts of non-encyclopedic *Etymologiae* are neither encyclopedias nor high-grade objects, nor were they always intended as library books. Most importantly, even if some of the manuscripts of non-encyclopedic *Etymologiae* — such as the eighteen items of this type that are classified as miscellanies — represent isolated instances of the appropriation of Isidore's text that defy comparison with other codices, many fit recognizable patterns that reveal the existence of several well-established non-encyclopedic transmission formats. These can be compared with the encyclopedic *Etymologiae* due to their textual, material, and functional homogeneity.

There is, for example, a non-encyclopedic format that I shall call the *Ars Isidori* using a name under which it appears in several early medieval manuscripts, a grammatical treatise that corresponds in content fully or to a significant extent to the first book of the encyclopedic *Etymologiae* (*De grammatica*).[60] It appears in early medieval grammatical compendia, explicitly evoking the teaching of grammar as a context of use.[61] The corpus preserves twenty-five early medieval manuscripts that transmit this entity.[62] Another type of an established non-encyclopedic for-

---

[60] The existence of the *Ars Isidori* is acknowledged in Maximilianus Manitius, *Geschichte der lateinischen Literatur des Mittelalters* (Munich: Beck, 1911), vol. 1, 67. I am currently preparing an article about this non-encyclopedic transmission format of the *Etymologiae*.

[61] For grammatical compendia, see Paolo de Paolis, "I codici miscellanei grammaticali altomedievali. Caratteristiche, funzione, destinazione," *Segno e testo* 2 (2004): 183–212, and Elizabeth Archibald, "Methods and Meaning of Basic Education in Carolingian Europe" (PhD Diss., Yale University, 2010). See also her essay in this volume.

[62] In addition, a cluster of grammatical treatises including the *Ars Isidori* were copied into one manuscript of the encyclopedic *Etymologiae* (Berlin,

mat of the *Etymologiae* appears in Carolingian pastoral collections and handbooks for priests from the beginning of the ninth century onwards.[63] This type of early medieval book connected with the education of Carolingian clergy commonly features material from Books VI–IX, dealing with God, saints, the Bible, the Church, and the sacraments.[64] In many manuscripts of this type we find this material in the form of excerpt collections woven together from snippets of the *Etymologiae,* and sometimes also others of Isidore's works, and frequently having the form of *interrogationes* and *responsiones* (questions and answers).[65] Al-

---

Staatsbibliothek, MS lat. fol. 641, 9th century, med., northern Italy), and six fragments containing material from the first book of the *Etymologiae,* given their small dimensions, represent remnants of non-encyclopedic *Etymologiae* and thus perhaps of manuscripts transmitting the *Ars Isidori.* Manuscripts transmitting this text were mostly copied in Caroline minuscule and date to the ninth century, although the oldest witnesses come from the last decades of the eighth century and one, preserved in Regensburg, is copied in Irish half-uncial.

63 For this type of manuscript, see especially Susan Keefe, *Water and the Word: Baptism and the Education of the Clergy in the Carolingian Empire,* Publications in Mediaeval Studies, 2 vols. (Notre Dame: University of Notre Dame Press, 2002), and Carine van Rhijn, "Manuscripts for Local Priests and the Carolingian Reforms," in *Men in the Middle. Local Priests in Early Medieval Europe,* ed. Carine van Rhijn and Steffen Patzold (Berlin: De Gruyter, 2016), 177–98. Quite a few of the surviving manuscripts of this type transmitting the material from the *Etymologiae* can be dated to the first quarter or the first half of the ninth century. Among the earliest are Albi, Bibliothèque municipale, MS 38bis (9th century, ¼, southern France); Bern, Burgerbibliothek, MS 225 (fols. 88–103) (9th century, ¼, western France); Karlsruhe, Badische Landesbibliothek, MS Aug. Perg. 18 (9th century, ¼, Reichenau); and Paris, Bibliothèque nationale de France, MS lat. 2175 (9th century, in., SW Germany).

64 See Keefe, *Water and the Word,* vol. 1, 22–27, and Carine van Rhijn, "Royal Politics in Small Worlds. Local Priests and the Implementation of Carolingian Correctio," in *Kleine Welten. Ländliche Gesellschaften im Karolingerreich,* ed. Thomas Kohl, Steffen Patzold, and Bernhard Zeller, Vorträge und Forschungen 87 (Ostfildern: Thorbecke, 2019), 9–10.

65 To name but a few, the *Collectio Sangermanensis,* the core of which is constituted by a set of questions and answers taken from the *Etymologiae,* survives fully or partially in seven manuscripts from the corpus. It has been edited in Michael Stadelmaier, *Die Collectio Sangermanensis XXI titulorum: eine systematische Kanonessammlung der frühen Karolingerzeit,*

Taille range	Encyclopedic *Etymologiae* (93 mss.)	*Ars Isidori* (25 mss.)	Pastoral excerpt collections (34 mss.)
< 350 mm (13.82 in.)	0	6	7
351–400 mm (13.82–15.75 in.)	2	5	7
401–450 mm (15.75–17.72 in.)	9	3	10
451–500 mm (17.72–19.67 in.)	16	10	4
501–550 mm (19.67–21.65 in.)	24	1	4
551–600 mm (21.65–23.62 in.)	23	0	1
601–650 mm (23.62–25.59 in.)	14	0	0
651–700 mm (25.59–27.56 in.)	3	0	1
> 700 mm (27.56 in.)	2	0	0

Table 4.4. The distribution of the surviving early medieval manuscripts transmitting the encyclopedic *Etymologiae,* the *Ars Isidori* and the pastoral excerpt collections based on their page tailles.

Freiburger Beiträge zur mittelalterlichen Geschichte 16 (Frankfurt am Main: Peter Lang, 2004). The *Collectio Unde,* another set of questions and answers taken from the *Etymologiae* whose name I took from the *unde* with which the questions are introduced, survives in ten complete early medieval manuscripts and one fragment. It is discussed in Michael Gorman, "The Carolingian Miscellany of Exegetical Texts in Albi 39 and Paris Lat. 2175," *Scriptorium* 51 (1997): 336–54. The collection *Interrogationes et responsiones de diversis causis* survives in eight manuscripts. It is described in María Adelaida Andrés Sanz, "Una reelaboración de textos isidorianos en forma de interrogationes et responsiones," *Helmantica: Revista de filología clásica y hebrea* 57, no. 172 (2006): 29–48. The collection *De catholica ecclesia et eius minisitris et de baptismatis officio,* survives in at least thirteen manuscripts; see Michael Andrieu, *Les ordines romani du haut*

together, the corpus includes thirty-four manuscripts that can either be classified as pastoral collections or be connected with pastoral care due to the texts they contain (exegesis, excerpts from patristic authors, expositions of the Creed, the baptism, the mass, etc.).

A common trait of manuscripts transmitting the *Ars Isidori* and the catechetical excerpt collections is their small size (t. 4.4). The average taille of manuscripts that transmit the first book of the *Etymologiae* turned *ars grammatica* is 413 mm (16.38 in.), while pastoral collections built from the material from Isidore's encyclopedia have an average taille of 419 mm (16.5 in.). If, moreover, two exceptionally large outliers are excluded from among the manuscripts transmitting pastoral excerpt collections, their average taille drops to 406 mm (15.98 in.).[66] The tailles of these two types of non-encyclopedic *Etymologiae* are, thus, 12–13 cm (5.12 in.) less than the average taille of an early medieval codex of the encyclopedic *Etymologiae* (542 mm [21.34 in.]) and almost 15–16 cm (6.3 in.) less than the average taille of a Carolingian single-volume copy of the *Etymologiae* (572 mm [22.52 in.]). Furthermore, only one manuscript of *ars Isidori* and six codices containing pastoral excerpt collections (or four excluding the outliers) have a taille above 500 mm (19.59 in.), which is true for 66 of the 95 surviving early medieval copies of the encyclopedic *Etymologiae* (70%) and thirty-four out of the thirty-six single-volume copies produced in Caroline minuscule (94%). By contrast, eleven manuscripts transmitting the *Ars Isidori* and fourteen codices containing the pastoral excerpt collection compiled from the *Etymologiae* have a taille below 400 mm (15.75 in.), which is true for only two surviving early medieval copies of the encyclopedic *Etymologiae*, both of

---

Moyen Âge, vol. 1, Spicilegium sacrum Lovaniense 11 (Leuven: Spicilegium sacrum Lovaniense, 1931), 338 and 479–80.

66 These are Karlsruhe, Badische Landesbibliothek, MS Aug. Perg. 18 (9th century, ¼, Reichenau) with a taille of 695 mm (27.36 in.), and Montecassino, Archivio dell'Abbazia, MS 205 (11th century, southern Italy) with a taille of 565 mm (22.24 in.).

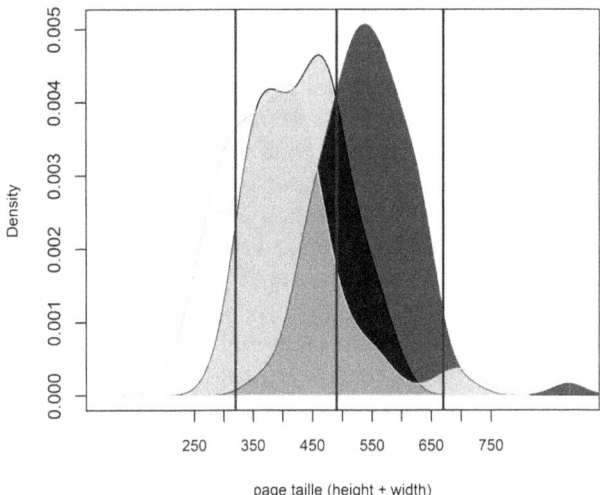

Fig. 4.2. The distribution of page tailles of the surviving early medieval manuscripts transmitting the encyclopedic *Etymologiae* (dark grey, ninety-five manuscripts), the non-encyclopedic *Etymologiae* in grammatical compendia (grey, forty-three manuscripts), and the non-encyclopedic *Etymologiae* in pastoral collections (light grey, twenty-nine manuscripts). The vertical lines mark the borders of Bozzolo and Ornato's typological categories: *petits* (<320 mm [12.6 in.]), *petit-moyens* (320–490 mm [12.6–19.29 in.]), *moyen-grands* (491–670 mm [19.33–26.38 in.]), and *grands* (>670 mm [26.38 in.]). This density graph was plotted with R.

a multi-volume kind.[67] Manuscripts transmitting both types of non-encyclopedic *Etymologiae* belong mostly to Bozzolo and Ornato's *petit-moyens* category (320–490 mm [12.6–19.3 in.]) rather than to the *moyen-grands* (491–670 mm [19.33–26.38 in.]) like the majority of the encyclopedic *Etymologiae* (fig. 4.2).

---

67 It should, moreover, be observed that the 43 manuscripts from the corpus that can be classified as grammatical compendia, a category including the 25 manuscripts of the *Ars Isidori* as well as other manuscripts containing smaller bits of the *Etymologiae,* have an average taille of 433 mm (16.93 in.).

The two types of non-encyclopedic *Etymologiae* we just compared to the encyclopedic *Etymologiae* also circulated in the early Middle Ages in the humblest but also perhaps the most common material format available, namely as unbound small *libelli*.[68] Given the extremely low survival rate of such booklets, it is a miracle that the corpus preserves six of them: five of the *Ars Isidori* and one of a catechetical excerpt collection.[69] The practically-focused design is immediately apparent from the fact that five of the six *libelli* have a taille in the range of 300–350 mm (11.81–13.79 in.), making them among the smallest surviving early medieval manuscripts transmitting the *Etymologiae*.[70] These *libelli* are all that survives of what once may have been a sizable but highly perishable population of handbooks used in education and clerical instruction.[71] Materially, they repre-

---

68 On *libelli,* see Pamela Robinson, "The 'Booklet': A Self-contained Unit in Composite Manuscripts," in *Codicologica* 3: *Essais typologiques,* ed. A. Gruys and J.P. Gumbert (Leiden: Brill, 1980), 46–69; Patrick Andrist, Paul Canart, and Marilena Maniaci, *La syntaxe du codex: essai de codicologie structurale,* Bibliologia 34 (Turnhout: Brepols, 2013), 15–17; and Pascale Bourgain, "The Circulation of Texts in Manuscript Culture," in *The Medieval Manuscript Book: Cultural Approaches,* ed. Michael Robert Johnston and Michael Van Dussen, Cambridge Studies in Medieval Literature 94 (Cambridge: Cambridge University Press, 2015), 144.

69 The four grammatical booklets are Leiden, Universiteitsbibliotheek, MS Voss. Lat. O 41 (9th century, ¼, NE France); London, British Library, MS Harley 2713 (fols. 1–34) (9th century, ¼, NE France); Oxford, Bodleian Library, MS Junius 25 (fols. 134–151) (9th century, Murbach); Paris, Bibliothèque nationale de France, MS lat. 11278 (9th century, ½, southern France or Italy?); and Trier, Bibliothek des Bischöflichen Priesterseminars, MS 100 (fols. 1–16) (9th century, ¾, northern France). The catechetical booklet is St. Gall, Stiftsbibliothek, Cod. Sang. 879 (9th century, ⅔, Lyon). Perhaps also to be counted among these *libelli* is St. Gall, Stiftsbibliothek, Cod. Sang. 876, bound together from originally separate booklets; see De Paolis, "Un manuale scolastico da Corbie," 82.

70 The exception is the Junius manuscript with a taille of 498 mm (19.60 in.). Its size and other features suggest that it may represent quires removed from a manuscript of the encyclopedic *Etymologiae*, to be circulated separately as a *libellus*.

71 See Keefe, *Water and the Word,* vol. 1, 16, and Cardelle de Hartmann, "Uso y reception de las *Etymologiae* de Isidoro," 489. As Keefe notes, the early medieval pastoral *libelli* were produced from model books that served as

sent the extreme opposite of the codex *nimiae magnitudinis* assembled by Isidore, making it possible for the contents of the *Etymologiae* to reach a substantially broader audience than the encyclopedic format.

However, not all non-encyclopedic formats are notable for their small dimensions. For example, certain collections of canon law acquired chapter 16 of Book VI of the *Etymologiae* (*De canonibus conciliorum*, "On the accepted councils") as a preface in the Carolingian environment.[72] The average taille of the eleven surviving manuscripts of canon law with this preface is 537 mm (21.14 in.), that is, it resembles the average taille of extra-Iberian encyclopedic *Etymologiae* (534 mm [21.02 in.]) rather than the average tailles of grammatical compendia and pastoral collections containing material from Isidore's encyclopedia (413 mm [16.38 in.] and 419 mm [16.5 in.], respectively). The six manuscripts of the Bible included in the corpus, because they feature excerpts from the *Etymologiae*, have an even larger average taille of 556 mm (21.89 in.). As these two examples make clear, the physical size of manuscripts transmitting the non-encyclopedic *Etymologiae* did not depend on whether they transmit material from Isidore's encyclopedia but rather on the purpose they served and audiences to which they catered. Canon law collections and Bibles transmitting the material from the *Etymologiae* are large-format because they are canon law collections and Bibles, which tend to be among the larger early medieval books,[73] just as grammatical compendia and pastoral collections transmitting non-encyclopedic formats of the *Etymologiae* are

---

exemplars for their copying. As in the case of bishops' and priests' books, some of the surviving early medieval grammatical compendia are clearly such model books. In one rare case, we possess both the model book (Bern, Burgerbibliothek, MS 207, 9th century, ½, Fleury), and a teacher's book containing an *Ars Isidori* copied from it (Leiden, Universiteitsbibliotheek, MS Voss. Lat. Q 86, 9th century, med., Fleury).

72 See Friedrich Maassen, *Geschichte der Quellen und der Literatur des Canonischen Rechts im Abendlande* I: *Die Rechtssammlungen bis zur Mitte des 9. Jahrhunderts* (Graz: Leuschner & Lubensky, 1870), 352.

73 Bibles tend to have large page dimensions; see Bozzolo and Ornato, *Pour une histoire du livre manuscrit au Moyen Âge*, 265.

small in size because this is the general property of early medieval grammatical compendia and pastoral collections. It was therefore the marriage of the *Etymologiae* with these types of medieval books that led Isidore's work to inhabit ever smaller pages.

Crucially, the incorporation of the *Etymologiae* into books that were by nature small, light, portable, relatively inexpensive to produce, and practical for certain kinds of uses may have released some of the pressure that, as we have seen, drove early medieval scribes to look for ways to make manuscripts of the encyclopedic *Etymologiae* smaller in size. Indeed, the de-canonization of the *Etymologiae* was, alongside segmentation, another viable strategy to bring Isidore's work below the minimal threshold taille of 450 mm (17.72 in.) that few encyclopedic copies of the *Etymologiae* surpassed in the early Middle Ages. The occasional surviving pre-Carolingian manuscripts of non-encyclopedic *Etymologiae* demonstrate that this strategy was developed before the advent of the Carolingian period.[74] Yet, as the dates of the oldest witnesses of many formats of non-encyclopedic *Etymologiae* suggests, their boom came in the ninth century. The explosion of the *artes Isidori*, Isidorian question-and-answer collections, and other iterations of the non-encyclopedic *Etymologiae* that followed in the wake of the Carolingian reform movement indicate that production of non-encyclopedic *Etymologiae* was the Carolingian strategy of choice. Segmentation, on the other hand, seems to have been favored in the pre-Carolingian world, but to have lost its appeal at the same time as the production of non-encyclopedic formats gathered pace.

The fact that non-encyclopedic *Etymologiae* were able to fill niches that the encyclopedic format could not may partially explain the increase in the size of the encyclopedic *Etymologiae* in the Carolingian period. The non-encyclopedic *Etymologiae* in

---

[74] The Irish, in particular, seem to have been pioneers, compiling several computistic non-encyclopedic formats as a result of their interest in time reckoning. See Immo Warntjes, "Isidore of Seville and the Formation of Medieval Computus," in *A Companion to Isidore of Seville,* ed. Andrew Fear and Jamie Wood (Leiden: Brill, 2020), 25–26.

its many new shapes and context-specific appropriations satisfied the needs of Carolingian users who wished to use Isidore's work as a schoolbook, a pedagogical aid, an instructional manual for priests-in-training, an introduction to specific disciplines, or a technical text on this or that subject. As a result, the encyclopedic *Etymologiae* profiled more clearly as a scholarly library book — that is, a book with one specific use. As two centuries of pressure exerted on the encyclopedic *Etymologiae* were lifted, it began to increase in size again. Paradoxically, this bifurcation of encyclopedic and non-encyclopedic *Etymologiae* may have reinforced the material differentiation of the two branches of transmission and driven them further apart. The more *artes Isidori* and Isidorian catechetical collections circulated in the Carolingian period, the less need there was for the encyclopedic *Etymologiae* to leave their natural habitat in monastic and cathedral libraries.

Who Was Reading the *Etymologiae* in the Early Middle Ages and How?

The trajectories of the material development of the *Etymologiae* in the early Middle Ages leads to the question of the intended and actual audiences of the encyclopedic and non-encyclopedic formats. When we wish to consider the role of users on the material properties of the manuscripts transmitting the *Etymologiae,* we must not forget that it was a two-sided exchange. Scribes and readers determined how a medieval manuscript text looked, but their copying and reading habits were also shaped by the physical format of a text. On the one hand, the material evolution of the *Etymologiae* described above reflects the conditions and intentions of particular social, cultural, and economic milieux. It sketches a story, in which many pre-Carolingian *scriptoria* may have struggled to reproduce the lavishness of Isidore's much-sought-after text or not to invest too much parchment into its production, as well as of the ambition of Carolingian *scriptoria* to increase the prestige of Isidore's encyclopedia just as his status was rising among Carolingian intellectuals.

On the other hand, however, the material form of a book also exerted influence on users, affecting who had access to certain authors, genres, texts, or constellations of texts, how they were read, and even how users interpreted them. As the hundreds of surviving early medieval manuscripts transmitting non-encyclopedic *Etymologiae* attest, the early Middle Ages, and the Carolingian period in particular, recognized many Isidores besides Isidore the Encyclopedist. Many Carolingian schoolboys (and perhaps also the odd schoolgirl) knew Isidore as a grammarian akin to Donatus, or perhaps their schoolmasters. Many Carolingian clerics-in-training and priests were familiar with Isidore the Catechist akin to the reforming Carolingian bishops, and their seniors. There were also several other Isidores who had little to do with the historical bishop of Seville and his seventh-century oeuvre, but were a fixture of the ninth-century intellectual landscape.[75] Many of the early medieval users of the *Etymologiae* would never encounter Isidore in other guises because their limited education never took them beyond the *Ars Isidori* or a question-and-answer collection serving the bettering of their Christian souls.[76] Thus, the material properties of the surviving early medieval manuscripts of the *Etymologiae* not only reveal a history consisting of downsizing and growth, but

---

[75] Book IV of the canonical *Etymologiae* (*De medicina*, "On medicine") is, for example, transmitted in Carolingian and later Beneventan medical compendia, sometimes as an epistle of Hippocrates; see Arsenio Ferraces Rodríguez, "Isidoro de Sevilla y los textos de medicina," in *"Isidorus medicus": Isidoro de Sevilla y los textos de medicina,* ed. Arsenio Ferraces Rodríguez, Monografías 113 (A Coruña: Universidade da Coruña, 2005), 11–37. The first two sections of Book III (*De arithmetica* and *De geometria*, known together as *De mathematica*) began to circulate as a preface to Boethius's *Institutio arithmetica* in Carolingian environments by mid-ninth century, perhaps as a result of the introduction of Boethius's works to schools; see John J. Contreni, "The Pursuit of Knowledge in Carolingian Europe," in *The Gentle Voices of Teachers: Aspects of Learning in the Carolingian Age*, ed. Richard Sullivan (Columbus: Ohio University Press, 1995), 124–25.

[76] Compare with the description of schools in Contreni, "The Pursuit of Knowledge," 111–14.

also show that medieval users of this text perceived it rather differently both from how its author envisaged it, and from how we have been taught to see it as a consequence of attitudes fostered by nineteenth-century scholarship.[77]

Even though the survival of ninety-five early medieval copies of the encyclopedic *Etymologiae* suggests that several hundred of these encyclopedic manuscripts were produced in the early Middle Ages, these were, for the most part, in-house scholarly copies preserved in monastic and cathedral libraries.[78] It is unclear who exactly had access to these scholarly copies. The few users that can be identified based on their marginalia or literary activity are overwhelmingly highly literate elite users, including well-known scholars.[79] Indeed, we should not assume that anyone beyond the learned few read and used the encyclopedic *Etymologiae* in a manner envisaged by some modern scholars. By contrast, an average user of the non-encyclopedic formats of the *Etymologiae* described above was not an elite intellectual, nor did they necessarily have access to a monastic or cathedral

---

77 See most recently John Henderson, *The Medieval World of Isidore of Seville: Truth from Words* (Cambridge: Cambridge University Press, 2007). The author espouses a view that the *Etymologiae* was read in a continuous manner. However, the *Etymlogiae* were meant to be consulted, not read.

78 Many of them have never left the walls of the institutions that produced them, making it clear that they were among the most travel-resistant books in the early Middle Ages; see Steinová, "The Oldest Manuscript Tradition of the *Etymologiae*," 112.

79 Hrabanus Maurus used the *Etymologiae* as a source of several of his works, notably of *De rerum naturis*. Walahfrid Strabo excerpted parts of Book I into his *collectaneum;* see Cardelle de Hartmann, "Uso y reception de las *Etymologiae* de Isidoro," 487–88. Martin of Laon included bits from the *Etymologiae* into his *collectaneum* in Laon, Bibliothèque municipale Suzanne Martinet, MS 468 (9th century, ¾, Laon); see John J. Contreni, *Codex Laudunensis 468: A Ninth-Century Guide to Virgil, Sedulius and the Liberal Arts,* Armarium Codicum Insignium 3 (Turnhout: Brepols, 1984), 17–18. Marginal annotations of Paul the Deacon are preserved in the twelfth-century Rome, Biblioteca Vallicelliana, A 18; see Claudia Villa, "Uno schedario di Paolo Diacono. Festo e Grauso di Ceneda," *Italia medioevale e umanistica* 27 (1984): 56–80. The *Etymologiae* were also annotated by Leo of Vercelli; see Simona Gavinelli, "Leone di Vercelli postillatore di codici," *Aevum* 75 (2001): 233–62.

library. It is true that none of the established non-encyclopedic formats of the *Etymologiae* identified in this chapter survives in numbers comparable to the encyclopedic *Etymologiae*. However, we need to keep in mind that material properties affected the rates of survival of early medieval manuscripts. As many of the most influential non-encyclopedic formats of the *Etymologiae* were small, of modest quality, designed to be portable, and perhaps even unbound, they likely disappeared at substantially higher rates than encyclopedic *Etymologiae*. Indeed, the smaller and more modest they were, the more significant this difference in the number of surviving witnesses may be in comparison with the manuscripts of the encyclopedic *Etymologiae* — the *libelli* discussed above are just one example. For this reason, we must seriously consider the possibility that some of the non-encyclopedic formats rivaled the encyclopedic *Etymologiae* in the extent of their diffusion and importance in the early Middle Ages. The *Ars Isidori* and the various embodiments of Isidore the Catechist, in particular, may have had a transformative effect on the status of Isidore as an author in the Carolingian period.

Paradoxically, while the *Etymologiae* became the encyclopedia of the Carolingian age *par excellence,* it was also regularly treated as an educational text, utilized for teaching on various levels by generations of schoolmasters, reformers, and other education specialists.[80] The more these two distinct domains of uses solidified in the Carolingian period, the more manuscripts embodying them differed materially and the more they reinforced the separation of these domains. Thus, the codices of the encyclopedic *Etymologiae* grew larger, more ornate, and more majestic, reverting to the ideal envisaged for them by Isidore after having broken away from it in the seventh and the eighth centuries. Many formats of the non-encyclopedic *Etymologiae,* on the other hand, acquired a life of their own, circulating as

---

80 As is observed in John J. Contreni, "The Carolingian Renaissance: Education and Literary Culture," in *The New Cambridge Medieval History,* ed. Rosamond McKitterick (Cambridge: Cambridge University Press, 1995), vol. 2, 726, and Codoñer Merino, "Transmisión y recepción de las Etimologías," 23.

self-sufficient texts for centuries after the decline of the Carolingian *scriptoria* that created them.[81] We must ask whether even those who moved between these two domains, as many Carolingian scholars did in different stages of their lives, saw the non-encyclopedic formats of the *Etymologiae* as related to Isidore's encyclopedia. It is possible that medieval users saw them as categorically different because they rarely treated a text as an abstract object that could be separated from its material embodiment. Instead, they thought with their hands, which would tell them that the big, heavy, and immobile encyclopedia perched on a lectern in their monastery was unlike the small and light *libellus* that they carried to school in their youth.

Sometimes, we should follow the example of those medieval scholars, and peek from behind our laptop screens to think with our hands (and backs). Only once we are forced to carry those early medieval books back and forth in libraries and wrestle with their pages, trying to keep them open on our desks, does something as abstract as the physical dimensions, or even worse, the taille of a manuscript, acquire real significance. It is one thing to read that an average one-volume manuscript of the *Etymologiae* copied in Caroline minuscule has a taille of 572 mm (22.52 in.), and quite another to have to use such a manuscript *in situ*, being forced to consider the operations for which such a large and heavy book could be used. It is only then that one can appreciate a taille difference of 5, 10, or 15 cm (1.97, 3.94, or 5.91 in.). For those who cannot immediately rush to a library, it may be enlightening to know that an average Carolingian one-vol-

---

[81] The *Ars Isidori* can be encountered as a model for the teaching of grammar up until the twelfth century; see Roger Baron, "La grammaire de Hugues de Saint-Victor," *Studi medievali* 7 (1966): 835–55, and Evina Steinová, *"Notam superponere studui": The Use of Annotation Symbols in the Early Middle Ages* (Turnhout: Brepols, 2019), 154. The Carolingian catechetical collections likewise continued to be transmitted well into the central Middle Ages. The excerpt collection *Interrogationes et responsiones de diversis causis*, for example, survives in six manuscripts dating from the eleventh to the fifteenth century and the collection *De catholica ecclesia et eius minisitris et de baptismatis officio* appears in nine eleventh- to thirteenth-century codices.

ume copy of the *Etymologiae* has pages slightly larger than Aris's *Explicatio formarum litterarum* (but is substantially thicker and heavier given the weight of parchment and wooden boards). At the same time, those non-encyclopedic *Etymologiae* with tailles of around 400 mm (15.75 in.) are roughly the equivalent of Bischoff's *Latin Paleography,* and perhaps not much heavier, depending on the number of folios and whether they were bound or not.

The shrinking of the *Etymologiae* in the early Middle Ages was neither accidental nor haphazard. It was a marvelous development, stimulated by a cocktail of factors. Early medieval scribes emerge from this story as enthusiastic and intelligent innovators, challenging the idea that the early Middle Ages was an era of conservativism and limited progress. We may be further surprised by their creativity if we study the material aspect of other early medieval textual traditions.

Bibliography

Manuscripts
Albi, Bibliothèque municipale, MS 38bis. https://cecilia.mediatheques.grand-albigeois.fr/idurl/1/113.
Berlin, Staatsbibliothek, MS Dep. Breslau 16.
Berlin, Staatsbibliothek, MS Ham. 689.
Berlin, Staatsbibliothek, MS lat. fol. 641.
Bern, Burgerbibliothek, MS 207. https://www.e-codices.unifr.ch/en/searchresult/list/one/bbb/0207.
Bern, Burgerbibliothek, MS 225.
Brussels, Koninklijke Bibliotheek, MS II 4856. https://uurl.kbr.be/1558122.
Cambridge, Trinity College, MS B.15.33. https://mss-cat.trin.cam.ac.uk/Manuscript/B.15.33.
Cambridge, University Library, MS Add. 5948. https://cudl.lib.cam.ac.uk/view/MS-ADD-05948/1.
Chartres, Bibliothèque municipale, MS 16. https://arca.irht.cnrs.fr/ark:/63955/md71ng451q9n.
Einsiedeln, Stiftsbibliothek, MS 167.
El Escorial, Monasterio San Lorenzo, MS D.I.1. https://rbdigital.realbiblioteca.es/s/rbme/item/13263.
El Escorial, Monasterio San Lorenzo, MS D.I.2. https://rbdigital.realbiblioteca.es/s/rbme/item/13432.
El Escorial, Monasterio San Lorenzo, MS P.I.6. https://rbdigital.realbiblioteca.es/s/rbme/item/14046.
El Escorial, Monasterio San Lorenzo, MS P.I.7. https://rbdigital.realbiblioteca.es/s/rbme/item/14048.
El Escorial, Monasterio San Lorenzo, MS T.II.24. https://rbdigital.realbiblioteca.es/s/rbme/item/14115.
El Escorial, Monasterio San Lorenzo, MS &.I.14. https://rbdigital.realbiblioteca.es/s/rbmc/itcm/13281.
Karlsruhe, Badische Landesbibliothek, MS Aug. Perg. 18. https://digital.blb-karlsruhe.de/id/20869.
Karlsruhe, Badische Landesbibliothek, MS Aug. Perg. 57. https://digital.blb-karlsruhe.de/id/1560019.

Krakow, Biblioteka Jagiellońska, MS 484. https://jbc.bj.uj.edu.pl/publication/239495.

Laon, Bibliothèque municipale Suzanne Martinet, MS 468. https://bibliotheque-numerique.ville-laon.fr/idurl/1/1473.

Leiden, Universiteitsbibliotheek, MS Voss. Lat. F 74. https://primarysources.brillonline.com/browse/vossiani-latini/vlf-074-isidorus-hispalensis.

Leiden, Universiteitsbibliotheek, MS Voss. Lat. O 41. https://primarysources.brillonline.com/browse/vossiani-latini/vlo-041-eutyches-grammaticalia-isidorus-alphabeta.

Leiden, Universiteitsbibliotheek, MS Voss. Lat. Q 86. https://primarysources.brillonline.com/browse/vossiani-latini/vlq-086-arator-prosper-sedulius-pstertullianus-cato-avianus-anthologia-latina-martialis-avitus-isidorus.

London, British Library, MS Add. 34389.

London, British Library, MS Egerton 267.

London, British Library, MS Harley 2713.

Madrid, Biblioteca Nacional, MS Vitr. 14-3. http://bdh.bne.es/bnesearch/detalle/bdh0000051810.

Madrid, Real Academia de la Historia, MS 25. https://bibliotecadigital.rah.es/es/consulta/registro.do?id=58.

Milan, Biblioteca Ambrosiana, MS L 99 sup. https://ambrosiana.comperio.it/opac/detail/view/ambro:catalog:77314.

Modena, Biblioteca Capitolare, MS O.I.17. https://www.archiviodiocesano.mo.it/opere-digitalizzate/cat/20-o-i-17-sancti-isidori-episcopi-liber-etimologiarum.

Montecassino, Archivio dell'Abbazia, MS 205.

Munich, Bayerische Staatsbibliothek, MS Clm 6275. https://daten.digitale-sammlungen.de/~db/0006/bsb00065380/images/.

Oxford, Bodleian Library, MS Junius 25. https://digital.bodleian.ox.ac.uk/objects/4df4cdd2-14d8-4256-ae07-a09917b3408e/.

Paris, Bibliothèque nationale de France, MS lat. 2175. http://archivesetmanuscrits.bnf.fr/ark:/12148/cc60068x.

Paris, Bibliothèque nationale de France, MS lat. 7587. http://archivesetmanuscrits.bnf.fr/ark:/12148/cc668233.
Paris, Bibliothèque nationale de France, MS lat. 7670. https://gallica.bnf.fr/ark:/12148/btv1b525190518.
Paris, Bibliothèque nationale de France, MS lat. 11278. http://archivesetmanuscrits.bnf.fr/ark:/12148/cc728933.
Paris, Bibliothèque nationale de France, MS lat. 13028. http://archivesetmanuscrits.bnf.fr/ark:/12148/cc74149k.
Paris, Bibliothèque nationale de France, MS lat. 14085.
Paris, Bibliothèque nationale de France, MS lat. 17159. https://gallica.bnf.fr/ark:/12148/btv1b52517128v.
Rome, Biblioteca Vallicelliana, MS A 18.
Schaffhausen, Stadtbibliothek, MS Min. 42.
Schaffhausen, Stadtbibliothek, MS Min. 43. https://www.e-codices.unifr.ch/en/list/one/sbs/min0043.
St. Gall, Stiftsbibliothek, Cod. Sang. 231–232. https://www.e-codices.unifr.ch/en/list/one/csg/0231.
St. Gall, Stiftsbibliothek, Cod. Sang. 233. https://www.e-codices.unifr.ch/en/list/one/csg/0233.
St. Gall, Stiftsbibliothek, Cod. Sang. 236. https://www.e-codices.unifr.ch/en/list/one/csg/0236.
St. Gall, Stiftsbibliothek, Cod. Sang. 876. https://www.e-codices.unifr.ch/en/list/one/csg/0876.
St. Gall, Stiftsbibliothek, Cod. Sang. 879. https://www.e-codices.unifr.ch/en/list/one/csg/0879.
Trier, Bibliothek des Bischöflichen Priesterseminars, MS 100. http://dfg-viewer.de/v3/?set[mets]=http%3A%2F%2Fzimks68.uni-trier.de%2Fstmatthias%2FS0100%2FS0100-digitalisat.xml.
Tours, Bibliothèque municipale, MS 844. https://arca.irht.cnrs.fr/ark:/63955/md60cv43qw34.
Turin, Biblioteca Universitaria, MS D.III.19.
Vatican City, Biblioteca Apostolica Vaticana, MS Vat. lat. 5763. https://digi.vatlib.it/view/MSS_Vat.lat.5763.
Vatican City, Biblioteca Apostolica Vaticana, MS Vat. lat. 7803. https://digi.vatlib.it/view/MSS_Vat.lat.7803.
Vercelli, Biblioteca Capitolare, MS CCII (29).

Wiesbaden, Landesbibliothek, MS 242.
Wolfenbüttel, Herzog August Bibliothek, MS Guelf. 64 Weiss. http://diglib.hab.de/?db=mss&list=ms&id=64-weiss.
Würzburg, Universitätsbibliothek, MS M.p.th.f. 143. http://vb.uni-wuerzburg.de/ub/mpthf143/index.html.
Zofingen, Stadtbibliothek, MS Pa 32. https://www.e-codices.unifr.ch/en/zos/pa0032.

Secondary

Amsler, Mark E. *Etymology and Grammatical Discourse in Late Antiquity and the Early Middle Ages.* Amsterdam: John Benjamins Publishing, 1989. DOI: 10.1075/sihols.44.

Andrés Sanz, María Adelaida. "Una reelaboración de textos isidorianos en forma de interrogationes et responsiones." *Helmantica: Revista de filología clásica y hebrea* 57, no. 172 (2006): 29–48. DOI: 10.36576/summa.29381.

Andrist, Patrick, Paul Canart, and Marilena Maniaci. *La syntaxe du codex: essai de codicologie structurale.* Bibliologia 34. Turnhout: Brepols, 2013.

Archibald, Elizabeth. "Methods and Meaning of Basic Education in Carolingian Europe." PhD Diss., Yale University, 2010.

Baron, Roger. "La grammaire de Hugues de Saint-Victor." *Studi medievali* 7 (1966): 835–55.

Bischoff, Bernhard. "Die europäische Verbreitung der Werke Isidors von Sevilla." In *Isidoriana: colección de estudios sobre Isidore de Sevilla,* edited by Manuel C. Díaz y Díaz, 317–44. León: Centro de estudios San Isidoro, 1961.

———. *Katalog der festländischen Handschriften des neunten Jahrhunderts: (mit Ausnahme der wisigotischen).* Edited by Birgit Ebersperger. 4 Volumes. Veröffentlichungen der Kommission für die Herausgabe der mittelalterlichen Bibliothekskataloge Deutschlands und der Schweiz. Wiesbaden: Harrassowitz, 1998–2017.

Bourgain, Pascale. "The Circulation of Texts in Manuscript Culture." In *The Medieval Manuscript Book: Cultural Approaches,* edited by Michael Robert Johnston and Michael

Van Dussen, 140–59. Cambridge Studies in Medieval
Literature 94. Cambridge: Cambridge University Press, 2015.
DOI: 10.1017/CBO9781107588851.008.

Bozzolo, Carla, and Ezio Ornato. *Pour une histoire du livre
manuscrit au Moyen Âge: Trois essais de codicologie
quantitative*. Equipe de recherche sur l'humanisme français.
Textes et études 2. Paris: Editions du CNRS, 1980.

Brown, T. Julian. "The Oldest Irish Manuscripts and their Late
Antique Background." In *Irland und Europa. Die Kirche
im Frühmittelalter,* edited by Próinséas Ní Chatháin and
Michael Richter, 311–27. Stuttgart: Klett-Cotta, 1984.

Büren, Veronika von. "La place du manuscrit Ambr. L 99 sup.
dans la transmission des *Étymologies* d'Isidore de Séville." In
Nuove ricerche su codici in scrittura latina dell'Ambrosiana,
edited by Mirella Ferrari and Marco Navoni, 25–44. Milan:
Vita e Pensiero, 2007.

Cardelle de Hartmann, Carmen. "Uso y reception de las
Etymologiae de Isidoro." In *Wisigothica. After M. C. Díaz
y Díaz,* edited by Carmen Codoñer Merino and Paulo
Farmhouse Alberto, 477–502. mediEVI 3. Florence: SISMEL
Edizioni del Galluzzo, 2014.

———. "Wissensorganisation und Wissensvermittlung im
ersten Teil von Isidors *Etymologiae* (Bücher I–X)." In
*Exzerpieren — Kompilieren — Tradieren: Transformationen
des Wissens zwischen Spätantike und Frühmittelalter,* edited
by Stephan Dusil, Gerald Schwedler, and Raphael Schwitter,
85–104. Millenium-Studien 64. Berlin: De Gruyter, 2017.
DOI: 10.1515/9783110516340-007.

Castro Correa, Ainoa. "Online Catalogue of Visigothic Script
Codices." http://www.litteravisigothica.com/visigothic-
script-topics/codicology.

Cinato, Franck. "Que nous apprennent les écritures des plus
anciens témoins du *Liber Glossarum* sur l'archétype?"
Dossiers d'HEL 10 (2016): 59–124.

Codoñer Merino, Carmen. *Introducción al Libro X de las
"Etymologiae": su lugar dentro de esta obra, su valor como*

diccionario. Logroño: Fundación San Millán de la Cogolla, 2002.

———. "Transmisión y recepción de las Etimologías." In *Estudios de latín medieval hispánico. Actas del V Congreso Internacional de Latín Medieval Hispánico,* edited by José Martínez Gázquez, Óscar Luis de la Cruz Palma, and Cándida Ferrero Hernández, 5–26. Florence: SISMEL Edizioni del Galluzzo, 2011.

Codoñer Merino, Carmen, José Carlos Martín Iglesias, and María Adelaida Andrés Sanz. "Isidorus Hispalensis Ep." In *La trasmissione dei testi latini del medioevo/Medieval Texts and Their Transmission,* Mediaeval Latin Texts and Their Transmission 2, edited by Paulo Chiesa and Lucia Castaldi, 274–417. Florence: SISMEL Edizioni del Galluzzo, 2005.

Colombi, Emanuela. "Assetto librario ed elementi paratestuali nei manoscritti tardoantichi e carolingi del 'De civitate dei'di Agostino: alcune riflessioni." *Segno e testo* 11 (2013): 183–272.

Contreni, John J. *Codex Laudunensis 468: A Ninth-Century Guide to Virgil, Sedulius, and the Liberal Arts.* Armarium Codicum Insignium 3. Turnhout: Brepols, 1984.

———. "The Carolingian Renaissance: Education and Literary Culture." In *The New Cambridge Medieval History,* Volume 2: *c. 700–c. 900,* edited by Rosamond McKitterick, 709–57. Cambridge: Cambridge University Press, 1995. DOI: 10.1017/CHOL9780521362924.030.

———. "The Pursuit of Knowledge in Carolingian Europe." In *The Gentle Voices of Teachers: Aspects of Learning in the Carolingian Age,* edited by Richard E. Sullivan, 106–41. Columbus: Ohio University Press, 1995.

De Paolis, Paolo. "I codici miscellanei grammaticali altomedievali. Caratteristiche, funzione, destinazione." *Segno e testo* 2 (2004): 183–212.

———. "Un manuale scolastico da Corbie." In *Vestigia notitiai. Scritti in memoria di Michelangelo Giusta,* edited by Edoardo Bona, Carlos Levy, and Giuseppina Magnaldi, 81–106. Alessandria: Edizioni dell'Orso, 2012.

Díaz y Díaz, Manuel Cecilio. "Introdución." In *San Isidoro de Sevilla. Etimologías: edicion bilingüe*, ed. José Oroz Reta and Manuel-A. Marcos Casquero, 1–2. Madrid: Biblioteca de Autores Cristianos, 2004.

Dorofeeva, Anna. "Reading Early Medieval Miscellanies." In *Scribes and the Presentation of Texts (from Antiquity to c. 1550)*, edited by Barbara A. Shailor, Consuelo W. Dutschke, Kyle Conrau-Lewis, Kristen Herdman, Carson Koepke, and Alexander Peña, 495–514. Turnhout: Brepols, 2021. DOI: 10.1484/M.BIB-EB.5.124988.

Elfassi, Jacques. "Isidore of Seville and the *Etymologies*." In *A Companion to Isidore of Seville*, edited by Andrew Fear and Jamie Wood, 245–78. Leiden: Brill, 2020. DOI: 10.1163/9789004415454_010.

Fear, Andrew, and Jamie Wood, eds. *A Companion to Isidore of Seville*. Brill's Companions to the Christian Tradition 87. Leiden: Brill, 2020.

———, eds. *Isidore of Seville and His Reception in the Early Middle Ages: Transmitting and Transforming Knowledge*. Late Antique and Early Medieval Iberia 2. Amsterdam: Amsterdam University Press, 2016. DOI: 10.5040/9789048551224.

Ferraces Rodríguez, Arsenio. "Isidoro de Sevilla y los textos de medicina." In *"Isidorus medicus": Isidoro de Sevilla y los textos de medicina*, edited by Arsenio Ferraces Rodríguez, Monografias 113, 11–37. A Coruña: Universidade da Coruña, 2005.

Fontaine, Jacques. *Isidore de Séville et la culture classique dans l'Espagne wisigothique*. 2nd edition. Paris: Études augustiniennes, 1983.

Ganz, David. "Book Production in the Carolingian Empire and the Spread of Caroline Minuscule." In *The New Cambridge Medieval History, Volume 2: c. 700–c. 900*, edited by Rosamond McKitterick, 786–808. Cambridge: Cambridge University Press, 1995. DOI: 10.1017/CHOL9780521362924.032.

Gorman, Michael. "The Carolingian Miscellany of Exegetical Texts in Albi 39 and Paris Lat. 2175." *Scriptorium* 51 (1997): 336–54. DOI: 10.3406/scrip.1997.1813.

Greenia, George D. "The Bigger the Book: On Oversize Medieval Manuscripts." *Revue Belge de Philologie et d'histoire* 83 (2005): 723–46. DOI: 10.3406/rbph.2005.4940.

Gumbert, Johan Peter. "Livre grand, livre petit: un problème de taille." *Gazette du livre médiéval* 38 (2001): 55–58. DOI: 10.3406/galim.2001.1519.

———. "Sizes and Formats." In *Ancient and Medieval Book Materials and Techniques,* Volume 1, edited by Marilena Maniaci and Paola F. Munafò, 227–63. Studi e Testi 357. Vatican City: Biblioteca Apostolica Vaticana, 1993.

———. "The Bearable Lightness of Parchment." *Gazette du livre médiéval* 59 (2012): 70–72. DOI: 10.3406/galim.2012.2018.

———. "The Sizes of Manuscripts. Some Statistics and Notes." In *Festschrift Wytze Hellinga,* edited by Anthony R.A. Croiset van Uchelen, 277–88. Amsterdam: Nico Israel, 1980.

Henderson, John. *The Medieval World of Isidore of Seville: Truth from Words.* Cambridge: Cambridge University Press, 2007.

Herren, Michael W. "Storehouses of Learning: Encyclopaedias and Other Reference Works in Ireland and Pre-Bedan Anglo-Saxon England." In *Practice in Learning: The Transfer of Encyclopaedic Knowledge in the Early Middle Ages,* edited by Rolf H. Bremmer and Kees Dekker, 1–18. Mediaevalia Groningana 16. Paris: Peeters, 2010.

Keefe, Susan A. *Water and the Word: Baptism and the Education of the Clergy in the Carolingian Empire.* 2 Volumes. Publications in Mediaeval Studies. Notre Dame: University of Notre Dame Press, 2002.

Lindsay, Wallace M. *Etymologiarum sive Originum libri XX.* 2 Volumes. Oxford: Clarendon Press, 1911.

———. "The Editing of Isidore *Etymologiae.*" *The Classical Quarterly* 5, no. 1 (1911): 42–53. DOI: 10.1017/S0009838800019273.
Lowe, Elias A. *Codices Latini Antiquiores: A Palaeographical Guide to Latin Manuscripts Prior to the Ninth Century.* 11 Volumes. Oxford: Clarendon Press, 1953–1966.
———. "Some Facts about Our Oldest Latin Manuscripts." In *Palaeographical Papers,* Volume 1, edited by Ludwig Bieler, 187–202. Oxford: Clarendon, 1972.
Maassen, Friedrich. *Geschichte der Quellen und der Literatur des Canonischen Rechts im Abendlande bis zum Ausgange des Mittelalters I: Die Rechtssammlungen bis zur Mitte des 9. Jahrhunderts.* Gratz: Leuschner & Lubensky, 1870.
Maniaci, Marilena. *Archeologia del manoscritto: metodi, problemi, bibliografia recente.* Rome: Viella, 2002.
———. "Costruzione e gestione dello spazio scritto fra Oriente e Occidente: principi generali e soluzioni specifiche." In *Scrivere e leggere nell'alto Medioevo,* 473–512. Settimane di studio del Centro italiano di studi sull'alto Medioevo 59. Spoleto: Centro Italiano di Studi sull'Alto Medioevo, 2012.
Manitius, Maximilianus. *Geschichte der lateinischen Literatur des Mittelalters.* Volume 1. Munich: Beck, 1911.
Martín Iglesias, José Carlos, ed. *Scripta de vita Isidori Hispalensis episcopi.* Corpus Christianorum Series Latina 113B. Turnhout: Brepols, 2006.
Mortensen, Lars Boje. "Change of Style and Content as an Aspect of the Copying Process. A Recent Trend in the Study of Medieval Latin Historiography." In *Bilan et perspectives des études médiévales en Europe. Actes du premier Congrès européen d'études médiévales (Spoleto, 27–29 mai 1993),* edited by Jacqueline Hamesse, 265–76. Textes et Études du Moyen Age 3. Turnhout: Brepols, 1995. DOI: 10.1484/M.TEMA-EB.4.00480.
Muzerelle, Denis, and Ezio Ornato, "The Third Dimension of the Book: Codicological Aspects of Multi-Textuality." In *Trends in Statistical Codicology,* edited by Marilena Maniaci,

Studies in Manuscript Cultures 19, 377–412. Berlin: De Gruyter, 2022. DOI: 10.1515/9783110743838-012.

Ornato, Ezio et al. *La face cachée du livre médiéval: l'histoire du livre vue par Ezio Ornato, ses amis et ses collègues.* Rome: Viella, 1997.

———. "The Application of Quantitative Methods to the History of the Book." In *The Oxford Handbook of Latin Palaeography,* edited by Frank T. Coulson and Robert G. Babcock, 651–68. Oxford: Oxford University Press, 2020.

Petrucci, Armando. "Dal libro unitario al libro miscellaneo." In *Scrivere e leggere nell'Italia medievale/Writers and Readers in Medieval Italy,* translated by Charles M. Radding, 15–42. New Haven: Yale University Press, 2007.

Pohl, Walter. "History in Fragments: Montecassino's Politics of Memory." *Early Medieval Europe* 10, no. 3 (2001): 343–74. DOI: 10.1111/1468-0254.00095.

Porzig, Walter. "Die Rezensionen der *Etymologiae* des Isidorus von Sevilla. Vorbemerkung." *Hermes* 72, no. 2 (1937): 129–70.

Reydellet, Marc. "La diffusion des Origines d'Isidore de Séville au Haut Moyen âge." *Mélanges d'archéologie et d'histoire* 78, no. 2 (1966): 383–437. DOI: 10.3406/mefr.1966.7523.

Rhijn, Carine van. "Manuscripts for Local Priests and the Carolingian Reforms." In *Men in the Middle: Local Priests in Early Medieval Europe,* edited by Carine van Rhijn and Steffen Patzold, 177–98. Berlin: De Gruyter, 2016. DOI: 10.1515/9783110444483-012.

———. "Royal Politics in Small Worlds. Local Priests and the Implementation of Carolingian Correctio." In *Kleine Welten. Ländliche Gesellschaften im Karolingerreich,* edited by Thomas Kohl, Steffen Patzold, and Bernhard Zeller, 237–52. Vorträge und Forschungen 87. Ostfildern: Thorbecke, 2019.

Rigg, George. "The Manuscript Miscellany." In *The Oxford Handbook of Latin Palaeography,* edited by Frank T. Coulson and Robert G. Babcock, 879–84. Oxford: Oxford University Press, 2020. DOI: 10.1093/oxfordhb/9780195336948.013.18.

Robinson, Pamela. "The 'Booklet': A Self-contained Unit in Composite Manuscripts." In *Codicologica* 3: *Essais typologiques,* edited by A. Gruys and J.P. Gumbert, 46–69. Leiden: Brill, 1980.

Ruzzier, Chiara. "The Miniaturisation of Bible Manuscripts in the Thirteenth Century: A Comparative Study." In *Form and Function in the Late Medieval Bible,* edited by Laura Light and Eyal Poleg, Library of the Written Word 27, 105–25. Leiden: Brill, 2013. DOI: 10.1163/9789004248892_006.

Ryan, Martin J. "Isidore amongst the Islands: The Reception and Use of Isidore of Seville in Britain and Ireland in the Early Middle Ages." In *A Companion to Isidore of Seville,* edited by Andrew Fear and Jamie Wood, 424–56. Brill's Companions to the Christian Tradition 87. Leiden: Brill, 2020. DOI: 10.1163/9789004415454_016.

Smyth, Marina. "Isidorian Texts in Seventh-Century Ireland." In *Isidore of Seville and His Reception in the Early Middle Ages: Transmitting and Transforming Knowledge,* Late Antique and Early Medieval Iberia 2, edited by Andrew Fear and Jamie Wood, 111–30. Amsterdam: Amsterdam University Press, 2016. DOI: 10.1017/9789048526765.007.

Stadelmaier, Michael. *Die Collectio Sangermanensis XXI titulorum: eine systematische Kanonessammlung der frühen Karolingerzeit.* Freiburger Beiträge zur mittelalterlichen Geschichte 16. Frankfurt am Main: Peter Lang, 2004.

Steinová, Evina. *Notam superponere studui: The Use of Annotation Symbols in the Early Middle Ages.* Turnhout: Brepols, 2019.

———. "The Oldest Manuscript Tradition of the *Etymologiae* (Eighty Years after A.E. Anspach)." *Visigothic Symposia* 4 (2020): 100–143. https://works.hcommons.org/records/4x39t-kdw29.

———. "Two Carolingian Redactions of the *Etymologiae* from St. Gallen." *Mittellateinisches Jahrbuch* 56, no. 2 (2021): 298–376. DOI: 10.36191/mjb/2021-56-2-4.

Stoppacci, Patrizia. "Cassiodorus Senator. *Expositio Psalmorum.*" In *La trasmissione tei testi latini del medioevo/ Mediaeval Latin Texts and Their Transmission,* Mediaeval Lation Texts and Their Transmission 2, edited by Paolo

Chiesa and Lucia Castaldi, 143–59. Florence: SISMEL Edizioni del Galluzzo, 2005.

Tardif, Ernest-Joseph. "Un abrégé juridique des *Étymologies* d'Isidore de Séville." In *Mélanges Julien Havet*, 659–81. Paris: Ernest Leroux, 1895.

Turner, Eric. *The Typology of the Early Codex*. Haney Foundation Series 18. Philadelphia: University of Pennsylvania, 1977. DOI: 10.9783/9781512807868.

Warntjes, Immo. "Isidore of Seville and the Formation of Medieval Computus." In *A Companion to Isidore of Seville*, edited by Andrew Fear and Jamie Wood, 457–523. Leiden: Brill, 2020. DOI: 10.1163/9789004415454_017.

5

Commented Editions of the Bible in Carolingian Europe: Otfrid's Approach to the Book of Isaiah

Cinzia Grifoni

The explanation of the Bible and the dissemination of its message were certainly major concerns of the monk and priest Otfrid (d. after 871).[1] Known as the first named author of German literature, Otfrid was raised at the East Frankish monastery of Wissembourg, in modern Alsace, and worked there as a teacher and exegete from the 830s to his death. At Wissembourg he completed a well-known Gospel harmony in Old High German

---

1 The research leading to this article has received funding from the Austrian Science Fund (FWF) under the Elise Richter Programme, Project No. V-811G, "Margins at the Centre." On Otfrid's life see Wolfgang Haubrichs, "Eine prosopographische Skizze zu Otfrid von Weißenburg," in *Otfrid von Weißenburg*, ed. Wolfgang Kleiber (Darmstadt: Wissenschaftliche Buchgesellschaft, 1978), 397–413, and Wolfgang Haubrichs, "Otfrid de Wissembourg, élève de Raban Maur, et l'héritage de l'école de Fulda au monastère de Wissembourg," in *Raban Maur et son temps*, ed. Philippe Depreux, Stéphane Lebecq, Michel J.-L. Perrin, and Olivier Szerwiniack, Collection Haut Moyen Âge 9 (Turnhout: Brepols, 2010), 155–72.

rhymes, the so-called *Evangelienbuch*,[2] and produced at least five commented editions in Latin of several Biblical books.[3] With these works Otfrid intended to facilitate his audience's understanding of the text of the Bible. On the one hand, his poetic reworking and interpretation of the Gospels in the vernacular addressed those members of the East Frankish laity and clergy who had difficulties in understanding the Bible in Latin and therefore needed a version in their mother tongue. On the other hand, he produced commented editions, which contain both the biblical text and an apparatus of pertinent explanations in Latin on each page, for an audience which had at least some command of Latin and would profit from short annotations to access the Bible.

There is a remarkable imbalance in the studies concerning Otfrid's output. While the *Evangelienbuch* has been the subject of numerous in-depth investigations given its capital significance for the history of German language and literature, Otfrid's Latin commented editions have been analyzed only as far as to establish their relation to his vernacular poem. Once modern scholarship assessed that the Latin annotations did not

---

2   For the most recent edition of the work and related studies, see Otfrid von Weißenburg, *Evangelienbuch*, vol. 1.1: *Edition nach dem Wiener Codex 2687* and vol. 1.2: *Einleitung und Apparat* (Tübingen: Max Niemeyer Verlag, 2004); vol. 2.1: *Edition der Heidelberger Handschrift P (Codex Pal. Lat. 52) und der Handschrift D (Codex Discissus: Bonn, Berlin/Krakau, Wolfenbüttel)* (Tübingen: Max Niemeyer Verlag, 2006); and vol. 2.2: *Einleitung und Apparat* (Tübingen: Max Niemeyer Verlag, 2010), ed. Wolfgang Kleiber and Ernst Hellgardt. See also Otfrid von Weißenburg, *Das "Evangelienbuch" in der Überlieferung der Freisinger Handschrift: (Bayerische Staatsbibliothek München, cgm. 14). Edition und Untersuchungen*, ed. Karin Pivernetz, 2 vols. (Göppingen: Verlag Kümmerle, 2000).

3   Wolfgang Kleiber, *Otfrid von Weißenburg. Untersuchungen zur handschriftlichen Überlieferung und Studien zum Aufbau des Evangelienbuches*, Bibliotheca Germanica 14 (Bern: Franke Verlag, 1971), 103–7, and Cinzia Grifoni, "Reading the Catholic Epistles: Glossing Practices in Early Medieval Wissembourg," in *The Annotated Book in the Early Middle Ages: Practices of Reading and Writing*, ed. Mariken Teeuwen and Irene van Renswoude, Utrecht Studies in Medieval Literacy 38 (Turnhout: Brepols, 2017), 709–29.

constitute a relevant exegetical source of the *Evangelienbuch*, that they do not contain Old High German words, and that they are mostly derivative with regard to their contents, they were no longer considered to be an interesting research topic.[4]

Yet Otfrid's commented editions deserve more consideration. Firstly, their Latin annotations are interesting from a linguistic point of view. The *Evangelienbuch* shows that Otfrid was particularly attentive to the difficulties his East Frankish, "German" speaking audiences had in understanding the Bible and its interpretations in Latin. With his Latin annotations he addressed "German-speaking" users, too, since he compiled them most likely for the members of his own monastic community. In fact, each commented edition is a *codex unicus*, that is, a work transmitted by only one manuscript, which was produced in the Wissembourg scriptorium and probably never left the shelves of the monastic library afterwards. Therefore, their linguistic peculiarities reveal which kind of Latin Otfrid regarded as adequate for his East Frankish audience. Secondly, it is interesting to analyze which sort of biblical interpretation the annotations convey and which sources Otfrid reproduced. This enables us to understand which level of exegetical expertise and which knowledge he regarded as standard. Finally, it is worth reflecting about the reasons that led Otfrid to prefer the complex codicological layout of a commented edition, which required much more time to be prepared, to simpler and more common formats of biblical commentaries, such as running commentaries. To this end, his choice needs to be contextualized in the framework of similar developments in the exegetical practice of Carolingian Europe by taking into particular account the cultural networks in which Otfrid was involved.

---

4 For the study of Otfrid's commented editions in relation to his *Evangelienbuch*, see Kleiber, *Otfrid*; Paul Michel and Alexander Schwarz, *Unz in obanentig. Aus der Werkstatt der karolingischen Exegeten Alcuin, Erkanbert und Otfrid von Weißenburg* (Bonn: Bouvier Verlag Herbert Grundmann, 1978), and Ernst Hellgardt, *Die exegetischen Quellen von Otfrids Evangelienbuch. Beiträge zu ihrer Ermittlung,* Hermaea N.F. 41 (Tübingen: Niemeyer Verlag, 1981).

The present contribution engages with these issues. After an overview of the characteristics and spread of commented editions of the Bible in Carolingian Europe, I will examine the features of Otfrid's books and discuss the possible reasons that led him to choose this codicological format instead of others. Special attention will be paid to his collection practices, to his privileged use of abridgments of authoritative treatises as a main source for his annotations, and to the implications of this choice with regard to his targeted audience. My observations will rest on the analysis of Otfrid's commented edition of the Book of Isaiah, which is transmitted in Wolfenbüttel, Herzog August Bibliothek, MS Guelf. 33 Weissenburg (hereafter 33w).

Commented Editions of the Bible from the Ninth Century

Following Louis Holtz's definition, an *édition commentée* (commented edition) is a manuscript designed and ruled for accommodating both a primary text and a substantial amount of related annotations at its sides.[5] This particular codicological format allots a relevant portion of the manuscript page to the marginalia, which were usually added before the codex would have left the scriptorium where it was produced.[6] The scholars who chose to employ the medium of the commented edition evidently regarded the presence of the annotations in the margins to be as essential as the primary text itself for finishing their book project and accomplishing their educational purposes. Through manuscripts of this sort, they provided their intended readers with a copy of a primary text, be it a collection of laws or the Bible, and a first exegetical introduction to it. The explana-

---

5 Louis Holtz, "Les manuscrits latins à gloses et à commentaires: de l'antiquité à l'époque carolingienne," in *Il libro e il testo*, ed. Cesare Questa and Renato Raffaelli (Urbino: Arti Grafiche Editoriali, 1984), 156.

6 See Michele Camillo Ferrari, "Before the *Glossa Ordinaria*. The Ezekiel fragment in Irish Minuscule, Zürich, Staatsarchiv W3.19.XII, and Other Experiments towards a *Bible commentée* in the Early Middle Ages," in *Biblical Studies in the Early Middle Ages*, ed. Claudio Leonardi and Giovanni Orlandi (Firenze: SISMEL Edizioni del Galluzzo, 2005), 289.

tion included in the marginal apparatus could be more or less basic depending on the contents and sources of the annotations.

Commented editions have a long history. They were developed in various layouts probably in eastern Roman scriptoria in the course of late antiquity and were used originally for the issue of legal texts and Greek Classics, such as the works of Ulpian or Callimachus.[7] To judge from the extant manuscripts, the Bible was not the subject of commented editions from the outset. Indeed, biblical books featuring this *mise-en-page* date to the eighth century at the earliest, both in the Byzantine East and in the Latin West. In particular, the earliest known biblical commented edition produced in the eastern Mediterranean is the catena commentary on the Gospel of Luke contained in the inferior layer of the palimpsest Codex Zacynthius (Cambridge, University Library, MS Add. 10062), whose writing is cautiously dated between the year 700 and the middle of the ninth century.[8]

As for the Latin West, on which the present contribution shall concentrate, the oldest witness of a commented edition of the Bible dates to the late eighth century and possibly stems from Ireland. It is a two-folio fragment held at the Staatsarchiv in Zurich, in which the ruled space is arranged in three columns: the biblical text (the Book of Ezekiel) occupies the central column, while dense annotations selected from the corresponding *Homilies* of Gregory the Great flank it at both sides. It has been posited that the volume to which this fragment belonged reached the monastery of St. Gall in the first half of the ninth century and remained part of the local library until the eleventh

---

7   Kathleen McNamee, "Another Chapter in the History of Scholia," *Classical Quarterly* 48, no. 1 (1998): 277–85; Nigel G. Wilson, "The Relation of Text and Commentary in Greek Books," in *Il libro e il testo*, ed. Cesare Questa and Renato Raffaelli (Urbino: Arti Grafiche Editoriali, 1984), 106; and Holtz, "Les manuscrits latins," 150 and 154.

8   David C. Parker, "The Undertext Writing," in *Codex Zacynthius: Catena, Palimpsest, Lectionary,* ed. Hugh A.G. Houghton and David C. Parker, Text and Studies 3.21 (Piscataway: Gorgias Press, 2020), 31.

century, when its relevance shrank and its leaves were re-used as binding material.[9]

Due to the Irish origin of the Zurich fragment, modern scholars, Louis Holtz *in primis,* assumed that insular teachers played a prime role in the production and use of commented editions for the study of the Bible. Similarly, insular scholars are regarded as responsible for the application of this codicological format to the study of Latin grammar and literature, and for its dissemination in western Europe.[10] As far as the Bible is concerned, it is indeed remarkable that the earliest extant commented editions produced in continental scriptoria of the Latin West stem from centers with well-known Insular connections, such as Fulda and St. Amand (see table 1, items 2 and 3). Although there are still too few specific studies on the paths of dissemination of this book type in the early Middle Ages, the number of pertinent manuscripts alone shows that commented editions enjoyed an increasing success in the Carolingian and post-Carolingian period until they became the privileged medium for the spread of the so-called *Glossa Ordinaria* at the turn of the twelfth century.[11]

No survey of the extant commented editions of biblical books produced In the Latin West before the twelfth century has so far been undertaken. For the ninth century, I have traced twenty-eight manuscripts of this kind, which are listed in table

---

9 Ferrari, "Before the *Glossa Ordinaria,*" 284–87. The fragment bears the shelf mark Zurich, Staatsarchiv, MS W I 3.19 (fols. 24r–25v).

10 Louis Holtz, "Le rôle des commentaires d'auteurs classiques dans l'émergence d'une mise en page associant texte et commentaire (Moyen Âge occidental)," in *Le commentaire entre tradition et innovation,* ed. Monique Goulet-Cazé et al. (Paris: Librairie Philosophique J. Vrin, 2000), 107–8; Holtz, "Les manuscrits latins"; and Louis Holtz, "Glosse e commenti," in *Lo spazio letterario del Medioevo. Medioevo Latino,* vol. 3: *La ricezione del testo,* ed. Guglielmo Cavallo, Claudio Leonardi, and Enrico Menestò (Roma: Salerno Editrice, 1995), 59–112.

11 Ferrari, "Before the *Glossa Ordinaria,*" 304–6, and Lesley Smith, *The Glossa Ordinaria: The Making of a Medieval Bible Commentary,* Commentaria: Sacred Texts and Their Commentaries: Jewish, Christian and Islamic 3 (Leiden: Brill, 2009), 91–105.

5.1. In this, the codices are ordered chronologically through the reference number of the first column. Information about their shelfmark, their place and date of production according to modern catalogues, and their content is included in the second, third, and fourth columns respectively. The fifth column notes the available studies in short form, while the full list occurs in the bibliography.[12]

No.	Signature	Date and Origin	Content	Available studies
1	Zurich, Staatsarchiv, W I 3.19 (fols. 24r–25v)	end of 8th c., Ireland?	Ezekiel	Ferrari 2005; Gorman 2004
2	Frankfurt, Stadt- und Universitätsbibl., Barth 32	c. 800, Fulda	Psalter	Gibson 1994; Cantelli 2008; Macaluso 2010
3	Ivrea, BC, LXXIX (28)	c. 815, Saint-Amand	Pauline Ep.	Mirella Ferrari 1998
4	St Gall, Stb, Cod. 1395, pp. 440–441	9th c., ¼, Fulda? St. Gall?	Pauline Ep.	Hawk 2012
5	Dillingen, Studienbibl., XV fragm. 26 + Oslo, SC, 74	9th c., Milan (?)	Psalter	Gibson 1994; Wunderle 2006

Table 5.1. Commented editions of the Bible to the end of the ninth century.

---

12 The table draws primarily on the information contained in Bernhard Bischoff, *Katalog der festländischen Handschriften des neunten Jahrhunderts (mit Ausnahme der wisigotischen)*, 4 vols. (Wiesbaden: Harrassowitz Verlag, 1998–2017). For the Wissembourg manuscripts I have followed Hans Butzmann, *Die Weißenburger Handschriften,* Kataloge der Herzog August Bibliothek Wolfenbüttel, Neue Reihe 10 (Frankfurt am Main: Klostermann, 1964).

No.	Signature	Date and Origin	Content	Available studies
6	Vatican City, BAV, Cod. Reg. lat. 307	800–850	Gospels of Luke and John	Bischoff Katalog 3, 6653, Catalogue Wilmart, 155–58. 2 columns!
7	Augsburg, Diözesanmuseum St. Afra 1002 (olim Bistumsarchiv 6)	Lyon	Gospels	Frank 1984; Schiegg 2015; Schiegg 2017
8	St Gall, Stb, Cod. 27	9th c., ½, Würzburg?	Psalter	Gibson 1994; Tibbetts 2002; Euw 2010
9	Fragments in Munich, Regensburg and Prague*	Glosses: 10th c., ½, Fulda?	Psalter	Gibson 1994; Tibbetts 2002; Crivello 2001
10	Göttweig, Stb, Cod. 30 (rot) / 2 (schwarz)	9th c., ⅔, St Gall	Psalter	Gibson 1994; Tibbetts 2002; Euw 2010

* These are the fragments: München, Bayerische Staatsbibliothek, Clm 29315/3 + Regensburg, Bischöfliche Zentralbibliothek, fragm. IV.2.1 + Praha, Národní galerie Inv. Nr. K 7314, originally belonging to the same manuscript.

No.	Signature	Date and Origin	Content	Available studies
11	Eremo Camaldoli, Arch., s.n. + Washington DC, Museum of the Bible, Leaf from the "Psalter of St. Romuald" (formerly Oslo, Schøyen Coll., 620)	9th c., 2nd third, northern or central Italy; or: South Germany; or: Saint-Amand? Salzburg, 9th. c., 1/3	Psalter	Andrei 2002; Stoppacci 2013; Tristano 2019
12	Laon, BmSM, Ms. 14	9th c., 2/3, St. Denis?	Psalter	Gibson 1994; Cantelli 2008
13	Colmar, Archives d'Alsace, Archive du Haut Rhin, Fragm. 86 (13)	9th c., 2/3, probably Murbach	Psalter	Bischoff, Katalog 1, 937
14	Strasbourg, Archives d'Alsace, Archive du Bas Rhin, Fragm. 151-J-60	9th c. 2/4(?), Wissembourg?	Psalter	Bischoff, Katalog 3, 6020

No.	Signature	Date and Origin	Content	Available studies
15	Wolfenbüttel, HAB, Cod. 26 Weiss.	c. 840–870, Wissembourg	Gospels	Kleiber 1971; Hellgardt 1981; Grifoni 2003; Gamberini 2011; Grifoni 2017; Grifoni 2019.
16	Wolfenbüttel, HAB, Cod. 32 Weiss.		Jeremiah	
17	Wolfenbüttel, HAB, Cod. 33 Weiss.		Isaiah	
18	Wolfenbüttel, HAB, Cod. 36 Weiss.		Min. Proph.	
19	Wolfenbüttel, HAB, Cod. 59 Weiss.		Acts; Cath. Ep.; Rev.	
20	Vercelli, BC, CXLIX (136)	9th c., 2nd–3rd qu., Salzburg	Psalter	Gibson 1994; Crivello 2001; Cantelli 2008
21	St Gall, Stb, Cod. 41	9th c., 3rd qu., St Gall	Prophets (Isaiah, Hosea, Zechariah, Daniel)	De Blic 1949
22	St Gall, Stb, Cod. 50	9th c., ¾, St Gall	Gospels	D'Imperio 2000
23	Vienna, ÖNB, Cod. 1239	9th c., ¾, Wissembourg	Pauline and Cath. Ep.	Grifoni 2017
24	Firenze, Bibl. Medicea Laurenziana, Cod. Ashb. 54	end of 9th c., northeastern France	Psalter	Cantelli 2008

No.	Signature	Date and Origin	Content	Available studies
25	Vercelli, BC, LXII (2)	middle to end of 9th c., northern Italy?	Psalter	Unterkircher 1974; Gibson 1994; Cantelli 2008
26	Munich, BSb, MSS Clm 7665 + Clm 7673 + Clm 7679	9th c., ⅔, Germany	Psalter	Bischoff, Katalog 2, 3090, p. 243; Bischoff, Schreibschulen II, 2, 233
27	Troyes, Médiathèque Jacques-Chirac, Ms. 615	end of 9th c., Paris?	Psalter	Gibson 1994
28	Orléans, Médiathèque, Ms. 48 (45)	end of 9th c., Fleury	Psalter	Gibson 1994; Cantelli 2008; Rädle 1974, 97–112

Though provisional, the list reveals some interesting particularities.[13]

Firstly, twenty-seven out of twenty-eight commented editions of biblical books were ruled in three columns (t. 5.1; the only exception is item 6): the central column was designed to accommodate the biblical text, while the two side-columns allowed space for a substantial number of annotations. This ruling scheme appears in the oldest fragment (item 1, probably of Irish origin), recurs in all but one manuscript of the list with

---

13 I am currently undertaking a systematic study of all commented editions of biblical books produced in Carolingian Europe in the framework of my research project "Margins at the Centre: Book Production and Practices of Annotation in the East Frankish Realm."

minor or no discrepancies, and was used for commented editions of the Bible until the twelfth century, as the copies of the *Glossa Ordinaria* in the so-called "simple format" show.[14] Around 1160, "more freedom and invention" were applied to create a "more complex formatting model," as Leslie Smith put it.[15] Ninth-century commented editions designed for the study of Latin, and of Virgil's poems in particular, are not so consistent. Here the three-column layout is predominant, but not exclusive.[16] This means — not surprisingly — that at least until the twelfth century, the scholars who created commented editions were more likely to reproduce their codicological models, and so more conservative, when they explained the Bible than when they engaged with the study of Latin. Otfrid was no exception in this respect: he too stuck to the three-column pattern in all his commented editions.

Secondly, in order to contextualize Otfrid's output it is important to remark that the East Frankish scriptoria specialized in the production of commented editions of several biblical books from the second third of the ninth century onward, roughly when the region fell under the control of Louis the German. As table 5.1 shows, nineteen of the twenty-eight manuscripts on the list were produced in scriptoria located in the eastern part of the Carolingian Empire (Fulda, Murbach, Salzburg, St. Gall, Wissembourg, and maybe Würzburg). All these codices provide crucial evidence of the cultural exchange and mutual influence between East Frankish scholarly centers. In particular, the scrip-

---

14 Smith, *The Glossa Ordinaria*, 94–105.
15 Ibid., 105.
16 Louis Holtz, "La typologie des manuscrits grammaticaux latins," *Revue d'Histoire des Textes* 7 (1977): 261–65, mentions Orléans, Médiathèque, MS 295 (9th century, ¾, from the Reims region: Donatus's *Ars Maior* with Muretach's explanations). Louis Holtz, "Le rôle," refers to following manuscripts: Bern, Burgerbibliothek, MS 167 (9th century, med., from Auxerre: Virgil, two columns); Bern, Burgerbibliothek, MS 165 (9th century, ⅔, from Tours: Virgil, three columns); Bern, Burgerbibliothek, MS 172 (9th century, ⅔, from either Fleury or St. Denis: Virgil, three columns); and Hamburg, Universitätsbibliothek, MS in scrinio 52 (c. 850, from the Paris region: Virgil, three columns).

toria of Wissembourg, with six (maybe seven) manuscripts, and St. Gall, with perhaps five manuscripts, intensively pursued the production of commented editions of the Bible precisely in Otfrid's time, that is, roughly during the period of Grimald's joint abbacy over the two monasteries.[17] Conversely, there are very few examples of ninth-century biblical commented editions from western Carolingian scriptoria, which knew and used this codicological tool, but apparently preferred to reserve it for the study of classical authors.[18]

Thirdly, the most common book of the commented Bible, especially in the second half of the ninth century, was the Psalter — probably on account of its centrality to elementary education and the liturgical office. Indeed, fifteen out of the twenty-eight items of table 5.1 are commented psalters. Moreover, commented editions produced outside East Francia almost exclusively contain psalters (see items 5, 12, 24, 25, 27, and 28); the only exception is the St. Amand manuscript dating to around 815 (item 3). Although East Frankish scriptoria applied this format to the issue of several books of the Bible (as Otfrid's manuscripts demonstrate), commented psalters also constituted a significant portion of the output in this region. In particular, the St. Gall scriptorium became a hub for the creation and dissemination of commented editions of the psalter, as items 8, 9, and 10 on the list demonstrate. The Vercelli psalter from Salzburg (item 20)

---

17 Grimald held the joint abbacy of Wissembourg and St. Gall from 847 until his death in 872. He had already led Wissembourg from 833 to 839. After a two-year pause he became abbot of St. Gall in 841 and was entrusted with leading Wissembourg once again from 847. See Dieter Geuenich, "Beobachtungen zu Grimald von St. Gallen, Erzkapellan und Oberkanzler Ludwigs des Deutschen," in *Litterae Medii Aevi. Festschrift für Johanne Autenrieth*, ed. Michael Borgolte and Herrad Spilling (Sigmaringen: Thorbecke, 1988), 55–68.

18 Louis Holtz, "Le rôle," 108. See also Silvia Ottaviano, "Reading between the Lines of Virgil's Medieval Manuscripts," in *The Annotated Book in the Early Middle Ages. Practices of Reading and Writing*, ed. Mariken Teeuwen and Irene van Renswoude, Utrecht Studies in Medieval Literacy 38 (Turnhout: Brepols 2017), 397–426.

also draws on the St. Gall model.[19] Moreover, East Frankish centers influenced the production of commented psalters abroad, as shown by the marginalia in the other Vercelli psalter (item 22), which depend directly on explanations produced at the monastic school of Mondsee.[20]

One possible reason for the predominant number of commented editions of the Psalms might lie in the fact that some of them (items 9 and 10) were created possibly at the request of lay commissioners.[21] The presence of short annotations surrounding the text of the Psalms, narrative drawings, and prayers intended for private devotion, and the overall elegance of some of these manuscripts, do hint at an external audience. However, this does not imply that all commented Psalters exclusively addressed non-monastic readers. As Silvia Cantelli Berarducci highlighted, each commented edition should be examined for its own peculiarities. The contents and sources of the annotations, the paratexts framing the commented edition itself, and the traces of use left by its readers provide relevant clues for understanding who may have been the audience addressed by these manuscripts.[22]

From these observations it is clear that commented editions spread with moderate success in Carolingian Europe and were produced primarily for a monastic audience and, perhaps in two cases, also for the lay elite. While outside East Francia the

---

19 Margaret Gibson, "Carolingian Glossed Psalters," in *The Early Medieval Bible: Its Production, Decoration and Use,* ed. Richard Gameson (Cambridge: Cambridge University Press, 1994), 80, and Sinéad O'Sullivan, "Book as Bibliotheca: The Emergence of the Commented Edition," *Speculum* 100, no. 2 (2025): forthcoming. My thanks to the author, who kindly provided me with a pre-print version of her article.

20 Silvia Cantelli Berarducci, "L'esegesi ai Salmi nel sec. IX. Il caso delle edizioni commentate del Salterio," in *Präsenz und Verwendung der Heiligen Schrift im christlichen Frühmittelalter,* ed. Patrizia Carmassi (Wiesbaden: Harrassowitz Verlag, 2008), 81.

21 Cantelli Berarducci, "L'esegesi," 87. See also Gibson, "Carolingian Glossed Psalters," 79–89. On the production of psalters for the lay elite see Rosamond McKitterick, *The Carolingians and the Written Word* (Cambridge: Cambridge University Press, 1989), 252–53.

22 Cantelli Berarducci, "L'esegesi," 88.

focus was set on commenting the Psalter, East Frankish scholars also applied this format to other books of the Bible. According to their origin, commented editions might be regarded as a product peculiar to East Francia, since East Frankish scriptoria produced two thirds of the Carolingian commented editions currently known. In particular, both the scriptoria of Wissembourg and St. Gall contributed significantly to their spread in the second half of the ninth century, as table 5.1 shows. Modern scholarship regards Otfrid of Wissembourg and Hartmut, head librarian, dean and (from 872) abbot of St. Gall, as the proponents of books of this sort in their respective monasteries.[23] Wolfgang Haubrichs suggested that the two scholars got to know each other maybe around 833–836 at Fulda, where they were both taught by Hrabanus Maurus.[24] If his hypothesis is correct, we may assume that it was at Fulda that Otfrid and Hartmut became familiar with the book format of the commented edition, which the local scriptorium had produced since the beginning of the ninth century (see items 2 and 4 in table 5.1). Once returned to their respective communities, they fostered its dissemination by supervising the production of similar books.

Their choice and, more generally, the remarkable success of commented editions in East Francia could be explained as a mere "cultural trend" concerning a limited group of intellectuals and scriptoria well connected to each other (Fulda, Wissembourg, and St. Gall). Conversely, it might have resulted from a purposeful pedagogical choice.

In this latter case, the remarkable spread of commented editions in Louis the German's realm could have originated from the shared intention of several scholars to resolve linguistic difficulties peculiar to East Francia. Thus, the spread of these commentaries would result from the same concern which led Otfrid among other teachers to write texts in the vernacular. Was a commented Bible regarded as a particularly fitting support for

---

23 Kleiber, *Otfrid,* 158.
24 Wolfgang Haubrichs, "Otfrids St. Galler 'Studienfreunde,'" *Amsterdamer Beiträge zur älteren Germanistik* 4 (1973): 74.

the study of theology in East Francia? Did its relatively short and strictly text-related Latin annotations match better the skills of readers whose mother-tongue was very different from Latin? Were the vocabulary and syntax of the scholia particularly suitable for the Latin command of the average East Frankish ecclesiastical or lay reader of the Bible? Producing an answer to these questions requires a systematic investigation and comparison of all items in table 5.1.[25]

The commented editions from Wissembourg provide a good starting point for the analysis. In contrast to all other books listed in table 5.1, which are regarded as anonymous exegetical works, their production can be attributed to a named teacher, the monk and priest Otfrid, whose scholarly career, networks, and interests are well-known. Their investigation enables us, on the one hand, to enrich our knowledge about Otfrid's working methods; on the other, we can contextualize his Latin output in the broader framework of Carolingian exegesis and understand whether and to what extent the scholarly networks in which he was involved influenced his choices.

According to Wolfgang Kleiber, Otfrid designed five commented editions and wrote an impressive number of annotations in their margins.[26] His project included the explanation of the Gospels as well as of the Books of Jeremiah, Isaiah, Minor Prophets, Acts, Catholic Epistles, and Revelation (items 15–19 in table 5.1). As mentioned above, Otfrid's commented editions are each transmitted by a single manuscript which probably never left Wissembourg. This implies that he wrote his books for the monks of his community. The detail-driven analysis of the codicological setting, contents, and sources of these volumes provides evidence for reflecting about Otfrid's aims, the exegetical expertise he regarded as adequate for his confreres and pupils, and the command of Latin he could expect of them.

---

25 I am carrying out this type of study as part of my current research project. See above, n13.

26 Kleiber, *Otfrid,* 102–60.

In this respect, his commented edition of the Book of Isaiah (manuscript 33W, item 17) provides us with a useful case study, which enables us to understand Otfrid's peculiar codicological and exegetical choices and to compare them with other contemporary practices. The codex 33W, along with the majority of the extant volumes from the medieval library of Wissembourg, is now in the possession of the Herzog August Bibliothek (HAB) in Wolfenbüttel; images of it are available online in the digital repository of the HAB.[27]

Otfrid's Commented Edition of the Book of Isaiah

Otfrid's commented edition of the Book of Isaiah consists of 78 folios of medium size (approximatively 300 × 260 mm [11.81 × 10.24 in.]).[28] The leaves are gathered into an initial binion (fols. 1r–4v), eight quaternions until fol. 68v, and a final quinion. The binion is ruled according to a two-column scheme. It contains an incomplete *capitulatio,* that is, a table of contents ordered by chapters (fols. 1v–2v) and three prefatory texts selected from Jerome's Letters 18 and 53 as well as from his preface to the Book of Isaiah included in the Vulgate (fols. 3v–4v). Paratexts of any kind revealing the identity of the designer of the commented edition, his purposes, and the addressee of the book are lacking. The nine gatherings containing the text of the Bible and the related marginalia are ruled according to the three-column scheme which is typical for early medieval commented editions of the Bible (see fig. 5.1).

---

27 See the website: Herzog August Bibliothek Wolfenbüttel, Handschriftendatenbank, "Cod(ices) Weiss(enburgenses)," http://diglib.hab.de/?db=mss &list=collection&id=weiss.

28 The description of the manuscript is based on my own analysis and differs in some respects from the information provided by both Butzmann, *Weißenburger Handschriften,* 143–44, and Roger Gryson in the introduction to his edition of Joseph Scot's Epitome. See Iosephus Scottus, *Epitome explanationum in Isaiam beati Hieronymi presbyteri,* ed. Roger Gryson, Corpus Christianorum, Continuatio Mediaevalis 284 (Turnhout: Brepols, 2018), 20–21.

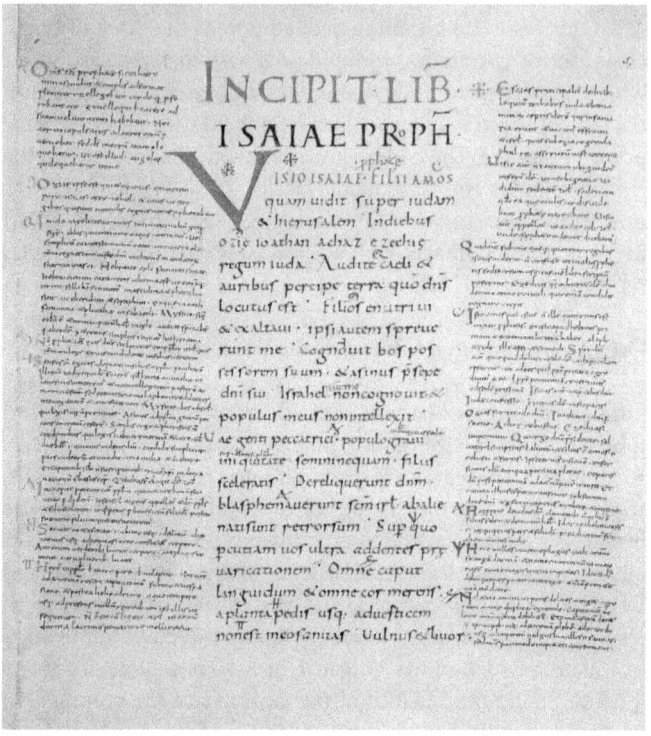

Fig. 5.1. MS Wolfenbüttel, Herzog August Bibliothek, 33. Weiss., fol. 5r. Source: Herzog August Bibliothek.

The central column accommodates 27 writing lines. The side-columns are not ruled, as is common to all of Otfrid's commented editions. The size of the script used for the marginalia is smaller than that of the primary text and two lines of scholia normally correspond to one line of Isaiah's text in the central column. Both the text of the Bible and the annotations are written in a neat Caroline minuscule. According to the paleographical analysis conducted by Wolfgang Kleiber, one scribe penned the incomplete *capitulatio,* including 126 of the 180 chapters into which Isaiah's text is divided in 33w.[29] Folio 3r, which should have contained the missing chapter titles, was left blank. A second copyist wrote the prefaces on folios 3v–4v as well as the entire biblical text, its chapters and a small number of red titles in the margins before the annotations were copied (fols. 5r–78r). When his work was completed, a further scribe, whom Kleiber identified as Otfrid himself, added all the scholia, the interlinear glosses, and the reference signs of 33w in his own hand.[30]

Despite the accumulation of text in the margins, the manuscript page does not intimidate the reader. Otfrid made use of various expedients to ensure the readability and the harmonious elegance of 33w (see fig. 5.1). Firstly, the disposition of the scholia is very ordered. Otfrid selected and copied the single annotations so that their length would not exceed the justification lines of the side-columns. Except for rare occasions, the scholia were never penned beyond the planned writing space and at least two sections of the page, that is, the top and the bottom margins, were usually left blank. Secondly, the scholia are easy to read. Otfrid penned them throughout the manuscript in a small but neat and uniform minuscule. Moreover, he made systematic use of punctuation signs and initials, with which he marked the beginning of each new annotation and its subparts. Thirdly, it is easy to spot which explanation pertains to a given word of the primary text, since Otfrid drew *signes de renvoi* (reference signs), that is, distinctive symbols, both above the biblical lemma in the central column and at the beginning of the corresponding scholion. When writing these tie marks, Otfrid probably developed and enriched a model he had come across

---

29 See Donatien De Bruyne, *Summaries, Divisions and Rubrics of the Latin Bible* (Turnhout: Brepols, 2014), 184–92: Series A.

30 Kleiber, *Otfrid,* 103. I refer to the distinction between "scholia" and "glosses" made by James E.G. Zetzel, *Marginal Scholarship and Textual Deviance. The "Commentum Cornuti" and the Early Scholia on Persius* (London: Institute of Classical Studies, 2005), 4. Accordingly, scholia are annotations of varying length, which were "keyed to the text by proximity or by reference signs"; glosses are interlinear annotations "linked to the text by placement alone."

at Fulda, as the strikingly similar reference signs occurring in the St. Gall fragment of possible Fulda origin demonstrate (item 4 in table 5.1).[31] Moreover, he drew both the initials and the reference signs in red. The resulting alternation between red and dark inks (concerning also the incipit of Isaiah's text in the central column) enhances the clarity of the *mise-en-page* while aiding its readability.

This short analysis of the codicological and paleographical characteristics of 33w shows that the book was the result of a well-thought-out plan and accurate execution. In this, the *capitulatio* alone, which was perhaps penned last, shows signs of incompleteness. Alongside the overall elegance of the volume, the scarcity of later additions suggests that 33w had been intended (and was actually regarded by its users) as a prestigious reference tool for the explanation of the Book of Isaiah, which a teacher could read to his pupils in the classroom or the monks could consult in their private study.[32] The investigation of the cultural context in which this book originated and of the contents of its annotations enables us to appreciate Otfrid's purposes and to characterize his intended audience more precisely.

As for the contemporary cultural context, Otfrid's choice to engage with the Book of Isaiah can be understood in the framework of the renewed interest of Carolingian scholars for the prophetic texts of the Old Testament.[33] Any exegetical approach to Isaiah's text in the eighth and ninth centuries had to come to terms with the monumental and extremely detailed explanation

---

31 See the manuscript St. Gall, Stiftsbibliothek, Cod. Sang. 1395, pp. 440–41, https://www.e-codices.unifr.ch/de/csg/1395/440.

32 Roger Gryson points out that the twelfth-century manuscript Wolfenbüttel, Herzog August Bibliothek, MS Guelf. 58 Weiss. (which contains a commented edition of the Book of Isaiah in the first six folios) includes the same prefatory texts and a part of the marginalia occurring in 33w. Gryson suggests either a direct dependence of Guelf. 58 Weiss. from 33w or a shared model: see Iosephus Scottus, *Epitome,* ed. Gryson, 22–24 and 32. If the first case applies, 33w was demonstrably an exegetical reference book.

33 Raffaele Savigni, "Il commentario a Isaia di Aimone di Auxerre e le sue fonti," in *Biblical Studies in the Early Middle Ages,* ed. Claudio Leonardi and Giovanni Orlandi (Firenze: SISMEL Edizioni del Galluzzo, 2005), 215.

provided by Jerome around 410 CE. However, the ways in which Jerome's text was read and re-used in the Carolingian period varied considerably. Several scholars, both named and unknown, excerpted and included a few passages of Jerome's treatise in their exegetical compilations. Further scholars, and in particular Joseph Scottus (d. around 795), abridged Jerome's explanation by reproducing verbatim only a selection of its contents.[34] Moreover, two well-known teachers created new commentaries of Isaiah based on Jerome's around the middle of the ninth century. One of them was Hrabanus Maurus, who completed a compendium of earlier patristic exegesis on Isaiah according to the literal and spiritual sense. To this end, he abridged Jerome's text and added pertinent extracts culled from a variety of other sources, primarily from Gregory the Great.[35] His intended audience, Hrabanus wrote in the preface, were students of the Bible at the beginning of their career, who were not skilled enough to engage with Jerome's philological and linguistic observations.[36] Besides Hrabanus, Haimo of Auxerre authored what is regarded as the first original explanation on the Book of Isaiah since the fifth century. In this, he built on Jerome's and several other works with an unprecedented independence of thought, and wrote a running commentary for proficient students of the Bible.[37] Finally, only two Carolingian scholars chose to write an explanation of the Book of Isaiah by adapting Jerome's exegetical background to the medium of the commented edition. One of them was Otfrid, who used an epitome of Jerome's treatise for

---

34 Iosephus Scottus, *Epitome,* ed. Gryson, 7–13.

35 Silvia Cantelli Berarducci, *Hrabani Mauri Opera Exegetica. Repertorium Fontium* (Turnhout: Brepols, 2006), vol. 1: *Rabano Mauro esegeta. Le fonti. I commentari,* 54–55 and 315–17; vol. 2: *Apparatus Fontium (In Genesim – in librum Macchabeorum),* 787–820. Hrabanus's commentary has not yet been edited.

36 Iosephus Scottus, *Epitome,* ed. Gryson, 9–10.

37 Haymo Autissiodorensis, *Annotatio libri Isaiae prophetae,* ed. Roger Gryson, Corpus Christianorum, Continuatio Mediaevalis 135C (Turnhout: Brepols, 2014), 6 and 95–110. On Haimo's biography and exegetical methods see Sumi Shimahara, *Haymon d'Auxerre, exégète carolingien* (Turnhout: Brepols, 2013), 59–81 and 435–45.

his annotations as discussed below; the other was an unknown teacher who produced a commented edition of Isaiah and three other prophets (Hosea, Zechariah, Daniel) at St. Gall in the third quarter of the ninth century. The manuscript in question is item 18 in table 5.1.[38]

Otfrid himself planned and completed his explanation of Isaiah, as well as his further commented editions, applying exegetical methods which he had learned from his teacher Hrabanus. Accordingly, his scholia are entirely derivative and reproduce a reasoned selection and adaptation of earlier exegesis. The marginalia of each commented edition draw primarily on one main model, which consists of an *abbreviatio,* an abridgement of patristic or Carolingian commentaries on the concerned biblical books.[39] Otfrid chose *abbreviationes* as the main source for his annotations because they captured the core of authoritative explanations and potentially fit into the limitations of space imposed by the side-columns of his books. In the case of the Gospels of Matthew and John, as well as for the Books of Jeremiah and Isaiah, Otfrid relied on near-contemporary Carolingian epitomes of earlier treatises, which he evidently regarded as authoritative texts and intended to disseminate.[40]

---

38 St. Gall, Stiftsbibliothek, Cod. Sang. 41. See Cinzia Grifoni, "Commented Editions of the Bible from Ninth-Century St. Gall: The Psalms, the Prophets, the Gospels," in *L'expérience exégétique au Moyen Âge et durant la première modernité,* ed. Frédérique Lachaud, Marielle Lamy and Sumi Shimahara (Leiden: Brill, forthcoming). It is noteworthy that, according to Roger Gryson, Haimo's commentary also circulated in the form of a commented edition in the ninth century (Haymo Autissiodorensis, *Annotatio,* ed. Gryson, 51–54).

39 Grifoni, "Reading the Catholic Epistles," 715–18.

40 For a description of the characteristics of Carolingian *abbreviationes* see Cantelli Berarducci, *Hrabani Mauri Opera Exegetica,* vol. 1, 11–14. Otfrid's scholia on the Gospel of Matthew drew primarily on an anonymous Carolingian commentary, which abbreviated and reworked Hrabanus's commentary. See Otfridus Wizanburgensis, *Glossae in Matthaeum,* ed. Cinzia Grifoni, Corpus Christianorum, Continuatio Mediaevalis 200 (Turnhout: Brepols, 2003), VIII–XI. For the Gospel of John, he used the *abbreviatio* of Alcuin's corresponding treatise, which Ercanbert of Fulda completed prob-

He usually added further text-related explanations to the annotations selected from the main source, which he extracted from other exegetical works and mostly copied in a darker ink during a later writing stage. When such additions stemmed from patristic commentaries, Otfrid followed in Hrabanus's footsteps and put an acronym for the author of the source at the side of the scholion in question.[41] Explanations of this sort are remarkably numerous in the commented editions of the Gospels, which formed Otfrid's main interest, as testified by his *Evangelienbuch*. Conversely, his other commented editions contain only a few additional scholia.[42]

Otfrid's explanation of Isaiah reproduces primarily the epitome of Jerome's commentary, which Joseph Scottus had completed at the request of his teacher Alcuin around the end of the eighth century. As Joseph himself stated in the dedicatory letter to Alcuin, his task was to select the core of Jerome's arguments and to make them available to both unmotivated readers, who were intimidated by the length of Jerome's work, and to smart and willing ones, who could attain the truth more quickly through his abridgment. The latter remained free to consult Jerome's "overflowing river," if more details were needed than those "in his rivulet."[43] As the investigation conducted by Roger Gryson shows, Joseph skipped Jerome's comparisons of the various translations of the Bible as well as his numerous erudite

---

ably around 830. His annotations on Jeremiah consist of an abridgment of Hrabanus's commentary.

41 On the use of the *nomina auctorum* in Carolingian works see Sita Steckel, "Von Buchstaben und Geist: Pragmatische und symbolische Dimensionen der Autorensiglen (*nomina auctorum*) bei Hrabanus Maurus," in *Karolingische Klöster: Wissenstransfer und kulturelle Innovation,* ed. Julia Becker, Tino Licht, and Stefan Weinfurter (Berlin: De Gruyter, 2015), 99–104.

42 Grifoni, "Reading the Catholic Epistles," 718–23.

43 Iosephus Scottus, *Epitome,* ed. Gryson, 492, 6–14: "Duabus autem causis, ut reor, haec ita fieri voluisti, ut vel fastidiosis tepidisque lectoribus tam longos libros legendi labor levaretur, vel ingeniosis et ardentis animi hominibus promptior breviorque quaerendae veritatis via redderetur. Si quis autem haec quasi breviora et ob id obscuriora despiciat, [...] ad fontem unde haec hausimus erecto cervice currat, et cui rivulus iste non sufficit, de super ripis suis inundanti flumine potet."

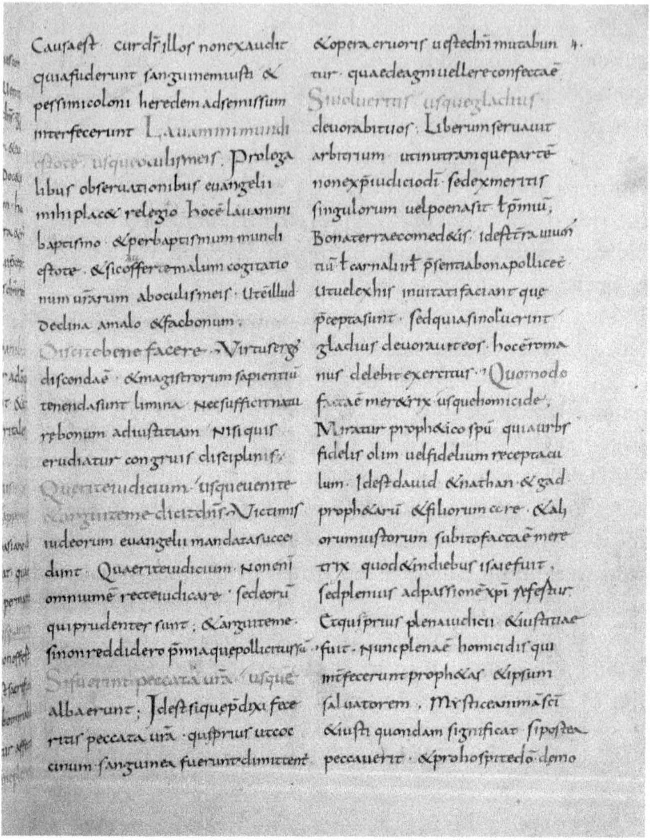

Fig. 5.2. Wolfenbüttel, Herzog August Bibliothek, 49. Weiss., fol. 4r. Source: Herzog August Bibliothek.

digressions. Through such drastic pruning, Joseph granted his readers access to the essence of Jerome's interpretation, focusing in particular on the literal and spiritual sense.[44] Although his explanations simplify the form and content of Jerome's sentences, they still presuppose some command of Latin and a familiarity

---

44 Iosephus Scottus, *Epitome,* ed. Gryson, 51–53.

with both the Bible and the various exegetical approaches to its text.

Joseph's work enjoyed a considerable success in East Francia. Six of the nine extant manuscripts transmitting the *Epitome* were produced in eastern Frankish scriptoria for local audiences. Of these six, five date to the second half of the ninth century.[45] A further, now lost, copy probably dating to this same period is listed among the entries of the tenth-century catalogue of the library of Lorsch.[46] Remarkably, the scriptorium of Wissembourg became a hub for the dissemination of Joseph's work. According to Gryson's reconstruction, a now-lost manuscript of Joseph's *Epitome* was available in Otfrid's time and served as a model for two locally produced copies. The first is the codex Wolfenbüttel, Herzog August Bibliothek, MS Guelf. 49 Weissenburg (hereafter 49W), transmitting the *Epitome* in its original form of a running commentary (see fig. 5.2);[47] the second is our 33w, in which Otfrid parceled out Joseph's text into scholia.[48] Evidently, East

---

45 See Iosephus Scottus, *Epitome,* ed. Gryson, 14–24. The five ninth-century east Frankish manuscripts containing Joseph's epitome are: Munich, Bayerische Staatsbibliothek, MS Clm 6296 (produced at Freising in the second quarter of the ninth century); Wolfenbüttel, Herzog August Bibliothek, MS Guelf. 49 Weissenburg (produced at Wissembourg around 850); 33w; St. Gall, Stiftsbibliothek, Cod. Sang. 254 (completed locally in the third quarter of the ninth century); and Fulda, Hessische Landesbibliothek, MS Aa 13 (produced at St. Gall around 900). The sixth extant east Frankish manuscript was produced at Wissembourg in the twelfth century.

46 Iosephus Scottus, *Epitome,* ed. Gryson, 14n1, quoting *Catalogi bibliothecarum antiqui,* ed. Gustav Becker (Bonn: Cohen, 1885), 108n370: "excerptio super Esaiam Iosephi Scoti."

47 Joseph's text reached St. Gall via Wissembourg. Roger Gryson regards 49w as the very exemplar from which the manuscript St. Gall, Stiftsbibliothek, Cod. Sang. 254 was copied in the third quarter of the ninth century. This information provides us with a further piece of evidence of the close intellectual networks between Wissembourg and St. Gall in Otfrid's and Hartmut's time: Iosephus Scottus, *Epitome,* ed. Gryson, 22.

48 Roger Gryson included Otfrid's scholia of 33w into the *stemma codicum* of his edition of Joseph's *Epitome.* Unfortunately, his critical apparatus does not give an account of the readings of 33w, which show how Otfrid abbreviated, corrected, and adapted his antigraph. In particular, the metric prologue, the metric epilogue, the hexameters closing the seventeen

Frankish scholars appreciated Joseph's concerns for his inexpert readers more than their colleagues elsewhere in Carolingian Europe, and regarded his abridgment as particularly adequate to address the average skills and needs of their own audience.

Otfrid himself reproduced Joseph's *Epitome* almost entirely, as far as both content and form were concerned. Thus, he provided his readers with explanations of a mostly literal and spiritual nature, avoiding both doctrinal arguments and erudite digressions, in short, strictly text-related sentences.

In some cases, however, the limitations of space imposed by the margins, and the necessity to place pertinent scholia alongside the biblical text, forced him to adapt, shorten, or even skip portions of it. Often, he simply preferred to write *et reliqua* ("and the rest") instead of copying a biblical quotation occurring in the model. In other, more significant cases, he left parts of Joseph's text out because he regarded the explanations pertaining to other biblical verses contained on the same page as more important.[49] Such occurrences demonstrate that Otfrid did not copy one segment of the *Epitome* after the other without thought. Rather, he had previously established how many of the available interpretations pertaining to the biblical text of a given page it could contain, and calculated how to position them tidily into the side-column according to their length. The ordered disposition of the annotations within the writing space was more important to Otfrid than the faithful reproduction of all the explanations conveyed by his model. His aim was to provide his audience with an easily readable tool, even if this meant that some "less important" biblical verses contained on the page remained unexplained.

---

books of Joseph's work, and the dedicatory letter to Alcuin placed after the epilogue are not transmitted in 33w. See Iosephus Scottus, *Epitome*, ed. Gryson, 20–21, 32, 37, and 64.

49 The scholia occurring on fol. 12v of 33w and explaining Isaiah 8, 1–12 provide a good example of Otfrid's *modus operandi*. Here he foresaw the lack of space for the spiritual interpretation of the verses 1–4 contained in Iosephus Scottus, *Epitome*, ed. Gryson, 115, 328–35.

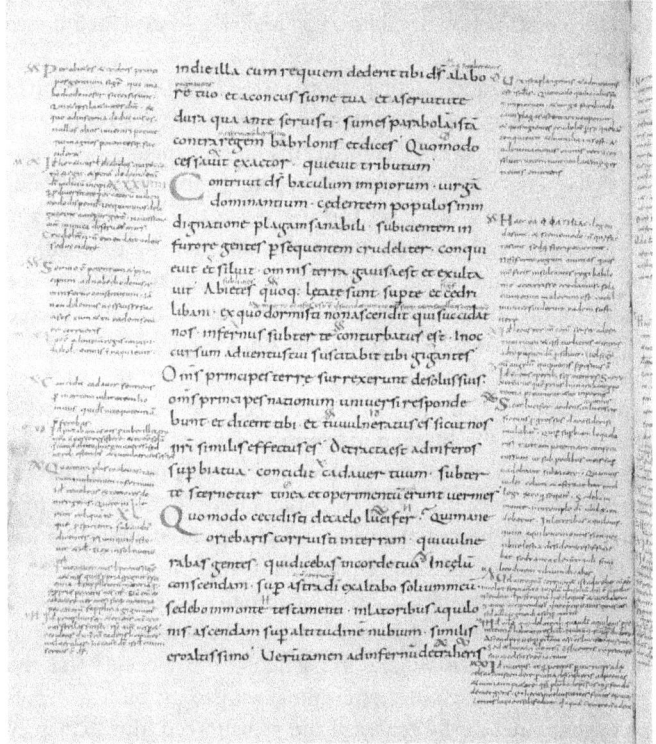

Fig. 5.3. Wolfenbüttel, Herzog August Bibliothek, 33 Weiss., fol. 18v. Spiritual annotations introduced by a red "M" for "mystice" both in the interlinear space and in the margins. Source: Herzog August Bibliothek.

Therefore, not just the content and linguistic features of Otfrid's annotations, but also his selection and copying practices reveal that his audience was not proficient students of the Bible. Rather, he worked for readers who would profit from a handy companion to Isaiah, one which conveyed a basic interpretation placed right beside the concerned verses. This intention is particularly clear in his handling of chapters 13 to 23 of Isaiah's text, which required him to make a particularly skilled rearrangement of the explanations of the *Epitome* in order to main-

235

tain the combination of biblical text and related explanations on each page.

Both Jerome and Joseph had organized their interpretation of chapters 13 to 23 according to a peculiar narrative structure. In Jerome's treatise, Book 5 contains his literal explanation of Isaiah's chapters 13 to 23; Book 6 his spiritual explanation of chapters 13 to 16; and Book 7 his spiritual explanation of chapters 17 to 23. Joseph, in contrast, drastically changed the disposition, but not the contents, of Jerome's text to bring together in one place the literal and spiritual interpretation, which he ordered by groups of verses. As a result, his Book 6 contains the literal and spiritual explanation of Isaiah's chapters 13 to 16. What Joseph dubbed his "Book 5 and 7" (referring to Jerome's disposition) contains the literal and spiritual explanation ordered by groups of verses of Isaiah's chapters 17 to 23. Thus, for instance, Joseph provided a literal and spiritual interpretation of the first 10 verses of chapter 13, then a literal and spiritual interpretation of verses 11–16 of the same chapter, and so on.

Otfrid took Joseph's revision of Jerome's text as a reference for this complicated section. However, the material setting of the commented edition, and in particular the necessity that the scholia in the side-columns pertain exactly to the biblical verses accommodated in the center of the page, forced him to display the text of his source according to yet another pattern. Otfrid rearranged Joseph's text in order to obtain, when possible, both a literal and a spiritual explanation for every single verse, and not for groups of verses as Joseph had done. In general, he excerpted two distinct annotations from the *Epitome* for each biblical verse — one for the literal, one for the spiritual interpretation — and attached them through distinct reference signs to the relevant *lemma* (see fig. 5.3). Otfrid copied them in two different writing stages. In the first phase, he wrote all the annotations containing the literal interpretation and placed them at approximately the same height as the relevant biblical verse, taking care to leave some space in between for the corresponding spiritual explanation. In the second writing phase, he copied the spiritual annotations into the space he had left blank and marked them

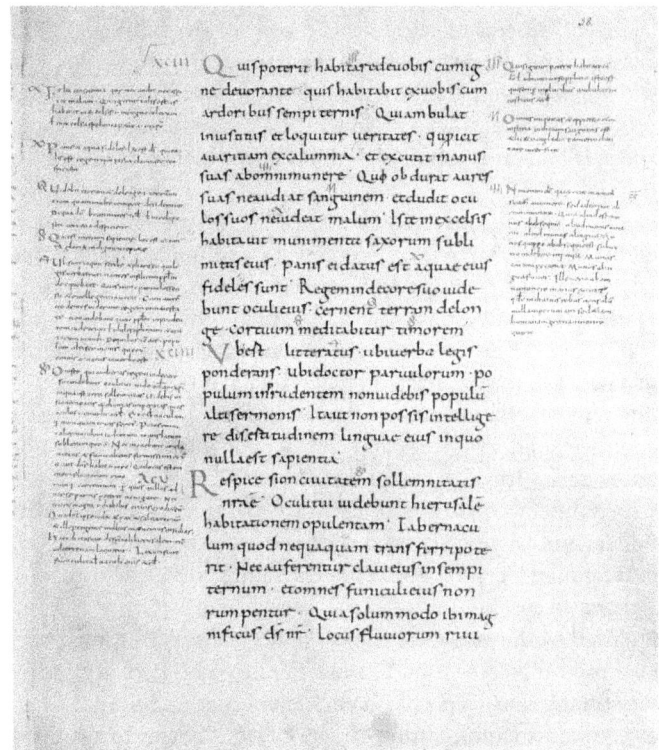

Fig. 5.4. Wolfenbüttel, Herzog August Bibliothek, 33 Weiss., fol. 38r. Additional scholion (third on the right) flanked by the acronym GG for Gregory the Great. Source: Herzog August Bibliothek.

with a capital "M" for *mystice* ("according to the spiritual sense," see fig. 5.3).[50] In this way, he signaled to his readers in advance what they would find in the ensuing sentence and granted an easy orientation within the many annotations contained on the page. Moreover, the lack of space in the margins led him to place a considerable amount of the spiritual expositions of this section in the interlinear space, which he otherwise left blank. This

---

50 Butzmann, *Weißenburger Handschriften*, 144, erroneously regarded the occurrences of the capital letter "M" as an acronym of Hrabanus Maurus.

laborious process of selection and copy of the right exegetical passage onto the right place of the page clearly shows that Otfrid aimed to simplify the narrative structure of his sources and provide his readers with an immediate access to both the literal and spiritual explanation of the biblical verses displayed on each page.

On two occasions Otfrid enriched the interpretation provided by Joseph's *Epitome* of Jerome with additional explanations taken from the *Homilies* of Gregory the Great. In both cases he marked these additions with the acronym "GG," following Hrabanus's use.[51] The first occurrence concerns Isaiah 11:2 (fol. 16r of 33w). Although he had already explained this verse in three different scholia taken from his main source, Otfrid chose to contravene his own rules and copied a long, text-related annotation taken from Gregory's *Homilies on Ezekiel* into both the upper and lower margins of folios 15v and 16r.[52] It is not easy to understand why he attached such importance to this addition, even though it completes the interpretation provided by Joseph's *Epitome* according to the moral sense. Perhaps Otfrid was influenced by the exegetical choices of his teacher Hrabanus, who also used this Gregorian passage to enrich his own commentary on the same verse of Isaiah.[53] The second occurrence of an integration stemming from Gregory's work relates to the third pericope of Isaiah 33:15, in particular the words "ab omni munere" (see fig. 5.4). Otfrid copied a short passage from Gregory's *Homilies on the Gospels,* in which the Church Father mentioned this pericope and briefly surveyed the various sorts of *munus* (gift).[54] Since Joseph's *Epitome* did not include any explanation

---

51 Gryson was incorrect when he suggested that these acronyms were an optical illusion of Hans Butzmann, who in fact spotted only one of them. See respectively: Iosephus Scottus, *Epitome*, ed. Gryson, 20, and Butzmann, *Weißenburger Handschriften*, 144.

52 The annotation reproduces Gregorius Magnus, *Homiliae in Hiezechielem*, ed. Marc Adriaen, lib. 2, hom. 7, ll. 204–48, Corpus Christianorum, Continuatio Mediaevalis 142 (Turnhout: Brepols, 1971).

53 See Cantelli Berarducci, *Hrabani Mauri Opera Exegetica*, vol. 2, 795.

54 Gregorius Magnus, *Homiliae in Evangelia,* ed. Raymond Étaix, 141, lib. 1, hom. 4, ll. 118–24, Corpus Christianorum, Continuatio Mediaevalis 142

of this portion of Isaiah's verse and there was still enough space on the page, presumably Otfrid added this passage with the aim of filling the gap in the main source. It is unclear why he decided to enrich Joseph's *Epitome* only on these two occasions, since he could have easily spotted further verses of the Book of Isaiah which the *Epitome* had either ignored or not exhaustively explained. As we have seen above, Otfrid did not strive to obtain a complete interpretation of Isaiah. These sporadic, even fortuitous integrations indicate that he had them gathered in a self-crafted dossier of patristic extracts, probably in the form of *schedulae* (slips of parchment), which he had ordered according to the relevant biblical verse and could use if a suitable opportunity arose.

Conclusions

The codicological features, the compilation practices, and the content of the annotations of Otfrid's commented edition of the Book of Isaiah enable us to speculate about his purposes and intended audience. Otfrid planned 33w to serve as a reference book for the monks of his community, whom he provided with the text of Isaiah and an exegetical first orientation according to the literal and spiritual sense. His purpose was to support his confreres' study of this biblical book with a tool, which transmitted an authoritative explanation and was at the same time easy to consult and to understand. To this end, he relied upon Joseph Scottus's epitome, which reproduced the core of Jerome's interpretation in simplified form, in terms of both its contents and the syntax of its Latin sentences. He did not aim to provide his readers with an explanation of all the verses of Isaiah. Rather, he shortened the text of the epitome when space limitations imposed it. On only two occasions, he enriched it with passages culled elsewhere. Though usually short and strictly text-related, his annotations did not include elementary explanations: they addressed an audience that was able to understand this kind of

---

(Turnhout: Brepols, 1999).

Latin and was familiar with the exegetical techniques (metaphor, typology, etc.) leading to a spiritual interpretation. Otfrid wrote neither for pupils at the beginning of their career nor for experts in the biblical studies, but rather for those members of his community who already had some introductory theological training and could profit from the basic approach provided by his annotations.

When comparing Otfrid's explanation of the Book of Isaiah with those of his contemporaries, we can observe that many other Carolingian scholars shared his choice to use or produce an abridgment of Jerome's treatise. However, Otfrid was one of only two Carolingian scholars who decided to transform such an abridgment into scholia and to attach them skillfully to the text of Isaiah in the framework of a commented edition. What advantages did he see in this layout over an epitome arranged in the usual form of a running commentary (see fig. 5.3)?

One might speculate that Otfrid opted for the production of commented editions for material or economic reasons, such as the need to combine two books (the Bible and its interpretation) into one due to lack of resources. But the case of his edition of Isaiah shows that this hypothesis cannot hold, since the text of Joseph's epitome, which Otfrid reproduced in his annotations, was available at Wissembourg in two other copies in his time (one is now lost, the other is 49w). Moreover, it was exactly in this period that the monastery reached the peak of its wealth and the local scriptorium increased its output considerably, particularly with regard to biblical studies.[55] If material resources played no role in Otfrid's decision, I would conclude that he regarded the combination of biblical text and authoritative short notes, typical of this book format, as particularly useful for those members of his community who did not have the skills or the motivation to read exhaustive commentaries, but, being monks, were nevertheless supposed to engage with the study of the Latin Bible. His commented edition provided them with the text of Isaiah and related annotations in close proximity, which

---

55 Grifoni, "Reading the Catholic Epistles," 707–8.

they could copy and meditate upon without too much effort, at least in Otfrid's vision.

Otfrid's effort in producing commented editions would therefore be in line with the concern that led him to write his vernacular Gospel harmony, with which he addressed a different, wider East Frankish audience whose command of Latin was poor or nonexistent. His commented editions therefore provide us with further evidence of his general commitment to granting East Frankish lay and ecclesiastical audiences access to certain books of the Bible, despite their linguistic difficulties with Latin.

Otfrid's use of commented editions as analyzed in this contribution invites us to widen the scope of the investigation and to engage for the first time with the reasons leading to the spread of this type of book in the Carolingian period. As we have seen, commented editions of the Bible were planned all across Western Europe to contain the biblical text and related explanations in Latin. According to the origin of the extant manuscripts and to the few available studies, however, they were particularly widespread exactly in those regions, such as the British Isles and the eastern part of the Carolingian Empire, in which Latin was a foreign language. The study of all manuscripts listed in table 5.1 will show whether this apparent imbalance in their spread was a mere coincidence or, conversely, whether commented editions were regarded — not only by Otfrid — as the most suitable tool to enable less educated readers to access the Latin Bible.

Bibliography

Manuscripts

Augsburg, Diözesanmuseum St. Afra., MS 1002 (*olim* Archiv des Bistums, MS 6).
Cambridge, University Library, MS Add. 10062. https://cudl.lib.cam.ac.uk/view/MS-ADD-10062/1.
Colmar, Archives d'Alsace, Archive du Haut Rhin, Fragm. 86 (13).
Dillingen, Studienbibliothek, MS XV Fragm. 26 + Oslo, Schøyen Collection, MS 74. https://www.digitale-sammlungen.de/de/view/bsb00005812?page=,1. https://www.schoyencollection.com/palaeography-collection-introduction/latin-book-scripts/carolingian-minuscule/ms-074.
Eremo Camaldoli, Archivio storico, MS s.n. + Washington, DC, Museum of the Bible, Leaf from the "psalter of St. Romuald" (formerly Oslo, Schøyen Collection, MS 620). https://collections.museumofthebible.org/artifacts/24711-leaf-from-the-psalter-of-st-romuald?&tab=description.
Florence, Biblioteca Medicea Laurenziana, MS Ashb. 54.
Frankfurt, Stadt- und Universitätsbibliothek, MS Barth 32. https://sammlungen.ub.uni-frankfurt.de/msma/content/titleinfo/3591450.
Fulda, Hessische Landesbibliothek, MS Aa 13. https://fuldig.hs-fulda.de/viewer/image/PPN321275837/1/LOG_0000/.
Göttweig, Stiftsbibliothek, Cod. 30 (rot) / 2 (schwarz). https://manuscripta.at/diglit/AT2000-30/0001.
Ivrea, Biblioteca Capitolare, MS LXXIX (28).
Laon, Bibliothèque Patrimoniale Suzanne-Martinet, MS 14.
Munich, Bayerische Staatsbibliothek, MS Clm 6296. https://www.digitale-sammlungen.de/en/details/bsb00049256.
Munich, Bayerische Staatsbibliothek, MS Clm 29315/3 + Regensburg, Bischöfliche Zentralbibliothek, MS fragm. IV.2.1 + Prague, Národní galerie Inv. Nr. K 7314. https://nbn-resolving.org/urn:nbn:de:bvb:12-bsb00061158-3.
Munich, Bayerische Staatsbibliothek, MSs Clm 7665 + Clm 7673 + Clm 7679.

Orléans, Médiathèque, MS 48 (45). https://mediatheques.orleans-metropole.fr/ark:/77916/FRCGMBPF-452346101-01A/D18010574.locale=fr.
St. Gall, Stiftsbibliothek, Cod. Sang. 27. https://www.e-codices.unifr.ch/en/list/one/csg/0027.
St. Gall, Stiftsbibliothek, Cod. Sang. 41. https://www.e-codices.unifr.ch/en/list/one/csg/0041.
St. Gall, Stiftsbibliothek, Cod. Sang. 50. https://www.e-codices.unifr.ch/en/list/one/csg/0050.
St. Gall, Stiftsbibliothek, Cod. Sang. 254. https://www.e-codices.unifr.ch/en/list/one/csg/0254.
St. Gall, Stiftsbibliothek, Cod. Sang. 1395, pp. 440–441. https://www.e-codices.unifr.ch/en/list/one/csg/1395.
Troyes, Médiathèque Jacques-Chirac, MS 615. https://portail.mediatheque.grand-troyes.fr/iguana/www.main.cls?surl=search#RecordId=2.2573.
Vatican City, Biblioteca Apostolica Vaticana, Cod. Reg. lat. 307. https://digi.vatlib.it/mss/detail/217807.
Vercelli, Biblioteca Capitolare, MS LXII (2).
Vercelli, Biblioteca Capitolare, MS CXLIX (136).
Vienna, Österreichische Nationalbibliothek, MS 1239.
Wolfenbüttel, Herzog August Bibliothek, MS Guelf. 26 Weissenburg. https://diglib.hab.de/?db=mss&list=ms&id=26-weiss&catalog=Westphal.
Wolfenbüttel, Herzog August Bibliothek, MS Guelf. 32 Weissenburg. https://diglib.hab.de/?db=mss&list=ms&id=32-weiss&catalog=Butzmann.
Wolfenbüttel, Herzog August Bibliothek, MS Guelf. 33 Weissenburg. http://diglib.hab.de/?db=mss&list=collection&id=weiss.
Wolfenbüttel, Herzog August Bibliothek, MS Guelf. 36 Weissenburg. https://diglib.hab.de/?db=mss&list=ms&id=36-weiss.
Wolfenbüttel, Herzog August Bibliothek, MS Guelf. 49 Weissenburg. https://diglib.hab.de/?db=mss&list=ms&id=49-weiss&catalog=Westphal.

Wolfenbüttel, Herzog August Bibliothek, MS Guelf. 59 Weissenburg. https://diglib.hab.de/?db=mss&list=ms&id=59-weiss.

Zurich, Staatsarchiv, MS W I 3.19 (fols. 24r–25v).

Primary

Catalogi bibliothecarum antiqui. Edited by Gustav Becker. Bonn: Cohen, 1885.

Codices Reginenses Latini. Tomus II: Codices 251–500, edited by Andreas Wilmart. Vatican City: Bibliotheca Apostolica Vaticana, 1945.

Gregorius Magnus. *Homiliae in Evangelia.* Edited by Raymond Étaix. Corpus Christianorum Series Latina 141. Turnhout: Brepols, 1999.

———. *Homiliae in Hiezechielem.* Edited by Marc Adriaen. Corpus Christianorum Series Latina 142. Turnhout: Brepols, 1971.

Haymo Autissiodorensis. *Annotatio libri Isaiae prophetae.* Edited by Roger Gryson. Corpus Christianorum, Continuatio Mediaevalis 135C. Turnhout: Brepols, 2014.

Iosephus Scottus. *Epitome explanationum in Isaiam beati Hieronymi presbyteri.* Edited by Roger Gryson. Corpus Christianorum, Continuatio Mediaevalis 284. Turnhout: Brepols, 2018.

Otfridus Wizanburgensis. *Glossae in Matthaeum.* Edited by Cinzia Grifoni. Corpus Christianorum, Continuatio Mediaevalis 200. Turnhout: Brepols, 2003.

Otfrid von Weißenburg. *Das "Evangelienbuch" in der Überlieferung der Freisinger Handschrift: (Bayerische Staatsbibliothek München, cgm. 14).* Edition und Untersuchungen. Edited by Karin Pivernetz. 2 Volumes. Göppingen: Verlag Kümmerle, 2000.

———. *Evangelienbuch.* Edited by Wolfgang Kleiber and Ernst Hellgardt, Volume 1.1: *Edition nach dem Wiener Codex 2687;* Volume 1.2: *Einleitung und Apparat.* Tübingen: Max Niemeyer Verlag, 2004; Volume 2.1: *Edition der Heidelberger Hand-*

schrift P (Codex Pal. Lat. 52) und der Handschrift D (Codex Discissus: Bonn, Berlin/Krakau, Wolfenbüttel). Tübingen: Max Niemeyer Verlag, 2006; Volume 2.2: *Einleitung und Apparat.* Tübingen: Max Niemeyer Verlag, 2010.

Secondary

Andrei, Filippo. "Il Salterio glossato di San Romualdo." *Benedictina* 49 (2002): 23–52.

Bischoff, Bernhard. *Die südostdeutschen Schreibschulen und Bibliotheken in der Karolingerzeit,* Volume 2: *Die vorwiegend österreichischen Diözesen.* Wiesbaden: Harrassowitz, 1980.

———. *Katalog der festländischen Handschriften des neunten Jahrhunderts (mit Ausnahme der wisigotischen).* 4 Volumes. Wiesbaden: Harrassowitz, 1998–2017.

Butzmann, Hans. *Die Weißenburger Handschriften,* Kataloge der Herzog August Bibliothek Wolfenbüttel. Neue Reihe 10. Frankfurt am Main: Klostermann, 1964.

Cantelli Berarducci, Silvia. *Hrabani Mauri Opera Exegetica. Repertorium Fontium.* 3 Volumes. Instrumenta Patristica et Mediaevalia 38. Turnhout: Brepols, 2006. DOI: 10.1484/M.IPM-EB.5.112148.

———. "L'esegesi ai Salmi nel sec. IX. Il caso delle edizioni commentate del Salterio." In *Präsenz und Verwendung der Heiligen Schrift im christlichen Frühmittelalter,* edited by Patrizia Carmassi, 59–115. Wiesbaden: Harrassowitz, 2008.

Crivello, Fabrizio. "Ein weiteres Fragment eines karolingischen Prachtpsalters aus Regensburg." *Bulletin of the National Gallery in Prague* 11 (2001): 58–64.

De Blic, Jacques. "L'oeuvre exégétique de Walafrid Strabon et la *Glossa ordinaria.*" *Recherches de théologie ancienne et médiévale* 16 (1949): 5–28.

De Bruyne, Donatien. *Summaries, Divisions and Rubrics of the Latin Bible.* Turnhout: Brepols, 2014. DOI: 10.1484/M.STT-EB.5.107417.

D'Imperio, Francesca Sara. "Le glosse ai quattro Vangeli nel ms. St. Gallen, Stiftsbibliothek 50." *Studi Medievali* 41, no. 2 (2000): 549–90.

Euw, Anton von. "Psalmenkommentare und kommentierte Psalter aus dem frühen Mittelalter." In *Mittelalterliche Handschriften der Kölner Dombibliothek*, edited by Heinz Finger, 201–41. Libelli Rhenani 34. Cologne: Erzbischöfliche Diözesan- und Dombibliothek, 2010.

Ferrari, Michele Camillo. "Before the *Glossa Ordinaria:* The Ezekiel Fragment in Irish Minuscule, Zürich, Staatsarchiv W3.19.XII, and Other Experiments towards a *Bible commentée* in the Early Middle Ages." In *Biblical Studies in the Early Middle Ages*, edited by Claudio Leonardi and Giovanni Orlandi, 283–307. Firenze: SISMEL Edizioni del Galluzzo, 2005.

Ferrari, Mirella. "Libri e testi prima del Mille." In *Storia della Chiesa di Ivrea dalle origini al XV secolo*, edited by Giorgio Cracco and Andrea Piazza, 511–33. Chiese d'Italia 1. Rome: Viella, 1998.

Frank, Irmgard. *Aus Glossenhandschriften des 8. bis 14. Jahrhunderts. Quellen zur Geschichte einer Überlieferungsart.* Heidelberg: Universitätsverlag Winter, 1984.

Gamberini, Roberto. "Il commento a Geremia e alle Lamentazioni di Rabano Mauro. Composizione, diffusione e fortuna immediate." *Studi Medievali* 52, no. 1 (2011): 1–30.

Geuenich, Dieter. "Beobachtungen zu Grimald von St. Gallen, Erzkapellan und Oberkanzler Ludwigs des Deutschen." In *Litterae Medii Aevi. Festschrift für Johanne Autenrieth zu ihrem 65. Geburtstag*, edited by Michael Borgolte and Herrad Spilling, 55–68. Sigmaringen: Thorbecke, 1988.

Gibson, Margaret. "Carolingian Glossed Psalters." In *The Early Medieval Bible: Its Production, Decoration and Use*, edited by Richard Gameson, 78–100. Cambridge: Cambridge University Press, 1994.

Gorman, Michael M. *"La plus ancienne édition commentée:* The Ezechiel Fragment in Irish Minuscule, Now in Zurich (CLA 7.1008)." *Revue Bénédictine* 114, no. 2 (2004): 276–88. DOI: 10.1484/J.RB.5.100588.

Grifoni, Cinzia. "Auf Otfrids Spuren in der frühmittelalterlichen Bibliothek Weißenburg." In *Marginalien im Bild und Text: Essays zu mittelalterlichen Handschriften*, edited by Patrizia Carmassi and Christian Heitzmann, 79–101. Wolfenbütteler Forschungen 156. Wiesbaden: Harrassowitz Verlag, 2019.

———. "Commented Editions of the Bible from Ninth-Century St. Gall: The Psalms, the Prophets, the Gospels." In *L'expérience exégétique au Moyen Âge et durant la première modernité,* edited by Frédérique Lachaud, Marielle Lamy and Sumi Shimahara. Leiden: Brill, forthcoming.

———. "Reading the Catholic Epistles: Glossing Practices in Early Medieval Wissembourg." In *The Annotated Book in the Early Middle Ages: Practices of Reading and Writing,* edited by Mariken Teeuwen and Irene van Renswoude, 705–42. Utrecht Studies in Medieval Literacy 38. Turnhout: Brepols, 2017. DOI: 10.1484/M.USML-EB.5.115039.

Haubrichs, Wolfgang. "Eine prosopographische Skizze zu Otfrid von Weißenburg." In *Otfrid von Weißenburg,* edited by Wolfgang Kleiber, 397–414. Darmstadt: Wissenschaftliche Buchgesellschaft, 1978.

———. "Otfrid de Wissembourg, élève de Raban Maur, et l'héritage de l'école de Fulda au monastère de Wissembourg." In *Raban Maur et son temps,* edited by Philippe Depreux, Stéphane Lebecq, Michel J.-L. Perrin, and Olivier Szerwiniack, 155–72. Collection Haut Moyen Âge 9. Turnhout: Brepols, 2010. DOI: 10.1484/M.HAMA-EB.3.4641.

———. "Otfrids St. Galler 'Studienfreunde.'" *Amsterdamer Beiträge zur älteren Germanistik* 4 (1973): 49–112. DOI: 10.1163/18756719-004-01-90000003.

Hawk, Brandon W. "A Fragment of Colossians with Hiberno-Latin Glosses in St. Gall, Stiftsbibliothek, Cod. Sang. 1395." In *Sacris Erudiri* 51 (2012): 233–56. DOI: 10.1484/J.SE.1.103175.

Hellgardt, Ernst. *Die exegetischen Quellen von Otfrids Evangelienbuch. Beiträge zu ihrer Ermittlung.* Hermaea N. F. 41. Tübingen: Niemeyer, 1981.

Holtz, Louis. "Glosse e commenti." In *Lo spazio letterario del Medioevo. Medioevo Latino,* Volume 3: *La ricezione del testo,* edited by Guglielmo Cavallo, Claudio Leonardi, and Enrico Menestò, 59–112. Rome: Salerno Editrice, 1995.

———. "La typologie des manuscrits grammaticaux latins." *Revue d'Histoire des Textes* 7 (1977): 247–69. DOI: 10.3406/rht.1978.1167.

———. "Le rôle des commentaires d'auteurs classiques dans l'émergence d'une mise en page associant texte et commentaire (Moyen Âge occidental)." In *Le commentaire entre tradition et innovation,* edited by Marie-Odile Goulet-Cazé 101–17. Paris: Librairie Philosophique J. Vrin, 2000.

———. "Les manuscrits latins à gloses et à commentaires: de l'antiquité à l'époque carolingienne." In *Il libro e il testo,* edited by Cesare Questa and Renato Raffaelli, 139–67. Urbino: Università degli studi, 1984.

Kleiber, Wolfgang. *Otfrid von Weißenburg. Untersuchungen zur handschriftlichen Überlieferung und Studien zum Aufbau des Evangelienbuches.* Bibliotheca Germanica 14. Bern: Francke, 1971.

Macaluso, Andrea. "Rabano Mauro e il Salterio glossato di Fulda (Frankfurt am Main, Stadt- und Universitätsbibliothek, Barth. 32." In *Raban Maur et son temps,* edited by Philippe Depreux, Stéphane Lebecq, Michel J.-L. Perrin, and Olivier Szerwiniack, 325–54. Collection Haut Moyen Âge 9. Turnhout: Brepols, 2010. DOI: 10.1484/M.HAMA-EB.3.4651.

McKitterick, Rosamond. *The Carolingians and the Written Word.* Cambridge: Cambridge University Press, 1989. DOI: 10.1017/CBO9780511583599.

McNamee, Kathleen. "Another Chapter in the History of Scholia." *Classical Quarterly* 48, no. 1 (1998): 269–88. DOI: 10.1093/cq/48.1.269.

Michel, Paul, and Alexander Schwarz. *Unz in obanentig. Aus der Werkstatt der karolingischen Exegeten Alcuin, Erkanbert und Otfrid von Weißenburg.* Bonn: Bouvier Verlag Herbert Grundmann, 1978.

O'Sullivan, Sinéad. "Book as Bibliotheca: The Emergence of the Commented Edition." *Speculum* 100, no. 2 (2025): forthcoming.

Ottaviano, Silvia. "Reading between the Lines of Virgil's Medieval Manuscripts." In *The Annotated Book in the Early*

Middle Ages: Practices of Reading and Writing, edited by Mariken Teeuwen and Irene van Renswoude, 397–426. Utrecht Studies in Medieval Literacy 38. Turnhout: Brepols, 2017. DOI: 10.1484/M.USML-EB.5.115029.

Parker, David C. "The Undertext Writing." In *Codex Zacynthius: Catena, Palimpsest, Lectionary*, edited by Hugh A.G. Houghton and David C. Parker, 19–32. Text and Studies 3.21. Piscataway: Gorgias Press, 2020. DOI: 10.31826/9781463241087-007.

Rädle, Fidel. *Studien zu Smaragdus von Saint-Mihiel*. Munich: Wilhelm Fink Verlag, 1974.

Savigni, Raffaele. "Il commentario a Isaia di Aimone di Auxerre e le sue fonti." In *Biblical Studies in the Early Middle Ages*, edited by Claudio Leonardi and Giovanni Orlandi, 215–38. Florence: SISMEL Edizioni del Galluzzo, 2005.

Schiegg, Markus. *Frühmittelalterliche Glossen*. Heidelberg: Universitätsverlag Winter, 2015.

———. "Source Marks in Scholia: Evidence from an Early Medieval Gospel Manuscript." In *The Annotated Book in the Early Middle Ages: Practices of Reading and Writing*, edited by Mariken Teeuwen and Irene van Renswoude, 237–62. Utrecht Studies in Medieval Literacy 38. Turnhout: Brepols, 2017. DOI: 10.1484/M.USML-EB.5.115022.

Shimahara, Sumi. *Haymon d'Auxerre, exégète carolingien*. Collection Haut Moyen Âge 16. Turnhout: Brepols, 2013. DOI: 10.1484/M.HAMA-EB.5.106063.

Smith, Lesley. *The Glossa Ordinaria. The Making of a Medieval Bible Commentary*. Commentaria. Sacred Texts and Their Commentaries: Jewish, Christian and Islamic 3. Leiden: Brill, 2009.

Steckel, Sita. "Von Buchstaben und Geist: Pragmatische und symbolische Dimensionen der Autorensiglen (*nomina auctorum*) bei Hrabanus Maurus." In *Karolingische Klöster: Wissenstransfer und kulturelle Innovation*, edited by Julia Becker, Tino Licht, and Stefan Weinfurter, 89–130. Materielle Textkulturen 4. Berlin: De Gruyter, 2015. DOI: 10.1515/9783110371222.89.

Stoppacci, Patrizia. "'Per varietates translationum....' Il commento ai Salmi di Cassiodoro tra versioni del salterio e salteri glossati." *Filologia Mediolatina* 20 (2013): 89–142.

Tibbetts, Tanya Nicole Sidney. "Uses of the Psalter in Carolingian St Gallen." PhD thesis, University of Cambridge, 2002.

Tristano, Caterina. "I percorsi della spiritualità sui fogli di un libro: il Salterio di San Romualdo a Camaldoli." In *Ianuensis non nascitur sed fit. Studi per Dino Puncuh,* Volume 2: *1291–1339,* edited by Carlo Bitossi. Quaderni della Società Ligure di Storia Patria 7. Genoa: Status, 2019. DOI: 10.5281/zenodo.3462500.

Unterkircher, Franz. *Die Glossen des Psalters von Mondsee (vor 788).* Fribourg: Universitätsverlag, 1974.

Wilson, Nigel G. "The Relation of Text and Commentary in Greek Books." In *Il libro e il testo,* edited by Cesare Questa and Renato Raffaelli, 103–10. Urbino: Università degli studi, 1984.

Wunderle, Elisabeth. *Die mittelalterlichen Handschriften der Studienbibliothek Dillingen.* Wiesbaden: Harrassowitz, 2006.

Zetzel, James E.G. *Marginal Scholarship and Textual Deviance: The "Commentum Cornuti" and the Early Scholia on Persius.* London: Institute of Classical Studies, 2005.

6

Rechtsblöcke, Scribes, and Layout Strategies in a Ninth-Century Legal Collection: Modena, Biblioteca Capitolare MS O. I. 2

Thom Gobbitt

Introduction

Modena, Biblioteca Capitolare, MS O. I. 2 is a collection of early medieval legal texts, edited as the *Liber Legum,* highly decorated throughout, and produced in the mid- to late ninth century, probably at Modena, northern Italy.[1] For a long time, the entire manuscript was misdated in the scholarship to the late tenth century as the final quire includes a calendar beginning in 991 in

1   Older scholarship had opted for Nonatola as the place of origin, but more recently production in Modena has been argued. See the introduction to the manuscripts in the recent edition of the *Admonitio Generalis:* Hubert Mordek, Klaus Zechiel-Eckes, and Michael Glatthaar, eds., *Die Admonitio generalis Karls der Großen, Fontes iuris germanici antiqui in usum scholarum separatim editi* 16 (Hanover: Monumenta Germaniae Historica, 2012), 66. I would like to thank Dr. Britta Mischke for her informed comments on an earlier version of this chapter. I would also like to thank the Austrian Science Fund (FWF) who supported the research project in which this chapter was researched and prepared (Project No. P29968-G28).

a securely dateable hand. But more recent work has recognized the final quire as a self-contained addition,[2] and has pushed the date back for the main hand to the mid- to late ninth century.[3] While this last quire is mostly beyond the scope of this study, it has been argued elsewhere that underlying similarities in the script indicate that the manuscript was produced and retained within the same community (which in older scholarship was thought to be the monastery at Nonatola) across at least the first century of its existence.[4]

The early medieval legal collection itself comprises introductory prologues, a group of law codes — the *Lex Salica, Lex Ribuaria, Leges Langobardorum, Lex Alamannorum,* and *Lex Baiuvariorum* — and a selection of Carolingian capitularies of Charlemagne, Pippin of Italy, Louis the Pious, Lothar, and Louis

---

2   Guiseppe Russo, "Leggi Longobarde nel codice O.I.2. della Biblioteca Capitolare di Modena," in *Atti del VI Congresso internazionale di studi sull'alto medioevo, Milano, 21–25 ottobre 1978* (Spoleto: Presso la Sede del Centro Studi, 1980), 616; Walter Pohl, *Werkstätte der Erinnerung: Montecassino und die Gestaltung der langobardischen Vergangenheit* (Vienna: Oldenbourg, 2001), 123–24; and Hubert Mordek, *Bibliotheca capitularium regum Francorum manuscripta: Überlieferung und Traditionszusammenhangder fränkischen Herrschererlasse,* Monumenta Germaniae Historica, Hilfsmittel 15 (Munich: Hahn, 1995), 267.

3   Annalisa Bracciotti argues for a *terminus post quem* of 855 for the Modena manuscript. Moreover, Britta Mischke notes in a forthcoming article that this dating would overlap with the later years of Eberhard of Friuli's life, who is thought to have died somewhere between 864–866. See Annalisa Bracciotti, ed., *"Origo Gentis Langobardorum." Testo critico, commento,* Biblioteca di cultura romanobarbarica (Rome: Herder, 1998), 59–61; Britta Mischke, "Lupus *Liber Legum* Reconsidered: Connections Between a North Italian Fragment and the *Liber Legum,*" in *Books of Law in the Long Tenth Century,* ed. Thom Gobbitt [unpublished]. I would like to thank Colleen Curran, Anna Dorofeeva, and Evina Stein for their further paleographical insights into the dating of the various contributing hands, and for their independent confirmation of a late ninth-century date. Dr. Curran prefers the late ninth-century date for all hands, while Drs. Dorofeeva and Stein suggest a broader date of the mid- to late-ninth century for hand 3 (personal communication, November and December 2019). Any errors, as ever, remain my own.

4   Pohl, *Werkstätte der Erinnerung,* 126.

II.[5] The exemplar for the manuscript was a law book, now no longer extant, which belonged to one "Eurardus," as named in the first lines of both introductory poems in the Modena manuscript (fol. 10r, ll. 17 and 28) and thought to have been Count Eberhard of Friuli (c. 815–16 December 867).[6] The law book itself is a systemization and compilation attributed to a "Lupus" (fol. 10r, l. 28),[7] usually assumed with varying degrees of certainty to have been Lupus Servatus, abbot of Ferrières (c. 805–c. 862).[8] Pressing back gently against this argument is the observation that the "Lupus" in question only identifies himself as the composer of the two introductory poems (fol. 10r, ll. 15–26, and fol. 10r, l. 27–fol. 10v, l. 2), rather than of the collection as a whole.[9] Britta Mischke further argues that, rather than seeing the Modena manuscript as one surviving branch of the *Liber Legum*, a text that she argues exists only in modern editorial reconstruction, it is better to consider the Modena manuscript as a capitulary compilation in its own right.[10] Her ongoing work continues to position the manuscript in its north Italian contexts.

---

5 See Mordek, *Bibliotheca capitularium regum Francorum*, 257–67; "Modena, Biblioteca Capitolare, O. I. 2," in *Bibliotheca Legum: A Database on Carolingian Secular Law-Texts*, ed. Karl Ubl, http://www.leges.uni-koeln.de/en/mss/codices/modena-bc-o-i-2/; and "Modena, Biblioteca Capitolare, O. I. 2," in *Capitularia: Edition der fränkischen Herrschererlasse*, ed. Karl Ubl, https://capitularia.uni-koeln.de/en/mss/modena-bc-o-i-2/.

6 Russo, "Leggi Longobarde," 617 and 621; Pohl, *Werkstätte der Erinnerung*, 122; and Rosamond McKitterick, *The Carolingians and the Written Word* (Cambridge: Cambridge University Press, 1989), 260–61.

7 Johannes Merkel, *Die Geschichte des Langobardenrechts* (Berlin: Verlag von Wilhelm Hertz, 1850), 18–19.

8 Oliver Münsch, *Der "Liber Legum" des Lupus von Ferrières* (Frankfurt am Main: Peter Lang, 2001).

9 Mischke, "Lupus' *Liber Legum* Reconsidered," and Harald Siems, "Textbearbeitung und Umgang mit Rechtstexten im Frühmittelalter. Zur Umgestaltung der *Leges* im *Liber legum* des Lupus," in *Recht im frühmittelalterlichen Gallien. Spätantike, Tradition und germanische Wertvorstellung*, Rechtsgeschichtliche Schriften, 7, ed. Harald Siems, Karin Nehlsen-von Stryk, and Dieter Strauch (Cologne: Böhlau, 1995), 29–72.

10 Britta Mischke, "Manuscript of the Month December 2017: Modena, Biblioteca Capitolare, O. I. 2," in *Capitularia: Edition der fränkischen*

The laws and capitularies have sometimes been considered in modern scholarship as comprising two clearly divided and self-contained sections. Hubert Mordek stated that "the collection is clearly divided into two parts," describing each as a self-contained "law block" (*Rechtsblock*).[11] I would like to critically examine this assertion here and shall argue, against it, that the capitularies are better seen as one more collection of legal texts among many and that there is in fact no clear divide in the materiality, *mise-en-page,* or text between "barbarian" law and imperial capitulary in the manuscript contexts. While there are changes in the *mise-en-page* used to present the various legal texts, these divisions do not occur in relation to changes between the law and capitulary, or between the individual laws. Likewise, the major changes do not occur between the stints of the contributing scribes, so are not personal preference, but rather these changes are an ongoing development implemented throughout the production as the scribes reflect on their sources and materials and the needs of the law book and its (anticipated) readers. In addition to the developing *mise-en-page* throughout the collected legal texts, the anticipated layout and interrelationship of parts can also be inferred from how they are framed, notably in the introductory poems and the use of prologues. I shall show here how these, again, denote the scribes' perception of a homogeneous unity across the collection as a whole.

A second aim of this study is to clarify the stratigraphy of the main scribes' interaction with the law book throughout its ongoing production. The text and paratext of the legal collection are written by three near-contemporary scribal hands, with hand 1 having supplied the main text from the start of the

---

Herrscherelasse, ed. Karl Ubl, https://capitularia.uni-koeln.de/en/blog/handschrift-des-monats-dezember-2017/.

11 Mordek, *Bibliotheca capitularium regum Francorum,* 256–57: "Die Sammlung ist klar in zwei Teile gegliedert." The assumption of two self-contained parts is also made in Patrick Wormald, *The Making of English Law: King Alfred to the Twelfth Century, Legislation and its Limits* (Oxford: Blackwell, 1999), vol. 1, 33.

manuscript through to fol. 53v (51v), l. 28, and hand 3 from fol. 54r (52r), l. 1 to the end. This would appear to be a simple transition, but it is further complicated by the hands who provided the various elements of paratext: hand 1 only provided paratextual additions to the parts of the manuscript they had written themselves, while hand 2 made additions from the start of the legal collection (fol. 9r) through to fol. 85r (83r) and therefore bridges both of the main scribes' work. Hand 3 also provides many paratextual items, the earliest instance of which I have identified as being on fol. 47v (45v) and then throughout the remainder of the manuscript. A fourth, potential, hand supplied a section of the running headings from the middle of the ninth quire (around fol. 66v, although paleographic diagnosis is not completely certain here) to their conclusion at the start of the seventeenth quire.[12] In addition to these scribes, there is also an artist who supplied the miniatures throughout the manuscript, comprising portraits of the various lawgivers and most likely also the border decorations for the tree of consanguinity (*arbor cognationum*) in the first quire.[13] It is unclear whether this artist

---

12 This count excludes many of the later scribal hands who augmented the manuscript with notes, corrections and other additions in the margins, and a fourth contemporary scribal hand who provided the running headings from partway through the eighth quire to their conclusion at the start of the seventeenth. It should not be forgotten that many of the additions in the margins can also be attributed to these main hands, while others are difficult or impossible to diagnose with any certainty.

13 Russo, "Leggi Longobarde," 616. From the perspective of the stratigraphy of the manuscript production, the next vital element to consider is that all of the ruler portraits throughout the manuscript were supplied by a single artist, as can be seen from the stylistic features of human representation, the line-work, and the close similarity of the color palettes. As such, the artist must be contemporary or later in relation to both hand 1 and 3. At the same time, the titles in orange identifying the people depicted in the portraits were also copied by hand 2 for the *Lex Salica, Lex Ribuaria,* and the *Leges Langobardorum,* while the Carolingians were labeled by hand 3. In all cases, the rubricated names demonstrably post-date the production of the portrait, fitting around the figures and sometimes even physically overlapping, as with the G in both "vvisegast" and "bedegast" (fol. 11v). This confirms that the artist was working at the same time as hands 2 and 3, but as both scribes later added labels to the pictures, it seems unlikely

is one of the already mentioned scribes, although as both hands 2 and 3 provide titles for miniatures which were not anticipated from the outset, it seems more likely that the artist was a different person. Either way, the community directly involved in the production of the legal collection is sizable and, from their multiple phases of activity and ongoing interaction with it, they were deeply invested in the book and its contents.

Before turning to either of the main aims of this chapter, it will first be useful to present some broader information on the manuscript as a whole and make a small contribution to one of the other debates surrounding the underlying homogeneity of the manuscript. Scholarship to date has been divided as to whether quire 1, which contains a range of historiographical texts, formed an integral part of the manuscript from the outset or if it circulated independently first and was only later joined with it as a booklet. Walter Pohl explores the cumulative reading created in the manuscript contexts, in which law and historiographical texts read together form "texts of identity," with the sum conveying more than the individual parts.[14] Paleographic evidence demonstrating that it was also the product of hand 1

---

that either was actually the artist. The same artist also seems to have been responsible for supplying the decorations to the *arbor cognationum* on fol. 4v, in quire 1, as the color palette is identical. While there are no humans portrayed to allow direct comparison of the figural representation, the line style and overall proportions (especially for the heads of the birds) are closely similar. This, of course, does not confirm that the artist was active at the same time as hand 1, but if that quire had already become separated from the rest of the collection before the completion of quire 25 and joining of the two production blocks, as suggested previously, then the artist must have been involved in the manuscript's production prior to that removal.

14 Pohl, *Werkstätte der Erinnerung,* 108–51, focusing overall on the early eleventh-century law book, Cava de' Tirreni, Biblioteca della Badia, MS 4, but including within it a dedicated section on the Modena manuscript, 122–29. See also Walter Pohl, "Memory, Identity and Power in Lombard Italy," in *The Uses of the Past in the Early Middle Ages,* ed. Yitzhak Hen and Matthew Innes (Cambridge: Cambridge University Press, 2000), 9–28 (particularly 15–16, 24–25); for a discussion of the *Origo* itself, see Herwig Wolfram, *"Origo et Religio:* Ethnic Traditions and Literature in Early Medieval Texts," *Early Medieval Europe* 3 (1994): 19–38.

has been offered by Guiseppe Russo, who cautiously noted that it was a codicologically self-contained unit.[15] Here I shall first make some further codicological observations that detail the similarities between the production of this quire and those of the legal collection following.

Modena, Biblioteca Capitolare, MS O. I. 2

In its current form, Modena, Biblioteca Capitolare, MS O. I. 2 comprises 208 folios, distributed between some twenty-eight quires, as detailed in its appendix. The folios are foliated from 1 to 206 in Arabic numerals in a red ink in the upper outer corner of the recto of each folio. The discrepancy in foliation arises as folios 14 and 45 were originally omitted and then supplied slightly later in the same ink and hand as 13bis and 43bis, respectively. While folios will be given here with the correct foliation per the manuscript's materials, for convenience of cross-referencing to much of the extant scholarship on the manuscript, I also give the erroneous numbers in square brackets where they differ. There are two sets of quire signatures running throughout the manuscript, one running from quires 2–28, and the other with several of the quires (now) having been omitted, from quires 7–25. As the folios of the manuscript have been substantially trimmed, evidenced by truncated text in margins throughout, some of the gaps in the second set of quire signatures presumably represent later loss. The current binding is modern, in tooled leather on wooden boards, with paper pastedowns.[16]

The first folio and final quire, as just noted, are both later additions to the manuscript, with the original historiographic material filling fols. 2–8 and the legal collection filling fols. 9–207,

---

15 Russo, "Leggi Longobarde," 614.
16 A short catalogue description focused on the manuscript's material condition, along with digitized images, is available from the Modena-Nonatola archive's website: "O.I.2 - *Leges Salicae, Ripuariae, Longobardorum, Baioariorum, Caroli Magni,*" in *Archivio Storico Diocesano di Modena-Nonantola,* https://archiviodiocesano.mo.it/opere-digitalizzate/cat/16-o-i-2_leges_salicae_ripuariae-longobardorum-baioariorum-carolimagni.

comprising quires 1 to 27. Of these twenty-seven quires, eleven are produced in a regular format with eight folios apiece folded from four bifolia,[17] and a further eleven with a "coupled-leaf" construction in which the quire has eight folios folded from three bifolia and a pair of half-sheets effectively forming an ersatz bifolium.[18] In all cases, the parchment is aesthetically arranged, per the rule of Gregory, so that hair-side faces hair-side

---

17 The regular quires comprise nos. 2, 4, 9–11, 14, 16, 22–23, and 25–26.
18 Quires 3, 7–8, 12–13, 15, 17–19, 21, and 24. For further details on coupled-leaf constructions see Johann Peter Gumbert, "The Tacketed Quire: An Exercise in Comparative Codicology," *Scriptorium* 65 (2011): 299–320, and Johann Peter Gumbert, "Skins Sheets and Quires," in *New Directions in Later Medieval Manuscript Studies: Essays from the 1998 Harvard Conference,* ed. Derek Pearsall (York: York Medieval Press, 2000), 81–90. An interesting feature observable in quire 22 (fols. 166 [164] to 173 [171]), is that the third bifolium, fols. 168:171 [166:169], has its own ruling grid, disrupting the regular arrangement of the quire, so that its left-hand half is ruled from the verso while its right-hand half from the recto. Furthermore, this bifolium is ruled for thirty-nine long-lines, although these are ignored and the pages are still written for twenty-eight lines each throughout, per the scribes' regular practice throughout the manuscript. Materials originally prepared for another codex were apparently co-opted and incorporated into the production of this legal collection, presumably demonstrating the relative importance of this book within the broader contexts of the scriptorium and community that produced it.

Of the five remaining quires in the original phase of the Modena manuscript's production, three have lost a folio (quires 1, 6, and 20), which can be deduced from corresponding lacunae in the text, while one (quire 5) must have already lost its final folio before it was written (or was produced without it from the start), since the *Lex Ribuaria,* no. 59.4, spans the opening of fol. 39v [(38v)], l. 27 to fol. 40r [(39r)], l. 1, without any disruption. The other atypical quire is the last one of the legal collection (quire 27), and comprises only two folios, both of which are half-sheets (fols. 206 [204] and 207 [205]). These are, again, arranged according to the Rule of Gregory, but should not be considered as forming a quire produced from just a single coupled-leaf bifolium. In relation to the sewn spine of the quire, both leaves are in the first part to the left, while their *talons* or stubs are positioned to the right. That is to say, the quire has been cut down to its current form, rather than having been produced in this fashion from the outset. The reason for this is obvious, as the final capitulary for the collection, the *Capitulare Missorum,* ends on fol. 207r (205r), l. 15, and the remainder of that page and all the verso have been left blank. As this is the end of the collection, the quire has been cut down to fit the materials, and though the full extent of the original

and flesh-side faces flesh-side throughout and so that the outer faces of each quire are also consistently the hair-side.[19]

As previously noted, the question of whether the opening quire of the manuscript (fols. 2–8) was an integral part of the collection from the outset or else was a later addition has received some debate in the scholarship. The quire contains a number of usually non-legal but seemingly related items, including an extract from Isidore of Seville's *Etymologiae* that now begins abruptly (fol. 2r, l.–fol. 4r, l. 22) and his *arbor cognationum* (tree of consanguinity) extending to seven generations added as a full-page diagram with a modified ruling grid to accommodate it (fol. 4v),[20] the *Capitulare Olonnense ecclesiasticum primum*, no. "viii" (fol. 4r, ll. 23–28), the *Origo Gentis Langobardorum* (fol. 5v, l. 1–fol. 7v, l. 2), and a list of emperors from Christ to Louis the Pious (fol. 8r, l. 11–fol. 8v, l. 18 and l. 27). While somewhat debated, the current consensus in the scholarship of how these relate to the legal collection is the two parts are integral to each other. Mordek argued that it is not by chance that the text immediately preceding the laws is the list of emperors,[21] but he wrote this as part of a brief catalogue entry and unfortunately did not expand on the significance of that statement. The fact

---

quire cannot be known, the edges of the ruling grid still visible on the *talon* confirm that at least these two half-sheets were first produced as full bifolia.

19 This reflects regular practice in Western book production, up until about the thirteenth century. See Albert Derolez, *The Paleography of Gothic Manuscript Books: From the Twelfth Century to the Early Sixteenth Century* (Cambridge: Cambridge University Press, 2003), 33–34.

20 The ruling grid includes a further three vertical lines added to position the central column. While the regular horizontal lines in hardpoint are from the recto of the folio and are an imprint from the ruling made on the now-lost first quire folio, the vertical lines are from the verso and were freshly ruled. There is no imprint from these lines traveling back into the earlier folios, and the prickings used to guide the new lines are likewise confined to fol. 4. Perhaps the quire had not yet been sewn when it was re-ruled. However, as much of the codicological evidence points to these being what Gumbert terms a "tacketed quire," it seems more likely that the scribe folded and opened the quire in such a way that only this folio was exposed. See Gumbert, "The Tacketed Quire."

21 Mordek, *Bibliotheca capitularium regum Francorum*, 256–57.

that he only names the emperor list may reflect only the other similar, but not identical, manuscript witness of this legal collection, Gotha, Forschungsbibliothek, MS Memb. I. 84.[22] Produced at Mainz in the tenth or eleventh century, it begins with the same list on fol. 148r, ll. a1–b31 where it is also positioned immediately before the prologues beginning the legal collection. For Walter Pohl, the direct connections go back further into this quire, with all texts augmenting the manuscript contexts and with especial focus given to the interrelationship with the *Origo*: a historiographical text on the origins of the Lombard gens that also includes a list of previous Lombard kings, in which law and historiography are combined in the re-production and transmission of ethnic identities.[23] Pohl's analysis may also be read alongside Brigitte Pohl-Resl's more general argument that the emphasis after the conquest of Lombard Italy in the late eighth century may be more Frankish multi-legalism than "any strong sense of ethnic identity,"[24] a framing which certainly seems to reflect the multi-legal contents of the Modena manuscript a century later.

Arguments taking the other perspective, that is that the first quire was originally independent, have only been made cautiously. Russo noted that the quire is codicologically self-contained, describing it as "seemingly extraneous to the compilation," but adds also that the scribal hand is paleographically identical to hand 1 in the main body of the manuscript and both parts were written by the same scribe.[25] While I agree entirely

---

22 "Gotha, Forschungs- und Landesbibliothek, Memb. I 84," in *Bibliotheca Legum: A Database on Carolingian Secular Law-Texts*, ed. Karl Ubl, http://www.leges.uni-koeln.de/en/mss/codices/gotha-flb-memb-i-84/; "Gotha, Forschungsbibliothek, Memb. I 84," in *Capitularia: Edition der fränkischen Herrschererlasse*, ed. Karl Ubl, https://capitularia.uni-koeln.de/en/mss/gotha-flb-memb-i-84/; and Mischke, "Lupus' *Liber Legum* Reconsidered."

23 Pohl, *Werkstätte der Erinnerung*, 122–29. See also Pohl, "Memory, Identity and Power in Lombard Italy," 15–16 and 24–25.

24 Brigitte Pohl-Resl, "Legal Practice and Ethnic Identities in Lombard Italy," in *Strategies of Distinction: The Construction of Ethnic Communities, 300–800*, ed. Walter Pohl and Helmut Reimitz (Leiden: Brill, 1998), 219.

25 Russo, "Leggi Longobarde," 614: "quasi estranea alla compilazione."

with the paleographic assessment, I would argue that codicological examination of the quire construction and layout of texts in fact shows how closely integrated this quire was with the main production. The strongest argument against quire 1 being part of the original collection from the outset is only that it was omitted from the overall run of quire signatures, which begin at "i" in the lower margin of the first folio of the second quire (fol. 9r). However, as Pohl argued, the manuscript stratigraphy confirms that this reflects the ongoing use of the manuscript, rather than the way it was originally anticipated and produced, and moreover must post-date the addition of the calendar in the late tenth century.[26]

---

26 The quire numbering, written in Roman numerals, continues unbroken through to "xxiiii" on the first folio of quire 25 (fol. 190r [188r]). The following quire (quire 26) is also signed, but here the numbering jumps abruptly to "xxx." However, there is no corresponding lacuna in the text to suggest that five intervening quires have since been lost, and instead the *Episcoporum ad Hludowicum imperatorum relatio* spans the divide: Alfred Boretius and Victor Krase, eds., "No. 196, *Episcoporum ad Hludowicum imperatorum relatio*," in *Capitularia regum Francorum* 2, Monumenta Germaniae Historica, Leges (Hanover: Hahn, 1892), 42. The capitulum spanning the two quires, no. 50, is rubricated in the manuscript as "xvi" on fol. 197v (195v), ll. 19–28, and the next capitulum in reading order is rubricated as "xvii" in the space at the end of l. 28, again showing that the items continued directly from each other. It would seem, then, that the jump in quire signature numbering is simply an error. This error may have been introduced due to the lower outer corner of the quire's first folio having already been trimmed away, which can be demonstrated by the first two graphs of the signature, "xxx," being on the edge of fol. 198r [196r], while the third and final graph is written on the following folio, 199r [197r]. The following quire (quire 27), comprising the two half-sheets with the final part of the capitularies, has not been signed, but the final quire of the manuscript (quire 28) continues the (mis)numbered signature and gives it as "xxxii" in what appears to be the same ink and hand, on the lower outer corner of fol. 208r [206r]. This quire signature set, then, was either added to the manuscript at the same time as the calendar, or at some later point. As Pohl noted, since the late ninth-century quire 1 cannot post-date the late tenth-century quire 28, it must therefore indicate that the first quire had become separated from the codex during this phase and was only reunited with it later: Pohl, *Werkstätte der Erinnerung,* 126–28. The second set of quire signatures, again in Roman numerals, begins with "i" on the

From a codicological perspective, the similarities between quire 1 and the following legal collection are apparent. The overall dimensions of the folios in quire 1 average 261 mm (10.28 in.) high by 168 mm (6.61 in.) wide, which is the same average dimensions as the quires in the main body of the legal compilation. However, as the manuscript has been heavily trimmed, this is not conclusive in its own right. More compelling for seeing quire 1 as part of the same production is the observation that the ruled space is for twenty-eight long lines throughout and again with identical average dimensions: 214 mm (8.42 in.) high by 133 mm (5.24 in.) wide, in both quire 1 and across the following quires containing the laws and capitularies. A second point to consider when assessing if quire 1 was produced to be part of the same law book is the layout of the page: the scribes frequently left the remainder of a page blank preceding the start of a new text. It may seem peculiar here that, in addition to the lower third of fol. 8r, hand 1 also left all of fol. 8v blank. Pohl suggested that the now-lost first folio from quire 1 may origi-

---

final folio of quire 7, fol. 62v [60v], in the center of the lower margin. They are erratically attested in this position through to "xv" on the final folio of quire 173v [171v]. The next quire is omitted, and there is a jump again at quire 25, with the numbering now lining up once more with the first set of quire signatures discussed above. The scribe also signed it as "xxiiii" rather than as "xvii." From here on, no further quire signatures survive in this set, although whether they were subsequently lost to trimming or else never written remains uncertain. It pushes coincidence too far to speculate that a similar slip in the quire numbering happened here, which brought the numbering into alignment with the signatures added in or after the late tenth century. A more likely, if speculative, explanation would be further to extend Pohl's compelling argument that hand 3 began producing their run of quires in a self-contained phase. Beyond the time taken to complete the final folio of quire 6, the scribe may not have had the earlier parts of the law book to hand for much of the time, if at all. However, the change in quire signature numbering suggests that, at some point between finishing quires 23 and 25 (following the last extant numeral from the continuous set of signatures), the two parts were re-united and the numbering was rearranged accordingly. Most importantly, if this reconstruction is true, then it suggests that the first quire, containing the *Origo* and other framing items, had already become separated from the whole during the latter phases of production in the late ninth century.

nally have had an illustration on it, as the missing portion of Isidore's *Etymologiae* would probably have filled only a single page.[27] Hand 1 of the Modena manuscript also left fol. 5r, immediately preceding the start of the *Origo*, entirely blank. The possibility that each of these pages had or anticipated a portrait or related decoration that was ultimately never supplied cannot be dismissed. It is perhaps worth noting that of the two other surviving copies of the *Origo*, where it is transmitted alongside the Lombard laws, one also prefaces the historiographical text with a full-page miniature. The illustration, in the early eleventh-century Cava de' Tirreni, Biblioteca della Badia, MS 4,[28] fol. 2r, shows the mythological origins of the Lombard name. In the tenth-century Madrid, Biblioteca Nacional, MS 413[29] there is no corresponding illustration. However, the page preceding the *Origo* (fol. 1r) was again originally left blank, perhaps anticipating some form of decoration, although it is now filled with various shelfmarks and summaries of contents. If these blank spaces were left for miniatures, then the anticipation of further illustrations in the Modena manuscript would therefore make sense and the independent treatment of this quire is certainly not new either.

---

27 Pohl, *Werkstätte der Erinnerung*, 127–28.
28 "Cava de' Tirreni, Biblioteca della Badia, 4," in *Bibliotheca Legum: A Database on Carolingian Secular Law-Texts*, ed. Karl Ubl, http://www.leges.uni-koeln.de/en/mss/codices/cava-dei-tirreni-bdb-4/; "Cava de' Tirreni, Biblioteca della Badia, 4," in *Capitularia: Edition der fränkischen Herrschererlasse*, ed. Karl Ubl, https://capitularia.uni-koeln.de/en/mss/cava-dei-tirreni-bdb-4/; Sören Kaschke, "Manuscript of the Month August 2016: Cava de' Tirreni, BdB, 4," in *Capitularia: Edition der fränkischen Herrschererlasse*, ed. Karl Ubl, https://capitularia.uni-koeln.de/en/blog/handschrift-des-monats-august-2016/; and Mordek, *Bibliotheca capitularium regum Francorum*, 98–111.
29 "Madrid, Biblioteca Nacional, 413," in *Bibliotheca Legum: A Database on Carolingian Secular Law-Texts*, ed. Karl Ubl, http://www.leges.uni-koeln.de/en/mss/codices/madrid-bn-413/; "Madrid, Biblioteca Nacional, MS 413," in *Early Medieval Laws and Law-Books*, ed. Thom Gobbitt, https://thomgobbitt.files.wordpress.com/2018/04/madrid_bn_ms413_april2018.pdf. Digitized at http://bdh-rd.bne.es/viewer.vm?id=0000087627&page=1.

The Legal Collection: Quires 2–27

In addition to the historiographical texts as an introduction to the legal content, there are also a number of prologues and related items at the start of quire 2. These begin with the prologues from two of the following law codes in the legal collection—the *Lex Baiuvariorum* (fol. 9r, l. 1 to fol. 9v, l. 15), and the *Lex Salica* (fol. 9v, l. 16 — 10r, l. 15). None of the other legal texts have their prologues, either here or in the main body. The only partial exceptions to this are the two copies of Charlemagne's Herstal capitulary, which retain their prologues,[30] one for the *forma communis* variant added in red ink on fol. 158v (156v), ll. 20–24 in the larger collection of Charlemagne's capitularies, and the other for the *forma langobardica* variant in black ink on fol. 177r (175r), ll. 11–15, in the set of capitularies actually attributed in the manuscript to Pippin. But neither of these introduces its respective capitulary block. The prologue to the first capitulary of Louis II is also retained, with the first part containing the rubricated dating clause (fol. 205v [203v], ll. 10–12), while the remainder is as an unnumbered item in black ink (ll. 13–17). These have traditionally been viewed in the scholarship as extraneous to the *Liber Legum* collection itself, mainly because these capitularies are not included in the capitula list at the outset, but presumably also because the Louis named in the poem at the outset is assumed to be Louis the Pious, whose capitularies are copied in the same set as those of Lothar.[31] Prologues clearly retained a small yet significant role in the collection, but, overall, the strategy was to remove them. Where prologues were retained, they

---

30 Alfred Boretius, ed., "No. 20, *Capitulare Haristallense*," in *Capitularia regum Francorum* 1, Monumenta Germaniae Historica, Leges (Hanover: Hahn, 1883), 46–51. See also Thom Gobbitt, "Scribal Communities and Lombard Law-Books: Charlemagne's Herstal Capitulary Within the Eleventh-Century *Liber Papiensis*," in *Creating Communities and Others in Early Medieval Europe*, ed. Richard Broome (Leeds: Kismet Press, forthcoming).

31 Mordek, *Bibliotheca capitularium regum Francorum*, 265–67; Russo, "Leggi Longobarde," 617 and 621; and Wormald, *The Making of English Law*, 32.

are mostly general rather than specific, framing and homogenizing the collection as a whole rather than emphasizing the individual origins of the varying components.

The use of the *Lex Baiuvariorum* prologue as a more general introduction to early medieval legislation is not uncommon, as it explicitly names the Franks. In terms of the socio-legal contexts of promulgation, this could be taken to mean the Salic and Ripuarian law codes, and perhaps also the later capitulary legislation under Charlemagne, Pippin of Italy, and Lothar; it could also include the Alamanni, as well as the Bavarians themselves. Comparable approaches can be seen in other manuscripts. For example, an early eleventh-century copy of the *Lex Salica,* now truncated after the first quire, is introduced by the prologue to the *Lex Baiuvariorum*.[32] The prologue to the *Lex Baiuvariorum* in the Modena manuscript was therefore probably also read as an introduction for all of the collected legislation. Unless the *Origo* was seen as the specific introduction for the Lombard laws over Rothari's prologue, or those of any of the later lawgivers, this strategy subsumed the legislative contexts of the Lombard laws and the former Lombard kingdom into the broader whole. Multilegalism, here, then, becomes more than the physical association of multiple laws and related texts in one place, but sees the various parts integrated into a larger whole.

Following the two narrative prologues are the poems attributed to the Lupus mentioned above (fols 10r, ll. 16–26, and fol.

---

32 This now forms the final quire of a slightly later manuscript of the *Liber Papiensis,* produced in or around Pavia in the third quarter of the eleventh century, Paris, Bibliothèque nationale de France, MS lat. 9656, fols. 109–115. See Mordek, *Bibliotheca capitularium regum Francorum,* 578–80; Thom Gobbitt, *The Liber Papiensis in the Long Eleventh Century: Manuscripts, Materiality and Mise-en-page* (Leeds: Kismet, forthcoming), chap. 4; "Paris, Bibliothèque Nationale, Lat. 9656," in *Bibliotheca Legum: A Database on Carolingian Secular Law-Texts,* ed. Karl Ubl, http://www.leges.uni-koeln.de/en/mss/codices/paris-bn-lat-9656/; "Paris, Bibliothèque Nationale de France MS lat. 9656," in *Early Medieval Laws and Law-Books,* ed. Thom Gobbitt, https://thomgobbitt.files.wordpress.com/2017/04/paris-bnf-ms-lat-9656-final.pdf; and Mordek, *Bibliotheca capitularium regum Francorum,* 578–80.

10r, l. 27–fol. 10v, l. 2), and another set of extracts from Isidore focused on divine and human law,[33] again showing the interconnection of the start of the legal collection with the materials in the preceding quire. In addition to tying together the collected legislation, however, the poems also introduce the miniatures depicting the various lawgivers that can be found throughout the manuscript and which make the connection between the portraits and the following legal text.[34] The description of the miniatures must have been written before the miniatures themselves were produced, suggesting that the exemplar also included such images which were later used as a model by the artist. But they also show that the overall shape of the book had been well-anticipated from the outset — even if hands 2 and 3 and the artisan were working at a significantly later point in time than hand 1, and even if they emended much of the *mise-en-page* and layout in the process of their work, they were nevertheless fulfilling the anticipated production ideas. The poems specifically mentions the portraits and legal texts for the *Lex Salica, Lex Ribuaria, Leges Langobardorum,* and the *Lex Alamannorum,* but in the case of the *Lex Baiuvariorum* only the laws are mentioned, not portraits (fol. 10r, ll. 23–24); and the laws themselves, copied by hand 3, also do not include portraits at the outset.[35] As such, the poem already anticipates the otherwise atypical treatment of the onset of the Bavarian laws in comparison to the other laws in the manuscript. As the prologue to the Bavarian laws serves in this manuscript as a general prologue to the collected laws, it seems quite feasible that the lack of other framing materials for the *Lex Baiuvariorum* is due to the prologue already having

---

33 For a summary of *De legibus divinis et humanis,* see Mordek, *Bibliotheca capitularium regum Francorum,* 259.

34 Russo, "Leggi Longobarde," 617 and 621; and Wormald, *The Making of English Law,* 32.

35 Patrick Wormald reads the poem differently, and argues that the omission of the *Lex Baiuvariorum* portrait in both Modena, BC, MS O. I. 2 and Gotha, Forschungsbibliothek, MS Memb. I. 84, reflects a later change that is contrary to the underlying contents. Wormald, *The Making of English Law,* 33.

been separated from the main body of the law code, presumably even in or before the exemplar that preceded the predation of Eurardus's own law book.

After the introductory poems in the Modena manuscript, there follows a collection of extracts from Isidore, reflecting on human and divine law (fol. 10v, l. 4–fol. 11r, l. 10),[36] and then, added slightly later into some available line space by hand 2, the paraenesis on just jurisdiction on ll. 11–21.[37] The insertion of these items between the two prologues and the legal collection as a whole again underscores that the prologues should be read as abstract introductions to the entire legal collection, rather than as specific framing for the law codes and capitularies within them. Law as culture and contexts of multi-legalism outweigh the specific royal, imperial, or gens-led contexts in which each legal text had originally been produced. Following these come the collected laws — and capitularies, and I wish now to bring focus to the *mise-en-page* of the text and paratext in each, noting how the strategies were developed and how this relates to the change in scribal hand partway through the Lombard laws, but more importantly also to how differences are developed within the respective legal texts and how this ultimately positions the capitularies as a continuation of the multi-legal collection, rather than as a separate and self-contained *Rechtsblock*.

The *Lex Salica* begins with the portrait of the Salian lawgivers on fol. 11v, with the list of capitula on the facing page written in black ink by hand 1 in two columns, from fol. 12r, l. 2 to fol. 12v, l. 11, following an incipit in orange ink made by hand 2. Each of the titles begins with a majuscule that has been highlighted in a dark red ink, and majuscules beginning new titles and items within the law code itself are similarly highlighted. The capitula list includes two sets of numbering for the titles. The first was added into the interlinear space above each of the titles in black ink, apparently by hand 1. This set of interlinear numbers is not continuous but relates the order of the titles to their more regu-

---

36 Mordek, *Bibliotheca capitularium regum Francorum*, 259.
37 Ibid.

lar positions in the non-systemized variants of the *Lex Salica*.[38] In the main body of the law code, these capitula numbers also have been added in the same ink in the outer margin of the page, but not as guides for a rubricator since the numbers are continuous and match the systemized order of the capitula as presented in the Modena manuscript. There, the numbers are added in orange ink by hand 2, positioned in the space to the left of the majuscules in the capitula list, and a matching number within the main body of the law code usually begins the rubrics themselves. This orange ink appears to be very different from the red used for the highlighting, especially on the verso, and indicates that these two parts were added in different phases. The same separate use of red ink for highlighting majuscules and orange ink for the capitula numbers and rubrics is also used throughout the body of the following laws. Hand 1 anticipated that the reader would also need to know the original order of the titles, which suggests that the intended users of this specific law book communicated with other individuals with legal interests using the law code in its more regular arrangement.[39]

It is unclear whether hand 1 also anticipated the later supply of the text in orange ink by hand 2. In many cases, space has been demonstrably left for items to be added into the main body of the law code: sometimes an entire line was left blank, or only the first half of the first line of the new capitulum was written, and that space was used for the rubric instead. Where the previous capitulum ended partway through a line, the empty line space at

---

38 Karl August Eckhardt, ed., *Lex Salica*, Monumenta Germaniae Historica, Legum Nationum Germanicarum 4.2 (Hanover: Hahn, 1969).

39 A comparable strategy is briefly employed in two of the eleventh-century *Liber Papiensis* manuscripts, where a few of the laws at the start of Rothari's legislation have been re-ordered: Vienna, Österreichische Nationalbibliothek, MS 471, and Paris, Bibliothèque nationale de France, MS lat. 9656, which I discuss in Gobbitt, *The Liber Papiensis*, chapters 3 and 4, respectively. This strategy is employed more comprehensively throughout two twelfth-century manuscripts of the *Lombarda* systemization of the Lombard laws, which I hope to return to in greater detail in the future: Florence, Biblioteca Medicea Laurenziana, MS Plut.77.10, and Paris, Bibliothèque nationale de France, MS lat. 4615.

the end was sometimes used as well. In some cases, the supplied rubrics fit easily, in others hand 2 had to squeeze them in, and on occasion they extended into the outer margins. The numbers added to the capitula list in orange ink for the right-hand entry (fol. 11v, l. 8) are particularly compressed, as there was only a narrow amount of space available. The question of whether hand 2 worked together with or at some point (soon) after hand 1 is hard to answer. Hand 1 clearly anticipated some form of decoration or paratext being added to the manuscript later and in a different ink, but the way in which hand 2 produced them did not always conform to the space that had been left. This, however, is hardly unexpected, as the second scribe was working in their own, larger ductus and had agency in deciding how to use the paratext to frame the underlying legal content. There are no instances when the manuscript passed back to hand 1 after hand 2 had finished their work, strongly suggesting that either hand 2 came into contact with the manuscript later, or if the two scribes were broadly contemporary, then once hand 1 had completed their parts they handed the book over and had nothing further to do with its production and use. In either case, hand 1 would appear to have produced book materials for the use of others, rather than producing a book which they would make ongoing use of themselves.

The following law code, the *Lex Ribuaria,* again begins with a full-page portrait of the lawgivers (fol. 31r [30r]), followed by an incipit in orange ink made by hand 2 (fol. 31v [30v], l. 1) and the two-column capitula list (fol. 31v [30v], l. 2, to 32v [31v], l. 28). This time, there is little or no re-ordering of the capitula by or in association with Lupus,[40] and here only a single set of numbering is included in the capitula list and in the main body of the laws. However, the ink colors are used in the same way as before, and the squeezing of capitula numbers into the avail-

---

40 Wormald noted that Lupus's real focus — if the weight of personal interest can be inferred meaningfully from the extent that the materials were reordered — was on the *Lex Salica* and *Leges Langobardorum*. See Wormald, *The Making of English Law,* 33–34.

able space in the capitula list is even more pronounced, particularly for the entries in the right-hand column of fol. 31v [30v], ll. 20–23. Conversely, the spacing is more generous in other cases, and that this is intentional can be seen where the scribe splits a title in the left-hand column over two or more lines to ensure a wider space in the center of the page. In the main body of the law code no space has been left for the rubricated capitula titles, nor are they supplied. Moreover, the scribe normally begins a new capitulum continuously rather than on a new line, although some empty space is often left immediately before the pen-drawn initials marking the new capitula, and these gaps are usually used for the supply of capitula-numbering. These gaps not only marked the position of the new initial and capitula but also demonstrably anticipated the addition of numbers, as hand 1 frequently (but not exclusively) varied the width of the empty space in accordance with the length of the Roman numeral to be added. Again, the highlighting of the initials is in red, while the capitula numbers are in orange, and the evidence again suggests that while hand 1 may have anticipated the later addition of the numbers to the manuscript, it may not have been specifically hand 2 who they anticipated actually doing the work.

The next set of laws in the Modena manuscript is the *Leges Langobardorum*,[41] which again begins with the portraits first, followed by the capitula list. Here a folio is missing from the quire, between what are now fols. 42 [41] and 43 [42], which must have once contained the end of the *Lex Ribuaria* on its recto and, almost certainly, the portraits of the Lombard lawgivers Rothari, Grimwald, and Liutprand on its verso. Instead, only the final two of the Lombard lawgivers Ratchis and Aistulf are still represented in the manuscript, fol. 43r [42r], and the capitula list begins overleaf here, with an incipit written in majuscules by hand 1 and highlighted in dark red ink (fol. 43v [42v], ll. 1–6).

---

41 Friedrich Bluhme, ed., "*Edictus Langobardorum*," in *Monumenta Germaniae Historica, Leges* 4, ed. Georg Henry Pertz (Hanover: Monumenta Germaniae Historica, 1868), 1–206, and Friedrich Bluhme, ed., "*Liber Legis Regum Langobardorum,* Concordia Dictus," in *Monumenta Germaniae Historica, Leges* 4, ed. Georg Henry Pertz (Hanover: Hahn, 1868), 235–89.

The capitula list concludes with an explicit also by hand 1 with the same *mise-en-page* (fol. 45r [43bisr], ll. 19–21). The Lombard laws have been heavily systematized and organized according to legal themes. The capitula list is written as continuous text and is comprised of the titles given to these thematic groups rather than those of the individual capitula from the collected law codes of the Lombard lawgivers, which do not exist outside of the *Liber Legum*. The numbering here reflects the new arrangement of the titles per the *Liber Legum*, and although Lupus had re-worked the arrangement of these laws as heavily as he had those of the *Lex Salica*,[42] there is no second list of capitula numbers relating the laws back to their original order. Despite the Italian point of origin of Modena, MS O. I. 2, it would appear, then, that hand 1 anticipated that a reader would need to cross-reference to the original arrangement of the *Lex Salica* but not the *Leges Langobardorum*. Should we infer from this that hand 1 assumed the reader of this Italian manuscript would be more focused on the Salic laws than those of the Lombards? Or did they assume the reader would already be familiar with the content of the Lombard laws and that such an apparatus would therefore be unnecessary? I suspect there may be a more pragmatic answer, as the stint of hand 1 ended partway through the copying of the Lombard laws. In the case of the *Lex Salica,* the second set of numbers were added into the manuscript slightly later and were presumably also compiled later rather than being copied from an underlying exemplar. It may well have been that a concordance of capitula numbering to the original arrangement of the Lombard laws was not added as this scribe was no longer working on the project.

The titles of the capitula list for the Lombard laws are written in a single column, with space left before the majuscule introducing each capitulum. Again, the width of the space sometimes varies to suit the length of the Roman numeral anticipated, the highlighting is in red, and the capitula numbers are in orange. It is still unclear whether hands 1 and 2 were working together, or

---

42 Wormald, *The Making of English Law,* 33–34.

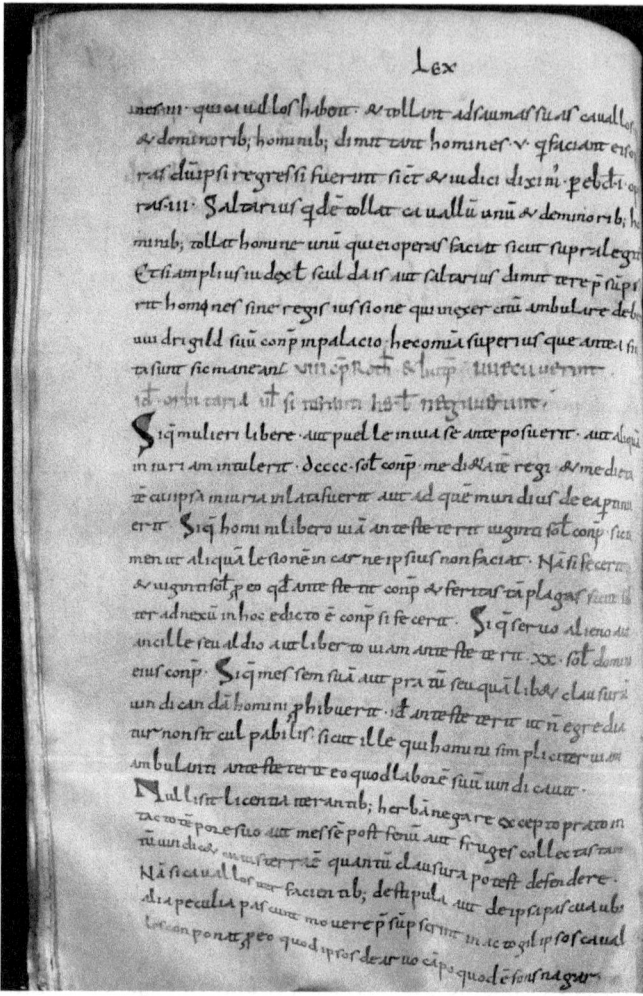

Fig. 6.1. Comparison of main contributing hands in Modena, Biblioteca Capitolare, O. I. 2, fol. 53v [51v]: hand 1 (main scribal hand); hand 3 (rubrics); and hand 2 (running heading).

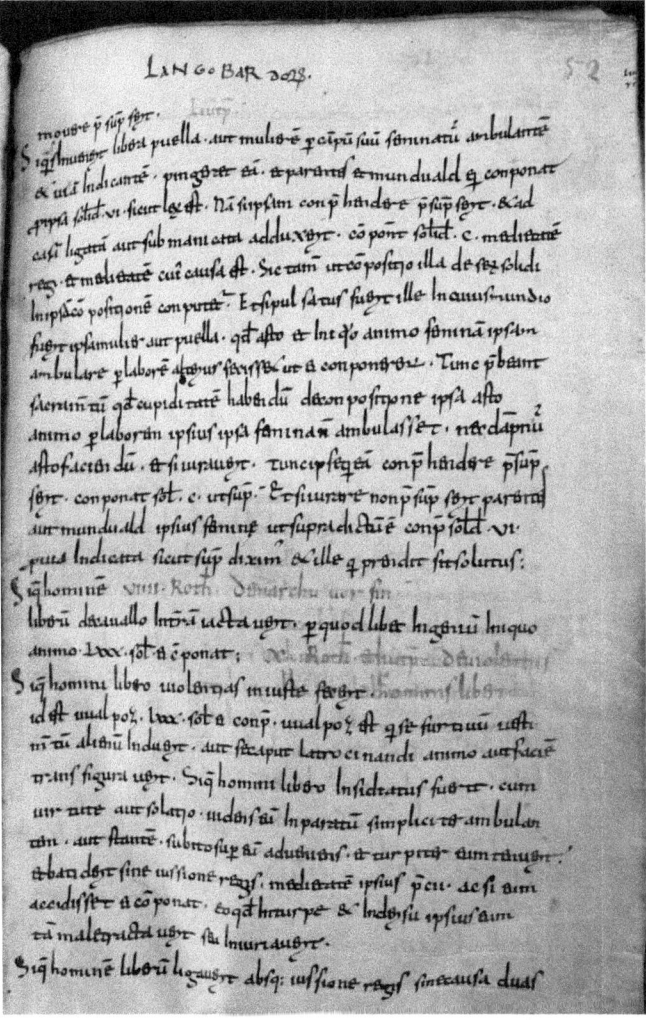

Fig. 6.2. Comparison of main contributing hands in Modena, Biblioteca Capitolare, O. I. 2, fol. 54r [52r]: hand 3 (main scribal hand, rubrics) and hand 2 (running heading).

if hand 2 added to the manuscript later in space that had been only loosely intended for some manner of decoration and paratextual apparatus. The change in layout strategy used by hand 1 for the Lombard capitula list, compared to previous law codes, is intriguing. It could have been drawn from an exemplar, but the overall similarity here to the *mise-en-page* used for the actual titles of the *Lex Ribuaria* immediately preceding cannot be ignored. Perhaps hand 1 had simply updated the layout of the Lombard laws to match. In so doing, they probably compressed the required length by at least one page, probably the better part of two, which could be taken as motivation in its own right. However, economy of parchment does not seem to have been a driving factor in the production of this law book, and the scribes regularly left empty space to position significant items so that they started on new pages. Resources, then, were hardly stretched.

The layout of the capitula themselves changes partway through the Lombard laws, corresponding to the change from hand 1 to hand 3 as the main writer (figs. 6.1 and 6.2), with the end of the first scribe's stint on the left-hand folio (fol. 53v [51v] to l. 28), and the start of the third scribe's stint on the right (fol. 54r [52r], from l. 1). The script of hand 3 here is at its "neatest." Pohl noted that the ductus of hand 3 gradually becomes "more hurried, much more crowded, and sometimes angular" as the writing progresses, and also that the overall appearance of the script, especially some of the graph forms, echo that seen in the final, additional quire added to the manuscript by the late tenth century.[43] Pohl also questioned whether there might have been some significant time jump between hands 1 and 3, raising the possibility that the production of the law book was paused for as much as a century and not continued until around the time when the calendar in quire 28 was copied.[44] In the light of the paleographic dating of the hands to the late ninth century, how-

---

43 Pohl, *Werkstätte der Erinnerung*, 126: "unruhigerer, viel gedrängterer, teils eckigerer."
44 Ibid., 127.

ever, any time jump here must at most be the matter of a decade or two.

In the section written by hand 1 (fol. 45r [43bis,r], l. 22 to fol. 53v [51v], l. 28), the new legal themes begin on a new line, with a pen-drawn initial in black, usually one line high, inset into the ruled area, and highlighted in the dark red ink. As before, rubrics and capitula numbering are in orange, generally copied by hand 2. Space has been anticipated in the written area for the titles of the legal sections, but as before sometimes this space is not enough for what was actually written, and the text has been squeezed in or extended into the margins. Individual capitula and sections within the new legal themes begin with a majuscule or small pen-drawn initial, again highlighted in red. Only a small amount of space is left before these initials, and it does not appear that any numbering or other paratextual item was anticipated. However, where the lawgiver responsible for the next capitulum changed, hand 2 has squeezed an abbreviation of their name into the gaps and interlinear space. This is almost certainly a later addition, reinventing the anticipated *mise-en-page* as produced by hand 1, but once more it is unclear how much later.

From fol. 54r [52r], l. 1, the main copyist of the legal collection changes to hand 3, and a new layout strategy is imposed. The main differences are that each new section of the law code — whether for an entire legal theme per the *Liber Legum* systematization, or for the capitula of specific Lombard lawgivers within it — is now begun on a new line, and the pen-drawn initial introducing it is now positioned in the margin immediately to the left of the ruled area, which facilitates the finding of individual capitula.[45] The initials are still highlighted in dark red,

---

45 The offsetting of initials becomes such a widely used strategy in the eleventh-century scholarly compilations of the Lombard laws, the *Liber Papiensis*, that Charles Radding argued it became one of the text's defining features. See Charles M. Radding, "Legal Manuscripts in Eleventh-Century Italy: From Royal Edict to Scholarly Compilation," in *Organizing the Written Word: Scripts, Manuscripts and Texts: Proceedings of the First Utrecht Symposium on Medieval Literacy, Utrecht, 5–7 June 1997*, ed. Marco

continuing that element of the preceding *mise-en-page*. Additional space is still retained for the addition of capitula numbers and rubrics, and, for the most part, these are done in orange.

The addition of many of the rubricated titles and capitula numbers in the second section is at first also the product of hand 2, confirming that their work bridges the activities of the two main scribes. In addition to facilitating the readability of the capitula, the re-worked layout by hand 3 also easily accommodates all of the developments in the *mise-en-page* and the paratextual strategies introduced by hand 2. Presumably, then, hand 2 advised or was perhaps even supervising the continuation work that was undertaken by hand 3. Hand 2 actively augments the content rather than simply supplying paratextual items, which reflects a clear and directed engagement with the legal materials. The addition of paratextual elements is therefore clearly far more than a passive decoration of the text, but rather an intensive and thorough engagement with the legal material.

While hand 2 continued to supply many of the rubrics in the parts of the law code copied by hand 3, their activity ends around fol. 85r [83r], towards the end of quire 11. At the same time, hand 3 also provided many of the rubrics throughout this production unit, and there is no clear division of labor. Moreover, hand 3 also contributed rubrics further back into the parts written by hand 1, from fol. 47v [45v] onwards — that is even then only within the earlier parts of quire 6 where their activity had first begun. There is no sign of hand 3 having emended or augmented any part of the first five quires. From fol. 85v [83v] onwards, that is, the penultimate folio of quire 11, hand 2 no longer contributes to the manuscript at all, and hand 3 is the sole copyist of the main text, capitula numbers and rubrics thereafter. The only exception to this is the running headings, which change to a different hand — identifiable by the distinctive curve on the upper part of the stroke of the *a* — partway

---

Mostert, Utrecht Studies in Medieval Literacy 2 (Turnhout: Brepols, unpublished). I would like to thank Prof. Radding for allowing me advance access to this chapter. See also Gobbitt, *The Liber Papiensis*.

through quire 9. Even here it is not entirely certain that this is a distinct scribal hand, and this may in fact be hand 3 using a specific display script. A pen trial in the upper margin of fol. 63r [61r] in fact shows a scribe developing this particular form of *a*, showing how hand 3 (or somebody else) might perfect their display script before they added the other running headings from the middle of that quire onwards.

The next law code, the *Lex Alamannorum*,[46] is written and decorated throughout by hand 3 only. The scribe here changed the layout, beginning with the capitula list (from fol. 110r, l. 2, following an incipit on fol. 110r [108r], l. 1) to fol. 111v [109v], l. 17), rather than with the portrait miniatures. This reversal of hand 1's layout of these two elements becomes the norm from here onwards. After the end of the capitula list, the remainder of the page (fol. 11v [109v], ll. 18–28) is left empty, and the portraits of the Alamannic lawgivers, comprising 160 faces and upper torsos set in pairs across multiple rows, then fill the three following pages (fol. 112r [110r] to 113v [111v]). The layout of the capitula lists is again written in a single column, with each new item beginning on a new line. Some features are carried over: initials beginning the titles are again highlighted in dark red, while the capitula are numbered in orange, although the capitula numbering does still appear to be done by hand 3. On the first page of the capitula list, the numbers are placed neatly in the inner margin to the left of the ruled space, but from then on they are positioned somewhat haphazardly at the end of each written line. That they were not added at the same time, even if they are by hand 3, is apparent from fol. 110v [108v], where one title spreads over two lines (ll. 6–7) but each line has been given its own number ("xxiii" and "xxxiiii," respectively). This means that the following numbers are one number out of place and do not match those added in the same color to the main body of the laws. The addition of capitula numbers therefore remains a later phase in the production and does not represent the scribe sim-

---

46 Karl August Eckhardt, ed., *Lex Alamannorum*, Monumenta Germaniae Historica, Legum Nationum Germanicarum 5.1 (Hanover: Hahn, 1966).

ply switching between ink pots. This can also be inferred from the main body of the laws, as many of the capitula have guide numbers or even the entire rubric written in the adjacent margins in the main dark ink by hand 3.

The final law code is the *Lex Baiuvariorum*,[47] which begins with a paired explicit and incipit (fol. 127r [125r], ll. 7–8). It follows immediately from the conclusion of the *Lex Alamannorum* rather than beginning on a new page, and is therefore highly atypical for the manuscript. The capitula list, again in a single column, runs from fol. 127r [125r], l. 9 through to 131r [129r], l. 22, ending with an explicit on l. 27. The initials for each title are highlighted in dark red through the first seven pages to fol. 130r [128r], but not thereafter, while the capitula numbers and rubrics for organizational divisions in the text are in orange. The positioning of the capitula numbers varies between the margin immediately to the left of the ruled area and the end of the line following the title. Occasionally, as on fol. 129r [127r], both methods were used on a single page.

The *Lex Baiuvariorum* does not include a portrait for the lawgivers, an omission which unlike the presumably stolen portrait from the *Leges Langobardorum* does not correspond to a missing folio, but instead is already indicated in the introductory poem, as discussed previously. This could, theoretically, be taken to suggest that the poem was composed and added after the rest of the manuscript had already been produced. In such a case, this would be an instance of hand 1 making a contribution after hand 3 had done their layers, and indirectly showing them both to be contemporary. However, the materiality and *mise-en-page* of quire 2, which contains the poem and prologue materials, make this very unlikely, if not impossible, and a more compelling interpretation is that both the poem and the paratextual framing of the *Lex Baiuvariorum* were copied from their exemplar. The biggest question remaining is why the compiler of

---

47 Ernst Maria Augustin Schwind, ed., *Lex Baiwariorum*, Monumenta Germaniae Historica, Legum Nationum Germanicarum 5.2 (Hanover: Hahn, 1926).

the Modena manuscript, and its exemplar, chose not to include a portrait for the *Lex Baiuvariorum*. I suspect the reason can be found in the separation of the prologue to the *Lex Baiuvariorum* from the main body of the laws themselves, and that this separation may predate even Eurardus's law book, which served as the exemplar for the Modena manuscript. In separating the written prologue from the laws' other paratextual elements — with the exception of the capitula list — the portrait framing the new set of legislation may also have been removed, which at the least would suggest that the aggregation of multiple law codes into multi-legal contexts was already an ongoing process by the mid-ninth century. Without having a model portrait to work from, later artisans may perhaps have felt it was inappropriate to create one. There seems little reason to speculate that the scribes of the Modena manuscript, and definitely not those of its exemplar, saw the Alamannic and Bavarian laws as being a single law code: the capitula list for the *Lex Baiuvariorum* stands at the beginning of the Bavarian laws, starting on fol. 128r [126r], rather than the beginning of the twin set of laws. That there may have been some room for confusion, however, might have been anticipated by hand 4, the scribe who added the running headings in this part of the manuscript. The last of the running headings is on the final folio with the *Lex Alamannorum,* and uniquely with the final one reading *Lex aLaMaNNorum FINITa eST* (the *Lex Alamannorum* is ended) spreading across the upper margins (fol. 126v [124v]–127r [125r]). The end of the Alamannic laws, then, is strongly emphasized. Conversely, the Bavarian laws do not receive running headings, and neither do any of the following capitularies. That so much development and augmentation of the texts as a whole took place during the production of the manuscript indicates how much the systematization of the *Liber Legum* was still a work in progress. The legal collection produced for the Eurardus named in the introductory poem may have had the larger decorations in the paratext, but it surely lacked many of the organizational features as introduced and developed here in the Modena manuscript.

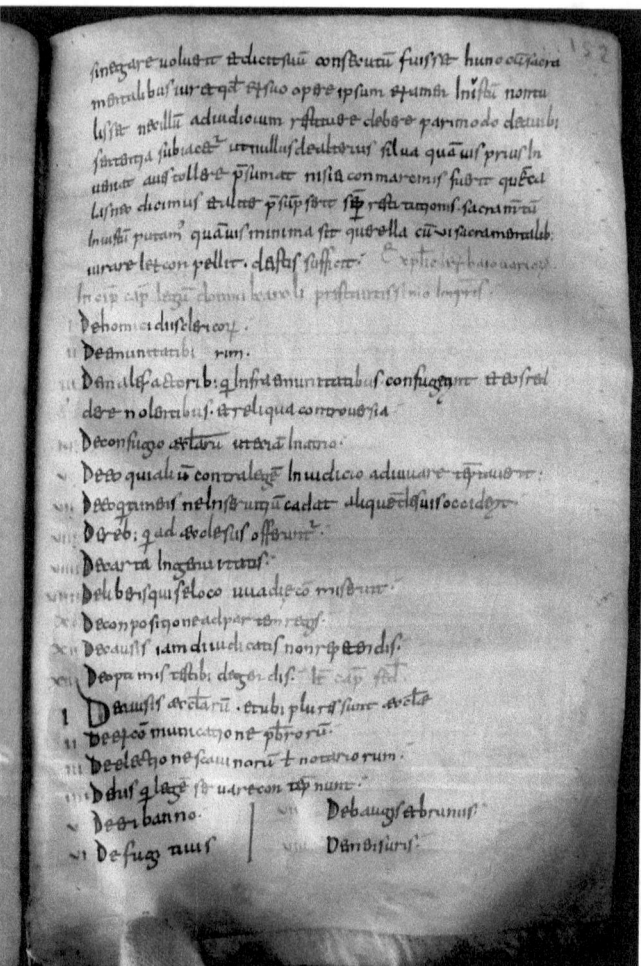

Fig. 6.3. Transition from *Lex Baiuvariorum* to Charlemagne's capitularies, Modena, Biblioteca Capitolare, O. I. 2, fol. 154r (152r).

Having come to the end of the law codes, it is now time to consider the capitularies, and the evidence for the pressing question of whether this should mark the transition from one self-contained *Rechtsblock* to another. The transition to the capitularies — as with the transition from the *Lex Alamannorum* to the *Lex Baiuvariorum* — occurs mid-page, that is, within a single, discrete piece of parchment. The two apparent parts are materially integrated, and consequently any argument for a discrete change between two types of legal text cannot be based on the codicology. Law and capitulary are demonstrably part of a single book. To what extent, then, is a discrete transition between the pair marked in the text, paratext, and overall *mise-en-page*?

The capitularies begin with an item in the paratext, written in orange-red ink by hand 3, that serves simultaneously as an explicit for the *Lex Baiuvariorum* and incipit for the capitula list for the *legum* (law) of Charlemagne, fol. 154r [152r], ll. 8–9. That the legal materials are described as *legum*, not as *capitula*,[48] again denotes that what modern scholars have split on editorial grounds into different types of legislative text were not seen as categories in that way by the producers of the Modena manuscript. Following the incipit, the text then leads directly into a capitula list, running from fol. 154r [152r], l. 10 through to fol. 156r [154r], l. 18, and the rest of the page is then left blank. Overleaf from the end of the capitula list, fol. 156v [154v], there is a full-page portrait of Charlemagne and Pippin. As this has been taken in the scholarship to represent a substantive break between the two types of legal text, law and capitulary, the fact that this transition occurs within the material context of a single page is of more than passing importance. Likewise, the shared *mise-en-page* and integration of the items is also significant, and the scribe's decision at this point to refer to the following legislation as "legum" rather than "capitulare" indicates that continuity

---

48 This contrasts with the wording used in, for instance, the capitulary collections of the eleventh-century manuscripts of the *Liber Papiensis*. See Gobbitt, *The Liber Papiensis*, and Radding, "Legal Manuscripts."

was being emphasized over change. This continuity and unity can be seen clearly in fig. 6.3, showing how the scribe laid out the transition from law to capitulary. From this alone it seems impossible to argue that they envisaged two clear *Rechtsblöcke* of the legal content, and to this we can add the evidence of the materiality and framing in the *mise-en-page*.

The capitula list is usually written in a single column, but changes to a two-column format towards the bottom on each of the first three pages. Again, majuscules are highlighted in dark red, while capitula numbers are written in orange. The capitula numbering is not continuous, restarting for each of the six specific capitularies contained within this set. When the main body of the legal text concludes (fol. 171r [169r], l. 2), it leads into an incipit for the capitularies of Pippin (l. 3), and a second set of capitula lists (l. 4 to 171v [169v], l. 10), again with majuscules highlighted in red. Capitula are also numbered (for ll. 2–10), restarting for each capitulary within the collection and written for the most part in a single line, but alternating to continuous text with space left for the numbers on the final page. The capitula themselves follow, concluding on fol. 178r [176r], l. 10, and the remainder of that page is then left blank.

The next incipit (fol. 178v [176v], l. 1) introduces the capitularies of Lothar, followed by a capitulary list written in two columns from fol. 178v [176v], l. 3 through to fol. 179r [177r], l. 10, and the rest of the page is left blank. The capitula then begin overleaf (l. 4, with an incipit on fol. 179v [177v], ll. 1–2). The positioning of these items on the pages is important, as each transition occurs within the material context of a single folio, which in turn is part of a full bifolium in a regularly formed quaternion (quire 23). That is to say, there is no disruption in the collation or in the text, and the portrait of Lothar and Louis mentioned in the poem cannot have been positioned here. Rather, as Mordek notes, it seems certain that that portrait page was on the now-lost folio immediately following on from those of Charlemagne and Pippin (fol. 158v [156v]), whose loss can be seen both in the collation of quire 20 and in the lacuna corresponding to the missing outset of the first capitulary.⁴⁹ All four of the Carolingian lawgivers depicted, then, must once have headed the entire capitulary collection. I suspect that they were already together in the exemplar, although they may instead only have been re-positioned together during the production of the Modena manuscript. Likewise, all of the capitulary lists may have been united in the exemplar but were probably, however, already split according to the works of their respective lawgivers, as the same division can be found in Gotha, Forschungsbibliothek, MS Memb. I. 84, and this later codex is not a direct descendant of the Modena manuscript.⁵⁰ The degree of intervention made by the Modena manuscript scribes, then, may well be significant, and considering how much was done to and with the paratext by this group, we cannot see an uncomplicated route through this law book to the variant made for and presumably used by Eurardus.

Does this mean then that the capitularies were treated, as Mordek argues, as a single and unified *Rechtsblock* by the Modena scribes, with the former part being a clear container of laws and the latter capitularies? The evidence presented here suggests not. Rather, I think we see the collected Carolingian rulers treated together as a self-contained group, similar to each of the preceding law codes. The closest parallel is the *Leges Langobardorum*, where all the Lombard lawgivers are presented at the start and a systematic breakdown of their collective legislation follows. However, where the Lombard laws were organized by legal theme, the Carolingian capitularies were structured by the lawgiver responsible, uniting their multiple capitularies into a single group. The three groups with capitula lists are identified by their incipits as being the legislation of Charlemagne first, Pippin second, and Lothar third. In practice, there is more division between them, as capitularies of Charlemagne are found

---

49 Alfred Boretius, ed., "No. 39: *Capitulare Legibus Additum*," *Capitularia regum Francorum* 1, Monumenta Germaniae Historica, Leges (Hanover: Hahn, 1883), 113–14, and Mordek, *Bibliotheca capitularium regum Francorum,* 261–62.

50 See Mischke, "Lupus' *Liber Legum* Reconsidered."

throughout those attributed to Pippin, and Louis the Pious is attested in those attributed to Lothar.[51] A fourth set of capitularies on the final folios of the manuscript represents those of Louis II (fol. 205v [203v], l. 10–207r [205r], l. 15). As these are not accompanied by a capitula list and are not present in the loosely comparable Gotha manuscript of the *Liber Legum* produced in the late tenth century, they have usually been treated in the scholarship as further additions made after the *Liber Legum* had ended. Certainly, the capitularies of Louis the Pious are integrated into the manuscript, in that they are also copied by hand 3, and, aside from missing a capitula list, share a comparable *mise-en-page*. Moreover, as Mischke argues, the differences between the Modena and Gotha manuscripts are substantial, and the Modena manuscript shows a clear intent to produce a systematized Italian capitulary collection.[52] In this way, the Modena manuscript foreshadows the production of a full Italian capitulary collection incorporated into the tenth-century manuscript of the Lombard laws — Paris, Bibliothèque nationale de France, MS lat. 4613[53] — or the self-contained Italian capitulary collection traveling in conjunction with the Lombard laws in the eleventh century, now edited under the name of the *Liber Papiensis*.[54]

---

51 See Mordek, *Bibliotheca capitularium regum Francorum*, 261–67. Mischke also addresses and adds further nuance to this seemingly clear-cut presentation in her forthcoming chapter, Mischke, "Lupus' *Liber Legum* Reconsidered."

52 Mischke, "Lupus *Liber Legum* Reconsidered," and Mischke, "Manuscript of the Month December 2017: Modena."

53 See Mordek, *Bibliotheca capitularium regum Francorum*, 469–76; "Paris, Bibliothèque Nationale, Lat. 4613," in *Bibliotheca Legum: A Database on Carolingian Secular Law-Texts*, ed. Karl Ubl, http://www.leges.uni-koeln.de/en/mss/codices/paris-bn-lat-4613/; and "Paris, Bibliothèque Nationale, Lat. 4613," in *Capitularia: Edition der fränkischen Herrschererlasse*, ed. Karl Ubl, https://capitularia.uni-koeln.de/en/mss/paris-bn-lat-4613/. Digitized at http://archivesetmanuscrits.bnf.fr/ark:/12148/cc634592.

54 Alfred Boretius, ed., *"Liber Legis Langobardorum* Papiensis Dictus," in *Monumenta Germaniae Historica, Leges* 4, ed. Georg Henry Pertz (Hanover: Monumenta Germaniae Historica, 1868), 290–585; Antonio Azara and Ernesto Eula, "Liber Papiensis," in *Novissimo Digesto Italiano*

Conclusion

Stepping back from the close consideration of the treatment of individual legal texts enables us to consider the patterns in how they are framed, and to see an overall unity of approach that develops continually throughout. When a given group has multiple lawgivers or legislative sessions by a single lawgiver, as in the *Leges Langobardorum,* all of the portraits are presented at the beginning of the collection. The same occurs with the collected capitularies, which suggests that they were interpreted collectively as a comparable, self-contained group of legislation. This group, however, is presented in the *mise-en-page* as being the equivalent of any one of the individual law codes or groupings of aggregate law, and there is no evidence in the manuscript to suggest that they were presented as a distinct group of legislative texts separate from and equivalent to the collected law codes. If there are *Rechtsblöcke* within the Modena manuscript, there are six such blocks,[55] one for each of the law codes and with the last being the capitularies. A potential counter to this is the insertion of individual capitula lists for the start of the legislation of each Carolingian lawgiver, rather than at the start of the capitularies as a whole. In this, the strategy contrasts with the Lombard laws, but again a direct comparison is not possible: these aggregate laws had already been systematized according to legal themes, so that any given title might include laws from several of the Lombard lawgivers. However, this reflects Lupus's organizational approach to systematizing the individual sets of laws, rather than a particular approach to different or abstracted kinds of legislative text.

Close consideration of the treatment both between and within each legislative text in its *mise-en-page* presents a clearer view of the manuscript's ongoing production and its develop-

---

9 ('Inve-L'), ed. Antonio Azara and Ernesto Eula, 3rd edn. (Turin: Unione Tipografico-Editrice, 1957), 829; and Gobbitt, *The Liber Papiensis.*

55 Or, if the *Lex Alamannorum* and *Lex Baiuvariorum* are considered as having been presented as a unified group, five such *Rechtsblöcke.*

ment by the three scribes as they reflected on their work. The stratigraphy of this community is relative, within the paleographic bounds of the mid- to later part of the ninth century, when all scribes were active. That, however, is a significant time range of potentially more than half a century, and there may well have been an extended time gap between the activities of hand 1, and hands 2 and 3. While hand 2 must clearly have worked with hand 3, the question of whether they were also contemporary to hand 1, or only added to that production phase later, is difficult to assess. Two main interpretations present themselves: if hands 1 and 2 were active at the same time, then they may have begun the project together and were joined by an artist; later, hand 1 handed over their own part of the production to hand 3, early in the copying of the Lombard laws (on fol. 54r [52r], l. 1). Hand 3 would have gradually taken up the work, first under the guidance of hand 2 who continued to provide most of the paratext, before hand 3 ultimately became responsible for text and paratext, finalizing the law book alongside the artist. Alternatively, it is also possible that hand 1 began the law book, then put it to one side when they completed what is now fol. 53v [51v]; then, at some later point, hand 2 picked up the project, introduced a number of revisions in the parts that had already been written, while working out what had been done and how best to continue the project, and brought hand 3 into the project. In the latter theory, hand 2 would have overseen hand 3, the new scribe, before hand 3 ultimately took over the production entirely. As neither hand 2 nor hand 3 appear to have given the manuscript back to hand 1 for further stints of activity, it is impossible to determine how long a period separated their respective activities: whether there was an overlap, uniting scribes and artist in a gradual transition, or if there was a significant time gap in the production during the mid- to late ninth century. Either way, the two phases are relatively close and it is hard to imagine that they could be divided by more than a few decades.

What is most interesting, however, is the way that hand 3 perpetuated their own developments in *mise-en-page*. It is apparent that this scribe made no major distinction between the collected barbarian law codes on the one hand and the Carolingian capitularies on the other. For hand 3, these comprised unified types of legislation and part of a homogeneous legal collection. Later scholarship has inserted an editorial break between what it considers as different types of legislative text, seeing a distinct pair of *Rechtsblöcke;* but for the medieval scribes of the Modena law book, and perhaps also those of Eurardus's law book, on which they drew, these were ultimately cumulative and comparable law texts.

Bibliography

Manuscripts

Cava de' Tirreni, Biblioteca della Badia, MS 4. http://www.internetculturale.it/jmms/iccuviewer/iccu.jsp?id=oai%3Awww.internetculturale.sbn.it%2FTeca%3A20%3ANT0000%3ACNMD0000205012&mode=all&teca=MagTeca+-+ICCU.

Florence, Biblioteca Medicea Laurenziana, MS Plut.77.10. http://mss.bmlonline.it/s.aspx?Id=AWOMMUQUI1A4r7GxMQ--&c=Leges%20Langobardorum#/book.

Gotha, Forschungsbibliothek, MS Memb. I. 84.

Madrid, Biblioteca Nacional, MS 413. http://bdh-rd.bne.es/viewer.vm?id=0000087627&page=1.

Modena, Biblioteca Capitolare, MS O. I. 2. http://archiviodiocesano.mo.it/archivio/flip/ACMo-OI-2/.

Paris, Bibliothèque nationale de France, MS lat. 4613. http://archivesetmanuscrits.bnf.fr/ark:/12148/cc634592.

Paris, Bibliothèque nationale de France, MS lat. 9656. http://archivesetmanuscrits.bnf.fr/ark:/12148/cc776464.

Primary

Capitularia regum Francorum 1. Edited by Alfred Boretius. Monumenta Germaniae Historica, Leges. Hanover: Hahn, 1883.

Capitularia regum Francorum 2. Edited by Alfred Boretius and Victor Krause. Monumenta Germaniae Historica, Leges. Hanover: Hahn, 1897.

"Cava de' Tirreni, Biblioteca della Badia, 4." In *Bibliotheca Legum: A Database on Carolingian Secular Law-Texts*, edited by Karl Ubl. http://www.leges.uni-koeln.de/en/mss/codices/cava-dei-tirreni-bdb-4/.

"Cava de' Tirreni, Biblioteca della Badia, 4." In *Capitularia: Edition der fränkischen Herrscherlasse*, edited by Karl Ubl. https://capitularia.uni-koeln.de/en/mss/cava-dei-tirreni-bdb-4/.

Edictus Langobardorum. In *Monumenta Germaniae Historica, Leges 4,* edited by Georg Henry Pertz, 1–206. Hanover: Hahn, 1868.

"Gotha, Forschungs- und Landesbibliothek, Memb. I 84." In *Bibliotheca Legum: A Database on Carolingian Secular Law-Texts,* edited by Karl Ubl. http://www.leges.uni-koeln.de/en/mss/codices/gotha-flb-memb-i-84/.

Lex Alamannorum. Edited by Karl August Eckhardt. Monumenta Germaniae Historica, Legum Nationum Germanicarum 5.1. Hanover: Hahn, 1966.

Lex Baiwariorum. Edited by Ernst Maria Augustin Schwind. Monumenta Germaniae Historica, Legum Nationum Germanicarum 5.2. Hanover: Hahn, 1926.

Lex Ribuaria. Edited by Franz Beyerle and Rudolf Buchner. Monumenta Germaniae Historica, Leges 3.1. Hanover: Hahn, 1954.

Lex Salica. Edited by Karl August Eckhardt. Monumenta Germaniae Historica, Legum Nationum Germanicarum 4.2. Hanover: Hahn, 1969.

Liber Legis Langobardorum Papiensis Dictus. In *Monumenta Germaniae Historica, Leges 4,* edited by Georg Henry Pertz, 290–585. Hanover: Hahn, 1868.

Liber Legis Regum Langobardorum, Concordia Dictus. In *Monumenta Germaniae Historica, Leges 4,* edited by Georg Henry Pertz, 235–89. Hanover: Hahn, 1868.

"Madrid, Biblioteca Nacional, 413." In *Bibliotheca Legum: A Database on Carolingian Secular Law-Texts,* edited by Karl Ubl. http://www.leges.uni-koeln.de/en/mss/codices/madrid-bn-413/.

"Madrid, Biblioteca Nacional, MS 413." In *Early Medieval Laws and Law-Books,* edited by Thom Gobbitt. https://thomgobbitt.files.wordpress.com/2018/04/madrid_bn_ms413_april2018.pdf.

"Modena, Biblioteca Capitolare, O. I. 2." In *Bibliotheca Legum: A Database on Carolingian Secular Law-Texts,* edited by Karl Ubl. http://www.leges.uni-koeln.de/en/mss/codices/modena-bc-o-i-2/.

"Modena, Biblioteca Capitolare, O. I. 2." In *Capitularia: Edition der fränkischen Herrschererlasse*, edited by Karl Ubl. https://capitularia.uni-koeln.de/en/mss/modena-bc-o-i-2/.

Mordek, Hubert. *Bibliotheca capitularium regum Francorum manuscripta: Überlieferung und Traditionszusammenhang der fränkischen Herrschererlasse.* Monumenta Germaniae Historica, Hilfsmittel 15. Munich: Hahn, 1995.

Mordek, Hubert, Klaus Zechiel-Eckes, and Michael Glatthaar, eds. *Die Admonitio generalis Karls der Großen.* Monumenta Germaniae Historica, Fontes iuris germanici antiqui in usum scholarum separatim editi 16. Hanover: Hahn, 2012.

Novissimo Digesto Italiano, 9 ('Inve-L'). Edited by Antonio Azara and Ernesto Eula. 3rd edition. Turin: Unione Tipografico-Editrice, 1957.

"O.I.2 - *Leges Salicae, Ripuariae, Longobardorum, Baioariorum, Caroli Magni.*" In *Archivio Storico Diocesano di Modena-Nonantola.* https://archiviodiocesano.mo.it/opere-digitalizzate/cat/16-o-i-2_leges_salicae_ripuariae-longobardorum-baioariorum-carolimagni.

"Paris, Bibliothèque Nationale, Lat. 4613." In *Bibliotheca Legum: A Database on Carolingian Secular Law-Texts*, edited by Karl Ubl. http://www.leges.uni-koeln.de/en/mss/codices/paris-bn-lat-4613/.

"Paris, Bibliothèque Nationale, Lat. 4613." In *Capitularia: Edition der fränkischen Herrschererlasse*, edited by Karl Ubl. https://capitularia.uni-koeln.de/en/mss/paris-bn-lat-4613/.

"Paris, Bibliothèque Nationale de France MS Lat. 9656." In *Early Medieval Laws and Law-Books*, edited by Thom Gobbitt. https://thomgobbitt.files.wordpress.com/2017/04/paris-bnf-ms-lat-9656-final.pdf.

"Paris, Bibliothèque Nationale, Lat. 9656." In *Bibliotheca Legum: A Database on Carolingian Secular Law-Texts*, edited by Karl Ubl. http://www.leges.uni-koeln.de/en/mss/codices/paris-bn-lat-9656/.

Secondary

Derolez, Albert. *The Palaeography of Gothic Manuscript Books: From the Twelfth Century to the Early Sixteenth Century.* Cambridge: Cambridge University Press, 2003.

Gobbitt, Thom. "Scribal Communities and Lombard Law-Books: Charlemagne's Herstal Capitulary within the Eleventh-Century Liber Papiensis." In *Creating Communities and Others in Early Medieval Europe,* edited by Richard Broome. Leeds: Kismet Press, forthcoming.

———. *The Liber Papiensis in the Long-Eleventh Century: Manuscripts, Materiality and Mise-en-page.* Leeds: Kismet Press, 2024.

Gumbert, Johan Peter. "Skins Sheets and Quires." In *New Directions in Later Medieval Manuscript Studies: Essays from the 1998 Harvard Conference,* edited by Derek Pearsall, 81–90. York: York Medieval Press, 2000.

———. "The Tacketed Quire: An Exercise in Comparative Codicology." *Scriptorium* 65, no. 2 (2011): 299–320.

Kaschke, Sören. "Manuscript of the Month August 2016: Cava de' Tirreni, BdB, 4." In *Capitularia: Edition der fränkischen Herrschererlasse,* edited by Karl Ubl. https://capitularia.uni-koeln.de/en/blog/handschrift-des-monats-august-2016/.

McKitterick, Rosamond. *The Carolingians and the Written Word.* Cambridge: Cambridge University Press, 1989. DOI: 10.1017/CBO9780511583599.

Merkel, Paul Johannes. *Die Geschichte des Langobardenrechts.* Berlin: Wilhelm Hertz, 1850.

Mischke, Britta. "Lupus' *Liber Legum* Reconsidered: Connections between a North Italian Fragment and the Liber Legum." In *Books of Law in the Long Tenth Century,* edited by Thom Gobbitt. Unpublished.

———. "Manuscript of the Month December 2017: Modena, Biblioteca Capitolare, O. I. 2." In *Capitularia: Edition der fränkischen Herrscherelasse,* edited by Karl Ubl. https://capitularia.uni-koeln.de/en/blog/handschrift-des-monats-dezember-2017/.

Münsch, Oliver. *Der "Liber Legum" des Lupus von Ferrières.* Frankfurt am Main: Peter Lang, 2001.

Pohl, Walter. "Memory, Identity and Power in Lombard Italy." In *The Uses of the Past in the Early Middle Ages,* edited by Yitzhak Hen and Matthew Innes, 9–28. Cambridge: Cambridge University Press, 2000. DOI: 10.1017/CBO9780511496332.002.

———. *Werkstätte der Erinnerung: Montecassino und die Gestaltung der langobardischen Vergangenheit.* Vienna: Oldenbourg, 2001. DOI: 10.7767/boehlau.9783205159995.

Pohl-Resl, Brigitte. "Legal Practice and Ethnic Identity in Lombard Italy." In *Strategies of Distinction: The Construction of Ethnic Communities, 300–800,* edited by Walter Pohl and Helmut Reimitz, 205–19. Leiden: Brill, 1998.

Radding, Charles M. "Legal Manuscripts in Eleventh-Century Italy: From Royal Edict to Scholarly Compilation." In *Organizing the Written Word: Scripts, Manuscripts and Texts. Proceedings of the First Utrecht Symposium on Medieval Literacy, Utrecht, 5–7 June 1997,* edited by Marco Mostert, Utrecht Studies in Medieval Literacy 2. Turnhout: Brepols, unpublished.

Radding, Charles M., and Antonio Ciaralli. *The "Corpus Iuris Civilis" in the Middle Ages: Manuscripts and Transmission from the Sixth Century to the Juristic Revival.* Leiden: Brill, 2007.

Russo, Guiseppe. "Leggi Longobarde nel codice O.I.2. della Biblioteca Capitolare di Modena." In *Atti del VI Congresso internazionale di studi sull'alto medioevo, Milano, 21–25 ottobre 1978,* 607–22. Spoleto: Presso la Sede del Centro Studi, 1980.

Siems, Harald. "Textbearbeitung und Umgang mit Rechtstexten im Frühmittelalter. Zur Umgestaltung der *Leges* im *Liber legum* des Lupus." In *Recht im frühmittelalterlichen Gallien. Spätantike, Tradition und germanische Wertvorstellung,* Rechtsgeschichtliche Schriften

7, edited by Harald Siems, Karin Nehlsen-von Stryk, and Dieter Strauch, 29–72. Cologne: Böhlau, 1995.

Wolfram, Herwig. *"Origo et Religio:* Ethnic Traditions and Literature in Early Medieval Texts." *Early Medieval Europe* 3, no. 1 (1994): 19–38. DOI: 10.1111/j.1468-0254.1994.tb00019.x.

Wormald, Patrick. *The Making of English Law: King Alfred to the Twelfth Century,* Volume 1: *Legislation and its Limits.* Oxford: Blackwell, 1999.

7

Sammelhandschriften and the *Breuiarium librorum* in Sankt Gallen 728

Mark Stansbury

Introduction

The *Breuiarium librorum de coenobio Sancti Galli,* a ninth-century list of books at the monastery of St. Gall now catalogued in St. Gall, Stiftsbibliothek, Cod. Sang. 728, has been studied as evidence for, among other things, the contents of the monastery's holdings, for the handwriting of Notker, and for the influence of Irish monks.[1] We can also look at how this text was compiled and what light its contents can throw on how texts were kept and assembled in the monastery. Central to this inquiry are *Sammelhandschriften,* the German term that has been adopted

---

1 For an edition of the catalogue and early bibliography, see Paul Lehmann, ed., *Mittelalterliche Bibliothekskataloge Deutschlands und der Schweiz,* vol. 1: *Die Bistümer Konstanz und Chur* (Munich: Beck, 1918), no. 16, 66–82. For Notker's handwriting, see Susan Rankin, *"Ego itaque Notker scripsi,"* *Revue Bénédictine* 101 (1991): 268–98. For Irish influence, see Cornel Dora and Franziska Schnoor, eds., Katherine Vanovitch, trans., *The Cradle of European Culture: Early Medieval Irish Book Art* (St. Gall: Klosterhof, 2018).

by scholars writing in English and other languages.[2] The word is a compound of *sammeln,* to collect, and *Handschrift,* manuscript, and is used to describe manuscripts whose contents seem to require explanation in a way that other manuscripts do not. For example, we would describe a manuscript containing Virgil's *Aeneid* or the Gospels as "a manuscript of the *Aeneid*" or "a Gospel book" because they correspond to other manuscripts with identical or similar contents and we are familiar with the sort of unity they represent. *Sammelhandschriften,* on the other hand, are so called because the collection of texts they contain is unique (or at least uncommon). In other words, we need an explanation for such manuscripts because the unity implied by the single physical object (a codex) is at odds with the disunity — or the uncommon unity — of the parts that make it up. This mismatch can result either from the contents of the manuscript (various subjects or authors) or its material constituents (written by different scribes at different times or in different places).

Yet the codex is, by its very nature, a unity assembled from parts: in Cassiodorus's formulation, a *corpus* (body) formed of *membra* (members).[3] Most codices consist of one or more codicological units bound together, and these units may be written by varying scribes across a number of different settings. The same applies to the contents: the *Aeneid* may be a single work by a single author, but it is composed of *libri* (units) assembled by the author. Indeed, in a letter to Firmus sending a copy of the *City of God* in gatherings, Augustine shows us that authors accustomed to the codex form were sensitive to the ways the material and textual forms matched:[4]

---

[2] There are several English terms that might also be used to describe manuscripts like these, such as "composite codices" or "miscellanies." I have chosen *Sammelhandschrift* because the focus here is on collecting.

[3] Cassiodorus, *Institutiones,* ed. Roger A.B. Mynors (Oxford: Clarendon Press, 1961), 1.2.1. See also Augustine, *Epistulae nuper in lucem prolatae,* Corpus Scriptorum Ecclesiasticorum Latinorum 88, ed. Johannes Divjak (Vienna: Hoelder-Pichler-Tempsky, 1981), 1a.

[4] Augustine, *Epistulae nuper in lucem prolatae,* 1a. Letter to Firmus: "libros de ciuitate Dei quos a me studiosissime flagitasti etiam mihi relectos, sicut

As promised, I have sent the books on the city of God that you eagerly demanded of me (and also reread them) […]. There are twenty-two gatherings [*quaterniones*], which is a great deal to collect into one codex [*corpus*], so if you want to make two codices, they should be divided so that one has ten books and the other twelve, for in these ten the vanities of the impious have been refuted and in the rest our religion demonstrated and defended — although this has been done in the former group where it was more appropriate, as well as in the latter. If, on the other hand, you prefer to have more than two codices [*corpora*], you ought to make five, the first of which contains the first five books, which contain the arguments against those who say that the cult not of gods but of demons contributes to the happiness of this life. The second [codex] should have the next five against those who think that by worshiping however many gods with rites and sacrifices that they will have a life to come after death. Now each of the three following codices should have four books, since we have dealt with the subject so that four show the rise of that city, the same number the advance — or perhaps "movement" is better — and the final four the end.

The four works that we know as the Gospels are all by different authors and were written at different times, but Theodore C.

---

promiseram, misi […] quaterniones sunt xxii quos in unum corpus redigere multum est; et si duos uis codices fieri, ita diuidendi sunt, ut decem libros habeat unus, alius duodecim. decem quippe illis uanitates refutatae sunt impiorum, reliquis autem demonstrata atque defensa est nostra religio, quamuis et in illis hoc factum sit ubi opportunius fuit, et in istis illud. si autem corpora malueris esse plura quam duo, iam quinque oportet codices facias, quorum primus contineat quinque libros priores quibus aduersus eos est disputatum qui felicitati uitae huius non plane deorum sed daemoniorum cultum prodesse contendunt, secundus sequentes alios quinque <aduersus eos> qui uel tales uel qualescumque plurimos deos propter uitam quae post mortem futura est per sacra et sacrificia colendos putant. iam tres alii codices qui sequuntur quaternos libros habere debebunt; sic enim a nobis pars eadem distributa est, ut quattuor ostenderent exortum illius ciuitatis totidem que procursum, siue dicere malumus, excursum, quattuor uero ultimi debitos fines."

Skeat argued that collecting them together as the *ur-Sammelhandschrift* enforced their identity as a group and encouraged the Christian adoption of the codex.[5] In the case of the Gospels, the collection of disparate material was intended to create and reinforce a unity that had been contested. The fact that we do not see a Gospel book as a *Sammelhandschrift* shows how well the technique worked. Historically, therefore, the technological possibilities of the codex are central to *Sammlung*.

We are fortunate to have a few cases in which the reasons for creating *Sammelhandschriften* are made clear, such as the program that Cassiodorus outlined in the first book of his *Institutiones*. Cassiodorus divided his large Bible into nine volumes, and the first nine chapters of the first book of the *Institutiones* describe texts that Cassiodorus left to explain the biblical text in each of these nine codices. In these nine chapters Cassiodorus described the biblical books contained in each division of the Bible and then recommended works to explain them. For his second biblical codex, *De Regum*(!), for example, Cassiodorus first observed that he could find no commentary on any of these books and thus "I have woven together some scraps from learned men into a sort of clothing so that what could not be found in a single book [*corpus*] can be known piecemeal [*membratim*] in a united collection."[6] After listing works by Origen, Augustine, Jerome, and Ambrose, as well as a homily by Ori-

---

5 Theodore C. Skeat, "The Origin of the Christian Codex," *Zeitschrift für Papyrologie und Epigraphik* 102 (1994): 68: "But inevitably the selection of the Four and their physical unity in the Codex gave them, right from the start, an authority and prestige which no competitor could hope to rival. The Four-Gospel Canon and the Four-Gospel Codex are thus inseparable."

6 Cassiodorus, *Institutiones*, 1.2.1: "In secundo vero Regum codice, quoniam continui textus expositionem reperire non potui, quaedam frusta disertissimorum virorum velut in uno quodam vestimento contexui, ut membratim possit adunata collectione cognosci, quod sub uno corpore nequaquam potuit inveniri." Cassiodorus plays on the meanings of the words he uses: *contexui* (woven) refers both to weaving a garment and composing a text; *membratim* (piecemeal) also plays on the idea of *membrum* and *corpus* (body) as well as the *membrana* (parchment) on which the codex was written.

gen he could not find, Cassiodorus says that he has "gathered all these in the body of one codex, so that, with the Lord's guidance, you may refer in turn to the pertinent things of the commentators on these books. To this codex I have also appended blank gatherings so that the writings yet to be found may be added to the above-mentioned commentaries."[7] In other words, Cassiodorus created a separate codex of writings designed to serve the monks at Vivarium as a commentary on the second codex of the Bible. For other biblical codices Cassiodorus also simply suggested works to be read. For example, concerning the first codex, the Octateuch, Cassiodorus wrote that the last three books of Augustine's *Confessions* are a good commentary on Genesis. He did not say that he had included these in his book of commentaries, but simply that these may be read with profit. In this part of the *Institutiones,* then, Cassiodorus's aim was to make books serve as teachers. Cassiodorus and Pope Agapetus could not found the kind of school they wanted in Rome in the 530s, so Cassiodorus was forced to create a new sort of school for his monasteries in Calabria. In this school, the monks had to gain an understanding of the Bible from teachers who taught not orally but in writing — from texts, not from people. And the textual teachers are what we would call *Sammelhandschriften,* texts collected and united in a codex whose purpose is to clarify a parallel collection of biblical texts. As all commentaries, the texts through which Cassiodorus carried out this program are metatexts, that is, they can be read as texts in their own right, but they also are texts that refer to and explain another set of texts. Without the *Institutiones,* the metatextual *Sammelhandschriften* would still be useful, but their functions as metatexts would be inexplicit.[8] In his explanation, Cassiodorus articulated

---

7   Cassiodorus, *Institutiones*, 1.2.12: "Quae tamen omnia in unius codicis corpore congregavi, ut in vicem commentorum ad libros ipsos pertinentia Domino praestante relegatis. cui codici puros etiam quaterniones adiunxi, ut quod de praefato opere adhuc repertum fuerit praedictis expositionibus aggregetur."

8   For the relationship to biblical commentaries, see Mark Stansbury, "Early-Medieval Biblical Commentaries, Their Writers and Readers," *Frühmittel-*

the reasons and procedures for creating a *Sammelhandschrift*: first, deciding the purpose, then selecting the texts, and finally juxtaposing the texts (either by binding or copying) in a new context. Cassiodorus also showed that when he could not find an appropriate text, he created one by weaving together selections in a process similar to the creation of the codex itself. Once these texts were brought together, the reason for their selection could well be lost, which is often the position in which we find ourselves. The unity formed by such a collection was represented visually by the *bibliotheca,* the bookcase, as we see in the fifth-century mosaic, possibly of St. Lawrence,[9] in the mausoleum of Galla Placidia in Ravenna, and the seventh-century portrait of the scribe Ezra from the Codex Amiatinus, with the nine biblical codices based on Cassiodorus's division.[10]

To summarize, then, Cassiodorus's example shows that *Sammelhandschriften* are a group of texts selected and juxtaposed in a new context for a purpose. The purpose may be articulated by the compiler, inferable from the contents, or unknown. To explore these issues, the rest of this chapter turns to the ninth-century *Breuiarium librorum de Coenobio Sancti Galli* to ask how *Sammelhandschriften* were seen by those using them and to look at the material conditions in the monastery that may have fostered the creation of such manuscripts.

The Composition of the *Breuiarium*

The *Breuiarium librorum* in St. Gall, Stiftsbibliothek, Cod. Sang. 728 is written on a single gathering of five bifolia (the pages numbered 3 to 22), which forms the first codicological unit of the manuscript. Legal texts make up the remainder of the man-

---

alterliche Studien 33, no. 1 (1999): 49–82.

9 Gillian Mackie, "New Light on the So-Called Saint Lawrence Panel at the Mausoleum of Galla Placidia, Ravenna," *Gesta* 29, no. 1 (1990): 54–60, argues that the saint is Vincent of Zaragoza based on the life and passion of Vincent, the popularity of his cult, and Galla Placidia's personal and family ties to Spain.

10 Florence, Biblioteca Medicea Laurenziana, MS Amiatino I, fol. 5r.

uscript, so St. Gall, Stb, Cod. Sang. 728 is itself a *Sammelhandschrift*. The books listed in the *Breuiarium* are grouped under headings in capitalis, usually written in reddish orange ink, and these headings follow a fairly conventional order: books of the Bible come first, followed by books grouped by author, then by books grouped by subject. (For the contents of the Breuiarium, see the Appendix.)

This may sound orderly and straightforward, but if one looks more closely, at p. 5, to take one example, it is possible to see that underlying this order is something of a mess: lines have been left blank or erased, entries have been changed or added, and comments have been made. The purpose of the blank lines may be to facilitate the addition of new books to the list, but the changes made to the individual entries tell a more interesting story. Many of them are the result of comparing the written list to the actual books being described, which also may account for the erased lines. For example, the book of Prophets in line 6 (originally no. 35),[11] was listed as one volume, but this has been crossed out and "two" written above. A note in the margin of line 11 next to no. 39, the volume containing Chronicles, Tobias, Judith, and Esther, says *ad scolam* (at the school), which is presumably meant to indicate that the book was not at its expected location but in the monastery's school. One can multiply such examples on many pages, and especially interesting are the comments on the quality of the manuscripts and texts written by the hand that wrote *ad scolam,* with such remarks as *ad nihil utila* (completely useless), *nunquam uidi* (I have never seen it), and *uetus et falsatus* (old and corrupt).[12]

---

[11] Numbers refer to the items in the accompanying transcription of the *Breuiarium librorum*. The transcription uses the following conventions: item numbers with asterisks are *Sammelhandschriften;* modifications to entries are in bold; ligatures are underlined; letters marked for deletion are printed in strikethrough; /\ indicates above the line; \/ indicates below the line; abbreviations are expanded in parentheses; and proper nouns are capitalized. The text has been punctuated for clarity, not to follow the manuscript.

[12] Susan Rankin argued that Notker the Stammerer was the author and scribe of many of these comments in Rankin, *"Ego itaque Notker scripsi."*

Several entries have been marked using *notae* by someone collating the manuscript either with an exemplar or the physical books. For example, no. 161 on p. 12 was first written as an entry for Columbanus's commentary on Psalms. Then a collator wrote the *nota* R (*require*) in the margin, perhaps to indicate that they could not find the book. The response to this request was then written at the end of the entry: "I have seen that Ruodinus has the book; he says that it is his."[13]

Annotations in the *Breuiarium* also show, for example, that there seems to have been great interest in the works of Gregory the Great, listed on p. 6, especially on the part of Charles the Bald and his wife. One volume of the forty homilies had been given to Charles, one old copy of the *Dialogues* was in Rohrbach (property owned by the monastery), Rickart (Richilda, Charles's wife) had a volume of the twelve homilies on the first part of Ezekiel, and a volume of all twenty-two homilies had been returned to Reichenau, and a new copy made.

Although it is relatively easy to see how individual entries have been modified and annotated, it is relatively difficult to determine the exact order of all the individual entries. The *Breuiarium* was written by several hands and parts of it have been extensively revised. By examining these notes and revisions it is possible to see that the foundation for the *Breuiarium* must have been an earlier list of the monastery's books. This earlier list was copied into the gathering, with space left for additions. The newly copied list was then updated to eliminate books the monastery no longer had and to include ones it had since acquired. As part of this process the gathering seems to have been taken to the books in order to compare the list with the physical objects.[14] We can see from additions and changes in the list

---

13 "Ruodinum uidi habere qui dixit suum esse."

14 This is clear from such notes as: "nunquam uidi," p. 7; "hoc auditum est non uisum," p. 11; "Ruodinum uidi habere qui dixit suum esse," "hoc non uidi," p. 12; "non uidi," p. 13. Although we may assume that the default location for all books was the monastery's library, it is interesting to note that *bibliotheca* is used only once in the list (no. 31) and refers not to a location but a biblical pandect.

that at times the description of the books was not accurate, or the books were not present but their locations were known, or new books were located and added, or duplicate listings were eliminated, or descriptions of the manuscripts and their quality were added.

But there are also indications that the overall structure of the catalogue is deceptive. This is most easily seen in the use of color washes to highlight changes between items or within items. The use of these mostly red and green washes is consistent from the beginning of the *Breuiarium* on p. 5 to the beginning of no. 206 on p. 15, but it ends with no. 206's continuation on p. 16, which does not use washes. Their use practically disappears for the remainder of the manuscript.[15] This also corresponds to a breakdown in the seeming clarity of the manuscript classification. To take two examples, no. 219, Hrabanus on the lamentations of Jeremiah, seems to fall under the category of laws, while nos. 248–250, an old volume of the lives of the fathers, letters and works of Alcuin, and excerpts from the Psalms, seems to fall under the heading Orthography in no. 237. It would seem that once the exemplar that formed the basis for the *Breuiarium* had been copied and corrected on p. 16, other books were added in more or less sensible groups through p. 21.

From all these annotations it is clear that the first gathering of St. Gall, Stb, Cod. Sang. 728 represents a working copy, the notes, of several people engaged in updating and adding to an earlier list of the monastery's books. Later, a fair copy of the *Breuiarium* was made in St. Gall, Stiftsbibliothek, Cod. Sang. 267 (also a *Sammelhandschrift*), and the later list, called an *Adnotatio librorum,* was incorporated into the monastery's history written by the monk Ratpert.[16] The *Adnotatio* omits many of

---

[15] From p. 16 on, washes are used in writing only nine items: numbers 238, and 256–263.

[16] On the relationship between the *Breuiarium* and the *Adnotatio,* see the excellent discussion by Hannes Steiner, ed. and trans., *Ratpert. St. Galler Klostergeschichten (Casus sancti Galli),* Monumenta Germaniae Historica, Scriptores Rerum Germanicarum in Usum Scholarum Separatim Editi 85 (Hanover: Hahn, 2002).

the details recorded in the *Breuiarium* such as those discussed above in the *Breuiarium*'s list of Gregory's writings. This also might be the reason that the earlier, messier, but more informative copy was kept.

Being able to characterize this document and understand the importance of its form — the fact that it is a portable gathering — also helps us better understand the list of books written in the Irish manner, the *Libri scottice scripti*. This list is in an odd position in the gathering: it occupies twenty-one lines on the verso of the first folio and thus comes one page before the *Breuiarium* begins on the recto of the second folio. Because the *Breuiarium* was being updated and presumably handled and carried often, the outer pages served as guard leaves and were not written upon. The scribes began the *Breuiarium* by writing on the first protected recto (p. 5) and proceeded to the last protected recto (p. 21), after which there was only one protected page available for the *Libri scottice scripti*, p. 4, which was written last.

"Precarious" Forms and Texts in St. Gall, Stb 728

The *Breuiarium* uses several terms to describe the physical appearance of the monastery's books. When one thinks of the St. Gall library today, one may have in mind the rococo splendor of the hall designed by Peter Thumb and built between 1758 and 1767, but our catalogue lists fewer than 400 objects, which would fit within a single alcove of the current room. And many of them were not bound as neatly as the books now on view in the library. The *Breuiarium* gives these categories for the physical forms.[17]

- *Volumen*. This is the most common term for the physical form of the book. The *Breuiarium* lists 327 *uolumina* or 86%

---

[17] I have counted the number of objects, not the number of works, so "Item tractatus sancti Ambrosii in epistulas Pauli volum. IIII" counts as four *uolumina*.

of the total. Presumably this refers to bound codices. Originally the term meant papyrus book roll, and in antiquity this would have corresponded with *liber,* so one *liber* of Virgil would be contained in one *uolumen,* which meant that the two could be used interchangeably.[18] Even though the codex was firmly established as the usual form by Jerome's day, he continued to use *uolumen* and *liber* interchangeably.[19]

- *Quaternio.* There are at least 23 *quaterniones* in the *Breuiarium,* or 6% of the total. It is difficult to be precise about the number because some items are listed as "in quaternionibus" without specifying how many.[20] This presumably refers to a group of sewn and ruled parchment bifolia, like the ones upon which the *Breuiarium* itself was written. I am doubtful that it refers only to gatherings of exactly four bifolia, so if the *Breuiarium* had been listed in itself, the entry would have been something like "Breuiarium librorum in quaternione I."
- *Codex (15)* and *Codicilli (2).* There are fifteen *codices* listed in the *Breuiarium* or 4% of the total. It is difficult to say what the difference between a *codex* or *codicillus* and a *uolumen* is. The two terms are used throughout the *Breuiarium* and there seems to be no obvious way to differentiate them. Perhaps the *codicilli* are smaller codices, but the term also had legal meaning.[21]

The following formats comprise a relatively small number of items.

---

18 Cicero, *Tusculanae Disputationes. M. Tulli Ciceronis Scripta Quae Manserunt Omnia,* part 44, ed. Max Pohlenz (Berlin: De Gruyter, 1918), 3.3.6: "quoniam duobus superioribus [libris] de morte et de dolore dictum est, tertius dies disputationis hoc tertium volumen efficiet."
19 Gert Kloeters, "Buch und Schrift bei Hieronymus" (PhD Diss., University of Münster, 1957), 199; Evaristo Arns, *La technique du livre d'après Saint Jérôme* (Paris: de Boccard, 1953), 118.
20 I have counted these unspecified plurals as two *quaterniones,* so the actual number is likely to be higher.
21 On the legal meaning of *codicillus,* see the *Dictionary of Medieval Latin from British Sources,* s.v. *codicillus.*

- *Schedula (6)* and *Scheda (1)*. There are six *schedulae* listed in the Breuiarium (1.6%) and one example of a *scheda*. Perhaps these refer to individual folios or unsewn bifolia.
- *Libelluli (4)*. The diminutive usually means a small book, and in these four cases refers to the physical form of the book rather than the authorial division, which is the normal use of *liber* in the *Breuiarium*.
- *Rotulus (1)*. There is one *rotulus*, the "List of abbots of Reichenau in 1 *rotulus*" listed on p. 21, which may form the basis for the later catalogue of Reichenau abbots.[22]
- *Mappa (1)*. Englisch discussed two *mappae mundi* found in St. Gall manuscripts of Isidore's *Etymologiae*, but not this entry. She did note that catalogue entries for *mappae mundi* date from the ninth century.[23]

From this, it is clear that although bound books predominate, the *quaterniones, schedae, schedulae,* and perhaps *libelluli,* which account for 34 of the 380 objects in the monastery, are not bound between boards, which means that some 10% of the monastery's holdings were in what I would call "precarious" forms.[24] By that I mean that these are forms that have, for the most part, not survived without being bound into codices. In fact, the best-known recent survival of such a book is the Faddan More Psalter, found in a bog in 2006 and consisting of five quires contained in a leather folder.

---

22 "Commemoratio abbatum qui in Augia fuerunt in I rodulo." For the catalogue, see Georg Heinrik Pertz, ed., *Monumenta Germaniae Historica, Scriptores 2* (Hanover: Hahn, 1829), 37, where Pertz speculates that the St. Gall *rotulus* provides the basis for the Reichenau one.

23 Brigitte Englisch, *Ordo orbis terrae. Die Weltsicht in den Mappae mundi des frühen und hohen Mittelalters* (Berlin: De Gruyter, 2002), 37n20 for the catalogue. The Isidore manuscripts are St. Gall, Stiftsbibliothek, Cod. Sang. 236 and 237.

24 For a discussion of similar ideas, see also Martin Mulsow, *Prekäres Wissen: Eine andere Ideengeschichte der Frühen Neuzeit* (Berlin: Suhrkamp 2012), and Johan Peter Gumbert, "The Tacketed Quire: An Exercise in Comparative Codicology," *Scriptorium* 65 (2011): 299–320.

We have seen above that the organization of *Breuiarium* breaks down on page 16 and in a more-or-less disorganized way up to page 21. This "disorganized" part of the *Breuiarium* also has more "precarious" text formats than the "organized" one, including the *Libri scottice scripti,* which has half of the total *quaterniones* in the *Breuiarium,* which perhaps helps explain why few if any of these manuscripts survived.[25]

Texts could be in a precarious state for other reasons as well. No. 87, for example, is described as "Selections on the Psalms, by an author I do not know, in gatherings" while the person checking for the item has written "I have never seen it."[26] Perhaps these gatherings were also in a precarious state because they had neither *auctor* nor *auctoritas.* In the same way, the manuscripts described as "useless" or "puny" may be seen as precarious.

Sammelhandschriften in the Breuiarium

We can now return to our original question, the presence of *Sammelhandschriften* in the *Breuiarium.* There are many ways one might define *Sammelhandschriften,* but to construct a preliminary list (the asterisked items in the Appendix) I have chosen two criteria: first, items with uncommon or unique combinations of texts, such as those that contain works by more than one author (except where that combination is common, such as Jerome and Gennadius — even though that might fit one of the criteria); second, manuscripts described as using the terms "collection" and "excerptum." Applying these criteria to the books listed in the *Breuiarium* gives a list of 93 items listing at least 134 objects or about 35% of the objects in the entire *Breuiarium.* We can infer some reasons for the collections:

- *Collecting works on a common subject or in a common genre*: By far the most common reason for collecting works would

---

25 The list has 19 *uolumina,* at least 11 *quaterniones,* and 2 *codicilli.*
26 St. Gall, Stb, Cod. Sang. 728, p. 7: "Item nescio /nunquam uidi\ cuius tractatoris Eglogae in Psalterium in quaternionibus."

seem to be the fact that the works have a common subject or genre. Because of my criteria, most of these are found in the second part of the *Breuiarium,* which is organized by subject. For example, there are numerous collections of saints' lives and miracles, saints' rules, law, computus, orthography, *grammatica,* heresies, and biblical commentaries. These collections seem to be "open," by which I mean that they are assembled according to a principle and, providing the principle is respected, were thus open for additions. No. 53 offers an interesting contrast, where the lives of Paul and Anthony have been added to Gregory's *Dialogues,* treating the "closed" text of Gregory like an "open" collection.

- *Epitomes*: The biblical commentaries of Jerome (nos. 75, 77, and 80) are excerpted as is a work on the Psalter (no. 87).
- *Replacing missing text*: At times, the texts by different authors seem designed to provide missing works, such as no. 65, in which the commentary of Hrabanus replaces the missing Jerome.
- *Personal collections*: The "Collectio Eadberti" in no. 169 is interesting because the authority for it seems to come from Eadbert's name and, assuming that this is the current manuscript St. Gall, Stiftsbibliothek, Cod. Sang. 243, there is a colophon by Eadberct, the compiler and scribe, explaining the compilation.[27] The collection is known under a different name, the *Collectio canonum Hibernensis.*

---

27 St. Gall, Stiftsbibliothek, Cod. Sang. 243, p. 254: "Ego eadberct hunc librum de ueteris & noui instrum(en)ti testimoniis coaptatum & de s(an)c(t)orum exemplis patrum collectu(m) multisq(ue) scripturaru(m) floribus ornatum non sine corporis labore depingens, opitulante D(e)o ad fine(m) usque perduxi. Qui nescit scribere non putat esse laborem. Tres /eni(m)\ digiti scribunt totum corpus laborat. Obsecro quicumque hęc legens recitaueris ut propitium mihi fieri D(eu)m rogare digneris." "I, Eadberct, writing with physical labor, have carried this book to completion with the help of God, having joined together testimony from the Old and New Testaments and ornamented it with examples collected from the holy fathers and excerpts from many writings. Those who do not know how to write think that it is no work. Although three fingers write, the whole body labors. I beg

- *Open texts*: No. 216 is a *uolumen* with "capitula that are to be added to the laws." In this manuscript, the actual contents are not fixed, but portions added according to a rule. This is similar to, for example, Gennadius's continuation of Jerome's *De uiris inlustribus*: the text classifies certain things and selects them (*capitula* that are to be laws, people who are well-known) and once this pattern has been established, the text is "open" in the sense that additions can be made to bring it up to date.
- *Preservation*: We cannot ignore the example of St. Gall, Stb, Cod. Sang. 728 itself, which shows us that some *Sammelhandschriften* must have been assembled because the booklets were of similar size and thus easily bound into a more stable form.

Conclusion

As we have seen, the manuscript of the *Breuiarium librorum* contained in the first codicological unit of St. Gall, Stb, Cod. Sang. 728 transmits a text in progress. The first part (pages 5 to 15) is no doubt based on an earlier list that was copied into the gathering and then revised and commented upon; the second (pages 16 to 21 and the *Libri scottice scripti* on page 4) was then added to include new subject headings as well as new books. In both parts, the addition of new items, deletion of lost items, correction of inaccuracies, and comments, all seem intended to make the list's descriptions accurate and keep its contents current with the monastery's holdings. At some point, the community stopped updating the *Breuiarium,* possibly because there was no more room in the gathering after the last entries, the *Libri scottice scripti.* The manuscript transmitting the *Breuiarium* records the layers of this process, so we can see the elements involved such as checking the location of books, checking number of objects, and so on. The *Breuiarium* also allows us to

---

whoever is reading these words that you will have read them aloud so that you will find it worthy to ask that God be favorably inclined toward me."

see the words used to describe the physical form of the items in the monastery's collection (*uolumen, codex,* etc.), although it is sometimes difficult to know how to interpret the terms precisely. These physical forms seem to fall into three categories: bound codices, unbound parchment leaves and gatherings, and other forms (the *mappa* and *rotulus*). From this, we can sketch a picture of the monastery's book holdings: there were a substantial number of unbound objects, books could be found in several possible locations (or lost), books could be misidentified or their identity unknown, books could be loaned outside the monastery, or they could be employed for personal use within it or at its holdings. The *Breuiarium*'s list, revised over time, then served as the basis for static book lists, which were eventually incorporated into the monastery's account of its own history in the same way that the *Gesta Abbatum Fontanellensium* did, demonstrating how important the collection of books was for the monastery.

Among these books we can identify *Sammelhandschriften*, that is, manuscripts that collect unusual or unique combinations of texts. This somewhat impressionistic definition reflects the fluidity inherent in *Sammelhandschriften* themselves. For example, the *Breuiarium* lists (no. 162) the "*Collectio* of Eadbert from various little works of the holy fathers in one *uolumen*." By our criteria, this is a *Sammelhandschrift,* not only for the use of *collectio* in the description but also the act of collection described by the manuscript's scribe in the colophon. Yet in today's catalogue, the manuscript (St. Gall, Stb, Cod. Sang. 243) has a different title as a witness to the *Collectio canonum Hibernensium* because it has a complicated relationship with several other manuscripts with similar texts.[28] And, of course, all the manuscripts of the *Collectio canonum Hibernensium* are collections of texts of different origins because the *Collectio* is a *Sammeltext.* The difference between *Sammelhandschrift* and *Sammeltext*

---

28 See Roy Flechner, *Making Laws for a Christian Society: The "Hibernensis" and the Beginnings of Church Law in Ireland and Britain* (London: Routledge, 2021).

shows us how entangled the idea of text and manuscript are and how dependent upon the viewpoint of the observer their study remains.

Appendix 1

Item numbers with asterisks are *Sammelhandschriften*. Modifications to entries are printed in bold. Ligatures are underlined. Letters marked for deletion are printed in strikethrough. Letters printed /a\ are above the line and \a/ are below the line. Abbreviations are expanded in parentheses. Proper nouns are capitalized. The text is punctuated for clarity, not to follow the manuscript.

No.	Pg.	Entry	Format	No.
	4	LIBRI SCOTTICE SCRIPTI		
1	4	Metrum Iuvenci in uol(umine) I	Volumen	1
2	4	Ep(istu)lę Pauli in uol(umine) I	Volumen	1
3	4	Act(us) Ap(osto)lor(um) in uol(umine) I	Volumen	1
4	4	Ep(istu)lę canonicę VII in uol(umine) I	Volumen	1
5	4	Tractat(us) Bedę in p(ro)uerbia Salom(onis) in uol(umine) I	Volumen	1
6	4	Ezechiel p(ro)p(heta) in uol(umine) I	Volumen	1
7	4	Euang(elium) sec(un)d(u)m Ioh(annem) in uol(umine) I	Volumen	1
8	4	Enchiridion Aug(ustini) in uol(umine) I	Volumen	1
9	4	Ite(m) Iuuenci metru(m) in uol(umine) I	Volumen	1
10	4	Apocalypsis in uol(umine) I	Volumen	1
11	4	Ite(m) Apocalypsis in uol(umine) I	Volumen	1

Table 7.1. Contents of the *Breuiarium librorum* in St. Gall, Stiftsbibliothek, Cod. Sang. 728.

No.	Pg.	Entry	Format	No.
12	4	Metru(m) Sedulii in uol(umine) I	Volumen	1
13	4	De gradib(us) eclesiasticis in uol(umine) I	Volumen	1
14	4	Arithmetica Boetii in uol(umine) I	Volumen	1
15	4	Missalis in uol(umine) I	Volumen	1
16	4	Vita S(an)c(t)i Hilarii in codicillo I	Codicillum	1
17	4	Passio s(anctorum) martyru(m) Marcellini et Petri	?	1
18	4	Metru(m) Virg(ilii) in uol(umine) I	Volumen	1
19	4	Eius glosa in altero	Volumen	1
20	4	Q(ua)t(er)nio I de inventione corporis S(an)c(t)i Stephani	Quaternio	1
21	4	Quat(ernio) I de relatione translationis S(an)c(t)i Galli in nova(m) ecl(esi)am	Quaternio	1
22	4	Bedę de arte met(rica) in q(u)/a\t(ernione)	Quaternio	1
23	4	Instructio ecclesiastici ordinis in codicillo I	Codicillum	1
24	4	Lib(er) I Genesis in q(u)/a\t(er)nioni(bus)	Quaternio	2
25	4	Act(us) Ap(osto)lor(um) et Apocalypsis in uol(umine) I ueteri	Volumen	1
26	4	Quat(er)nio I in nat(a)l(e) innocentu(m) legend(um)	Quaternio	1
*27	4	Orationes et sententię varię in uol(umine) I	Volumen	1
*28	4	Orationes in q(u)/a\t(er)nion(ibus)	Quaternio	2
29	4	Expositio in Cantica Cant(icorum) in q(u)/a\tern(ionibus) II ⊣	Quaternio	2

313

No.	Pg.	Entry	Format	No.
30	4	Ite(m) in Regu(m) q(u)/a\t(ernio) I	Quaternio	1
	5	BREVIARIUM LIBRORUM DE COENOBIO S(AN)C(T)I GALLI CONF(ESSORIS) CHR(IST)I		
	5	DE LIBRIS VETERIS TESTAMENTI		
31	5	Bibliotheca una	Volumen?	1
32	5	Eptatici II	Volumen?	3
33	5	Regum uolumina V	Volumen	5
34	5	Salomonis uolum(ina) VI **et in uno ex his Iob et Tobias et in alio Esdras et Ne(he)mi(a) ℞**	Volumen	3
35	5	Libri omniu(m) p(ro)phetarum in **dvob(us) voluminib(us)** (corr. ex uno uolumine)	Volumen	2
36	5	Item Esaię et Hieremiae in uno uolumine	Volumen	1
37	5	Ezechihelis et Danihelis et XII p(ro)phetar(um) In uno uol(umine)	Volumen	1
38	5	Paralippomenon, Iudiht, Hester, Esdrae, Machabeorum In uno uolumine	Volumen	1
39	5	Ite(m) Parlippom(enon), **Tobias** Iudith, Hester In uol(umine) I ueteri **ad scolam**	Volumen	1
40	5	Item Machabeoru(m) uolumina duo	Volumen	2
41	5	Ite(m) Iob, Tobias, Ivdith, Hester, Ezras, Neemias in uol(umine) I	Volumen	1
42	5	Ite(m) Iob, Tobias, Iudith, Hester in uol(umine) I	Volumen	1

No.	Pg.	Entry	Format	No.
43	5	Ite(m) Iob, Tobias, Iud(ith), Hester in uol(umine) I	Volumen	1
44	5	Ite(m) Iob in uol(umine) I **ad Rorbach**	Volumen	1
45	5	Tobias, Iudith, Hester in codice I	Codex	1
	5	ITEM DE LIBRIS NOVI TESTAMENTI		
46	5	Euangeliorum uolumina IIII **ex his duo non inueni s(ed) I et tria uetera** [marg eras: defecsti]	Volumen	4
47	5	Epistolae Pauli et VII epistolae canonicae et Act(us) Apostoloru(m) atq(ue) Apocalipsis Ioh(annis) Apost(oli) uolum(ina) V	Volumen	5
48	5	Ite(m) Act(us) Ap(osto)lor(um) et Apocal(ypsis) in uol(umine) I	Volumen	1
49	5	Ite(m) Euangelia II S(e)c(un)d(u)m Ioh(annem) scottice scripta	?	2
	6	DE LIBRIS BEATI GREGORII PAPE		
50	6	In lectiones euangelicas homeliar(um) XL uolum(ina) IIII **unu(m) ex his datu(m) e(st) domino Karolo regi**	Volumen	4
*51	6	Item eiusde(m) Lib(er) pastoral(is) uolumina III/a\ **et in uno eor(um) ep(istu)lę Hieronimi**	Volumen	3
52	6	Moraliarum in Iob libri XXXV in uoluminibus VII	Volumen	7
*53	6	Dialogorum uolumina II **et in uno ex eis uita Pauli et Antonii**	Volumen	2
54	6	Ite(m) uetus I **ad Rorbach**	Volumen?	1

No.	Pg.	Entry	Format	No.
55	6	In Ezechi/h\el(em) prima(m) par̲tem ho̲mil(iae) XII in uol(umine) I **hab̲et** domna Rickart	Volumen	1
56	6	In ultima(m) pa̲rte(m) ei(us) de(m) p(ro)ph(etae) ho̲mil(iae) X in uolum(ine) I	Volumen	1
57	6	Eędem ho̲milię XXII In uolu̲mine uno **Redditę** s(unt) ad **Augia(m) e̲t** patrate s(unt) novę	Volumen	1
*58	6	Item libri XXX V excerpti ab eisde(m) moRaliar(um) libris in codice uno	Codex	1
59	6	Epistolarum Gregorii uolum(en) I **pusillum**	Volumen	1
60	6	~~Regul(a) pastoral(is) Gregorii uolum(ina) III~~	Volumen	3
61	6	VI partes ~~partes~~ in Iob singulae in singulis uolu̲minib(us) optimis	Volumen	6
	6	DE LIBRIS HIERONIMI PR(ES)B(YTER)I		
*62	6	Liber quęstionu(m) hebraicaru(m) in genesim e̲t expositio nescio cui(us) in p(ro)uerbia solomo- nis e̲t Hieroni̲mi de trib(us) inpossibilib(us) e̲t quarto in- cognito atq(ue) instructionu(m) Iunilii libri II **e̲t lib(er) locor(um)** hoc totu(m) in uol(umine) I	Volumen	1
*63	6	Iusti ep(iscop)i in Cantica Canticoru(m) e̲t Hieronimi in Eclesiasten in uol(umine) I	Volumen	1
64	6	Ite(m) Hieronimi in Esaia(m) libri XVIIII in uoluminib(us) trib(us)	Volumen	3

SAMMELHANDSCHRIFTEN AND THE *BREUIARIUM LIBRORUM*

No.	Pg.	Entry	Format	No.
*65	6	Ite(m) eiusde(m) in Hieremia(m) a capite libri V in uol(umine) I et Raba<u>ni</u> usq(ue) in fine(m)	Volumen	1
66	6	In Ezechiel p(ro)pheta(m) libri duodeci(m) in uoluminib(us) duob(us)	Volumen	2
67	6	Eiusde(m) sup(er) totu(m) Dani/h\ele(m) comm(en)tarioru(m) uolum(en) I	Volumen	1
68	6	In Oseę p(ro)pheta(m) libri III in uol(umine) I	Volumen	1
69	6–7	In Abdia(m) liber I, in Zacharia(m) libri III, in Malachia(m) | liber I, in Abbacuc libri II hoc totu(m) in uol(umine) I ┐	Volumen	1
70	7	In Amos libri III in uolum(ine) I	Volumen	1
71	7	Ite(m) in Iohel et Michea(m) libri III in uol(umine) I	Volumen	1
72	7	In Iona(m), Nau(m), Sophonia(m) et Aggeu(m) libri IIII in uol(umine) I **habet Rickart**	Volumen	1
73	7	Eiusde(m) expositio in om(n)es Psalmos uol(umina) magna II **n(on) sunt ei(us) sed invtiles**	Volumen	2
74	7	Ite(m) expositio sup(er) psalmos uol(umina) II **[eras] inutilia**	Volumen	2
*75	7	Eiusde(m) commentariu(m) **in Math(eum) libri IIII et** in Marcu(m) lib(er) excerptus uolu(men) I m(en)daciu(m)	Volumen	1
76	7	~~Ite(m) in Matheu(m) libri IIII in uol(umine) I~~ <u>uetus</u>	Volumen	1

317

No.	Pg.	Entry	Format	No.
*77	7	Ite(m) excerptio in Matheu(m) de comm(en)tariis Hieron(imi) uolumina tria **ad nihil utilia**	Volumen	3
*78	7	Liber locoru(m) et liber hebraicoru(m) nominu(m) et chosmographię liber prim(us) Aethici phlosophi et p(ro)fectio Antonini martiris in uol(umine) I **pittaciolu(m) inutile**	Volumen	1
79	7	Epistolaru(m) Hieronimi ad diuersos uolum(ina) IIII **duo Liutuuardus habet**	Volumen	4
*80	7	÷ ~~Ite(m) excerptio de libris Hieronimi in Esaiam libri XVIIII In uolumine uno~~ :	Volumen	1
*81	7	Liber inlustriu(m) uiroru(m) Hieronimi et Gennadii uolum(en) I	Volumen	1
82	7	In ep(istu)las Pauli id (est) ad Ephesios et ad Titu(m) et Philimonem libri V in uolum(ine) I	Volumen	1
83	7	Ite(m) in epistola(m) ad Galatas thomi tres in uol(umine) I	Volumen	1
84	7	Contra Iouinianu(m) hereticu(m) libri II in uol(umine) I	Volumen	1
*85	7	Ite(m) dialogus Iheron(imi) cum Crettobolo uolum(en) II **et in uno eorum s(unt) Aug(ustini) de vita chri(sti)ana et alt(er)catio singagogę et ecl(esi)ę**	Volumen	1
*86	7	Altercatio Athanasii cu(m) Arrio, Sabellio et Fotino hereticis et Hieron(im)i cu(m) Luciferiano in uol(umine) I	Volumen	1

No.	Pg.	Entry	Format	No.
*87	7	**Re** ÷ Ite(m) nescio cui(us) tractatoris eglogę in Psalteriu(m) in quaternionib(us) : **nunquam vidi**	Quaternio	2
88	7	Chronica Eusebii et Hieronimi uol(umen) I	Volumen	1
89	7	Ep(istu)la Hieronimi ad Eustochiu(m) in q(u)/a\ ternionib(us) **veterrimis et falsatis**	?	2
	8	DE LIBRIS S(AN)C(T)I AUGUSTINI EP(ISCOP)I		
90	8	Augustini sup(er) euang(e)l(iu)m Iohannis uolumina tria	Volumen	3
91	8	De sermone D(omi)ni in monte habito libri duo et quęstionu(m) in euang(e)l(iu)m Mathei et Lucę et Iohan(nis) libri III in uol(umine) I	Volumen	1
92	8	Omelię X in ep(istu)lam Iohan(nis) in uol(umine) I	Volumen	1
93	8	De consensu euangelistaru(m) libri IIII in uol(umine) I	Volumen	1
94	8	De doctrina chr(ist)iana libri IIII in uol(umine) I	Volumen	1
95	8	De s(an)c(t)a trinitate libri XV in uol(umine) I	Volumen	1
96	8	De civitate D(e)i libri XXII in uoluminib(us) duob(us)	Volumen	2
97	8	Decades s(an)c(t)i Augustini sup(er) /**om(n)es**\ Psalmos in uoluminib(us) sex	Volumen	6
98	8	De difinitionib(us) ecclesiasticor(um) dogmatu(m) et ad Petru(m) diaconu(m) de fide uolum(en) I	Volumen	1

No.	Pg.	Entry	Format	No.
99	8	In Apocalipsim omelię XVIII in uol(umine) I	Volumen	1
100	8	Contra Manicheos in Genesim libri II in uol(umine) I	Volumen	1
101	8	Soliloquioru(m) libri II in uol(umine) I	Volumen	1
*102	8	Ambrosii contra hereticos et Augustini contra Arrianos et epistulę duę Ambrosii ad Ualentinu(m) imp(erato)rem in uol(umine) I	Volumen	1
*103	8	Questiones diuersę s(an)c(t)i Augustini ep(iscop)i numero LXXXII	Volumen	2
104		Ite(m) excerpta de decad(ibus) s(an)c(t)i Aug(ustini) in II uol(uminibus)	Volumen	2
*105	8	Ite(m) lib(er) Eugippii uolum(en) I magnu(m)	Volumen	1
106	8	Lib(er) retractationu(m) s(an)c(t)i Augustini ep(iscop)i	?	1
107	8	Augustini in Genesim ad litteram XII LiB(ri)	?	1
108	9	[above first line] Questionu(m) in Heptatheucu(m) libri VII	?	1
109	9	Item lib(er) confessionum s(an)c(t)i Augustini	?	1
110	9	Augustini contra Faustum manicheum	?	1
111	9	Item lib(er) de baptismo s(an)c(t)i Augustini ep(iscop)i	?	1
*112	9	It(em) Aug(ustinus) de bono credulitatis et bono naturę et scolia Cyrilli in uol(umine) I	Volumen	1
	9	DE LIBRIS S(AN)C(T)I AMBROSII EP(ISCOP)I		

No.	Pg.	Entry	Format	No.
113	9	Ambrosii in evangeliu(m) Lucę uol(umen) I	Volumen	1
114	9	Ite(m) tractatus s(an)c(t)i Ambrosii in ep(istu)las Pauli uolumina IIII	Volumen	4
115	9	Exameron s(an)c(t)i Ambrosii uol(umen) I	Volumen	1
*116	9	~~Ambrosii et Augustini contra hereticos libri II in uol(umine) I~~ R	Volumen	
*117	9	Ite(m) Ambrosii de bono mortis et eiusde(m) sermo qui di(citu)r pastoralis et Hieronimi ad Anatholiu(m) in apocalipsin Ioh(annis) uol(umen) I	Volumen	1
118	9	Ite(m) s(ancti) Ambrosii lib(ri) III de officiis In uol(umine) I	Volumen	1
119	9	Amb(rosius) de fide lib(ri) III	Volumen?	1
120	9	Ite(m) de sp(irit)u s(an)c(t)o et incarnat(ione) D(omi)ni in singulis uoluminibus	Volumen	1
	9	DE LIBRIS PROSPERI EP(ISCOP)I		
121	9	Liber P(ro)speri p(ro)missionu(m) et p(ro)rędictoru(m) D(e)i uol(umen) I vet(us) et falsat(us)	Volumen	1
*122	9	Ite(m) de gratia et libero arbitrio ad Rufinu(m) et responsiones p(er) LV capitula et Augustini de octo questionib(us) ad Dulcitiu(m) et ypognosticon eusde(m) de p(rae)distinatione atq(ue) enchiridion hoc totu(m) in codice I	Codex	1
123	9	Ite(m) de actiua et c(on)templatiua uita libri III in cod(ice) I	Codex	1

No.	Pg.	Entry	Format	No.
124	9	Ite(m) eiusde(m) epigra(m)mata in uoluminib(us)/·I·\ duob(us) > vnu(m) fuit scotticu(m) pusillu(m) r.	Volumen	2
	9	DE LIBRIS BEDAE PRE(S)B(YTER)I		
125	9	Expositionis in euangeliu(m) Lucę libri VI in uolum(ine) I	Volumen	1
126	10	Omelię in lectiones euangelicas L in codice I	Codex	1
127	10	In Marcu(m) evangelista(m) libri IIII in uolu(mine) I	Volumen	1
128	10	In Actus Apostoloru(m) liber I et in Apocalipsim Iohan(nis) libri III in cod(ice) I	Codex	1
129	10	In septe(m) epistolas canonicas expos(itio) uolum(en) I	Volumen	1
130	10	De co(m)p/**u**\to et te(m)porib(us) volum(en) I	Volumen	1
*131	10	De exameron lib(er) I, Ite(m) lib(er) Ysidori ad Florentina(m) dat/**u**\s et Hieronimi de mansionib(us) filioru(m) Isr(ae)l in uol(umine) I	Volumen	1
132	10	Ite(m) in p(ro)uerbias Salomonis libri III in uol(umine) I	Volumen	1
133	10	Ite(m) liber allegorice expos(itio) de te(m)plo Salomonis uol(umen) I	Volumen	1
134	10	Ite(m) tractat(us) in hystoria(m) Tobię, Esdrę et Neemię libri IIII in uol(umine) I	Volumen	1
135	10	Eiusde(m) martyrlogium in uol(umine) I **ad sacrariu(m)**	Volumen	1

SAMMELHANDSCHRIFTEN AND THE *BREUIARIUM LIBRORUM*

No.	Pg.	Entry	Format	No.
136	10	In canticu(m) Abbacuc volumen I pusillulu(m) iuxta translation(e) antiqva(m)	Volumen	1
137	10	Gesta angloru(m) volum(en) I	Volumen	1
*138	10	Ite(m) de miracul(is) Gudp(er)ti ep(iscop)i et Althelmi de laude virginu(m) lib(er) I et note iuris, Ite(m)q(ue) uersus alii in uol(umine) I	Volumen	1
*139	10	In Cantica Canticoru(m) libri V et un(us) Gregorii in uolumine vno	Volumen	1
	10	DE LIBRIS YSYDORI EP(ISCOP)I		
*140	10	Aethimologiaru(m) libri XX et ratio horologii et glosa grecoru(m) uerbor(um) in uol(umine) I	Volumen	1
141	10	Ite(m) de libris Ysidori aethimologiaru(m) uolum(ina) II **corrupta**	Volumen	2
142	10	Expositio Ysidori in Eptaticu(m) et Regu(m) in uol(umine) I	Volumen	1
*143	10	Eiusde(m) de D(e)o liber I et de officiis lib(er) I differentiaru(m) Eucherii et de questiunculis s(an)c(t)i August(ini) et defloratib(us) diuersis et alia multa de s(an)c(t)oru(m) patru(m) opusculis exce/r\pta in uol(umine) I **vet(us)tissimo**	Volumen	1
*144	11	Ite(m) liber differentiaru(m) Ysidori et alia nonnulla In uol(umine) I **totu(m) mendacium et inutile**	Volumen	1
145	11	R Ite(m) de D(e)o libri III in uol(umine) I **hoc auditu(m) e(st) n(on) uisu(m)**	Volumen	1

323

No.	Pg.	Entry	Format	No.
146	11	Sententiaru(m) libri III in uol(umine) I **et alt(er) defect(us) et disiect(us)**	Volumen	1
147	11	Rotaru(m) lib(er) et lib(er) glosaru(m) in uol(umine) I et hoc inutile	Volumen	1
148	11	Ite(m) synonima Ysid(ori) de co(m)planctu hominis et ratione ei reddita libell(us) I ~~uolu(men)~~ I **hoc legi n(on) potest**	Volumen	1
*149	11	Ite(m) Isidori uolum(en) I hinc inde collectu(m) cuius p(r) incipiu(m) de scriptiorib(us) est ecclesiasticis **Vuolfkeri e(st)**	Volumen	1
150	11	TRACTAT(US) Origenis in Genesi(m), Exodu(m) et Leuiticu(m) in u(o)l(umine) I	Volumen	1
151	11	Expositio Pelagii sup(er) om(n)es ep(istu)las Pauli in uol(umine) I	Volumen	1
152	11	Item tractatus Origenis sup(er) ep(istu)lam ad Romanos uolum(en) optimu(m)	Volumen	1
	11	DE LIBRIS CASSIODORI		
*153	11	Cassiodori senatoris ecclesiasticę /h\istorię de tribus auctorib(us) sumptę id est Sozomeni, T/h\eodoriti atq(ue) Socratis libri XII in codice I	Codex	1
154	11	Ite(m) eiusde(m) sup(er) omnes Psalmos in uoluminib(us) trib(us) [2 blank lines follow]	Volumen	3
	11	DE LIBRIS EUSEBII		
155	11	Eusebii hystorię ecclesiasticę libri VIIII et Rufini interpretis eiusde(m) libri II in uolum(ine) I	Volumen	1

No.	Pg.	Entry	Format	No.
156	11	Ge<u>s</u>ta pontificu(m) romanoru(m) uol(umen) I	Volumen	1
157	11	Egesippi libri V excerpti de is<u>t</u>oria Ioseppi uol(umen) I	Volumen	1
	12	DE LIBRIS DIVERSORU(M) AUCTORUM		
158	12	Gregorii turonici liber miraculoru(m) I in gloria martyris Iuliani lib(er) I, de uirtutib(us) s(an)c(t)i Martini ep(iscop)i libri IIII, de vita patru(m) liber I, In gl(ori)a confessoru(m) lib(er) I, hoc totu(m) in uolumine uno	Volumen	1
159	12	Chronicę diuersoru(m) temporu(m) libri V et ge<u>s</u>ta Francoru(m) in uolumine I	Volumen	1
160	12	Ite(m) chronica Eusebii <u>et</u> Hieronimi in uol(umine) I int(er) libros Hiero<u>nimi</u> descript(us) e(st)	Volumen	1
161	12	R Expositi s(an)c(t)i /**Colu(m) bani**\ sup(er) om(ne)s Psalmos uol(umen) I **Ruodinu(m) uidi habere qui dix(it) suu(m) e(ss)e**	Volumen	1
162	12	R Ite(m) eiusde(m) in<u>s</u>tructio de fide <u>et</u> alia n(on)nulla in uol(umine) I **hoc non uidi**	Volumen	1
163	12	Libri Effrem diaconi VI de diuersis causis uol(umen) I	Volumen	1
164	12	÷ Iunilii in<u>s</u>tructionu(m) lib(ri) II, Ite(m) de caritate D(e)i <u>et</u> dilectione p(ro)ximi, Ite(m) de m(en) sib(us) <u>et</u> annis In uol(umine) I :	Volumen	1
165	12	Ferrandi diaconi qualis e(ss)e debeat dux religiosus in militarib(us) actib(us) uolum(en) I	Volumen	1

No.	Pg.	Entry	Format	No.
*166	12	Eucherii qu̧estionu(m) in uetus et nouu(m) testam(en)tu(m) et Ysodori lib(er) differentiaru(m) in uol(umine) I **inutile**	Volumen	1
167	12	Iuliani episcopi p(ro) gnosticor(um) futuri seculi libri III in uol(uminibus) II	Volumen	2
*168	12	Collectarii magni IIII homeliaru(m) seu sermonu(m) s(an)c(to)ru(m) patru(m) p(er) singulas festiuitates in anno [1 blank line following]	?	4
*169	12	Collectio Eadb(er)ti de diuersis opusculis s(an)c(t)oru(m) patru(m) in uolum(ine) I	Volumen	1
*170	12	Ite(m) collectio de uerb(is) Augustini, Hieronimi, Gregorii seu ceteroru(m) s(an)c(t)oru(m) patru(m) uol(umen) I **inutile**	Volumen	1
171	12	Expositio Tichonii /**donatisţe**\ in Apocalipsim uol(umen) I uetus	Volumen	1
*172	12	Expos(itio) Primasii in Apolipsim libri V Et glosuļe Gregorii in Apocalipsi(m) spi(ri)talis intellegenti̧e in uolumine I **corrupt(us)**	Volumen	1
	13	DE LIBRIS ALCHUUINI		
173	13	Alchuuini in euangeliu(m) Iohannis libri VI in uol(umine) I	Volumen	1
*174	13	Ite(m) eiusde(m) in Genesim qu̧estiones et metru(m) quorunda(m) sapientiu(m) in uol(umine) I R÷	Volumen	1
175	13	Ite(m) de fide et spe et caritate **non uidi**	?	

No.	Pg.	Entry	Format	No.
176	13	Ite(m) in septe(m) Psalmos penitentię et in centesimu(m) octauum decimu(m) Psalmum et in Psalmos XV graduu(m) expos(itio) et eiusde(m) epistola de confessione peccatoru(m) in uolum(ine) I	Volumen	1
	13	DE REGULIS S(AN)C(T)ORU(M) PATRU(M)		
*177	13	**Regulę s(an)c(t)i Benedicti** cum martyrlogiis in uol(uminibus) III	Volumen	3
*178	13	Ite(m) alię regulę ueteres cu(m) ymnariis et martyrologiis uolumana VIIII r ·I·	Volumen	9
*179	13	Ite(m) regulę s(an)c(t)oru(m) patru(m) i(d) s(unt) Basilii, rugula coenob/i\alis patru(m), rugula Colu(m)bani, regula Augustini, regula Pauli et Stephani, Ite(m) August(ini) de opere manuu(m), prouerbia s(an)c(t)i Euagrii, regula Macharii, Pinufii et Serapionis et alterius Macharii In uolu(mine) I	Volumen	1
*180	13	It(em) idem nouus in quat(er)nionib(us)	Quaternio	2
181	13	Vita canonicoru(m) uol(umen) I	Volumen	1
182	13	Antiphonarii III et ueteres II	?	1
*183	14	Coll(ectio) patrum uolumina IIII	Volumen	1
	14	DE VITA S(AN)C(T)OR(UM) PATRUM		
*184	14	Vitę patru(m) maiores uolum(en) I	Volumen	1
*185	14	Vitę patru(m) minores uolum(ina) II **unu(m) habet Liutuuart**	Volumen	2

No.	Pg.	Entry	Format	No.
*186	14	Vita s(an)c(t)orum patru(m) id (est) Pauli, Antonii et /H\ ilarionis atq(ue) Malchi et ho/me\lię Cęsarii XII et de inuentione basilicę s(an)c(t)i Michaelis et dicta Martini ep(iscop)i ad Polemiu(m) ep(iscopu)m in uol(umine) I	Volumen	1
*187	14	Ite(m) Pauli et Antonii ualde uetus uol(umen) I **inutile**	Volumen	1
188	14	Ite(m) [h eras]omelię Cesarii ep(iscop)i uol(umina) II parua **unu(m) aliqu(i)d alt(er) nihil**	Volumen	2
*189	14	Uita s(an)c(t)i Siluestri et s(an)c(t)i Gregorii, Hilarii ep(iscop)i et eiusde(m) ep(istu)la ad filia(m) sua(m) Abram et Lucii confessoris atq(ue) Lonochilidis ep(iscop)i et Goaris in uol(umine) I	Volumen	1
*190	14	Ite(m) uita s(an)c(t)i Siluestri et passio s(an)c(t)oru(m) Uiti, Modesti, Crescentię atq(ue) Goaris confes(soris) et passio s(an)c(t)i Chr(ist)o[eras]fori marti(ris) et co(m)memoratio /**de miracul(is)**\ s(an)c(t)i Genesii mar(tyris) in uol(umine) I	Volumen	1
*191	14	Uita s(an)c(t)orum patru(m) Colu(m)bani et Galli in uoluminib(us) II **antiq(ue) dictata**	Volumen	2
*192	14	Ite(m) uita s(an)c(t)oru(m) Galli et Martini atq(ue) Otmari abbatis in u(o)l(umine) I	Volumen	1
193	14	Uita s(an)c(t)i Colu(m)bę in codice I	Codex	1

No.	Pg.	Entry	Format	No.
194	14	Uita s(an)c(t)i Marcelli ualde uet(us) in uol(umine) I **gl….. r**	Volumen	1
195	14	Uita Aredii abbatis ualde uet(us) in cod(ice) I **legi non pote(st)**	Codex	1
*196	15	Vita s(an)c(t)o/**ru(m)**\ patru(m) id (est) Hieronimi, Ambrosii, Bonifacii et passiones s(an)c(t)oru(m) Abdon et Senes, Xisti, Laurentii, Ippoliti in codice I	Codex	1
*197	15	Ite(m) vita s(an)c(t)i Galli et Otmari nobiliter scripta	?	1
198	15	Vita s(an)c(t)i Siluestri Recens et bene c(on)scripta	?	1
199	15	Vita s(an)c(t)i Martini optime scripta	?	1
200	15	DE VIRTVTIB(VS) SEV PASSIONIB(VS) S(AN)C(T) OR(UM) APOSTOLOR(UM) VEL MARTIRV(M) uol(umina) magna II	Volumen	2
201	15	Miracula seu passiones Apostoloru(m) in uol(umine) I	Volumen	1
*202	15	Ite(m) passion(es) omniu(m) Apostoloru(m) nec non et quorunda(m) martyru(m) id (est) Geruasii, Protasii, Uictoris, Xisti, Laurentii, Ippoliti, Alexandri, Uiti, Modesti, Eusebii, /**Pelagii mar(tyris)**,\ Benigni pr(es)b(yter)i, Mauricii et socior(um) ei(us) et alia n(on)nvlla in uol(umine) I **antiquissimo**	Volumen	1

No.	Pg.	Entry	Format	No.
*203	15	Ite(m) liber passionu(m) id (est) S(an)c(t)i Sebastiani libri duo, Mammę, Nazari et Celsii, Saprici et Nicefori, Uincentii, Cosme et Damiani, Remedii ep(iscop)i, Genesii, Tharaci, Andronici p(res)b(yter)i, Agnę uirg(inis), Crisanti et Darię, Eugenie, P(ro)ti et Iacinci et alioru(m), Cecilię uirg(inis), Eufemię uirg(inis), Crisogoni mar(tyris), Teudote cu(m) tribus filiis P(er)petuę et Felicitatis, Pelagię, C/h\ristinę uir(ginis), Dorotheę hec om(ni)a in codice I **antiquo**	Codex	1
204	15	Ite(m) liber passionu(m) Crispini et Crispiniani et Quintini in uol(umine) I modico et mutili	Volumen	1
*205	15	Ite(m) libellus passionu(m) Dionisii, Rustici, Eleutherii et homelia de na(ta)l(ibus) eorunde(m) in cod(ice) I modico	Codex	1

No.	Pg.	Entry	Format	No.
*206	15–16	Ite(m) passiones s(an)c(t)aru(m) uirg(inum) et alioru(m) martyrum | Uincentię et Margaritę Domitillę, scripta Nerei et Achillei ad Marcellu(m), Rescriptu(m) Marcelli de obitu Petronellę et passione Feliculę, passio Nerei ET Achillei, Eufrosinę, Theodorę, Sulpicii ac Seruiliani sponsaru(m) ipsarum, de conuersatione Iustinę uirginis, passio Longini militis et Leudegarii ep(iscop)i, uita Apri ep(iscop)i, passio Iusti martiris, Agathę uirg(i)n(is), Lucię uirg(inis), Ite(m) Luceię hęc omnia in uol(umine) I **pittaciolu(m) e(st)**	Volumen	1
207	16	Historia Frecholfi in uol(umine) I grandi	Volumen	1
*208	16	Concilia principalia XII et decretales et ep(istu)lę pontificu(m) romanorum uol(umen) I	Volumen	1
*209	16	Ite(m) exce/r\ptum de canonibus uolumen I **ad scola(m)**	Volumen	1
*210	16	Ite(m) expositio missę romanę, Ite(m) ordo baptizandi Alchuuini ad Uitone(m) com(ite)m capitula XXXV Passio s(an)c(t)i Pantaleonis et hom(e)l(i)ę Augus(tini) et passio s(an)c(t)i Andreę ap(osto)li et de transitus s(an)c(t)i Martini ep(iscop)i Et benedictio fontis hęc om(ni)a in uol(umine) uno paruo ℞ **nihil est**	Volumen	1

No.	Pg.	Entry	Format	No.
*211	16	Liber canonu(m) ecclesia<u>st</u>icoru(m) siue <u>st</u>atutoru(m) sinodi Nicenę <u>et</u> capitula Gregorii pape quę transmisit ad Augu<u>st</u>inu(m) ep(iscopu)m in Saxonia(m) <u>et</u> homilię s(an)c(t)i Augu<u>st</u>ini Et Bedę pr(es)b(yter)i de remediis peccatoru(m) hoc totu(m) in uol(umine) I modico	Volumen	1
*212	16	Ite(m) lib(er) ymnoru(m) <u>et</u> penitential(is) in uolumine uno paruo	Volumen	1
	17	DE LEGIBUS		
*213	17	LEX Theodosiana, Lex Ermogeniana, LEX Papiani, LEX Francoru(m), LEX Alamannoru(m) in uolumine I	Volumen	1
214	17	Capitula Ludouuici imperatoris in cod(ice) I **R**	Codex	1
*215	17	CAPITVLA CAROLI Imperatoris <u>et</u> glose in Genesi(m) et Exodu(m) Et Leuiticu(m) <u>et</u> Numeru(m) <u>et</u> in Deuteronomiu(m) <u>et</u> Iesue <u>et</u> Iudicu(m) <u>et</u> Ruht <u>et</u> Regu(m) mediu(m) libru(m) in uol(umine) I	Volumen	1
*216	17	Ite(m) capitula quę legib(us) addenda sunt in uolu(men) I	Volumen	1
217	17	Ite(m) IN<u>st</u>itutiones imperatoru(m) romanoru(m) uol(umen) I	Volumen	1
*218	17	Capitula Hludouuici imperatoris de regula s(an)c(t)i Benedicti in quaternionibus **R**	Quaternio	2
219	17	Rabani in lam(en)tationes <u>Hi</u>eremię	?	1

No.	Pg.	Entry	Format	No.
220	17	LIBRI GLOSARVM uolumina VIII	Volumen	8
221	17	Ite(m) Uualafridi glosa in Leuiticu(m) et Numeru(m) in uol(umine) I	Volumen	1
*222	17	Ite(m) eiusde(m) **glosa** in septe(m) ep(istu)las canonicas et Hieronimi ad Marcella(m) de conexionib(us) litteraru(m), Ite(m) eiusde(m) ad Marcella(m) de hebraicis nominib(us), Ite(m) eglogae tractatoru(m) in Psalteriu(m) in I uolum(ine) **R**	Volumen	1
223	18	OMELIE Maximi ep(iscop)i per totu(m) annu(m) de diuersis festiuitatib(us) uolum(en) uetus ualde	Volumen	1
224	18	Expositio Ilarii e(piscop)i super Matheu(m) euang(e)l(i)am uolu(men) I	Volumen	1
225	18	Victorini de s(an)c(t)a trinitate uol(umen) I	Volumen	1
226	18	¬ Liber s(an)c(t)i Clementis et eiusde(m) epistola ad Iacobum ap(osto)l(u)m uol(umen) I	Volumen	1
*227	18	S(an)c(t)i Cipriani de XII abusiuis s(ae)c(u)li et de oratione dominica et de patientia et de opere et elemosinis, Dicta Gregorii Nazanzeni ep(iscop)i de Hieremia p(ro)pheta et alia n(on)nulla in uol(umine) I	Volumen	1

No.	Pg.	Entry	Format	No.
228	18	Expositu(m) sup(er) lectiones comitis pleniter p(er) totu(m) anni circulu(m) legendu(m), Ite(m) in lectiones homelię p(er) singulas festiuitates a na(ta)le D(omi)ni usq(ue) in ascensione(m) D(omi)ni uol(umen) I	Volumen	1
229	18	Ite(m) ab ascensione D(omi)ni usq(ue) in uigilia(m) nat(a)lis D(omi)ni uol(umen) I	Volumen	1
230	18	Sermones Iohannis Chrisostomi de diuersis reb(us) in I uol(umine)	Volumen	1
231	18	Duo uolumnia noua sermonu(m) et omeliaru(m) ab aduentu D(omi)ni usq(ue) in Pascha	Volumen	2
232	18	Tertiu(m) a Pascha usq(ue) in oct(aua) Pentecost(es)	Volumen?	1
233	18	Quart(us) usq(ue) de aduentu D(omi)ni	Volumen?	1
234	18	ORDO Roman(us) in duob(us) quaternionib(us)	Quaternio	2
235	18	Ite(m) aliud in quat(er)nionib(us)	Quaternio	2
*236	18	LIBER astrologię et co(m)pot(us) Rabani et alius co(m)pot(us) in uolumine I	Volumen	1
*237	18	ORTHOgraphia Capri, Acroetii et Bedę in uol(umine) I	Volumen	1
238	18	Libri pastoris uol(umen) I	Volumen	1
239	18	Glosa in Ioh(annem) euangelista(m)	?	1
*240	18	De remediis peccatoru(m) et alia collecticia in uol(umine) I	Volumen	1
241	18	Libri ethimologiaru(m) Isidori in sceda I tam(en) boni	Sceda	1

No.	Pg.	Entry	Format	No.
*242	18	Vita s(an)c(t)i Siluestri et sermones in uol(umine) ualde uetusto	Volumen	1
243	19	De custodia monachoru(m) et canonicoru(m) in scedula I uet(ere)	Scedula	1
244	19	De natiuitate s(an)c(t)ę Marię in scedula	Scedula	1
245	19	Passio martyru(m) Sergii et Bachi in scedula I	Scedula	1
246	19	Passio Pelagii in scedula parua	Scedula	1
*247	19	Passio Desiderii et alioru(m) mart(yrum) in uol(umine) I	Volumen	1
*248	19	Vitę patru(m) in uolumine uetustissimo	Volumen	1
*249	19	Duo libelluli epistolaru(m) Albini et alius [eras] fide et uirtutib(us)	Libellulus	3
*250	19	Psalteria XVI plena et V[?] excerpta	?	1
251	19	Ite(m) Bedę de arte metrica	?	1
*252	19	Passio Cyriaci et alioru(m) in libellulo I	Libellulus	1
253	19	Expos(itio) in passione(m) D(omi)ni sec(un)d(um) Ioh(annem) in scedula I	Scedula	1
*254	19	Sermones in uolumine scottico ueteri	Volumen	1
	19	DE METRIS		
*255	19	Metrum Iuuenti pr(es)b(yter)i et Sedulii ep(iscop)i uolumina IIII R ·I·	Volumen	4
256	19	Metrum Aurelii Prudentii libri VII in uol(umine) I	Volumen	1

No.	Pg.	Entry	Format	No.
257	19	Metrum Aratoris in Act(us) Apostolor(um) uolumina II	Volumen	2
258	19	Metrum Alcimi Auiti ep(iscop)i libri VII in uol(umine) I [marg: DELI]	Volumen	1
259	19	Epigra(m)mata Prosperi uol(umina) III in quaternionib(us) R ·I·	Quaternio	3
260	19	Metru(m) de uita s(an)c(t)i Galli in quaternionib(us) uol(umen) I [blank line follows]	Volumen	1
*261	19	Althelmi de metris et enigmatib(us) ac pedu(m) regulis uol(umen) I	Volumen	1
262	19	Ite(m) Althelmi de laude uirginu(m) uol(umen) I	Volumen	1
*263	19	Ite(m) Althelmi de enigmatib(us) et Bedę de metrica arte et metrum Simphosii et alia n(on) nulla s(an)c(t)oru(m) opuscula in uol(umine) I paruo	Volumen	1
*264	19	Sermo de epiphania et alius Cypriani et alia quę(dam) in libellulo ualde uetusto	Libellulus	1
265	19	Ep(istul)a s(an)c(t)i Aug(ustini) et eiusdem sermo de die iudicii In uol(umine) I paruo	Volumen	1
266	20	In uolumine I Iosepi hystoriaru(m) antiquitatis iudaicę libri XII	Volumen	1
267	20	In alio uolumine eiusde(m) hystoriographi de bello iudaico libri VII	Volumen	1
268	20	Ite(m) in tertio lib(ri) IIII	Volumen	1
269	20	Glosa in euangelium et alia diuersa in uolumine I	Volumen	1

No.	Pg.	Entry	Format	No.
270	20	Excerpta in Psalmos glosa in ep(istu)las Pauli et in Iob et Regu(m) in codice I	Codex	1
271	20	÷ Liber p(ro)hemioru(m) Isidori et ei(us)dem de uita (ue) l obitu s(an)c(t)oru(m) patru(m) utriusq(ue) testam(en)ti, de ratione dieru(m) ac m(en)siu(m), de natura reru(m), de officiis ecclesiasticis, de dieb(us) festis et ieiuniis, et ordinib(us) ecclesiasticis in uol(umine) I :	Volumen	1
	20	DE LIBRIS GRA(M)MATICĘ ARTIS		
272	20	LIBRI PRISCIANI DE OCTO PARTIB(US) XVI, Ite(m) eiusdem de constructione partiu(m) orationu(m) libri II, Ite(m) ad Simachu(m) de figuris numeroru(m) liber I, hęc om(ni)a in uol(umine) I	Volumen	1
*273	20	Ite(m) partes Donati minores atq(ue) maiores et Onorati de finalib(us) litteris Et declinationes Et comm(en)tariu(m) Sergii in partes Donati Et Ysidori liber Et liber Capri de ortographia Et Bedę de metrica arte hęc om(ni)a in uol(umine) I R	Volumen	1
*274	20	Ite(m) partes Donati minores atq(ue) maiores et Bedę de metrica arte et Alc/h\uuini de octo partib(us), Ite(m) Ysidori de octo partib(us), Ite(m) metru(m) Iuuenci et Sedulii, metru(m) Catonis libri IIII et alia nonnulla in uol(umine) I	Volumen	1

No.	Pg.	Entry	Format	No.
*275	20	Partes Asporii, Ite(m) partes Donati gra(m)matici, Ite(m) ars Honorati gra(m)matici, Diomedis de metro, Ite(m) Bedę pr(es)b(yter) i de metrica arte, Ite(m) partes Donati minores maioresq(ue), Ite(m) tractat(us) Pompegii in Donatu(m) et alia multa hęc om(ni)a in uol(umine) I	Volumen	1
*276	21	Ite(m) Priscian(us) minor et Donati pars maior et V declina(tiones) coniugation(es) et Bedę de metrica arte Isidori ars et cetera in uol(umine) I	Volumen	1
277	21	Alchuuini de octo partibus orationum uolumina II R ·I·	Volumen	2
278	21	Ite(m) partes Donati minores maioresq(ue) et declination(es) nominu(m) in uol(umine) I	Volumen	1
*279	21	Ite(m) partes Donati minores maioresq(ue) et Alchuuini in octo partes Donati in uol(umine) I	Volumen	1
280	21	Commemoratio abbatu(m) qui in Augia fuer(unt) in I rodulo	Rotulus	1
*281	21	Partes Donati maiores et minores, grammatica Albini, Bede de arte metrica et tropis atq(ue) scematib(us) in codice uno	Codex	1
*282	21	Grammatica Adaloldi in qua partes Donati et expositio Erchanberti sup(er) ipsas	?	1
*283	21	Ymnoru(m) uolum(en) I	Volumen	1
*284	21	Ite(m) in quaternionib(us) alius ymnar(um)	Quaternio	2

No.	Pg.	Entry	Format	No.
*285	21	Ite(m) diuersoru(m) ymnoru(m) uol(umen) uetus I	Volumen	1
286	21	Ite(m) grammatica sine auctore	Volumen?	1
*287	21	Versus undecumq(ue) collecti et glosę in om(ne)s libros diuinę auctoritatis in scedula una	Scedula	1
288	21	Solini polihistor(is)	?	1
289	21	Mappa mundi I	Mappa	1
290	21	Descriptio octo principalium uitioru(m)	?	1
291	21	Volumen I Alexandri Macedonis	Volumen	1
292	21	libri medicinal(is) artis uolumina II et I paruus r ·I·	Volumen	2
293	21	Ite(m) libri III medicinalis artis in quaternionibus	Quaternio	2
294	21	Expositio **Seruii** in Uirgiliu(m) uolumen I **perditu(m) es(t) R**	Volumen	1
*295	21	Excerptu(m) Iustini de Pompeio hystoriographo in uol(umine) I libri XLIIII	Volumen	1

Bibliography

Manuscripts

Florence, Biblioteca Medicea Laurenziana, Amiatino
I. http://mss.bmlonline.it/s.aspx?Id=AWOS3h2-I1A4r7GxMdaR&c=Biblia%20Sacra#/book.

St. Gall, Stiftsbibliothek, Cod. Sang. 236. https://www.e-codices.unifr.ch/en/list/one/csg/0236.

St. Gall, Stiftsbibliothek, Cod. Sang. 237. https://www.e-codices.unifr.ch/en/list/one/csg/0237.

St. Gall, Stiftsbibliothek, Cod. Sang. 243. https://www.e-codices.unifr.ch/en/list/one/csg/0243.

St. Gall, Stiftsbibliothek, Cod. Sang. 267. https://www.e-codices.unifr.ch/en/list/one/csg/0267.

St. Gall, Stiftsbibliothek, Cod. Sang. 728. https://www.e-codices.unifr.ch/en/list/one/csg/0728.

Primary

Augustine. *Epistulae nuper in lucem prolatae.* Corpus Scriptorum Ecclesiasticorum Latinorum 88. Edited by Johannes Divjak. Vienna: Hoelder-Pichler-Tempsky, 1981.

Cassiodorus. *Institutiones.* Edited by Roger A.B. Mynors. Oxford: Clarendon Press, 1961.

Cicero. *Tusculanae Disputationes. M. Tulli Ciceronis Scripta Quae Manserunt Omnia.* Part 44. Edited by Max Pohlenz. Berlin: De Gruyter, 1918.

Mittelalterliche Bibliothekskataloge Deutschlands und der Schweiz, Volume 1: *Die Bistümer Konstanz und Chur.* Edited by Paul Lehmann. Munich: Beck, 1918.

Monumenta Germaniae Historica, Scriptores 2. Edited by Georg Heinrik Pertz. Hanover: Hahn, 1829.

Ratpert. *St. Galler Klostergeschichten (Casus sancti Galli).* Edited and translated by Hannes Steiner. Monumenta Germaniae Historica, Scriptores Rerum Germanicarum in Usum Scholarum Separatim Editi 85. Hanover: Hahn, 2002.

Secondary

Arns, Paulo Evaristo. *La technique du livre d'après Saint Jérôme.* Paris: de Boccard, 1953.

Dora, Cornel, and Franziska Schnoor, eds. *The Cradle of European Culture: Early Medieval Irish Book Art.* Translated by Katherine Vanovitch. St. Gall: Klosterhof, 2018.

Duft, Johannes. "Einleitung I. Die Handschriften-Katalogisierung in der Stiftsbibliothek St. Gallen vom 9. bis zum 19. Jahrhundert." In *Die Handschriften der Stiftsbibliothek St. Gallen. Beschreibendes Verzeichnis. Codices 1726–1984 (14.-19. Jahrhundert),* edited by Beat Matthias von Scarpatetti, 9–99. St Gall: Stiftsbibliothek, 1983.

Englisch, Brigitte. *Ordo orbis terrae. Die Weltsicht in den Mappae mundi des frühen und hohen Mittelalters.* Berlin: De Gruyter, 2002. DOI: 10.1524/9783050048260.

Flechner, Roy. *Making Laws for a Christian Society: The "Hibernensis" and the Beginnings of Church Law in Ireland and Britain.* London: Routledge, 2021. DOI: 10.4324/9781351267243.

Gumbert, Johan Peter. "The Tacketed Quire: An Exercise in Comparative Codicology." *Scriptorium* 65 (2011): 299–320.

Kloeters, Gert. "Buch und Schrift bei Hieronymus." PhD Dissertation. University of Münster, 1957.

Mackie, Gillian. "New Light on the So-Called Saint Lawrence Panel at the Mausoleum of Galla Placidia, Ravenna." *Gesta* 29, no. 1 (1990): 54–60. DOI: 10.2307/767100.

Mulsow, Martin. *Prekäres Wissen: Eine andere Ideengeschichte der Frühen Neuzeit.* Berlin: Suhrkamp 2012.

Meeder, Sven. *The Irish Scholarly Presence at St. Gall: Networks of Knowledge in the Early Middle Ages.* Studies in Early Medieval History. London: Bloomsbury Academic, 2018. DOI: 10.5040/9781350038905.

Rankin, Susan. "Ego itaque Notker scripsi." *Revue Bénédictine* 101, nos. 3–4 (1991): 268–98. DOI: 10.1484/J.RB.4.01265.

Skeat, Theodore C. "The Origin of the Christian Codex." *Zeitschrift für Papyrologie und Epigraphik* 102 (1994): 263–68. https://www.jstor.org/stable/20189148.

Stansbury, Mark. "Early-Medieval Biblical Commentaries, Their Writers and Readers." *Frühmittelalterliche Studien* 33, no. 1 (1999): 49–82. DOI: 10.1515/9783110242317.49.

8

Sharing Alphabets: Early Medieval Grammatical Miscellanies and Their Networks

Elizabeth P. Archibald

Among the books that appear in the earliest library catalogues of medieval Europe, those designated by their catalogers as falling under the heading of *grammatica* have a distinctive format. In these catalogues, the *grammatica* section is characterized by the extreme length of the entries. Even conscientious catalogers appear to have been challenged by the miscellaneous nature of these codices: long lists of didactic works by many different authors often end with phrases like "and many other things [...] all these things in one volume."[1] In other words, the subject of

---

1 Characteristic is this entry from the ninth-century St. Gall library catalogue in St. Gall, Stiftsbibliothek, Cod. Sang. 728, p. 20: "Partes Asporii; item partes Donati grammatici; item ars Honorati grammatici; Diomedis de metro; item Bedae presbyteri de metrica arte; item partes Donati minores maioresque; item tractatus Pompegii in Donatum; et alia multa, haec omnia in uol. 1." ("The parts [of speech] of Asporius; also the parts of Donatus the grammarian; also the *ars* of Honoratus the grammarian; the work of Diomedes on meter; also the work of the priest Bede, *De metrica*

grammatica is closely linked with the miscellaneous codex in early catalogues.

This miscellaneous quality is prominent among the early medieval manuscripts containing grammatical and other elementary didactic material that survive today. For instance, among the codices in Bernhard Bischoff's list of twenty-nine grammatical manuscripts associated with Charlemagne (c. 742–814) and Louis the Pious (778–840), all but one are miscellanies, containing between a handful and dozens of short texts.[2] The chrestomathic profile of *grammatica* manuscripts is not inevitable — many works of *grammatica*, both late antique and early medieval, could fill a sizeable codex. In fact, they increasingly did, as substantial works like Priscian's (c. sixth century) monumental *Institutiones grammaticae* gained in prominence over the course of the ninth century. But the characteristic format of early medieval *grammatica* codices is the miscellany, and examination of these manuscripts suggests that their miscellaneous orientation was a deliberate result of instructors' and compilers' approach to *grammatica*, the most elementary subject of literate study.[3] As James E.G. Zetzel observes, the compilation of these manuscripts was motivated by utility rather than authority: "Grammatical manuscripts are frequently eclectic anthologies in which the contents matter more than the source."[4]

---

arte; also the *Ars minor* and *Ars maior* of Donatus; also the commentary of Pompeius on Donatus; and many other things, all these in one volume.") Printed in Paul Lehmann, *Mittelalterliche Bibliothekskataloge Deutschlands und der Schweiz*, vol. 1: *Die Bistümer Konstanz und Chur* (Munich: Beck, 1918), 66–82. See also the article by Mark Stansbury in this volume.

2 Bernhard Bischoff, "Libraries and Schools in the Carolingian Revival of Learning," in *Manuscripts and Libraries in the Age of Charlemagne*, trans. Michael Gorman (Cambridge: Cambridge University Press, 1994), 93–113.

3 On the wide-ranging subject of *grammatica* in the earlier Middle Ages and its material forms, see Martin Irvine, *The Making of Textual Culture: "Grammatica" and Literary Theory, 350–1100* (Cambridge: Cambridge University Press, 1994).

4 James E.G. Zetzel, *Critics, Compilers, and Commentators: An Introduction to Roman Philology, 200 BCE–800 CE* (Oxford: Oxford University Press, 2018), 162.

What priorities underlie the content selection that results in these eclectic anthologies? If the goal of those who compiled these manuscripts was not to preserve the integrity of authoritative texts but to create useful didactic compendia, the results are an important source of information about the purpose and techniques of elementary instruction. They are challenging sources: miscellanies are difficult to reckon with, codicologically and bibliographically, and many have not yet been catalogued sufficiently.[5] But the nature of these manuscripts provides a valuable opportunity to examine the contours of the curriculum and the logic of didactic compilation in a way that manuscripts of a simpler structure do not.

Examination of these manuscripts and the materials they include reveals that they are by no means a uniform group, but they are closely connected nevertheless. They draw from a

---

5   Louis Holtz, *Donat et la tradition de l'enseignement grammatical: Étude sur l'Ars Donati et sa diffusion (IVe-IXe siècle) et édition critique* (Paris: CNRS, 1981) provides a thorough accounting of the contents of manuscripts in which the works of Donatus appear. The Università di Cassino has become a center for the study and cataloging of early medieval grammatical manuscripts; see Paola Degni and Alessandra Peri, "Per un catalogo dei manoscritti grammaticali altomedievali," in *Manuscripts and Tradition of Grammatical Texts from Antiquity to the Renaissance. Proceedings of a Conference held at Erice, 16-23 October 1997*, ed. Mario De Nonno, Paolo De Paolis, and Louis Holtz (Cassino: Edizioni dell'Università, 2000), 719-45; Paolo De Paolis, "I codici miscellanei grammaticali altomedievali. Caratteristiche, funzione, destinazione," in *Il codice miscellaneo. Tipologie e funzioni. Atti del Convegno internazionale, Cassino, 14-17 maggio 2003*, ed. Edoardo Crisci and Oronzo Pecere (Cassino: Edizioni dell'Università, 2004), 183-211; Paolo De Paolis, "Per un catalogo delle opere e dei manoscritti grammaticali tardoantichi e altomedievali," in *Priscien. Transmission et refondation de la grammaire. De l'Antiquité aux modernes. États des recherches à la suite du colloque international de Lyon, 10-14 octobre 2006*, ed. Marc Baratin, Bernard Colombat, and Louis Holtz (Turnhout: Brepols, 2009), 653-67; and Paolo De Paolis, "Il progetto di catalogazione dei codici grammaticali latini e la tradizione delle opere ortografiche latine," in *Libri e testi: Lavori in corso a Cassino. Atti del Seminario internazionale Cassino, 30-31 gennaio 2012*, ed. Roberta Casavecchia, Paolo De Paolis, Marilena Maniaci, and Giulia Orofino (Cassino: Edizioni dell'Università, 2013), 13-51. The Università di Cassino catalogue is available at http://codicigrammaticali.unicas.it/.

common menu of materials, but the results vary widely. For instance, returning to Bischoff's list of grammatical manuscripts associated with Charlemagne and Louis the Pious, twenty-nine in all, if we list all of the texts represented in this group of manuscripts, we find that sixty percent of the texts are unique to a single manuscript — a relatively centrifugal set of materials.[6] On the other hand, some of the other texts are rather common, shared by nearly half of the group. The *grammatica* curriculum in the early part of the ninth century, judging from the texts that appear most often in miscellanies, was anchored by a small number of significant texts: the *Ars minor* and *Ars maior* of Aelius Donatus (c. mid-fourth century), Book I of Isidore of Seville's (c. 560–636) *Etymologies,* and several well-known commentaries on Donatus, including Pompeius and Servius (c. late fourth and fifth centuries). However, the fixity of these common texts is elusive. All of them appear in many different forms, manipulated and remixed, another characteristic that confounds efforts to study, let alone edit, them.

Identifying these "anchor texts" helps us to understand the didactic goals of the instructional compilations. The less canonical texts, from a pedagogical perspective, constitute the apparatus applied to help learners with the common elements of the curriculum. Not a gloss or a commentary, exactly, but an infinitely variable conglomeration of short, mutable, usually unattributed texts that assist in the digestion of the main dish. These materials, lacking in authority, stature, and textual stability, are often overlooked in assessments of manuscript culture and educational history. But the same qualities that cause them to be overlooked can prove helpful when it comes to reconstructing practices of knowledge selection and the pedagogical goals that informed them. To examine the ways that didactic materials circulated and transformed, and what these transformations can show about the goals and strategies that informed didactic compilations in early medieval educational contexts, this study will trace the circulation of a single "less canonical" text, a short

---

6 Bischoff, "Libraries and Schools," 99–113.

exposition of the letters of the alphabet, to see how its many travels illuminate a larger intellectual landscape.

A Text and its Contexts

The text in question, like many others that appear in didactic compilations, is a short, anonymous introduction to the letters of the alphabet; it is preserved in five manuscripts dating from around the beginning of the ninth century. In two of the manuscripts the work appears under the promising but rather vague heading "A certain wise person expounded on the Latin letters."[7] As is common for early medieval instructional texts, the versions of this text appear with significant variations in the manuscripts. These variations impede efforts to edit the text or even to conclude definitively that the manuscripts present the "same" text, but precisely because of their variation they offer an opportunity to trace the way that instructional materials were compiled, manipulated, and used in the early Middle Ages. In its basic outline, this text proceeds letter by letter through the alphabet, bringing together apparently disparate crumbs of information from linguistics, Christian doctrine, and hermeneutics. About the letter A, the text offers the following: it is called *A* in Latin, *alpha* in Greek, and *aleph* in Hebrew; it is the first letter because Adam was the first man and the words *anima* and *angelus* also begin with A; it represents the adverb *quingenties* (500 times); and it is formed from three graphical strokes, representing both its three names in the *tres linguae sacrae* and the three persons of the Trinity, with the three strokes comprising one letter.[8] This short but encompassing exposition follows a traditional scheme in late-antique grammatical writing that assesses the letters according to three qualities: *nomen* (the letter's name), *potestas* (its phonic value), and *figura* (its written form).

---

[7] "De litteris Latinis quidam sapiens interpretatus est." The title appears in the manuscripts Bern, Burgerbibliothek, MS 417 (fol. 94r), and Paris, Bibliothèque nationale de France, MS lat. 13025 (fol. 24r).

[8] See the version published by Hermann Hagen in *Anecdota Helvetica quae ad grammaticam latinam spectant* (Leipzig: Teubner, 1870), 302–5.

Elements of its approach derive very loosely from Martianus Capella (earlier fifth century), who presents the letters in Book 3 of *De nuptiis Philologiae et Mercurii,* not according to alphabetical order but according to functional linguistic categories.[9]

The text is brief and appears in the company of numerous other texts in its manuscript witnesses. Several of the manuscripts include it among a common group of other short, anonymous texts on the letters, as found in Paris, Bibliothèque nationale de France, MS lat. 13025, a *grammatica* miscellany originating at Corbie in the early ninth century that has been the subject of various investigations including a recent in-depth study by Paolo De Paolis.[10] Among the material in this codex (and in Paris, Bibliothèque nationale de France, MS lat. 14087, another component of the original miscellany) De Paolis identified thirty-three main textual components, along with fourteen additional textual sub-sections.[11] Among these are the prominent didactic texts of *grammatica* around the turn of the ninth century, including material from Donatus and Isidore. It is clear that the manuscript was the result of an attempt to fortify these core components with additional useful materials. Our text begins a group of anonymous material inserted between two chapters of Donatus's *Ars maior (De syllabis* and *De pedibus),* divided into four sub-sections beginning with our text as follows:

a) fols. 24v–25v: "A certain wise person expounded on the Latin letters"
b) fols. 25v–26r: "It is asked who first discovered the letters"
c) fol. 26r–v: "Likewise about the Hebrew letters"

---

9   *De nuptiis* 3.234–60. Martianus's many references to classical names are not retained in this text, with the exception of "Tanaquil."
10 See Paolo De Paolis, "Un manuale scolastico da Corbie," in *Vestigia notitiai: Scritti in memoria di Michelangelo Giusta,* ed. Edoardo Bona, Carlos Lévy, and Giuseppina Magnaldi (Alessandria: Edizioni dell'Orso, 2012), 81–106.
11 De Paolis, "Un manuale scolastico," 92–94.

d) fol. 26v: "Here begins the Greek alphabet with numbers"[12] Together, these four texts provide an introduction and brief reference manual on the Latin, Greek, and Hebrew letters, their visual forms and significance, their sound values, their reported history, and their numerical equivalents—all of which is common, in one form or another, in *grammatica* manuscripts of the period.

These four texts appear in close proximity in at least two other early ninth-century miscellanies. In Bern, Burgerbibliothek, MS 417, a manuscript from the region of Tours that consists of primarily computistical material, these texts on the letters form a small *grammatica* component under the heading "Here begins an introduction to the letters, what they are called and what sound each one has."[13] The texts appear in the order: b. "It is asked who first discovered the letters" (fols. 94r–95r), c. "On the main parts of the Hebrew letters" (fols. 95r–v, corresponding with "Likewise about the Hebrew letters" in Paris, BnF, MS lat. 13025), d. "Here begins the Greek alphabet" (fols. 95v), then our text, a. "A certain wise person expounded on the Latin letters" (fols. 95v–98v).[14] This group is followed by an excerpt from Donatus and concludes with a text beginning "All the letters derive

---

12 "De litteris latinis quidam sapiens interpretatus est"; "Quaeritur enim quis primus litteras [...] adinvenit"; "Item de hebreis litteris"; "Incipit abcdis grece cum numero." On this section of the manuscript, see Luigi Munzi, *Littera legitera: Testi grammaticali latini dell'Alto Medioevo*, Annali dell'Università di Napoli l'Orientale 11 (Naples: Istituto universitario orientale, 2007), 39–41; De Paolis, "Un manuale scolastico," 97–98; and Zetzel, *Critics, Compilers, and Commentators*, 360–61.

13 "Incipit expositio de litteris quomodo nominantur vel quale sonum habeant inter se." This is the manuscript used by Hagen in *Anecdota Helvetica*. See Bernhard Bischoff, *Katalog der festländischen Handschriften des neunten Jahrhunderts (mit Ausnahme der wisigotischen)*, vol. 1: *Aachen-Lambach* (Wiesbaden: Harrassowitz, 1998), no. 592, p. 127 ("Umkreis von Tours"), and Marco Mostert, *The Library of Fleury: A Provisional List of Manuscripts* (Hilversum: Verloren, 1989), no. 185, 76.

14 "Quaeritur enim quis primus"; "Hebraicarum litterarum primae" and "Item de hebreis litteris"; "Incipit abcdis grece"; "De litteris latinis quidam sapiens interpretatus est."

their forms from their relationship with sounds" drawn from Martianus Capella (fols. 98v–99r).[15]

Paris, Bibliothèque nationale de France, MS lat. 1750, a collection of material assembled from disparate sources, includes twelve folios with an early ninth-century Fleury origin.[16] In this section is a cluster of material on the letters, under the heading "Here begins an excerpt on the letters" (fol. 140r) which begins with an introduction drawn from the *De littera* section of Donatus's *Ars maior,* then continues with the text we are tracing (without a title, fols. 140r–41r), followed by the same Martianus-based excerpt as in Bern, Bb, MS 417 (fol. 141r–v), a short "On orthography" (fols. 141v–42r), and then the same group of three sequential texts found in the other two manuscripts.[17] It is clear that, although each of these manuscripts is a miscellany, containing other instructional texts relating mostly to the letters and *grammatica,* these four texts form a coherent little lesson on the letters of the alphabet in their various aspects (names, forms, phonic values, and the *tres linguae sacrae*). In Paris, BnF, MS lat. 13025, our text directly precedes the triad of shorter texts, while in the Bern manuscript it follows the group, and in turn is followed by the text on the letters drawn from Martianus Capella, from whom it also borrows. In Paris, BnF, MS lat. 1750, it is followed by the same Martianus-based text, in proximity with the same triad I have been discussing but not directly adjacent. In these manuscripts, we see the way that a short, useful introduction, perhaps originating as a standalone *schedula,* could find

---

15 "Omnes vero litterae ad similitudinem vocis characteras acceperunt." Luigi Munzi outlines these contents in *Littera legitera,* 38.

16 See Philippe Lauer, *Catalogue general des manuscrits latins,* II (Paris: Bibliothèque nationale, 1940), 154–55; Munzi, *Littera legitera,* 39–40; and Bischoff, *Katalog der festländischen Handschriften des neunten Jahrhunderts,* vol. 2: Laon-Paderborn, ed. Birgit Ebersperger (Wiesbaden: Harrassowitz, 2004), 54.

17 "Incipit de litteris excerptum"; "De orthographia." The three texts appear as follows: "Queritur enim quis primus litteram [...] adinvenit" (fol. 142r–v), "Item de Ebreis litteris" (fols. 142v–43r), and "Incipit abcdis grece cum numero" (fol. 143r). Lists of *voces animantium* (Latin verbs denoting the sounds of various animals) and abbreviations round out the section.

a home amidst material designed to contextualize and supplement the standard and more authoritative curriculum (in this case, the *Ars maior* of Donatus).

Extended Contexts

These compilations, in their variety, hint at the freedom scribes and compilers exercised in assembling materials for particular and immediate didactic purposes. However, the text also appears in even more widely varying forms and manuscript contexts reflective of other didactic goals and compilation strategies.[18] An abridged version of the text appears in Leiden, Universiteitsbibliotheek, MS BPL 135, where it is appended to the end of the odd, perhaps seventh-century, grammar known as the *Ars Sergi{li}i*, with which it shares an interest in letter forms and their significance.[19] At the other extreme, there also exists an expanded version, which Luigi Munzi edited on the basis of the late eighth or early ninth-century Reichenau manuscript Karlsruhe, Badische Landesbibliothek, MS Aug. 112.[20] As Munzi notes, the version in Leiden, Ub, MS BPL 135 seems to offer "a sort of reduced and 'skeletal' version of the text printed by Hagen," whereas the version in Karlsruhe, BLb, MS Aug. 112, by contrast, offers an amplified version, enriched not by grammatical material but by

---

18 The known versions of the text are discussed in Zetzel, *Critics, Compilers, and Commentators*, 360.

19 The second codicological section of the manuscript, fols. 66r–86v, is the one in question (the text appears at fols. 73r–74v); see Bischoff, *Katalog*, vol. 2, no. 2154, 44. The version of the text in this manuscript was edited by Luigi Munzi, *Littera legitera*, 95. The text has also been edited by Richard M.A. Marshall as part 4 of the *Ars Sergi{li}i* in whose proximity it appears in the manuscript, but without certainty regarding its identity as an integral part of that text and its tradition. Richard M.A. Marshall, "Studies on the *Ars Grammatici Sergi{li}i* with an Edition," *Journal of Medieval Latin* 20 (2010): 167–231.

20 The text appears on fols. 3v–12v; some of the folios in question are a palimpsest of a Gallican psalter. Bischoff, *Katalog* 1, no. 1642, p. 344; Alfred Holder, *Die Handschriften der Badischen Landesbibliothek in Karlsruhe. Die Reichenauer Handschriften*, vol. 1 (Wiesbaden: Harrassowitz, 1970), 289–95.

"materials tending to monastic devotion, particularly aphorisms and *sententiae* of biblical and patristic origin."[21]

One particular feature of texts about the letters of the alphabet is that they provide a structure that invites manipulation. A scribe might omit some material about any or each letter without disrupting the integrity of the text, and, on the other hand, the alphabetical structure also presented an organizational filing system that could expand to accommodate various other kinds of material. In the Karlsruhe manuscript, the already wide-ranging treatments of each letter are fortified with edifying material organized according to this alphabetical scheme. Thus, the *grammatica*-based doctrine also served as a way to organize *sententiae* and other useful and edifying extracts from other sources. It has not been previously noted that the text, with similar insertions, also appears in St. Gall, Stiftsbibliothek, Cod. Sang. 230, a fascinating and monumental miscellany but not a *grammatica* compilation or instructional manuscript strictly speaking, likely produced in the region of St. Gall in the later part of the eighth century.[22] In this manuscript the text is introduced as follows: "In the name of the Holy Trinity, here begins the volume on the 17 [sic] letters of the alphabet."[23] This is the fullest version of the text — including a good deal more interpolated material than the version in the Karlsruhe manuscript — but it is also incomplete, breaking off after the letter O. From the existence of this text it can be surmised that the version in the Karlsruhe

---

21 "una sorta di versione ridotta e 'scheletrica' del testo stampato da Hagen" and "materiali attinenti la devozione monastica, in particolare aforismi e *sententiae* di origine biblica e patristica." Munzi, *Littera legitera*, 95–96.

22 Bernhard Bischoff, *Katalog der festländischen Handschriften des neunten Jahrhunderts (mit Ausnahme der wisigotischen)*, vol. 3: *Padua-Zwickau*, ed. Birgit Ebersperger (Wiesbaden, 2014), 316; Gustav Scherrer, *Verzeichniss der Handschriften der Stiftsbibliothek von St. Gallen* (Halle: Verlag der Buchhandlung des Waisenhauses, 1875), 83–84; and see Anna Dorofeeva, "Miscellanies, Christian Reform and Early Medieval Encyclopaedism: A Reconsideration of the Pre-Bestiary Latin Physiologus Manuscripts," *Historical Research* 90, no. 250 (2017): 665–82.

23 "In nomine sanctae trinitatis incipit volumen de litteris abcnariis xvii." The text appears on pp. 549–63.

manuscript is not actually an original elaboration of the "base" text that appears among the grammatical material in Paris, BnF, MS lat. 13025 and elsewhere, but an abridgment of a still longer version that is partially preserved in St. Gall, Stb, Cod. Sang. 230. The version in the Karlsruhe manuscript provides a clue that it is an abridgment by ending several of its sections with the phrase "and the rest"; and comparison with St. Gall, Stb, Cod. Sang. 230 shows that the expanded text continues in each case.[24]

Examination of this ampler version of the text offers an interesting glimpse of intellectual selection processes. The version of the text represented in this manuscript is not the original compilation, as is clear from the fact that it breaks off at the letter O with no material disruption to the manuscript, while the abridged Karlsruhe version continues on to the end of the alphabet.[25] Instead, a small flourish and some blank space end the text, which is the main scribe's last contribution to the manuscript (another hand is responsible for the text in its final seven pages); perhaps a defective exemplar was to blame. But it is still possible to detect some of the strategies employed by the compiler of the text. Beginning with the brief introduction to the letters of the alphabet and their forms that we have been tracing, as well as other textual resources, the compiler used the alphabetical text as a framework for inserting *sententiae* of a moral-didactic nature.

Collections of *sententiae,* whether from biblical, patristic, or classical sources, or all of the above, had a relatively wide circulation in the early Middle Ages. Those who assembled them took different approaches to their organization, including compiling *sententiae* in the order in which they appear in their original texts, arranging material alphabetically based on the first words of the *sententiae,* and organizing material themati

---

24 "Et reliqua." The letters *a, f,* and *g* end this way; see Munzi, *Littera legitera,* 126–27.
25 The Reichenau and St. Gall associations and contemporaneity of these two manuscripts hint at their connections, perhaps indicating a point of origin for the compilation.

cally by subject. Given that the first word of the *sententia* is also sometimes its conceptual subject, alphabetical organization can also result in thematic groupings.[26] Thus, among the sentential texts that early medieval readers could choose from were works like the *Liber scintillarum* of Defensor, arranged in many chapters according to theme (with sub-sections for quotations from individual *auctores*); the *Synonyma* of Isidore of Seville, also organized by subject; and works arranged alphabetically like the popular *Liber de moribus,* an early medieval compilation drawn from Senecan and Pseudo-Senecan works. All of these texts circulated in the ninth century and all were incorporated into other collections of *sententiae.*

The compiler of the *sententiae* in St. Gall, Stb, Cod. Sang. 230 took a somewhat hybrid approach, achieving a mostly alphabetical and somewhat thematic compilation, whose curious character is probably due in part to the fact that it was compiled from sources with disparate agendas. Many of the sections, upon concluding the grammatical material of the base text, continue with the phrase "Concerning A" (about the letter in question) as an introduction to the sentential component.[27] Having considered the moral and spiritual significance of the letter forms themselves, the compilation moves on to include moral material pegged to each letter.

The compiler leaned heavily on several sources. Most prominent among these is Isidore's *Synonyma,* which offers a number of appealing qualities for the purposes of a compendium like this. The second book of the *Synonyma,* in particular, features a rhetorical style characterized by the heavy use of parallel structures, including repetition of specific words.[28] It therefore lends itself to excerpting in a text emphasizing the letter with which the repeated words begin. (In the St. Gall manuscript, this feature is

---

26 Barry Taylor, "Medieval Proverb Collections: The West European Tradition," *Journal of the Warburg and Courtauld Institutes* 55 (1992): 26–27, outlines the possible arrangements.

27 "De A."

28 See Claudia Di Sciacca, *Finding the Right Words: Isidore's* Synonyma *in Anglo-Saxon England* (Toronto: University of Toronto Press, 2008), 24.

highlighted visually by the coloring of initial letters throughout the text.) For instance, Isidore's passage on the benefits of *lectio* was suitable for excerpting in the L section of the text: "Through reading (*lectio*), understanding and intellect are increased; for reading teaches what to avoid, reading shows what you should pursue."[29] Because the parallel structures of Isidore's *Synonyma* were not motivated by concerns of alphabetization, the compiler of the text sometimes adjusted Isidore's text to emphasize the alphabetical organization. Therefore, Isidore's line "you should read frequently; you should contemplate the law daily" becomes "you should read frequently; your reading should be a daily meditation," with a corresponding adjustment in meaning.[30]

If the compiler was seeking to present moral material in a pedagogically effective manner, the *Synonyma* was a good resource. It straddles the line between rhetorical handbook and moral instruction treatise.[31] As Claudia di Sciacca notes, "the rhythmical prose of the *Synonyma* itself serves a pedagogic aim, since aural effects such as assonance, homoeoteleuton, and rhyme represent an effective support to memory."[32] In incorporating the *Synonyma* into an alphabetical compendium, the compiler took Isidore's mnemonically beneficial rhetoric and added to it the additional mnemonic benefit of an alphabetical arrangement. At the same time, the *Synonyma* could serve as a kind of sourcebook for virtuous behavior; its appearance in

---

29 "Lectio<ne> sensus et intellectus augetur: lectio enim docet quod caveas, lectio ostendit quo tendas." St. Gall, Stiftsbibliothek, Cod. Sang. 230, p. 560, and Isidore, *Synonyma* 2.19.

30 "Sit tibi frequens lectio, sit quotidiana legis meditatio"; "Lectio sit tibi frequens; Lectio sit tibi cotiditana meditatio." Ibid.

31 To understand whether early medieval readers viewed the *Synonyma* as moral or *artes* instruction, Jacques Elfassi analyzed their reception and concluded that while they were sometimes perceived and used as a grammatical text, they were more generally regarded as moral and spiritual works. Jacques Elfassi, "Les *Synonyma* d'Isidore de Séville: manuel de grammaire ou de morale? La réception médiévale de l'œuvre," *Revue d'études augustiniennes et patristiques* 52 (2006): 167–98.

32 Di Sciacca, *Finding the Right Words*, 30.

this grammatical framework suggests that the compiler saw its double utility for rhetorical and moral instruction.[33]

The compiler also drew from scripture (unsurprisingly, the sapiential books loom large, especially Proverbs), as well as some less-common sources like the sermons of Ephrem the Syrian. In many of the sections, it is possible to detect not only the sources of the compiler, but also the method of compiling the excerpts. For instance, under the heading "Concerning A," the compilation, headed with "Solomon says," begins with a robust selection of phrases from Proverbs 1 (1:1, 1:4, 1:8), then excerpts from later chapters of Proverbs, followed by excerpts from Sirach, Isidore's *Synonyma,* and Gregory the Great's *Regula pastoralis* — all of them beginning with the letter *a*.[34] The organization of these selections seems consistent with a compilation process of sifting through sources more or less in their textual order, and excerpting material starting with *a*-words. The abridged version of the compilation that appears in the Karlsruhe manuscript gives little opportunity to observe this process, preserving only a fragment of the first quotation followed by "and the rest."[35]

In the section on the letter B, under the heading "Effrem dicta," the compiler drew from two of Ephrem's sermons that circulated in Latin in the early Middle Ages ("De compunctione cordis" and "De beatitudine animae"); these appear together in some of the early manuscripts of Ephrem.[36] The excerpts in our alphabetical compilation appear in the order that they are found in the original texts, although the excerpts are necessarily selective, in order to conform to the requirement of presenting mate-

---

33 Felice Lifshitz observed that Isidore "developed a unique way of doing theology through grammar, putting the techniques of ancient rhetoric in the service of Christian morality," and that the early medieval manuscript tradition reveals links between the *Synonyma* and florilegia. Felice Lifshitz, *Religious Women in Early Carolingian Francia: A Study of Manuscript Tradition and Monastic Culture* (New York: Fordham University Press, 2014), 149–51.

34 "Salamon ait."

35 "Et reliqua." Munzi, *Littera legitera,* 123.

36 David Ganz, "Knowledge of Ephrem's Writings in the Merovingian and Carolingian Ages," *Hugoye: Journal of Syrian Studies* 2 (1999): 37–46.

rial beginning with *b*. Still, the compilation is once again consistent with a selection process that involved leafing through the texts of the sermons in order and selecting phrases that began with *b* as they appeared. The abbreviated version of the compilation in the Karlsruhe manuscript omits the *sententiae* entirely for *b*, offering only the original doctrine about the letter itself.

The letter *o* provides a particularly interesting example of textual transmission, practices of selection, and the circulation of instructional content. In the two manuscripts that include the amplified version of the text, Karlsruhe, BLb, MS Aug. 112 and St. Gall, Stb, Cod. Sang. 230, the section on the letter *o* includes a component where the prompt "Men disparage you" is repeated, in keeping with the *o* theme, and furnished with possible responses like "This is the habit of bad people, not good."[37] There are seventeen possible responses provided in the St. Gall manuscript. Nine of those seventeen appear in the abridged Karlsruhe manuscript. These selections function as a rhetorical exercise in paraphrase (not entirely different from the rhetorical aspect of Isidore's *Synonyma*) and reach back to the intellectual and textual tradition of the Senecan *De remediis fortuitorum*. Pieces of that text circulated in the early Middle Ages along with other material in the *Liber de moribus,* where the relevant prompt is not "Men disparage you" but "Men think / speak badly of you" and is supplied with six possible responses.[38]

Tracing the relationships of the compilation that appears in St. Gall, Stb, Cod. Sang. 230 takes us to the text of *Liber de moribus* in St. Gall, Stb, Cod. Sang. 238, where the usual six responses are supplemented with two additional responses to the

---

37 "Obtrectant tibi homines"; "Hoc est malorum, non bonorum."
38 "Male de te opinantur / loquuntur homines." Friedrich Haase, *L. Annaei Senecae Opera quae supersunt* (Leipzig: Teubner, 1895), 136–48. On the early tradition of *De moribus,* see Veronika von Büren, "La transmission du *De moribus* du ps. Sénèque, de Winithar de S. Gall à Sedulius Scottus," in *Ways of Approaching Knowledge in Late Antiquity and the Early Middle Ages: Schools and Scholarship,* ed. Paulo Farmhouse Alberto and David Paniagua (Nordhausen: Traugott Bautz, 2012), 206–44. On *De remediis fortuitorum,* see Robert J. Newman, "Rediscovering the *De Remediis Fortuitorum,*" *The American Journal of Philology* 109, no. 1 (1988): 92–107.

prompt.³⁹ This manuscript, an interesting miscellany compiled by a monk named Winithar at St. Gall at the end of the eighth century, shares some general interests with the alphabetical text found in St. Gall, Stb, Cod. Sang. 230. At the end of the *Liber de moribus* in Winithar's manuscript follows (without separation) a *florilegium* of material from various sources, including some of the same excerpts from Isidore's *Synonyma* that are found in the alphabetical collection of *sententiae* in St. Gall, Stb, Cod. Sang. 230.⁴⁰ Both of the supplemental answers to the adversarial prompt in Winithar's text of the *Liber de moribus* also appear in a freestanding text in two other early ninth-century manuscripts, arranged as thirty-six responses to "Men disparage you" with the title "The noisy blathering of the detractors and the praiseworthy advice of reason."⁴¹ All of the responses inserted into the alphabetical framework of Karlsruhe, BLb, MS Aug. 112 and St. Gall, Stb, Cod. Sang. 230 also appear in this freestanding text, which Luigi Munzi describes as a rhetorical exercise. Given that the character of the compilation in the Karlsruhe and St. Gall manuscripts straddles moral and *artes* instruction, the inclusion of this rhetorical-moral content fits the theme well, and, at a textual level, the entanglements between these various versions of the rhetorical material hint at the complex practices of borrowing, editing, and compiling that produced these miscellanies.

---

39 St. Gall, Stiftsbibliothek, Cod. Sang. 238, p. 400: "Gaudeo si menciunt, doleo si uera dicunt" and "Dum me lazerant se maculant."

40 Veronika von Büren elucidates the connections between this compilation and other material, including Paris BnF Lat. 10138 (*Codex Salmasianus*), in "La transmission du *De moribus*," 210–14.

41 "Obtrectatorum murmurosa garrulitas et rationis laudabile consilium." This text was edited by Luigi Munzi on the basis of three manuscripts, of which two date from the early ninth century: Paris, Bibliothèque nationale de France, MS lat. 2449, fol. 48r, and Vatican City, Biblioteca Apostolica Vaticana, MS Reg. lat. 1625, fol. 65r, which was originally connected with Paris, Bibliothèque nationale de France, MS lat. 10307 and which contains other typical *grammatica* material including Priscian and Martianus Capella; as well as an eleventh-century manuscript, Paris, Bibliothèque nationale de France, MS lat. 4886. Munzi, *Littera legitera*, 160–61.

Conclusion

To summarize, the little text with which this chapter begins ("A certain wise person expounded on the Latin letters") appears in instructional compilations in many different forms. It is found with and without an introduction drawn from Donatus and a conclusion drawn from Martianus Capella, sharing company with long menus of grammatical texts. It is found concealed between chapters of Donatus. It is found supplemented with numerous moral-didactic *sententiae,* and then trimmed down to present fewer of these *sententiae.* The *sententiae* it incorporates are also found in a variety of other forms, both freestanding and otherwise contextualized. Its most extreme versions are hardly recognizable as textually related, although they are clearly preoccupied with the same general issues about the letters and their greater significance.

To examine the manuscript world of this little text is to enter into a dynamic intellectual landscape. Its many permutations make clear the freedom that individual compilers exercised when faced with the task of creating a useful didactic compilation. As has been shown, much of the activity in *grammatica* miscellanies aims at complementing a relatively small number of core texts which serve as magnets for these manipulations and insertions. Even for these core components, creating a useful text was more important than maintaining a stable text. As Zetzel observes, this approach results in a kind of "fuzzy authorship" that preserves the general sense of core texts but not the precise words of revered *auctores.*[42] The title applied to our text in two of the manuscripts ascribes it to "A certain wise person," an attribution that on the one hand seems to acknowledge the role of *auctoritas,* but on the other hand makes it clear that it is the utility of the text that really matters. The compilers evidently did not feel bound to protect and preserve a stable text. At each moment of copying, they omitted and expanded, rearranged

---

42 Zetzel, *Critics, Compilers, and Commentators,* 162.

and supplemented, presumably for purposes that were fundamentally local and individual.

As various scholars have shown, in other spheres of activity of this period it is possible to identify groups of compilations that demonstrate concrete efforts to bring together specific texts for copying as a corpus.[43] Precisely because of the variety we have observed, the *grammatica* miscellanies of the early ninth century do not give the impression of a coordinated effort at creating a standardized corpus or curriculum. Among the *grammatica* miscellanies, no two are alike. Furthermore, despite high-minded discussions of the seven liberal arts in contemporary texts, early medieval compilations rarely touch on all of these disciplines, an apparent shortcoming that has caused scholars to discount the idea of serious efforts at standardization in elementary education. Looking past the variety and mutability of the texts and the relaxed approach of the compilers to authority, however, we can detect the contours of a surprisingly coherent approach to the *grammatica* curriculum. The compilations, at once less and more than stable copies of a single authoritative textbook, demonstrate an interest in bringing together instruction on grammar, the alphabet, poetry, orthography, and

---

43 For instance, the corpus identified by Michael Gorman, "The Carolingian Miscellany of Exegetical Texts in Albi 39 and Paris lat. 2175," *Scriptorium* 51 (1997): 336–54. See also Dorofeeva, "Miscellanies, Christian Reform and Early Medieval Encyclopaedism." In other areas the standardization efforts of reformers seem more illusory: as Susan Keefe notes of Carolingian baptismal instructions, the manuscript material "reflects an extraordinary lack of standardization across Carolingian Europe throughout the time when it has been thought that standardization was the achievement of the reformers." Susan Keefe, *Water and the Word: Baptism and Education of the Clergy in the Carolingian Empire* (Notre Dame: University of Notre Dame Press, 2002), vol. 2, 154. On the many possibilities of local use of such instructional materials, see Carine van Rhijn, "Manuscripts for Local Priests and the Carolingian Reforms," in *Men in the Middle: Local Priests in Early Medieval Europe,* ed. Steffen Patzold and Carine van Rhijn (Berlin: De Gruyter, 2016), 177–98, at 182, who emphasizes both the variety and the anonymity of the texts in such compilations — analogous to the *grammatica* miscellanies.

computus.⁴⁴ Moral and religious instruction are often interwoven with these subjects, as we find with the *sententiae* inserted into the alphabetical text. Scholars have sometimes questioned the rationale for dividing didactic material into "schoolbooks" and other sorts of miscellaneous compilation, given the difficulty in determining whether a glossed manuscript (of an author used in teaching, such as Prudentius) should be considered a "schoolbook."⁴² The example of St. Gall, Stb, Cod. Sang. 230 (a miscellany, but not a *grammatica* compilation) and its alphabetic *sententiae* reminds us that this can be an elusive distinction. In both texts and compilations, the boundary between grammatical, moral, and ascetic teaching was permeable, as exemplified by Isidore's *Synonyma*, now generally regarded as a moral rather than grammatical work.

The blending of grammatical material with other types of didactic content, particularly moral instruction, is in fact a common feature of the curriculum as it appears in the miscellanies. A similar illustration of this blending of didactic purpose is apparent in another early medieval school text, the "Interrogationes de litteris et de singulis causis," a dialogue which begins with a section on the letters of the alphabet and then pivots to a discussion of the Bible. The text, like the alphabetical compilation in St. Gall, Stb, Cod. Sang. 230, combines a grammatical introduction with a didactic text of another genre. The grammatical portion circulates separately (as with our text) and in the amplified version the interlocutors of the dialogue seem to acknowledge the abrupt change of subject.⁴⁵ In some of the

---

44 Alphabetical, orthographical, and poetic instruction can all be considered part of the discipline of *grammatica*.

42 The problems are outlined in Gernot Wieland, "The Glossed Manuscript: Classbook or Library Book?" *Anglo Saxon England* 14 (1985): 153–73.

45 "Si te de litteris cuncta quae interrogari possunt interrogem, ante credo mihi dies quam sermo cessavit [...] incipiamus de sancta scriptura." ("If I were to ask you all the things that could be asked about the letters, we would be here all day, believe me [...] let us begin concerning the holy scripture.") Nicholas Everett, "The *Interrogationes de littera et de singulis causis:* An Early Medieval School Text," *Journal of Medieval Latin* 16 (2006): 259.

manuscripts the text achieves this pivot by suggesting that that the letters of the alphabet and God form a continuum, inasmuch as the letter is the "smallest part," according to Donatus's definition, and eternal God is the "greatest part."[46] As surprising as this rhetorical point is, the notion that grammatical instruction might be integrated with religious and moral instruction is in keeping with some of the broadly stated goals of education in the early Middle Ages, and all of these texts start from the assumption that *grammatica* has an ethical and religious valence. In the text on the letters that we have been considering, the didactic content appended to the grammatical framework in two manuscripts is not doctrinal but moral and ascetic, in keeping with the contemporary tendency to pair rhetoric with the virtues, or the ideal of the "good man, skilled in speaking" inherited from ancient *auctoritates* that informed attitudes toward study in early medieval Europe.[47]

Despite broadly discernible goals and strategies like this, it is clear that the scribes of early medieval Europe felt little pressure to copy, and instructors felt little pressure to teach, a standard textbook. The relatively common materials, like the *Ars minor* and *Ars maior* of Donatus, are elaborated in an innumerable variety of ways in the manuscripts through reformulations, commentaries, interpolations, and the juxtaposition of a widely ranging menu of useful texts like our own. However, as we have seen, close examination of the texts and their contexts reveals not merely fragmentation but also a highly interconnected intellectual network. Our text on the letters of the alphabet is not common, but a thorough examination of its echoes throughout the corpus of Carolingian compilations requires a surprising journey through textual genres and manuscripts of widely varying origins. And in some of these manuscripts our text is just one among dozens. Tracing each of the others also leads

---

46 "Pars minima." Ibid.: "Quid est pars minima quid est pars maxima pars minima est littera pars maxima est Deus in aeternum." ("What is the smallest part and what is the greatest part? The smallest part is the letter and the greatest part is God eternal.")

47 "Vir bonus, dicendi peritus."

to a multiplicity of manipulated versions and sub-texts, each of which highlights connections with different groups of manuscripts. The heterogeneity of the *grammatica* anthologies suggests a centrifugal intellectual landscape, but this heterogeneity, upon closer inspection, allows us to perceive their dense interconnections.

Rather than laboring in local isolation without access to materials, compilers were evidently well integrated into a wide textual network but chose to exercise autonomy in assembling their materials. Variety and independent approaches to compilation, rather than a drive for standardization and deference to authority, characterize early medieval *grammatica* manuscripts, but this variety emerged from a closely connected textual world. Regarding the somewhat unruly intellectual legacy of the Carolingians, John Contreni has argued that to observe meaningful continuity in education we should look at the books: "The continuity of Carolingian education, so difficult to observe in human and institutional terms, is implicit in the texts teachers and scholars created."[48] The production of standard compilations on computus and exegesis, for instance, testify to an intellectual interconnectivity that transcended institutional discontinuity. *Grammatica,* as we have seen, is not a field where compilers seem to have prioritized the creation of a standard or uniform compendium; personal and local preferences seem to have taken precedence over any impulse to standardize. However, despite the variety, closer examination of the grammatica manuscripts also reveals the complex contours of a robust and enduring intellectual network transcending institution and place.

---

48 John J. Contreni, "Learning for God: Education in the Carolingian Age," *Journal of Medieval Latin* 24 (2014): 128–29.

Bibliography

Manuscripts

Bern, Burgerbibliothek, MS 417.
Karlsruhe, Badische Landesbibliothek, MS Aug. 112. https://digital.blb-karlsruhe.de/blbhs/content/pageview/11129.
Leiden, Universiteitsbibliotheek, MS BPL 135. http://hdl.handle.net/1887.1/item:1616565.
Paris, Bibliothèque nationale de France, MS lat. 1750. http://archivesetmanuscrits.bnf.fr/ark:/12148/cc12931x.
Paris Bibliothèque nationale de France, MS lat. 13025. http://archivesetmanuscrits.bnf.fr/ark:/12148/cc8514n.
Paris, Bibliothèque nationale de France, MS lat. 14087. http://archivesetmanuscrits.bnf.fr/ark:/12148/cc75552x.
St. Gall, Stiftsbibliothek, Cod. Sang. 230. https://www.e-codices.unifr.ch/de/list/one/csg/0230.
St. Gall, Stiftsbibliothek, Cod. Sang. 238. https://www.e-codices.unifr.ch/de/list/one/csg/0238.
St. Gall, Stiftsbibliothek, Cod. Sang. 728. https://www.e-codices.unifr.ch/de/list/one/csg/0728.

Primary

Bischoff, Bernhard. *Katalog der festländischen Handschriften des neunten Jahrhunderts (mit Ausnahme der wisigotischen)*, Volume 1: *Aachen-Lambach*. Wiesbaden: Harrassowitz, 1998.

———. *Katalog der festländischen Handschriften des neunten Jahrhunderts*, Volume 2: *Laon-Paderborn*. Edited by Birgit Ebersperger. Wiesbaden: Harrassowitz, 2004.

———. *Katalog der festländischen Handschriften des neunten Jahrhunderts (mit Ausnahme der wisigotischen)*, Volume 3: *Padua-Zwickau*. Edited by Birgit Ebersperger. Wiesbaden: Harrassowitz, 2014.

Università di Cassino grammar manuscript catalogue. https://iris.unicas.it/handle/11580/28063.

Secondary
Bischoff, Bernhard. "Libraries and Schools in the Carolingian Revival of Learning." In *Manuscripts and Libraries in the Age of Charlemagne*, translated by Michael Gorman, 99–113. Cambridge: Cambridge University Press, 1994.

Contreni, John J. "Learning for God: Education in the Carolingian Age." *The Journal of Medieval Latin* 24 (2014): 89–129. DOI: 10.1484/J.JML.5.103276.

De Paolis, Paolo. "I codici miscellanei grammaticali altomedievali. Caratteristiche, funzione, destinazione." In *Il codice miscellaneo: Tipologie e funzioni. Atti del Convegno internazionale, Cassino, 14–17 maggio 2003*, edited by Edoardo Crisci and Oronzo Pecere, 183–211. Cassino: Edizioni dell'Università, 2004.

———. "Il progetto di catalogazione dei codici grammaticali latini e la tradizione delle opere ortografiche latine." In *Libri e testi: Lavori in corso a Cassino. Atti del Seminario internazionale Cassino, 30–31 gennaio 2012*, edited by Roberta Casavecchia, Paolo De Paolis, Marilena Maniaci, and Giulia Orofino, 13–51. Cassino: Edizioni dell'Università, 2013.

———. "Per un catalogo delle opere e dei manoscritti grammaticali tardoantichi e altomedievali." In *Priscien. Transmission et refondation de la grammaire. De l'Antiquité aux modernes. États des recherches à la suite du colloque international de Lyon, 10–14 octobre 2006*, edited by Marc Baratin, Bernard Colombat, Louis Holtz, and Christine Melin, 653–68. Turnhout: Brepols, 2009. DOI: 10.1484/M.SA-EB.3.1238.

———. "Un manuale scolastico da Corbie." In *Vestigia notitiai: Scritti in memoria di Michelangelo Giusta*, edited by Edoardo Bona, Carlos Lévy, and Giuseppina Magnaldi, 81–106. Alessandria: Edizioni dell'Orso, 2012.

Degni, Paola, and Alessandra Peri. "Per un catalogo dei codici grammaticali altomedievali." In *Manuscripts and Tradition of Grammatical Texts from Antiquity to the Renaissance. Proceedings of a Conference held at Erice, 16–23 October 1997,* edited by Mario De Nonno, Paolo De Paolis, and Louis Holtz, 719–45. Cassino: Edizioni dell'Università, 2000.

Di Sciacca, Claudia. *Finding the Right Words: Isidore's Synonyma in Anglo-Saxon England.* Toronto: University of Toronto Press, 2008. DOI: 10.3138/9781442688117.

Dorofeeva, Anna. "Miscellanies, Christian Reform and Early Medieval Encyclopaedism: A Reconsideration of the Pre-Bestiary Latin *Physiologus* Manuscripts." *Historical Research* 90, no. 250 (2017): 665–82. DOI: 10.1111/1468-2281.12198.

Elfassi, Jacques. "Les *Synonyma* d'Isidore de Séville: manuel de grammaire ou de morale? La réception médiévale de l'œuvre." *Revue d'études augustiniennes et patristiques* 52, no. 1 (2006): 167–98. DOI: 10.1484/J.REA.5.100907.

Everett, Nicholas. "The *Interrogationes de littera et de singulis causis*: An Early Medieval School Text." *The Journal of Medieval Latin* 16 (2006): 227–75. DOI: 10.1484/J.JML.2.303236.

Ganz, David. "Knowledge of Ephrem's Writings in the Merovingian and Carolingian Ages." *Hugoye: Journal of Syrian Studies* 2 (1999): 37–46. DOI: 10.31826/9781463214074-004.

Gorman, Michael. "The Carolingian Miscellany of Exegetical Texts in Albi 39 and Paris Lat. 2175." *Scriptorium* 51 (1997): 336–54. DOI: 10.3406/scrip.1997.1813.

Haase, Friedrich. *L. Annaei Senecae Opera quae supersunt.* Leipzig: Teubner, 1895.

Hagen, Hermann. *Anecdota Helvetica quae ad grammaticam latinam spectant.* Leipzig: Teubner, 1870.

Holder, Alfred. *Die Handschriften der Badischen Landesbibliothek in Karlsruhe. Die Reichenauer Handschriften.* Volume 1. Wiesbaden: Harrassowitz, 1970.

Holtz, Louis. *Donat et la tradition de l'enseignement grammatical: Étude sur l'Ars Donati et sa diffusion (IVe–IXe siècle) et édition critique.* Paris: CNRS, 1981.

Irvine, Martin. *The Making of Textual Culture: "Grammatica" and Literary Theory, 350–1100.* Cambridge: Cambridge University Press, 1994.

Keefe, Susan. *Water and the Word: Baptism and Education of the Clergy in the Carolingian Empire.* 2 Volumes. Notre Dame: University of Notre Dame Press, 2002.

Lauer, Philippe. *Catalogue general des manuscrits latins.* Volume 2. Paris: Bibliothèque nationale, 1940.

Lehmann, Paul. *Mittelalterliche Bibliothekskataloge Deutschlands und der Schweiz,* Volume 1: *Die Bistümer Konstanz und Chur.* Munich: Beck, 1918.

Lifshitz, Felice. *Religious Women in Early Carolingian Francia: A Study of Manuscript Tradition and Monastic Culture.* New York: Fordham University Press, 2014. DOI: 10.5422/fordham/9780823256877.001.0001.

Marshall, Richard M.A. "Studies on the *Ars Grammatici Sergi{li}i* with an Edition." *The Journal of Medieval Latin* 20 (2010): 167–231. DOI: 10.1484/J.JML.1.102104.

Mostert, Marco. *The Library of Fleury: A Provisional List of Manuscripts.* Hilversum: Verloren, 1989.

Munzi, Luigi. *Littera legitera: Testi grammaticali latini dell'Alto Medioevo.* Annali dell'Università di Napoli l'Orientale 11. Naples: Istituto universitario orientale, 2007.

Newman, Robert J. "Rediscovering the *De Remediis Fortuitorum.*" *The American Journal of Philology* 109, no. 1 (1988): 92–107. DOI: 10.2307/294763.

Scherer, Gustav. *Verzeichniss der Handschriften der Stiftsbibliothek von St. Gallen.* Halle: Verlag der Buchhandlung des Waisenhauses, 1875.

Taylor, Barry. "Medieval Proverb Collections: The West European Tradition." *Journal of the Warburg and Courtauld Institutes* 55, no. 1 (1992): 19–35. DOI: 10.2307/751418.

Van Rhijn, Carine. "Manuscripts for Local Priests and the Carolingian Reforms." In *Men in the Middle: Local Priests in Early Medieval Europe,* edited by Steffen Patzold and Carine van Rhijn, 177–98. Berlin: De Gruyter, 2016. DOI: 10.1515/9783110444483-012.

Von Büren, Veronika. "La transmission du *De moribus* du ps. Sénèque, de Winithar de S. Gall à Sedulius Scottus." In *Ways of Approaching Knowledge in Late Antiquity and the Early Middle Ages: Schools and Scholarship,* edited by Paulo Farmhouse Alberto and David Paniagua, 206–44. Nordhausen: Traugott Bautz, 2012.

Zetzel, James E.G. *Critics, Compilers, and Commentators: An Introduction to Roman Philology, 200 BCE–800 CE.* Oxford: Oxford University Press, 2018.

9

What Is a Vademecum? The Social Logic of Early Medieval Compilation

Anna Dorofeeva

Did vademecums exist in the early Middle Ages?[1] This question raises several important issues. The term "vademecum" literally means "go with me," but has been attested as denoting a reference book or manual only since the seventeenth century.[2] In

---

1   I am very grateful to Erik Kwakkel for the initial impetus to work on this subject, and to Claire Burridge, Jeremiah Coogan, Colleen Curran, Roy Flechner, Thom Gobbitt, Brandon Hawk, Eleanor Jackson, Jesse Keskiaho, Aaron Macks, Sinéad O'Sullivan, Carine van Rhijn, Evina Stein, Mariken Teeuwen, Carolyn Twomey, Bastiaan Waagmeester, and Arthur Westwell for invaluable comments and advice on various ideas and drafts of this article. I would also like to thank Annkathrin Sonder, Bastian Politycki, Niklas Fröhlich, Oliver Glaser, and Bart van Hees of the DFG-Graduiertenkolleg 2196 "Dokument — Text — Edition" at the University of Wuppertal for the invitation to speak at the conference "Der Text und seine (Re-) Produktion" on September 29–30, 2021, which shaped some of the ideas presented here. The research for this article was supported by the Gladys Krieble Delmas Foundation and an IRC Government of Ireland postdoctoral research fellowship (GOIPD/2017/1348).
2   *OED Online*, s.v. "vade-mecum, n.," https://www.oed.com/view/Entry/220967. First use: Daniel Tuvill, *Vade Mecum: A Manuall of Essayes Morrall, Theologicall. Inter-wouen with Moderne Obseruations, Historicall, Politicall* (London: Nicholas Okes, 1629).

scholarship, it has often been used loosely to mean a companion book, owned and used by an individual, whether named or unnamed, but sometimes it has also meant a generally useful book, a reference text, or even a kind of girdle book.[3] The fuzziness of the term has, paradoxically, tended to obscure the role of individuals in the compilation of multi-text books or miscellanies.[4] Scholarship over the past few decades, in fields ranging from New Philology to codicology, has shown that the process of selection and arrangement of pre-existing texts in early medieval miscellanies was creative and innovative, rather than simply a way of avoiding writing original works. This means that new miscellanies created new contexts for their contents through the coordinated activity of everyone involved in the book production and reception process. Helmut Reimitz, following Gabrielle Spiegel, has proposed that early medieval texts have a "social logic": every text represents a situated use of language and is therefore essentially local. As a result, texts are embedded within the systems of communication and power that produced them, and they exercise influence on them in turn.[5] Reimitz applied this poststructuralist interpretation to historiographical compendia, but it can and should be applied to all early medieval compilations, or multi-text books (which can themselves be seen as texts), and their contents. But if some compilations were created as companion books for specific individuals, a dichotomy exists between compilations as collaboratively produced and read on the one hand, and as books directed by the needs and wants of a brilliant individual on the other hand. This

---

[3] Hans-Georg Beck, *Vademecum des byzantinischen Aristokraten. Das sogenannte Strategikon des Kekaumenos,* Byzantinische Geschichtsschreiber 5 (Graz: Verlag Styria, 1956), and Raymond Clemens and Timothy Graham, *Introduction to Manuscript Studies* (Ithaca: Cornell University Press, 2007), 56.

[4] For a discussion of the various kinds of miscellany, see the essay on *Sammelhandschriften* by Mark Stansbury in this volume.

[5] Helmut Reimitz, "The Social Logic of Historiographical Compendia in the Carolingian Period," in *Herméneutique du texte d'histoire,* ed. Osamu Kano (Nagoya: Graduate School of Letters, Nagayo University, 2012), 17–28.

is a methodological rather than a contextual historical problem, but it leads to two interesting questions: how and to what extent did individuals shape the compilation of whole books? And what is the precise connection between individual intellectuals, their manuscript books, and the communities in which both operated?

To begin to answer these questions, this chapter looks at a case study of a set of famous "vademecums" from the ninth and tenth centuries. All of them are known as vademecums or personal handbooks (terms which are treated as synonyms here) in scholarship. The below discussion examines and compares their contents as well as their codicological and paleographical features, with a focus on the effect individual intervention or direction had on the resulting book. The analysis foregrounds multi-text manuscripts from both the perspective of structural codicology — as Gumbert's work on mono-, homo- and allogenetic manuscripts has shown, this is vital for understanding compilations — and of textual criticism.[6] It should be noted that the latter approach has an inherent emphasis on originality and individuality, as seen from its terminology: holograph (an author's texts copied by that author), autograph (texts written by a known hand), and idiograph (an author's texts produced under their supervision). These terms and the ideas behind them can be useful, but, as I will argue, the material context of texts is equally important, and it highlights, instead, the collaborative nature of text and manuscript production.

The following case study analysis considers this tension between text and material carrier in the context of personal hand-

---

6 Johan P. Gumbert, "Zur Kodikologie und Katalographie der zusammengesetzten Handschrift," in *La descrizione dei manoscritti: esperienze a confronto,* Studi e richerche del Dipartimento di Filologia e Storia 1, ed. Edoardo Crisci, Marilena Maniaci, and Pasquale Orsini (Cassino: University of Cassino, 2010), 4. See also Orietta Da Rold, "Codicology, Localization and Oxford, Bodleian Library, MS Laud Misc. 108," in *Makers and Users of Medieval Books: Essays in Honour of A.S.G. Edwards,* ed. Carol M. Meale and Derek Pearsall (Cambridge: Cambridge University Press, 2014), 48–59.

books. Three features receive particular attention: codicology, autograph writing, and contents. Manuscript size is discussed in the following section, "Did vademecums really exist in the early Middle Ages?," which also considers the case study in the context of social logic.

List of Vademecums

The nine manuscripts described below have been identified as vademecums or personal handbooks by various scholars. Their inclusion in this list, which is by no means exhaustive, is intended to highlight the disparities between them, showing them to have few real features in common, and to raise a set of issues with the way that personal or individual involvement in early medieval book production has been treated to date.[7] The broad textual and material features of these vademecums will also be examined, however, to see whether it is possible to understand the relationship between individuals, "handbooks," and community-run early medieval book centers in a more productive way. Ultimately, the question to be answered here is: "What makes a personal book personal?"

The key features of these manuscripts are briefly provided below and compared in the following section. These short descriptions are based on the catalogues and other publications which provide full details of the manuscripts and which are listed in the footnotes to the classmarks. I have therefore omitted any information not directly relevant to the present discussion, since it is available elsewhere. Although the list of contents for each manuscript cannot be examined in detail in this overview, it is provided in order to give the reader an idea of the collection, especially for those manuscripts whose catalogue descriptions abridge their contents lists.

---

7   The vademecum of Ademar of Chabannes (Leiden, Universiteitsbibliotheek, MS Voss. Lat. Oct. 15), for example, has been omitted due to its late date, but there are many others which could also be added to this list. It is therefore intended only as a representative example.

An Episcopal Pastoral Manual: St. Gall, Stiftsbibliothek, Cod. Sang. 222[8]

This manuscript was described as a bishop's pastoral manual by Susan Keefe.[9] Made in a small format (130–134 × 173–174 mm [5.11–5.27 × 6.81–6.85 in.]), it was copied by several different hands around the second half of the ninth century. Contemporary quire marks list quires A–K to p. 132 (with quire F missing). A final quire contains the end of Isidore's *De ecclesiasticis officiis* and the remaining texts in the manuscript. Although the manuscript's codicology indicates that it is a single unit, the paleography suggests there may be a break: the same scribe continued Isidore's text from p. 133 and a similar hand copied the text on p. 135, but the remaining works were copied by two early medieval scribes with very different training, from p. 138 probably by a student. Since these texts were also copied unsystematically, onto blank and largely unruled leaves, they may represent unplanned additions.

- 2–134: Isidore of Seville, *De ecclesiasticis officiis* (partial, due to missing quire and lacking the two final chapters)
- 135: Baptismal blessing of the Cross
- 136: Blank
- 137–39: Commentary on the baptismal rite
- 139–42: List of chapters from the Aachen capitulary of 813 (lacking final two chapters)
- 143–45: Blank
- 146–47: Prayer to St. Gall (thirteenth-century addition)

---

8   Gustav Scherrer, *Verzeichniss der Handschriften der Stiftsbibliothek von St. Gallen* (Halle: Verlag der Buchhandlung des Waisenhauses, 1875), 79, and Albert Bruckner, *Schreibschulen der Diözese Konstanz: St. Gallen II*, Scriptoria Medii Aevi Helvetica: Denkmäler schweizerischer Schreibkunst des Mittelalters 3 (Geneva: Roto-Sadag, 1938), 84.
9   Susan A. Keefe, *Water and the Word: Baptism and the Education of the Clergy in the Carolingian Empire*, vol. 1: *A Study of Texts and Manuscripts*, Publications in Medieval Studies (Notre Dame: University of Notre Dame, 2002), 163.

- 148: Blank (with mirror-image offset of later medieval pastedown, no longer present)

An Episcopal Handbook: Munich, Bayerische Staatsbibliothek, MS Clm 6426[10]

This five-part manuscript (255 × 205 mm [10.04 × 8.07 in.]) was copied by twenty scribes in the circle of the missionary bishop Abraham of Freising (950–993/994) over at least thirteen years. Despite the disparate nature of the five different codicological parts, the codicological and paleographical evidence indicates that they were created and used within the same tenth-century production context. This context was most likely Abraham's chancery, which traveled with him on his journeys to Germany (including Freising and the places frequented by Otto II's court), Italy (including the Veneto), and various locations in Slovenia. The manuscript contains autograph writing by Abraham as well as Liutprand of Cremona and Rather of Verona. Most studies of this manuscript consider it to be Abraham's vademecum, due to its strong focus on episcopal liturgy and canon law. The contents may have been shaped by Abraham's own personal interests. As other scholars have noted, the many sermons on Easter are a particular focus.[11] That Abraham had an interest in sermons generally is also supported by the copy of an otherwise unknown sermon delivered by Liutprand (fols. 27r–33r), which Abraham seems to have attended and whose transmission it ap-

---

10 Karl Leyser, *Communications and Power in Medieval Europe: The Carolingian and Ottonian Centuries*, ed. Timothy Reuter (London: Bloomsbury, 1994), 113, calls it an episcopal vademecum with blessings, formulae, and missionary aids in Slavonic. I have examined this manuscript in detail in Anna Dorofeeva, "Reading Early Medieval Miscellanies," *Scribes and the Presentation of Texts (From Antiquity to c. 1550): Proceedings of the 20th Colloquium of the Comité international de paléographie latine, Beinecke Rare Book & Manuscript Library, Yale University (New Haven, September 6–8, 2017)*, ed. Consuelo W. Dutschke et al., Bibliologia 65 (Turnhout: Brepols, 2021), 495–514.

11 Despite this, the strong focus on Lent and Easter can also be explained by the importance of this period in the Christian liturgical year.

pears he ensured.[12] Mentions of Abraham's name in parts IV and V also indicate that this manuscript was closely linked with the bishop.

Part I
- 1v: Notes recording property in Godego (see fol. 152vb) and about the income of Freising free tenants in Regensburg and Ergolding
- 2r–21r: Rather of Verona, *sermones* 2 and 4 on Quadragesima and Easter; in his own hand on fols. 17r–21r
- 21r–23r: Pseudo-Augustine, *sermo* 2, *De consolatione mortuorum,* chaps. 1–4 (chap. 4 incomplete)[13]
- 23v–25r: *Ordo* for the excommunication of *incorrigibiles* (apostates)
- 25r–26r: Short version of an *Ordo Romanus qualiter concilium agatur,* based on Alcuin's letters, in the hand of Rather of Verona
- 26v: Synod of Tribur (895), chap. 46, on rape
- 27r–47r: Nine sermons, including by Liutprand of Cremona, Maximus of Turin, Gregory the Great, Leo the Great, Pseudo-Maximus of Turin, and Fulgentius of Ruspe; fols. 27r–39v are in Abraham's own hand, with a Greek title by Liutprand
- 47r–v: Pseudo-Clemens I, *Epistula* 3, on the duty of clerics to teach the Word of God (excerpt)
- 48r: Council of Carthage (419), chap. 32, asserting the right of bishops to inherit property
- 48r–49r: Sermon on Easter
- 49v: *Probationes pennae* and continuation of text on fol. 65r

---

12 Bernhard Bischoff, "Eine Osterpredigt Liudprands von Cremona (um 960)," in Bernhard Bischoff, *Anecdota novissima: Texte des vierten bis sechzehnten Jahrhunderts,* Quellen und Untersuchungen zur lateinischen Philologie des Mittelalters 7 (Stuttgart: Anton Hiersemann, 1984), 20–34.

13 The author of this sermon is now thought to be John Chrysostom.

Part II
- 50r–56v: *Ordo* for the blessing of the bells and crucifix of a church
- 56v–57v: Mass for the sick
- 58r–60v: Weather blessings
- 61r–62r: Leo the Great, *sermo* 94 on the fast of the seventh month
- 62v–64r: Sermon for the feast of the Purification of the Virgin (2 February)
- 65r: Council of Carthage (419), chap. 86, on the ordination of bishops; ends on fol. 49v
- 65v–71r: Alcuin, *Liber de virtutibus et vitiis*, chaps. 27–35, on the principal vices
- 71r–72r: Anonymous sermon on the advent of the Holy Spirit
- 72r: Short legal text on the obedience due to a bishop
- 72v–77r: Two *ordos* for visiting and anointing the sick
- 77v: Antiphonary for certain feast days and blessing for candles
- 78rv: Confession formula in Old Slavic (*Freisinger Denkmäler* 1)
- 79r: Jewish Oath

Part III
- 80r–84r: Regino of Prüm, *De synodalibus causis* Bk. II, chap. 407–16: on excommunication and removal of clergy from office
- 84v–86v: Sermon on St. Mary and St. Corbinian, patron saints of the Freising church (see also fols. 161v–162v)

Part IV
- 87r–108v: Diverse sermons, including by Maximus of Turin, Pseudo-Augustine, and Pseudo-Rather of Verona
- 108v–118r: Isidore of Seville, *De fide catholica contra Judaeos*, Bk. 1, chaps. 18–50
- 118rv–126v: Diverse sermons

- 126v: List of enslaved people of the Freising monastery in Ennstal
- 127r–145v: Seven sermons, five by Caesarius or Pseudo-Caesarius of Arles
- 145v–146r: Chapters from the decrees of the Synods of Vaison (442), Orléans (511), and Meaux-Paris (845–46), with a list of witnesses to a transaction made by bishop Abraham on fol. 146r
- 147v–148r: Extract from the decree of the assembly at Ranshofen (c. 990), on runaway slaves and servants

Part V
- 149ra–151ra: Sermon on Quadragesima
- 151ra–152ra: Nicetas of Remesiana, *De psalmodiae bono*, excerpt
- 152rb–152va: Explanations of the Alleluia and Gloria
- 152vb–153ra: Note of land near Godego in Treviso given to Bishop Abraham; fol. 1v repeats the first paragraph
- 153v–155v: Sermon on penitence
- 155v–157v: Gregory the Great, *Registrum epistularum*, Bk. 13, ep. 6, and Bk. 11, ep. 29, on sick bishops; and Bk. 9, ep. 139, on supporting bishops
- 158va–161va: Homily and formula for public confession in Old Slavic (*Freisinger Denkmäler* 2 and 3)
- 161v–162v: Sermon on St. Mary and St. Corbinian, patron saints of the Freising church (see also fols. 84v–86v)
- 163r–169r: Augustine, excerpts from sermons on the Gospel of John, on Easter and the Last Supper

Monastic Handbook for Teaching and Learning: St. Gall, Stiftsbibliothek, Cod. Sang. 878[14]

According to Bischoff's famous study of this manuscript, it was the vademecum of Walahfrid Strabo (c. 808–849), monk at

---

14 Gustav Scherrer, *Verzeichniss der Handschriften der Stiftsbibliothek von St. Gallen* (Halle: Verlag der Buchhandlung des Waisenhauses, 1875), 307–9;

Reichenau Abbey in the ninth century. Bischoff identified his hand among many others in the manuscript and showed that it evolved in four distinct stages from c. 825 to c. 849 (the period during which the contents were copied). The codex is 210 × 137 mm (8.27 × 5.4 in.) in size. It consists of five codicological units, added as need arose. At least one text (the calendar on pp. 324–27) may have been copied in Fulda during Walahfrid's stay there as a pupil of Hrabanus Maurus. According to Bischoff, the contents of the manuscript were determined by Walahfrid's interest in dreams, portents, monsters, and unusual events, whether they were things that he himself experienced (as with an earthquake in 849, his last year of life) or whether they were described in the extracts he selected and copied. The manuscript is carefully rubricated throughout and its contents were evidently well planned.

Part I
- 5–79: Donatus, with extracts from Priscian, *Institutiones,* and poems on 70–71
- 91–148: Bede, *De arte metrica* and *De schematibus et tropis*
- 148–71: Priscian, *Instititutiones* (extracts)
- 171–74: Isidore, *De officiis* 1.12 (= Hrabanus Maurus, *De institutione clericorum* 2.54)
- 174–76: Practice grammar sentences
- 176–77: Text on the twelve signs of the zodiac

Augusto Beccaria, *I codici di medicina del periodo presalernitano* (Rome: Ed. di Storia e Letteratura, 1956), 391–93; and Bernhard Bischoff, "Eine Sammelhandschrift Walahfrid Strabos (Cod. Sangall. 878)," in Bernard Bischoff, *Mittelalterliche Studien. Ausgewählte Aufsätze zur Schriftkunde und Literaturgeschichte,* vol. 2 (Stuttgart: Anton Hiersemann, 1967), 34–51. See also Wesley M. Stevens, *Rhetoric and Reckoning in the Ninth Century: The Vademecum of Walahfrid Strabo,* Studia Traditionis Theologiae: Explorations in Early and Medieval Theology 24 (Turnhout: Brepols, 2018), https://scholarworks.iu.edu/journals/index.php/tmr/article/view/31090.

Part II
- 178–240: Hrabanus Maurus, *De computo* (incomplete, beginning in chap. 13)
- 240: Text on the days of the week and signs of the zodiac

Part III
- 242–62: Bede, *De natura rerum,* with an added list of chapters to Bede's *De temporibus* on p. 243
- 262–76: Bede, *De temporibus*
- 277–84: World chronicle up to the year 809 with another brief chronicle from Adam to Christ on final page
- 284–302: Computistical material
- 302–5: Chronicle, *Fasti Vindobonenses, Chronicon* of Jerome (excerpts), and note of an earthquake from 849
- 306–7: Cassiodorus, *Historia tripartita* (excerpts)
- 308–15: Jerome, ep. 73
- 315–21: Isidore, *Etymologiae* (excerpts) and three alphabets (Hebrew, Greek, runic)

Part IV
- 322–23: Alcuin, *Disputatio de vera philosophia* and *De grammatica* (first half, continued below)
- 324–27: Calendar
- 327–31: Hippocrates, *Epistula ad Antiochum regem*
- 331–34: Medical recipes with some Old High German glosses (later additions), two incense recipes,[15] and an eleventh-century addition (a five-line epitaph of Adelbertus, a priest) on p. 333
- 335–39: Moralistic excerpts and a letter of Charlemagne
- 340–44: Alcuin, *Disputatio de vera philosophia* and *De grammatica*
- 344–47: Computistical and astronomical notes
- 348–50: Seneca, *Epistulae morales ad Lucilium* (excerpts)
- 351: Blank

---

15 Claire Burridge, "Incense in Medicine: An Early Medieval Perspective," *Early Medieval Europe* 28 (2020): 219–55.

Part V
- 352–65: Anthimus, *Epistula de observatione ciborum*
- 366–67: Text on good and bad days for bloodletting
- 368–77: Various excerpts on agriculture and medicine
- 378: Cassiodorus, *Historia tripartita* (excerpts)
- 378–80: Eusebius, *Historia ecclesiastica* (excerpts)
- 380–91: Orosius, *Historiarum adversum paganos* (excerpts)
- 392–93: Medical recipes
- 394: Verses and grammatical notes (twelfth-century addition)

Patristic Dossier for Intellectual Work: Vatican City, Biblioteca Apostolica Vaticana, MS Vat. lat. 3852[16]

This is a patristic miscellany compiled and copied by Florus of Lyon (c. 810–859). Its dimensions are 240 × 195 mm (9.45 × 7.68 in.). It has been called a vademecum by Pierre Chambert-Protat in his extensive study of Florus's work.[17] Its different parts were added to one another progressively from around 840, and the parts rearranged each time, which has caused some texts in the present manuscript to begin or continue in non-adjacent quires.

---

16   Anne-Marie Turcan-Verkerk, "Faut-il rendre à Tertullien l'*Ex libris Tertulliani de execrandis gentium diis* du manuscrit Vatican latin 3852?," Revue des Études augustiniennes 46 (2000): 205–34; Anne-Marie Turcan-Verkerk, "Florus de Lyon et le ms. Roma. Bibl. Vallicelliana, E 26. Notes marginales," in *La tradition vive. Mélanges d'histoire des textes en l'honneur de Louis Holtz*, ed. Pierre Lardet (Turnhout: Brepols, 2003), 307–16; and Pierre Chambert-Protat, "Le manuscrit Montpellier 157 de Mannon de Saint-Oyen et la collection *De pascha* de Florus de Lyon," *Revue bénédictine* 128 (2018): 95–141. Among the sources for this manuscript were Montpellier, Bibliothèque interuniversitaire. Section Médecine, MS H.308 and Montpellier, Bibliothèque interuniversitaire. Section Médecine, MS H.157. I am grateful to Pierre Chambert-Protat for useful discussions about these volumes, and for personally checking the dimensions of this Vatican manuscript.

17   Chambert-Protat, "Le manuscrit Montpellier 157," 11, and Pierre Chambert-Protat, "Florus de Lyon, lecteur des Pères: documentation et travaux patristiques dans l'église de Lyon au IXe siècle" (PhD Diss., École doctorale de l'école pratique des Hautes Études, 2016).

Anne-Marie Turcan-Verkerk has suggested that part I (codicologically the oldest part) may date to an early period in Florus's life. Many of the texts can be identified in other manuscripts annotated by Florus, from which this Vatican codex was evidently copied and which therefore represents a book closely linked to Florus's intellectual activity. The manuscript seems to be a typical "dossier" of texts, like others known to have been compiled by Florus; but it also appears to represent an early stage in the compilation of a miscellany, made over time according to the needs of the hour, and necessitating occasional rearrangement.[18]

Part I
- 1r–30v: Bede, *Chronica maiora* = *De temporum ratione* chap. 65 (excerpts)

Part II
- 31r–50v: Orosius, *Historiae adversum paganos* (excerpts)
- 50v–82v + 119r: Paul the Deacon, *Historia Langobardorum* books 1–6 (excerpts)
- [83–102: see part III]
- 103r–112v: Isidore, *Etymologiae,* Bk. XVI (excerpts)
- 113r–114v: Bede, *In I Samuhelem,* Bk. II (preface on chronology only)
- 114v–118v + 31r: Bede, *Explanatio Apocalypsis* (excerpt)
- 119r–125v: Three texts on weights and measures, among them Maecianus, *Distributio partium,* and Epiphanius of Salamis, *De mensuris et ponderibus*
- 125v–129v: Eucherius of Lyons, *Instructiones,* Bk. II (excerpts)
- 129v–130v: Tertullian, *De execrandis gentium diis* (excerpts)

Part III
- 83r–101v: Jerome, *epistulae* nos. 100 (end only), 91, 51, 83, 84, and 124
- 102r–v: Augustine, *epistula* 186 (excerpts)

---

18 Turcan-Verkerk, "Faut-il rendre à Tertullien," 220–26.

– 102v: Bede, *Historia ecclesiastica* (excerpt)

Custom-Made Bible Study Tool: Paris, Bibliothèque nationale de France, MS lat. 15679[19]

This is the collection of epitomes of biblical commentaries compiled by Theodulf of Orléans (c. 750–821). Originally intended to be two separate volumes, the collection was designed and executed under his supervision. It is 300 × 210 mm (11.81 × 8.27 in.) in size. The penultimate quire of the first volume is now missing, but this is not reflected in the pagination. Although the epitomes it contains include most books of the Bible, as Bischoff noted, it remained manageable because its scribes used the small minuscule script employed by the scribes of Theodulf's one-volume recensions of the Vulgate.[20] Michael Gorman suggested the manuscript gave the impression that it was "carried out over a considerable amount of time by many different scribes," but that it never fulfilled its intended function as a Bible study tool for Theodulf's monks. Theodulf's own hand may be preserved in a rubric on p. 219 and in a marginal correction on p. 167.[21] It was described as a "Vademecum der biblischen Kommentare" by Bonifatius Fischer.[22] Fischer meant only that this was a volume of "companion works" intended for consultation, assistance with reading the Bible and other scholarly tasks, which further highlights the indeterminate nature of the term "vademecum."

---

19   The most useful description of the manuscript is in Michael Gorman, "Theodulf of Orléans and the exegetical miscellany in Paris lat. 15679," *Revue bénédictine* 109 (1999): 278–323.

20   Bernhard Bischoff, "Libraries and Schools in the Carolingian Revival of Learning," *Manuscripts and Libraries in the Age of Charlemagne*, trans. Michael Gorman (Cambridge: Cambridge University Press, 1994), 109n8.

21   Gorman, "Theodulf of Orléans," 290, 293.

22   Bonifatius Fischer, "Bibeltext und Bibelreform unter Karl dem Großen," in *Karl der Große: Lebenswerk und Nachleben, II. Das geistige Leben*, ed. Bernhard Bischoff (Düsseldorf: L. Schwann, 1965), 177; repr. Bonifatius Fischer, *Lateinische Bibelhandschriften im frühen Mittelalter*, Vetus Latina: Aus der Geschichte der lateinischen Bibel 11 (Freiburg: Herder, 1985), 138.

Volume 1
- 1–63: Isidore's commentaries on the first seven books of the Old Testament
- 63–64: Life of St. Asclas (later ninth- or tenth-century addition)
- 65–75: Bede, *XXX Quaestiones in libros Regum*
- 75–83: A series of 31 excerpts on the Books of Kings
- 85–160: Epitomes of Jerome on Isaiah, Jeremiah, and Ezekiel 1:1–38.8
- 160–67: An epitome of Gregory's homilies on Ezekiel 2:1–10
- 169–82: An epitome of Bede on Ezra
- 183–99: Epitomes of Jerome on Jonah, Abdiah, Micah, and Naum
- 199–202: Life of St. Polycarp (addition, possibly from the second half of the ninth century)
- 202–225: Epitomes of Jerome on Sophonias, Aggaeus, Zachariah, and Daniel
- 226: Blank, except for ownership note
- 227–93: An epitome of Gregory, *Moralia in Iob*
- 293–94: A brief composition on the allegorical significance of the figure of Tobias
- 294–324: A commentary on Psalms 1–95 (incomplete at end due to missing quire)
- 325: An epitome of the translation made by Rufinus of Origen on the *Song of Songs* 2:13–15 (beginning lost)
- 325–226: The commentary of Justus of Urgel on the *Song of Songs* 2:16–8.14

Volume 2
- 337–50: An epitome of Jerome on Matthew
- 350–54: An epitome of the Pseudo-Jerome commentary on Mark
- 354: Gregory, *Homilia in Evangelia* 2:29
- 354–67: An epitome of Ambrose on Luke 1:1–22.42
- 369–402: An epitome of Augustine's *Tractatus in Ioannem*
- 402–64: Epitomes of the Pseudo-Jerome commentaries on Romans, 1–2 Corinthians, Galatians, Ephesians, Philippi-

ans, 1–2 Thessalonians, Colossians, 1–2 Timothy, Titus, and Philemon
- 464–74: An epitome of the translation made by Mutianus of John Chrysostom on Hebrews
- 475–85: Commentaries on the Epistle of James; the First and Second Epistles of Peter; the First, Second, and Third Epistles of John; and the Epistle of Judas
- 485–95: A set of brief comments on the Acts of the Apostles
- 496–504: Anonymous commentary on the Apocalypse (abbreviated)

Pastoral and Doctrinal Collection Used by a Cathedral Lay Brother: Laon, Bibliothèque municipale, MS 265[23]

John Contreni has shown that this collection of doctrinal and pastoral texts was known and used by Martin of Laon. Though he may not have compiled it himself, several of the texts evidently matched his interests and activities as a lay teacher at the cathedral in Laon.[24] Copied in the first half of the ninth century, the manuscript (c. 240 × 130 mm [9.45 × 5.12 in.]) consists of at least seven codicological parts which were bound together before Martin's death in 875, as a table of contents and small notes in his own hand attest.[25] Part VII (fols. 162–83) was rearranged

---

23 Described in John J. Contreni, *The Cathedral School of Laon from 850 to 930: Its Manuscripts and Masters*, Münchener Beiträge zur Mediävistik und Renaissance-Forschung 29 (Munich: Arbeo-Gesellschaft, 1978); Hubert Mordek, *Bibliotheca capitularium regum Francorum manuscripta: Überlieferung und Traditionszusammenhang der fränkischen Herrscherer-lasse* (Munich: Hahnsche Mordek, 1995), 200–5, 431, 895, 950–51, and 973; and Susan A. Keefe, *A Catalogue of Works Pertaining to the Explanation of the Creed in Carolingian Manuscripts*, Instrumenta Patristica et Mediaevalia 63 (Turnhout: Brepols, 2012), 251–52.

24 John Contreni, *The Cathedral School of Laon*, 130–34. Contreni noted on pp. 109–11 that Martin may have been a layman: there is no evidence he ever took orders or was ordained.

25 There are eight manuscript parts, but parts V and VII may once have formed a single codicological unit. Bernhard Bischoff, *Katalog der festländischen Handschriften des neunten Jahrhunderts (mit Ausnahme der wisigotischen)*, vol. 2: *Laon-Paderborn*, ed. Birgit Ebersperger (Wiesbaden:

out of its original order at some point before the current binding. According to Bischoff, parts I–III were probably copied at St. Amand in the first third of the ninth century, while the remainder were made in northeastern France in the second third of the ninth century.

Part I
- 2r–35v: The Gospel of Nicodemus (*Gesta Salvatoris*)

Part II
- 36r–50v: Gennadius of Marseille, *De ecclesiasticis dogmatibus*
- 51r–82r: Jerome, *Commentarii in Danielem* (epitome); two sermons of Gregory I on Ezekiel; excerpt from Gregory's *Moralia;* excerpt from Jerome's letter on penance to Rusticus; and Ps.-Jerome, *Epistula ad Oceanum* on the clerical life (fragment)
- 82v: Blank

Part III
- 83r–95r: Fulgentius of Ruspe, letters
- 95r–122r: Fulgentius of Ruspe, *De fide ad Petrum*
- 122v: Ps.-Augustine, *Expositio sancti Augustini de secreto gloriosae incarnationis Domini* (remainder illegible)

Part IV
- 123r–148v: Sermons on Mark 16:14–20 and Luke 11:5–13, and Isidore, *Liber differentiarum* 2.1–41

Part V
- 149r–156v: Bede, *Homilia subditia* 48 on the prodigal son

Harrassowitz, 2004), 30, did not distinguish between different codicological parts for fols. 123–91.

Part VI
- 157r–161v: Homilies on John 1:1–14, Matthew 4:1–11, and Luke 18:9–14

Part VII
- 162r–167r: Decrees from capitularies by Pippin and Charlemagne on marriage[26]
- 167v: Blank
- 168r–v: End of Ps.-Augustine *sermo* 242 on the Creed (with 182r–83v)
- 168v–171v: Isidore of Seville, *De ecclesiasticis officiis* 1.17–18 (largely without rubrics) on the benediction of the people and the sacrifice of the Mass
- 171v–176r: Canons on marriage and baptism from the Councils of Epaone (chap. 30) and Tours (chap. 22)[27]
- 176r–180v: Sermon, dubiously attributed to Nicetas of Remesiana
- 180v–182r: Commentary on the Lord's Prayer
- 182r–183v: Ps.-Augustine *sermo* 242 on the Creed (with fol. 168r–v)

Part VIII
- 184r–191v: Life of St. Clement and a fragment of a homily on Matthew 11:2–10 on John the Baptist

---

26 Mordek lists excerpts from the *Decretum Compendiense* and *Decretum Vermeriense* on fols. 162r–164v, and the penitential of Pseudo-Theodore of Canterbury on fols. 164v–167r.

27 Mordek also lists the *Epitome Aegidii* of the *Lex Romana Visigothorum: Sententiae* of Paul 4.10 on the seven degrees of kinship (short version) on fols. 174v–175v. The identification of the councils is also his.

Personal Miscellany of an Imperial Minister: St. Gall, Stiftsbibliothek, Cod. Sang. 397[28]

This manuscript (210 × 160 mm [8.27 × 6.3 in.]) was considered by Bischoff to be the vademecum of Grimald, abbot of both St. Gall and Wissembourg, as well as imperial chaplain and chancellor to Louis the German, but this has been disputed by Uwe Grupp. Notes from other manuscripts indicate that the book was owned by Grimald, or that it was closely associated with him, but not necessarily that he was the compiler.[29] Grupp contended that the manuscript consists of two separate parts, both dating from c. 830–872, but united only after Grimald's death (in 872) at the very earliest. According to Grupp's analysis, there is no evidence that Grimald contracted the manuscript to be made, nor that he significantly influenced its contents, nor that he was one of its principal users.

Part I
- 1: Blank
- 2–4: *Laudes regiae*
- 5–16: Augustine, *De excidio urbis* and *sermo* 135, both incomplete
- 17: Blank

---

28 The list of contents for this manuscript is adapted from Uwe Grupp, "Der Codex Sangallensis 397 — ein persönliches Handbuch Grimalds von St. Gallen?," *Deutsches Archiv für Erforschung des Mittelalters* 70 (2014): 453–63, and Anton von Euw, *St. Galler Buchkunst vom 8. bis zum Ende des 11. Jahrhunderts*, vol. 1: *Textband*, Monasterium Sancti Galli 3 (St. Gall: Verlag am Klosterhof, 2008), 181. See also Gustav Scherrer, *Verzeichnis der Handschriften der Stiftsbibliothek von St. Gallen* (Halle: Verlag der Buchhandlung des Waisenhauses, 1875), 135–36, and Rolf Bergmann and Stephanie Stricker, *Katalog der althochdeutschen und altsächsischen Glossenhandschriften*, vol. 2 (Berlin: De Gruyter, 2005), 543–44.

29 Bernhard Bischoff, "Bücher am Hofe Ludwigs des Deutschen und die Privatbibliothek des Kanzlers Grimalt," in Bernhard Bischoff, *Mittelalterliche Studien: Ausgewählte Aufsätze zur Schriftkunde und Literaturgeschichte*, vol. 3 (Stuttgart: Anton Hiersemann, 1981), 199, 201, and Grupp, "Der Codex Sangallensis 397," 425–63.

- 18: Blessing of iron for trial by ordeal (*ordines iudiciorum Dei*) and annalistic notes
- 19: Blessing of water for trial by ordeal (*ordines iudiciorum Dei*)
- 20: Blank (with erasure)
- 21: Poem on the planets and five death notices
- 22: Two recipes, two notices of moon eclipses (860, 864), short mathematical working-out of "seventy times seven" from Matthew 18:22, and four death notices
- 23: Death notices, fragmentary note, and Julianus Pomerius, *De vita contemplativa* 2:5
- 24–25: *Libri computi* 4.29a and Greek alphabet
- 26: Egyptian days, names of the months, and winds from Einhard, *Vita Karoli*
- 27: Annalistic notes, Augustine, *In Iohannis evangelium tractatus* 46 and Julianus Pomerius, *De vita contemplativa* 2:5
- 28: Epitaph of Hildegard, Louis the German's daughter, and a death notice
- 29–33: Orosius, *De sex cogitationibus sanctorum*, Easter Proclamation with neumes, blessing of fire for trial by ordeal (*ordines iudiciorum Dei*), blessings of fire and incense, and foundation dedication of the Zurich Fraumünster church founded by Louis the German for his daughter Hildegard
- 34: Blank
- 35–36: Bede, *De temporum ratione* 19, *Libri computi* 1.2

Part II
- 37: Boethius, *Liber contra Eutychen* on substance and essence, Pseudo-Seneca, *De moribus* 30 and *Proverbia* 43–44
- 38–39: List of Greek names for charitable institutions, followed by a set of quotations from various sources — two on grammar, from Isidore of Seville, *Etymologiae* II, 26.11, and Alcuin, *Ars grammatica;* and two on baldness, from Ausonius, *Epigrammaton* 68, and Ovid, *Ars amatoria* III, verses 249–50

- 40–42: Glossary from Fulgentius, *Expositio sermonum antiquorum,* Isidore of Seville *Etymologiae* VI, 19.10–12 on song, and a second glossary
- 43–44: Ps.-Ausonius, epigram on the rose, and a verse on an oak shoot growing from a bone attributed to Grimald
- 45–47: Three interpretations of "alleluia," "amen," and "hosanna" from various sources, followed by several glossaries and glossographic notes
- 48–51: *Notitia Galliarum,* and continuation listing the names of other Roman provinces; and four monograms of the sons of Louis the German
- 52: Verse from Einhard's residence in the Aachen palace complex, which mentions Grimald, and Grimald's tombstone inscription
- 53: Excerpts from Alcuin, *Dialogus de rhetorica et virtutibus,* followed by short anonymous excerpts on the soul and virtue
- 54: Table for calculating the moon's sidereal orbital period
- 55–66: Calendar with death notices and astronomical notes
- 67–68: Ausonius, verses: two on selected months and star signs, one on the number of days, and one on the astrological signs; followed by the popular alliterative mnemonic poem *Nonae aprilis* for remembering the dates of the Easter full moons
- 69–70: Ausonius, verse on the 12 months, and a list for remembering kalends, nones, and ides of each month (*De kalendis, nonis et idibus*)
- 71–73: Tables for various astronomical calculations, and methods for calculating planetary intervals
- 74–78: Table for calculating planetary intervals, and Greek alphabet with alphanumeric values
- 79: Table listing various alphabetic characters and their different possible numeric values, and list of Greek diphthongs
- 80: List of ordinal and cardinal numbers, and Augustine, *Soliloquiorum,* Bk. 1.3 (prayer)

- 81–85: Short astronomical *argumenta,* and Alcuin, *Conflictus veris et hiemis,* which is immediately followed by part of a verse in praise of the Church Fathers by Isidore of Seville
- 86–98: Bede, *De computo vel loquela digitorum* and *De temporum ratione,* and a variety of computistical texts from the *Libellus annalis*
- 98–102: Bede, *De temporum ratione,* chaps. 46, 45, 38; *Liber calculationis,* chap. 86; and *Libri computi* 3.6
- 102–114: Extracts from the *Libri computi, Liber calculationis,* and *Libellus annalis*
- 114: Boniface, *Ars metrica* (extract on metrical feet, later addition)
- 115–119: On weights and measures, from the *Libri computi* 7.2–4
- 119–21: Extracts from verses by Ovid, Pentadius, and Priscian
- 121–22: Bede, *De temporum ratione,* chap. 4; Isidore of Seville, *Etymologiae* V, 31.4–14 (list of the seven divisions of the night);[30] anonymous proverb about love; and extract from Ps. 10:5 on overcoming enemies
- 132–40: Bede, *De natura rerum* (partial) and *Libri computi* 7.1
- 141–44: Bede, *Chronicon breve* (excerpt of his *De temporum ratione,* also known as the Chronica maiora), also part of *Libri computi* 1.5, and list of the kinds of nymphs
- 145: Ps.-Ovid, short metrical preface to the *Argumenta Aeneidis* and the first lines of each of its twelve books, and excerpt from Martial, *De habitatione ruris*
- 146: *Libri computi* 4.29a, and a short note, possibly a caption for a miniature[31]

---

30 The partially cut-off marginal gloss read "*crepusculum*" (twilight) — the second division given by Isidore that seems to have been accidentally omitted from the main text and inserted into the margin instead. The eighth listed division is "*aurora*" (dawn), which is not technically part of Isidore's seven divisions but rather an additional category from his text.

31 Bischoff, "Bücher am Hofe," 206.

- 147: Calendrical poem ("Fonte lavat genitor [...]"); Ps.-Ausonius, *Catonis de musis versus* on the muses, and Isidore, *Etymologiae* III, 19.1, on the divisions of music
- 148: Several excerpts from Isidore, *Etymologiae* II, 25.1, on Porphyry's *Isagoge*, and II, 26.5–6, on Aristotle's *Categories*, as well as two unreadable passages (one of them possibly a list of bishops' names)

Partially Surviving Handbook on Monastic Virtue from Imperial Circles: Vatican City, Biblioteca Apostolica Vaticana, MS Reg. lat. 339 + St. Gall, Kantonsbibliothek, Vadianische Sammlung, MS 317[32]

Two parts of these multi-part manuscripts were identified by Bischoff as forming another vademecum from the circle of Grimald (the other is St. Gall, Stb, Cod. Sang. 397), copied in St. Gall in the second third of the ninth century.[33] The codicological and paleographical evidence for their unity is supported by a list of books from Grimald's private library, which gives texts present in both manuscript parts: "Books of Valerian, Bishop of Cimiez, and a text on the life of Charles the emperor, and the admonitions of St. Basil in one *sceda*."[34] The Vatican manuscript was assembled by Melchior Goldast in the sixteenth or seventeenth century from fragments of six other manuscripts. Part II of this manuscript is 227 × 177/180 mm (8.94 × 6.97/7.09

---

32 Bernhard Bischoff, *Katalog der festländischen Handschriften des neunten Jahrhunderts (mit Ausnahme der wisigotischen)*, vol. 3: *Padua-Zwickau*, ed. Birgit Ebersperger (Wiesbaden: Harrassowitz, 2014), 428–29.

33 Bischoff, *Mittelalterliche Studien* 3, 199. See also Matthias M. Tischler, *Einharts Vita Karoli. Studien zur Entstehung, Überlieferung und Rezeption*, Schriften der Monumenta Germaniae Historica 48 (Hanover: Hahn, 2001), vol. 1, 215.

34 "Librum Valerii Cimilensis episcopi et de vita Karoli imperatoris et admonitiones sancti Basilii in una sceda." The list is preserved on pp. 30–32 of St. Gall, Stiftsbibliothek, Cod. Sang. 267 (the relevant entry is on p. 32). Edited in Paul Ruf, Sigrid Krämer, and Christine Elisabeth Ineighen-Eder, eds., *Mittelalterliche Bibliothekskataloge Deutschlands und der Schweiz*, vol. 1 (Munich: Beck, 1918), 89, ll. 24–26.

in.) in size. It formed the beginning of the original vademecum, though the bifolium comprising folios 7 and 14 was replaced in the eleventh century.[35] It was copied by three hands, of which one (hand 2) also copied parts of the Pseudo-Basil text in the Vadiana manuscript. The Vadiana manuscript (230 × 180 mm [9.06 × 7.09 in.]) is also composed of six different parts, dating to the ninth and tenth centuries, and bound together around 1460 with two dividing paper bifolia. According to Bischoff, only part I of this manuscript, containing the pseudo-Basil text, belonged to the original vademecum. However, Susan Rankin noted that part VII matches part I in dimensions, number of lines, and ruling, and was copied by a similar hand to that of the Pseudo-Basil text.[36] Its contents also seem to match the hypothetical vademecum, which focuses on monastic virtue. I therefore include part VII in this discussion.

Vatican, Biblioteca Apostolica Vaticana, MS Reg. lat. 339; Part II
- 7r: Carolingian genealogy
- 7v–12r: Augustine, *De bono disciplinae* (author given as Valerian of Cemele)
- 12r–15v: Isidore of Seville, *Sententiarum libri tres,* four chapters: on priests, the principles of justice, patience, and law (3.48–51)
- 16r–18v: Sermon for the feast of the Archangel Michael
- 19r: Glossary on Prudentius, *Psychomachia* (tenth- or eleventh-century addition)
- 19v–38v: Einhard, *Vita Karoli Magni*

---

35 Rolf Bergmann and Stefanie Stricker, eds., *Katalog der althochdeutschen und altsächsischen Glossenhandschriften* (Berlin: De Gruyter, 2005), vol. 4, 1565–69, no. 821, 1–3, and André Wilmart, *Codices Reginenses Latini. II: Codices, 251–500* (Vatican City: Biblioteca Apostolica Vaticana, 1945), 263–67.

36 Susan Rankin, "The Earliest Sources of Notker's Sequences: St. Gallen, Vadiana 317, and Paris, Bibliothèque nationale lat. 10587," *Early Music History* 10 (1991): 208.

St. Gall, Kantonsbibliothek, Vadianische Sammlung, MS 317;
Part I
- 1r–13r: Pseudo-Basil of Caesarea, *Admonitio ad filium spiritualem*
- 13r: Isidore of Seville, *Etymologiae* XI, 1.13, on memory
- 13v–15v: Notker the Stammerer, six sequences with some neumes (early tenth-century addition)[37]
- 15v: Boethius, *Consolatio philosophiae,* Bk. 3, carmen 7, lines 1–6. In the same hand as the sequences; only a stub remains of the subsequent folio (last of the quire)

Part VII
- 70r–77v: Cassiodorus, *De anima,* chaps. 1–4

Personal Handbook of a Travelling Schoolmaster: Bern, Burgerbibliothek, MS lat. 363[38]

Giorgia Vocino has demonstrated that this travel-sized manuscript (240 × 185 mm [9.45 × 7.28 in.]) was copied and annotated by a schoolmaster in the circle of Sedulius Scottus in the mid-ninth century.[39] Although the texts in the manuscript are related to the liberal arts curriculum, it is clear that they were not intended for classroom use, but rather as a personal book. There is some internal evidence to suggest that the contents were compiled over time and in different locations (northeastern Francia and northern Italy), although there appear to be no codico-

---

37 On the musical contents of this manuscript, see Susan Rankin, "The Earliest Sources of Notker's Sequences," 205 and 209n20.
38 Described in Simona Gavinelli, "Per un'enciclopedia carolingia (Codice Bernese 363)," *Italia medioevale e umanistica* 26 (1983), 1–26, and Bernhard Bischoff, "Bücher am Hofe Ludwigs des Deutschen und die Privatbibliothek des Kanzlers Grimalt," in *Mittelalterliche Studien. Ausgewählte Aufsätze zur Schriftkunde und Literaturgeschichte,* vol. 3 (Stuttgart, 1981), 187–212. This manuscript has not been digitized.
39 Giorgia Vocino, "A Peregrinus's Vade Mecum: MS Bern 363 and the 'Circle of Sedulius Scottus,'" in *The Annotated Book in the Early Middle Ages,* ed. Mariken Teeuwen and Irene van Renswoude, Utrecht Studies in Medieval Literacy 38 (Turnhout: Brepols, 2017), 87–123.

logical caesuras. The annotations indicate that the compiler and scribe was very interested in contemporary debates, and that he may have known some of the nobles and clerics involved.

- 2r–27v: Servius, commentary on Virgil's *Eclogues* (with a lacuna at 1.37–2.11)
- 27v–28r: Epitaphs of Terence, Virgil, and Lucan; and epigrams by Eugenius of Toledo
- 28r–58r: Servius, commentary on Virgil's *Georgics*
- 58r: A life of Virgil
- 58r–143r: Servius, commentary on Virgil's *Aeneid* (stops at Bk. 7.12)
- 143r–153v: Consultus Fortunatianus, *Ars rhetorica*
- 153v–160v: Augustine, *De dialectica*
- 160v–165v: Augustine, *De rhetorica*
- 165v–166v: Clodianus, *Ars rhetorica de statibus*
- 167r–186v: Horace, *Odes* (with extracts from Pseudo-Acron's metrical commentary)
- 187r–188v: Ovid, *Metamorphoses* (excerpts)
- 188v–194r: Bede, *Historia ecclesiastica* (preface; list of chapters; Bk. I, chaps. 1–27)
- 194v–197v: Carolingian poems
- 195r: Priscian, *De laude Anastasii imperatoris* (verses 1–44)
- 195r–196r, 197r, 197v, 1v: Dioscorides, lists of chapters to *De materia medica,* Bks. 2–5

Features of Personal Handbooks
In summary, these are the nine vademecums of this case-study:

WHAT IS A VADEMECUM?

Manuscript	Owner
1. St. Gall, Stb, Cod. Sang. 222	Anonymous bishop
2. Munich, BSb, MS Clm 6426	Abraham of Freising
3. St. Gall, Stb, Cod. Sang. 878	Walahfrid Strabo
4. Vatican City, BAV, MS Vat. lat. 3852	Florus of Lyons
5. Paris, BnF, MS lat.15679	Theodulf of Orléans
6. Laon, BmSM, MS 265	Martin of Laon
7. St. Gall, Stb, Cod. Sang. 397	Grimald
8. Vatican City, BAV, MS Reg. lat. 339 + St. Gall, Stb, Cod. Sang. 317	Grimald
9. Bern, Bb, MS 363	Irish schoolmaster from the circle of Sedulius Scottus

Table. 9.1. The nine vademecums of this case study.

As is the nature of lists, this list of manuscripts elicits the desire to systematize, that is, to situate these handbooks within the known output of other individuals, both named and unnamed. There are, after all, a great many other manuscripts which might qualify as personal handbooks, as recent research has shown.[40] Why not include them? The terminology also seems dissatisfactory: although I have focused on "vademecums," "handbooks," or "manuals," other labels — "collectaneum," for example — can arguably also refer to "personal" manuscripts. But "collectaneum" is an even vaguer term than "vademecum." Indeed, the two well-known *collectanea* of named Carolingian scholars are problematic in this context. The *collectaneum* of Hadoard of Corbie in Vatican City, Biblioteca Apostolica Vaticana, MS Reg. lat. 1762 has recently been shown not to be associated with him or with any other Carolingian intellectual project, while the *collectaneum* of Heiric of Auxerre in Vatican City, Biblioteca Apostolica Vaticana, MS Vat. lat. 4929 was not necessarily compiled

---

40 Steffen Patzold and Carine van Rhijn, eds., *Men in the Middle: Local Priests in Early Medieval Europe* (Berlin: De Gruyter, 2016).

or directed by him.⁴¹ The terminology is ultimately not the issue, or rather, it reflects a similarly hard-to-define manuscript corpus. As the above list shows, a personal manuscript is essentially a miscellany, and the selection parameters of any medieval miscellany can be adjusted *ad infinitum* to produce more or less different lists of volumes. Miscellanies simply do not fit categories neatly, a problem that I have discussed elsewhere.⁴² The way out of this dilemma must be to consider the social logic behind the idea of an early medieval vademecum. In what way are some books more personal than other books, and *why* are they more personal? The following analysis raises three principal problems of personal books associated with multi-part codicology, autograph writing, and the planning of text contents, and discusses opportunities to advance the debate in useful directions.

1. Multi-Part Codicology

Seven of the nine manuscripts (with the exception of Bern, Bb, MS 363 and St. Gall, Stb, Cod. Sang. 222) are composed of multiple codicological parts which were copied by multiple scribes. Five of them were demonstrably compiled over a considerable period of time: decades, in the case of St. Gall, Stb, Cod. Sang. 878. It is clear that the compilation process of personal hand-

---

41 Clara Auvray-Assayas, "Qui est Hadoard? Une réévaluation du manuscrit Reg. lat. 1762 de la Bibliothèque Vaticane," *Revue d'histoire des textes* 8 (2013): 307–38; Claude W. Barlow, "Codex Vaticanus Latinus 4929," *Memoirs of the American Academy Rome* 15 (1939): 87–124; Giuseppe Billanovich, "Dall'antica Ravenna alle biblioteche umanistiche," *Aevum* 30 (1956): 319–62; and Jacqueline Hamesse, "Les florilèges philosophiques, instruments de travail des intellectuels à la fin du moyen âge et à la Renaissance," in *Filosofia e teologia nel Trecento: Studi in ricordo di Eugenio Randi,* ed. Luca Bianchi, Textes et Études du Moyen Âge 1 (Turnhout: Brepols, 1994), 479–508. Billanovich made the suggestion that Heiric compiled Vatican, City, BAV, MS Vat. lat. 4929, but this appears to be a supposition not positively supported by the evidence presented by Barlow.

42 Anna Dorofeeva, "Miscellanies, Christian Reform and Early Medieval Encyclopaedism: A Reconsideration of the Pre-Bestiary *Physiologus* Manuscripts," *Historical Research* 90, no. 250 (2017): 665–82, and Dorofeeva, "Reading Early Medieval Miscellanies."

books often took a long time to complete, that it was usually a group effort, and that the physical composition of the manuscript was therefore modular, that is, made of several parts, which could be (and sometimes, though not always, were) rearranged.[43]

However, these features are not exclusive to personal handbooks. The physical structure of any manuscript could also be altered at any time, by anyone, thereby changing how it was to be read. This is especially clear from the *scheda (sceda, ceda, schedula)*, "a strip of wood or papyrus," or "a small leaf or page."[44] Grimald's personal list of books, which describes Vatican, Biblioteca Apostolica Vaticana, MS Reg. lat. 339 + St. Gall, Kantonsbibliothek, Vadianische Sammlung, MS 317 as being "in una sceda," probably refers to the method of storing unbound

---

43 This has been observed by G.D. Hobson for medieval bindings, which were often many decades or even centuries younger than the manuscripts themselves: Geoffrey D. Hobson, *English Binding Before 1500* (Cambridge: Cambridge University Press, 1927), 56. In the interests of space, I have omitted a fuller discussion here about manuscript modularity and booklets, which has a very rich scholarly history and has been thoroughly studied especially in Pamela R. Robinson, "'The Booklet': A Self-Contained Unit in Composite Manuscripts," *Codicologica* 3 (1980): 46–69, repr. *The History of the Book in the West: 400 AD–1455*, ed. P.R. Robinson and J. Roberts, The History of the Book in the West: A Library of Critical Essays 1 (London: Routledge, 2016), 159–82; Patrick Andrist, Paul Canart, and Marilena Maniaci, *La syntaxe du codex: essai de codicologie structurale*, Bibliologia 34 (Turnhout: Brepols, 2013); and Johann Peter Gumbert, "Codicological Units: Towards a Terminology for the Stratigraphy of the Non-Homogeneous Codex," in *Il Codice Miscellaneo: Tipologie e funzioni. Atti del Convegno internazionale, Cassino, 14–17 Maggio 2003*, ed. Edoardo Crisci and Oronzo Pecere, Segno e Testo 2 (Turnhout: Brepols, 2004), 17–42. See also Brandon W. Hawk, *Preaching Apocrypha in Anglo-Saxon England*, Toronto Anglo-Saxon Series 30 (Toronto: University of Toronto Press, 2018), chap. 1, for a discussion of preaching collections.

44 Charlton T. Lewis and Charles Short, *A Latin Dictionary: Founded on Andrews' Edition of Freund's Latin Dictionary* (Oxford: Clarendon Press, 1879), s.v. *scida*. *Sceda* was also used to refer to something composed hastily or informally, and to the single sheets of papyrus or parchment on which charters were written (as in British Library, Stowe Charter 31): Mary Carruthers, *The Book of Memory: A Study of Memory in Medieval Cultures* (Cambridge: Cambridge University Press, 2008), 411n148.

or loosely bound quires within a folded sheet of parchment; but in general, the word refers to small sheets, often bound or sewn with the regular folios in a book, though sometimes left loose, as with textual amulets.[45] A range of *schedae* are still extant in early medieval manuscripts. The insertion of glosses was an important function of such sheets, as is apparent from a few manuscripts: a ninth-century copy of Priscian from Corbie, which was bound with *schedae* containing glosses by the principal glossator of the manuscript;[46] a ninth-century copy of the works of Virgil made in St. Amand, containing a *scheda* with additional glosses that would not have fit on the main page;[47] and an early eleventh-century, northern Italian copy of Virgil's Aeneid, glossed with Servius partly in the margins, partly on *schedae*.[48]

But the addition of glosses was not the only function of such leaves. One late eighth-century Irish copy of Matthew's Gospel contains ninth-century *schedae* which, though probably made for another Gospel codex, were carefully selected for their size and shape to receive pieces of commentary on the text, and were intended to be read with the full pages next to which they were bound.[49] A second eighth-century, Irish manuscript contains a

---

45 This use is distinct from the composition of texts on small sheets of parchment. Claudius of Turin, for example, compiled his Chronicle using notes on such slips: see Warren Pezé, "The Making of the *De Praedestinatione* of Ratramnus of Corbie (Including the Identification of a New Personal Manuscript)," in *The Annotated Book in the Early Middle Ages: Practices of Reading and Writing*, ed. Mariken Teeuwen and Irene van Renswoude, Utrecht Studies in Medieval Literacy 38 (Turnhout: Brepols, 2017), 148. Similarly, Hadoard of Corbie noted the numerous selections of his famous collection of Classical excerpts on wax tablets. On Grimald's manuscript, see Susan Rankin, "The Earliest Sources of Notker's Sequences," 209.

46 Paris, Bibliothèque nationale de France, MS lat. 7501. See Franck Cinato, *"Accessus ad Priscianum*. De Jean Scot Érigène a Létald de Micy," *Archivum Latinitatis Medii Aevi* 70 (2012): 27–90.

47 Valenciennes, Bibliothèque municipale, MS 407 (389), 17bis.

48 Basel, Universitätsbibliothek, F II 23: https://www.e-codices.unifr.ch/en/list/one/ubb/F-II-0023.

49 Würzburg, Universitätsbibliothek, MS M.p.th.f.61, http://vb.uni-wuerzburg.de/ub/mpthf61/index.html. See Michael Cahill, "The Würzburg Matthew: *status quaestionis*," *Peritia* 16 (2002): 1–25.

single *scheda,* inserted between fols. 8 and 9 as an extension of the previous page with an omitted part of the text.[50] Similarly, a ninth-century manuscript from Flavigny contains the accidentally omitted conclusion to Cassiodorus's commentary on Psalm 130 (131 in the Septuagint numbering) in a *scheda,* formatted as a miniature page with margins and ruling.[51] In a Luxeuil codex, a *scheda* (fol. 14ᵃ) containing an extract from Cassiodorus's commentary on the Psalms, with an explanation of the trembling of the Earth from Psalm 96 (97 in the Septuagint numbering), was inserted next to texts on land surveying by Julius Frontinus and Agennius Urbicus.[52] This manuscript was copied by a single scribe, the monk-priest Constantius, who left a subscription in which he stated that he completed the work within eleven days between June 15 and 26, 1004, at the command of his abbot Milo. The thematic association resulting from the juxtaposition of the Psalm commentary with land surveying is original to the compiler of this manuscript (whether Constantius or Milo). Other manuscripts with *schedae* await codicological study.[53]

---

50 Basel, Universitätsbibliothek, MS F III 15d: https://www.e-codices.unifr.ch/en/list/one/ubb/F-III-0015d.
51 Autun, Bibliothèque municipale, MS S 022 (020 A), fol. 191r–v: https://bvmm.irht.cnrs.fr/mirador/index.php?manifest=https://bvmm.irht.cnrs.fr/iiif/21896/manifest.
52 Bern, Burgerbibliothek, MS 87: https://www.e-codices.unifr.ch/en/list/one/bbb/0087. Constantius's subscription is on fol. 17v.
53 Among them are Angers, Bibliothèque municipale, MS Rés. 91, a tenth-century sacramentary from western France or Brittany, which contains two *schedae* after fol. 255 (https://commulysse.angers.fr/ark:/54380/a011504254863VZPMmB/e8cf7ecc9a), and Vatican City, Biblioteca Apostolica Vaticana, MS Pal. lat. 1341, a Lorsch manuscript from the second half of the tenth century which contains Helperic of Grandval's popular *Liber de computo* with two *schedae* after fols. 95 and 99 (https://bibliotheca-laureshamensis-digital.de/bav/bav_pal_lat_1341 and https://digi.vatlib.it/view/bav_pal_lat_1341). Some early medieval manuscripts also had *schedae* inserted in later centuries, indicating that this was a continuous practice. See, for example, Paris, Bibliothèque nationale de France, MS lat. 9085, fol. 26r, https://gallica.bnf.fr/ark:/12148/btv1b10511073x, and Paris, Bibliothèque nationale de France, MS lat. 9433, fols. 138, 156, 183: https://gallica.bnf.fr/ark:/12148/btv1b8479011k/f9.item.

Thus, although the insertion of *schedae* may have followed different practices, both codicologically and textually, in Insular and continental book-making centers, their main effect was always to introduce another layer of selection into the manuscript. This was the case even for those *schedae* that simply supplied an accidentally omitted part of the text, since their inclusion represented an editorial choice. Such *schedae* suggest that textual selection was routinely undertaken at various stages in the creation of a manuscript, and by different people. The relationship between the text and its material support in early medieval codices was therefore fluid and dependent on the social logic of the manuscript.

In fact, the existence of a codex composed entirely of *schedae* highlights the problem of the idea of "private" books. Paris, Bibliothèque nationale de France, MS lat. 2718 was copied on very short, wide scraps of parchment left over from large sheets used for charters. Produced at Tours, it is a typical legal, theological, and administrative handbook evidently hastily compiled for the needs of a large center handling not only its own daily affairs but also work for the chancery of Louis the Pious.[54] Manuscripts like this one and like Laon, BmSM, MS 265, which originally may have been kept as booklets, perhaps survived as bound volumes precisely because of the utility of their contents to others, while private or individual notes were lost like the more ephemeral supports on which they were written.[55]

2. Autograph Writing

The hands of the presumed owners can be positively identified in five of the manuscripts. Their direct intervention ranges from a few marginal annotations (Paris, BnF, MS lat. 15679) or a single

---

54 David Ganz, "Paris BN Latin 2718: Theological Texts in the Chapel and the Chancery of Louis the Pious," in *Scientia veritatis: Festschrift für Hubert Mordek zum 65. Geburtstag,* ed. Oliver Münsch and Thomas Zotz (Ostfildern: Thorbecke, 2004), 137–52.

55 I am grateful to Jesse Keskiaho for comments that informed this discussion.

text (Munich, BSb, MS Clm 6426; Laon, BmSM, MS 265) in one or two codicological parts, to a large number of texts throughout the various parts (St. Gall, Stb, Cod. Sang. 878) or the whole manuscript (Vatican City, BAV, Vat. lat. 3852). Evidently, some level of personal participation tended to occur in the production of early medieval individuals' handbooks. It may have been standard practice among professionally literate men and women directing a writing project. Autograph handwriting is indisputably valuable for understanding individuals' interests and intellectual practices (and it is even more important in diplomatic than in manuscript studies). But, as these codices demonstrate, an autograph hand did not automatically make a manuscript a personal handbook (as with Paris 15679), nor was it the only criterion necessary for a manuscript to qualify as a personal handbook (as with Munich 6426). Autograph writing as an indicator of authorship, ownership, or celebrity is not an early medieval phenomenon. It is, moreover, problematic as a tool for the identification and study of personal handbooks, since the vast majority of early medieval scribes are unnamed or unidentified.

3. Planned Contents

Thematic and other patterns are evident in some of the manuscripts listed above, but there is little commonality across the group, except the usual commonality of popular works by patristic authors such as Augustine, Isidore, and Jerome. Despite this, almost every manuscript shows evidence of extensive planning that defies sometimes chaotic production circumstances. This is the case with Munich, BSb, MS Clm 6426. It seems to have traveled extensively in several different pieces, and different groups of scribes added to all of these pieces over at least thirteen years. Yet the manuscript is carefully structured around its core topics: sermons, particularly those on Easter and Christmas, and other texts pertinent to Abraham's life and work (property notes, episcopal and pastoral works in Slavic and Latin, and excerpts on subjects related to Freising). The selection and organization of the contents for this and other handbooks leads to another important observation. Although the contents of St. Gall, Stb, Cod. Sang. 878 and Bern, Bb, MS 363, which are the closest thing on the list to personal notebooks, were clearly guided by an individual's interests, they are not intimate collections. As John Contreni has pointed out, St. Gall, Stb, Cod. Sang. 878 seems to have been intended (presumably by its compiler Walahfrid) for the use of more than one person.[56] In fact, there is very little in its contents that is inconsistent with the interests of Walahfrid's wider ninth-century intellectual context. The manuscript could easily be used by another scholar, and to judge from the additions it received up to at least the thirteenth century, it was.

The purposes for which these handbooks were intended do tend to be consistent with the professional activity of the individuals who directed their production. Classroom texts predominate in manuscripts produced by or for teachers. Martin of Laon may not have directed the production of the vademecum in our case-study, but he did direct the compilation of Laon, BmSM, MS 468, a teaching manual which, on his death in 875, passed to the two schoolmasters who succeeded him: Bernard, followed by Adelelm. The contents of Bern, Bb, MS 363 are strongly focused on the contemporary literary and linguistic canon, indicating that its owner, whether or not he was a schoolmaster, required these texts to fulfill a professional function among the literate elite. Walahfrid, a monk and keeper of the monastic garden, copied texts on astronomy, history, medicine, rhetoric, computus, and grammar (St. Gall, Stb, Cod. Sang. 878), topics that were the basis of learning in early medieval monasteries. Priests and bishops reproduced pastoral, liturgical, moral, dogmatic, and ecclesiastical texts (Vatican City, BAV, MS Reg. lat. 339 + St. Gall, Stb, Cod. Sang. 317; St. Gall, Stb, Cod. Sang. 222; and Munich, BSb, MS Clm 6426). In fact, the number of manuscripts made by or for priests, named and anonymous, is very large, and their

---

56 John J. Contreni, review of *Rhetoric and Reckoning in the Ninth Century: The Vademecum of Walahfrid Strabo,* by Wesley M. Stevens, *The Medieval Review,* June 18, 2020, https://scholarworks.iu.edu/journals/index.php/tmr/article/view/31090.

production seems to have begun earlier than other handbooks: among eighth-century local priests' handbooks are the Bobbio Missal and a Burgundian codex now in Brussels (although this may also be simply due to the randomness of survival).[57] Medical handbooks like St. Gall, Stiftsbibliothek, Cod. Sang. 761, and St. Gall, Stiftsbibliothek, Cod. Sang. 217 + fragment collection 1396, also form a separate category.[58]

However, this correlation between an individual's profession and their handbook indicates only that teachers, doctors,

---

57 Brussels, Bibliothèque royale de Belgique, MS 10127–10144, http://belgica.kbr.be/fr/coll/ms/ms10127_44_fr.html. On these late eighth-century books from Burgundy, see Yitzhak Hen, "A Liturgical Handbook for the Use of a Rural Priest (Brussels BR 10127–10144)," in *Organizing the Written Word: Scripts, Manuscripts and Texts. Proceedings of the First Utrecht Symposium on Medieval Literacy*, ed. Marco Mostert, Utrecht Studies in Medieval Literacy 30 (Turnhout: Brepols, 2022); the manuscript seems to agree with Carolingian prescriptions on what priests should know. Bobbio Missal (Paris, Bibliothèque nationale de France, MS lat. 13246): http://archivesetmanuscrits.bnf.fr/ark:/12148/cc743249. Yitzhak Hen, "The Church in Sixth-Century Gaul," in *A Companion to Gregory of Tours*, ed. Alexander C. Murray (Leiden: Brill, 2015), 250, stated that it is undoubtedly a vademecum. On priests' books in the early Middle Ages: Steffen Patzold and Carine van Rhijn, eds., *Men in the Middle: Local Priests in Early Medieval Europe* (Berlin: De Gruyter, 2016); Carine van Rhijn, *Leading the Way to Heaven: Pastoral Care and Salvation in the Carolingian Period*, The Medieval World (London: Routledge, 2022); and Steffen Patzold, *Presbyter: Moral, Mobilität und die Kirchenorganisation im Karolingerreich*, Monographien zur Geschichte des Mittelalters 68 (Stuttgart: Anton Hiersemann, 2020).

58 Augusto Beccaria, *I codici di medicina del periodo presalernitano* (Rome: Ed. di Storia e Letteratura, 1956), 19, called Vatican City, BAV, Stb, Cod. Sang 761 a "vademecum tascabile probabilmente per l'utilizzazione personale": "a portable vademecum probably for personal use." Vatican City, BAV, Stb, Cod. Sang 761: https://www.e-codices.unifr.ch/en/list/one/csg/0761. Vatican City, BAV, Stb, Cod. Sang 217: https://www.e-codices.unifr.ch/en/list/one/csg/0217. See Luanne Meagher, "The Gellius Manuscript of Lupus of Ferrières" (PhD Diss., University of Chicago, 1936), and Peter Köpp, ed., *Vademecum eines frühmittelalterlichen Arztes. Die gefaltete lateinische Handschrift medizinischen Inhalts im Codex 217 und der Fragmentensammlung 1396 der Stiftsbibliothek in St. Gallen*, Veröffentlichungen der Schweizerischen Gesellschaft für Geschichte der Medizin und der Naturwissenschaften 34 (Aarau: Sauerländer, 1980).

priests, and monks needed books to carry out some of their tasks. It is evident from the case-study manuscripts discussed here that there is a much stronger correlation between these books and wide-ranging networks of people rather than single individuals. The implications of this finding are discussed in the final section of this chapter.

A further problem that arises from the case-study manuscripts is that some of them were probably not made by or for those people who ended up using them as handbooks, whether in whole or in part (Laon, BmSM, MS 265; St. Gall, Stb, Cod. Sang. 397; and Vatican City, BAV, MS Reg. lat. 339 + St. Gall, Stb, Cod. Sang. 317). This was evidently not a problem for their early medieval users, but it is for us. What is personal about a handbook, if not in the texts that one carefully compiles for oneself? Yet the inherent recyclability of early medieval textual material for contemporary readers applied to handbooks too. These "inherited" handbooks underscore the importance of early medieval networks and communal contexts even for personal or individual modes of reading. As we shall see below, this ties in with the idea of social logic.

A final remark needs to be made about the role of women in the production and ownership of vademecums in the early Middle Ages. Although the evidence is scant, that which does exist complicates the picture of intellectual authority in handbooks in interesting ways. The eighth-century Ragyndrudis Codex is one example of a manuscript commissioned by a woman: the eponymous Ragyndrudis, a nun in the Main river valley.[59]

---

59 Fulda, Hochschul- und Landesbibliothek Fulda, MS 100 Bonifatianus 2 (also known as the Ragyndrudis Codex): https://fuldig.hs-fulda.de/viewer/!thumbs/PPN438486781/1/. Described in Regina Hausmann, *Die theologischen Handschriften der Hessischen Landesbibliothek Fulda bis zum Jahr 1600. Codices Bonifatiani 1–3, Aa 1–145a* (Wiesbaden: Harrassowitz, 1992), 7–10, and Lutz von Padberg and Hans-Walter Stork, eds., *Der Ragyndrudis-Codex des Hl. Bonifatius* (Paderborn: Bonifatius Druck-Buch-Verlag, 1994). Although fol. 2v names Aodulf, Wilhelm Levison suggested that this refers to Athuolf: see Günther Haseloff, "Der Einband des Ragyndrudis-Codex in Fulda—Codex Bonifatianus 2," in *Von der Klosterbibliothek zur Landesbibliothek: Beiträge zum zweihundertjährigen*

Her father Athuolf is listed in the manuscript as an owner, presumably before passing it on to the missionary (and later saint) Boniface. Ragyndrudis may have had the manuscript made for Boniface. The codex is a short miscellany of fourteen texts outlining and explaining the Catholic faith. Some dry-point glosses in the margins may have been made by Boniface himself. The volume may have been one of three manuscripts in his personal possession at the time of his martyrdom. The other two are a Gospel harmony and a pocket-sized Gospel (discussed below). As a group, these books are extremely well suited for the working requirements of a traveling missionary.[60] Did Ragyndrudis direct the contents of a book intended for someone else, and were these contents, as Felice Lifshitz believed, at least partly shaped by local female intellectual interests?[61] If so, this manuscript is an example of a handbook whose contents were the result of a social consensus — in which women played a pivotal role — on what texts it was suitable for a missionary to carry.

Did Vademecums Exist in the Early Middle Ages?

In order to answer this question, we must begin with the interesting problem of manuscript size. Most of the volumes discussed here fall within a taille (height + width) range of 320–490 mm (12.6–19.3 in.), which characterizes small/medium ninth- and

---

Bestehen der Hessischen Landesbibliothek Fulda, ed. Artur Brall, Bibliothek des Buchwesens 6 (Stuttgart: Anton Hiersemann, 1978), 46. See also Felice Lifshitz, *Religious Women in Early Carolingian Francia: A Study of Manuscript Transmission and Monastic Culture,* Fordham Series in Medieval Studies (New York: Fordham University Press, 2014), 31. I am very grateful to Rosamond McKitterick and Lutz von Padberg for their material help and useful discussions about this manuscript, and I owe a great debt to Matthew Hussey for enabling my access to some images of this codex before it was digitized.

60 Fulda, Hochschul- und Landesbibliothek Fulda, MS 100 Bonifatianus 1 or the Victor Codex: https://fuldig.hs-fulda.de/viewer/!thumbs/PPN325289808/1/, and Fulda, Hochschul- und Landesbibliothek Fulda, MS 100 Bonifatianus 3 or the Cadmug Gospel, https://fuldig.hs-fulda.de/viewer/!thumbs/PPN325292043/1/.

61 Lifshitz, *Religious Women in Early Carolingian Francia,* 31.

tenth-century manuscripts according to the criteria developed by Bozzolo and Ornato.[62] The taille of all of these is also between 20 and 143 mm (.79 and 5.63 in) less than 480 mm (18.9 in.), the average taille of Western manuscripts copied between the fourth and the tenth centuries.[63] As with any manuscript group, this one also has outliers. Only one of the volumes listed above — St. Gall, Stiftsbibliothek, Cod. Sang. 222 — has a small taille under 320 mm (12.6 in.). Similarly, only one volume — Paris, Bibliothèque nationale de France, MS lat. 15679 — has a medium/large taille of 510 mm [20.08 in.] (the range for this category is 491–670 mm [19.33–26.38 in.]). Nevertheless, these numbers suggest that personal manuscripts tended to be compact and therefore easily portable.

But are small manuscripts personal because they are portable, or portable because they are personal? Hyper-portability may have been an important criterion for some Insular manuscripts. Chief among them are Irish "pocket-book" Gospels, which are unusually small and include the Book of Armagh (195 × 145 mm [7.68 × 5.71 in]), the Book of Deer (157 × 108 mm [6.18 × 4.25 in.]), the Book of Dimma (175 × 142 mm [6.89 × 5.6 in.]), the Book of Mulling (165 × 120 mm [6.5 × 4.72 in.]), the Cadmug Gospel (125 × 100 mm [5.9 × 3.93 in.]), the St. Cuthbert Gospel (137 × 95 mm [5.39 × 3.74 in]), and the Stowe St. John

---

62 Carla Bozzolo and Ezio Ornato, *Pour une histoire du livre manuscrit au Moyen Âge: Trois essais de codicologie quantitative,* Equipe de recherche sur l'humanisme français, Textes et études 2 (Paris: CNRS, 1980), 265. See also Ezio Ornato, "The Application of Quantitative Methods to the History of the Book," in *The Oxford Handbook of Latin Palaeography,* ed. Frank T. Coulson and Robert G. Babcock (Oxford: Oxford University Press, 2020): 650–68. Manuscript taille is also discussed in the contribution by Evina Stein in this volume.

63 Marilena Maniaci, "Costruzione e gestione dello spazio scritto fra Oriente e Occidente: principi generali e soluzioni specifiche," in *Scrivere e leggere nell'alto Medioevo,* Settimane di studio del Centro italiano di studi sull'alto Medioevo 59 (Spoleto: Centro Italiano di Studi sull'Alto Medioevo, 2012), 484. For further discussion of manuscript size in the early Middle Ages, see the essay by Evina Stein in this volume.

(150 × 120 mm [5.9 × 4.72 in.]).[64] There is some evidence that such small books were private vademecums: they contain significant abbreviations as well as diagrammatic layouts appropriate for silent reading; some Gospels, like the Book of Armagh and Cuthbert Gospel, were later kept in satchels, raising the possibility that these replaced earlier personal book-bags like those around the necks of the Evangelist portraits in the Book of Deer; and some (the Cuthbert Gospel, Stowe St. John, and Book of Dimma) were probably at first stand-alone copies of the Gospel of John, while in the Book of Deer John's is the only unabridged text — probably due to its importance for private devotional reading and study (see below on the importance of John's Gospel as a talisman).[65]

Such small, personal Gospels were therefore an essential part of the missionary and private religious tool-kit of Insular *peregrini* (who travelled alone or in small groups). A *peregrinus* could, of course, also work as a copyist. In the colophon of the Stowe St. John (fol. 11r), for example, the scribe describes himself as a *peregrinus*. But the social logic of the text suggests that the small size of these Gospel books had less to do with their nature as "personal" books — in the sense that they probably belonged to and were used by individuals — and more with their Insular cultural context, as books produced by and for travellers with a spiritual mission. An example of this is St. Gall,

---

64 For more on these pocket Gospels, see Eleanor E. Jackson, "To Hold Infinity in the Palm of Your Hand: The Insular Pocket Gospel Books Re-Evaluated" (PhD thesis, University of York, 2017); Bernard Meehan, "Irish Pocket Gospel Books," in *The St Cuthbert Gospel: Studies on the Insular Manuscript of the Gospel of John,* ed. Claire Breay and Bernard Meehan (London: British Library, 2015), 83–102; Patrick McGurk, "The Irish Pocket Gospel Book," *Sacris Erudiri* 8 (1956): 249–70, repr. *Gospel Books and Early Latin Manuscripts,* Variorum Collected Studies Series 606 (Aldershot: Ashgate, 1998), 249–69.

65 Jackson, "To Hold Infinity in the Palm of Your Hand." Book satchels are also thought to be depicted on other early medieval sources, including the Papil 1 Stone (National Museums Scotland, Edinburgh, IB.46), Papil 2 or Monks Stone (Shetland Museum, Lerwick, ARC 6634), and the Cullingsburgh Stone (National Museums Scotland, Edinburgh, IB.109), all found on the Shetland Islands.

Stiftsbibliothek, Cod. Sang. 913.[66] This small (85 × 85 mm [3.35 × 3.25 in.]) manuscript is composed of rough scrap parchment, its leaves frequently sewn together rather than folded as part of regularly conjoined bifolia. Rather than Gospels, however, the codex contains a variety of theological, evangelical, and school texts in Latin and Old High German, including glossaries, questions and answers on various topics, explanations of names, and works on computus and grammar. Made in the second half of the eighth century in Germany, the manuscript was written by a single scribe in Insular half-uncial and minuscule. These features suggest that this scribe probably copied the manuscript for personal use more or less unaided, rather than in formal collaboration with others as part of institutional book-production.[67] The codex requires a great deal more study, but it was manifestly made by an Insular missionary who required a handbook and who created one in the image of the practical pocket Gospels with which they were familiar.[68]

Yet other small manuscripts produced in continental contexts do not seem to share any particular features apart from their size. A case in point is the Psalter of Bishop Rupert (probably worn as an amulet and not actually used by Rupert), made in ninth-century France. It measures only 37 × 31 mm (1.46 × 1.22 in.), but its extremely small size has more to do with the talismanic character of the Bible than with its personal nature.[69] The Christian context of such tiny talismans has a long history, as demonstrated by a copy of John's Gospel measuring 75 × 60

---

66 Thomas Klein, "Zu Herkunft, Sprache und Übersetzer des Vocabularius Sti. Galli," *Zeitschrift für deutsche Philologie* 1 (2012): 3–32, and Stefanie Stricker, "Vocabularius Sancti Galli," in *Althochdeutsche und altsächsische Literatur,* ed. Rolf Bergmann, De Gruyter Lexikon (Berlin: De Gruyter, 2013), 494–500.

67 Stricker, "Vocabularius Sancti Galli."

68 The manuscript has been studied almost exclusively as the carrier of the famous *Vocabularius Sancti Galli,* the oldest subject glossary in German, rather than as a whole book.

69 Salzburg, Archiv von St. Peter, MS A.I.0. See Florentine Mütherich, *Psalterium Sancti Ruperti: Handschrift a I O der Stiftsbibliothek St. Peter, Salzburg* (Graz: Akademische Druck- und Verlagsanstalt, 2007).

mm (2.95 × 2.36 in.). Copied in uncial script in the late fifth or early sixth century, this miniature book was probably originally made to serve as an amulet — a function that continued into the eleventh century, when it was placed in a reliquary in Chartres.[70]

Comparison between these kinds of books makes it clear that "personal" is a methodological rather than an empirical category. Both Irish pocket Gospels and the other manuscripts examined above are "personal" in one way or another, but all their ways of being personal are unrelated. Although individual intervention was expressed in the same ways (autograph writing, attribution as planner, etc.), individual participation in the text or book was governed by local networks of communication and power around that individual — that is, by the social logic of the text — and not by the individual themselves. This is true even for the multiple social logics of texts that arise in the course of the very long lives and mutability of medieval manuscripts.

An important element of this view of individual intervention in texts, expressed in post-modern theories like deconstruction, is that text (*écriture,* in its broadest sense) is inherently ambiguous. As Gabrielle Spiegel put it, "the inevitable clash of codes coexisting within the text fractures the apparently continuous, harmonious surface of the work to reveal the contradictions and pluralities of meanings that it harbors."[71] Because of this, it is impossible to derive a historically accurate understanding of either the individual associated with a particular book or text, or of a general set of features required by individuals from books and texts in the early Middle Ages. All that we have is an unreliable material artifact, whose rare survival was governed by chance and not by the importance of its contents. Its messages are further contingent on the questions and level of engagement brought to it by modern researchers.

---

70 Paris, Bibliothèque nationale de France, MS lat. 10439: https://gallica.bnf.fr/ark:/12148/btv1b52503882m. On the history of John's Gospel as a talisman, see Don C. Skemer, *Binding Words: Textual Amulets in the Middle Ages* (University Park: Pennsylvania State University Press, 2006).
71 Gabrielle M. Spiegel, "History, Historicism, and the Social Logic of the Text in the Middle Ages," *Speculum* 65, no. 1 (1990): 62.

But this plurality need not be an obstacle. It does not mean individuals did not exist. Rather, it forces us to investigate the individual as part of the communal and to regard the manuscript as a product of both. A case in point is a set of four books commissioned from the monks of St. Amand by Lotharius (d. 828), sacristan at the same monastery. These manuscripts contain Church canons and works by Lactantius, Eugippius, and Origen.[72] Lotharius ordered the manuscripts to be made, and may have selected the contents, but the books were copied by many scribes, and the contents were almost certainly intended for the use of all the monks. A range of aspects made this project unique, among them intellectual and political patronage at St. Amand, the status of its school, the politics of giving books as gifts there, and Lotharius's function within the monastery. The fact that we can detect Lotharius's presence in these books enables us to see his networks — not him — more clearly.

Another example of this is a note from Gunthar, the ninth-century Archbishop of Cologne, preserved on the back of a quire in Cologne, Erzbischöfliche Diözesan- und Dombibliothek, MS 117, 97v: "Make as many copies as possible of this quaternio; give one to the Archbishop Liutbert and distribute it to as many bishops as possible. Send a copy of it to Cologne, so that it may come into the hands of the brothers; let them copy and send it to the bishops also. Let Willibert in particular be provided with it, as well as Arnulf the provost, Madalfrid, Ingilfrid, Baldric and Erembold, and all the other brothers who want to be especially attached to us."[73] The quire contains a polemic pamphlet support-

---

[72] Vatican City, Biblioteca Apostolica Vaticana, MS Reg. lat. 1021 and MS Pal. lat. 161; Paris, Bibliothèque nationale de France, MS lat. 2109; and Laon, Bibliothèque municipal Suzanne Martinet, MS 298. Verses mentioning Lotharius at the end of these manuscripts describe him as *claviger* and priest. He was also described as "Hlotharius custos" by Alcuin. See Ludwig Traube, "Schreiber Lotharius von S. Amand," *Zentralblatt für Bibliothekswesen* 9 (1892): 87–88. With thanks to Arthur Westwell for drawing my attention to these manuscripts.

[73] Wilfried Hartmann, ed., *Die Konzilien der karolingischen Teilreiche, 860–874*, Monument Germaniae Historica, *Concilia* 4, (Hanover: Hahnsche, 1998), 189: "Istum quaternionem exemplari facite in aliis quaternionibus

ing Lothar II in his divorce from Theutberga, which Gunthar sought to use to persuade his audience.[74] It reveals a great deal about Gunthar's place and relationship to others within the debate — his social context — but much less about him as a person.

Ultimately, this social logic of the text ought to change how we interpret the excerpting and collecting practices of individuals. The manuscripts discussed in this chapter make it clear that the people responsible for the act(s) of selection that created handbooks worked in groups, over a long period of time, sometimes at a distance from each other; they may have been men or women who belonged to the clergy, the monastic orders, or, on occasion, the laity; the excerpts were taken from many different books and libraries within and outside monasteries, and there may have been more than one guiding principle behind their inclusion or it might have changed over time; and the act of selection could be altered by anyone at the codicological level. These features reflect an effort between compilers, scribes, and authors to work together. Individuals sought to connect to others, an early medieval process that has been described as the transition from late-antique "autarkic" to central-medieval "collectivized monasticism."[75] Brian Stock observed something similar for the collectivized textual culture of the eleventh and twelfth centuries: "What was essential to a textual community was not a written version of a text, although that was sometimes present, but an individual, who, having mastered it, then utilized it for

---

    quam pluribus et unum date Liutberto archiepiscopo et ad alios episcopos, quantum plus potestis pervenire facite. Ad Coloniam unum exemplar dirigite, ita ut in manus fratrum perveniat et illi etiam exemplari faciant et ad episcopos mittant. Willibertus specialiter inde provideat et Arnulfus praepositus et Madalfridus, et Ingilfridus et Baldricus et Eremboldus similiter inde provideant et ceteri, qui speciales esse volunt fratres."

74 Warren Pezé, "Nouvelles approches sur le fait controversial au haut Moyen Âge," Les régimes de polémicité au Moyen Âge, ed. Bénédicte Sère (Rennes: Presses universitaires de Rennes, 2019), 31–44.

75 Richard E. Sullivan, "The Context of Cultural Activity in the Carolingian Age," in The Gentle Voices of Teachers: Aspects of Learning in the Carolingian Age, ed. Richard E. Sullivan (Columbus: Ohio State University, 1995), 73.

reforming a group's thought and action."[76] Rutger Kramer has gone even further in his study of the Carolingian reforms, showing the political and social foundations of a process in which texts were constantly re-circulated as part of continuous conversations at all levels.[77] Individuals, their texts, and their books were active agents in the creation of their own social logics and are therefore better understood within these contexts than by comparison to each other alone.

Conclusion

Early medieval books were closely associated with their makers and owners not because these individuals were particularly authoritative — though abbots and bishops had a great deal of authority through their offices, and force of personality was important — but because this association enabled people to identify each manuscript book, to remember what it contained, and to recall whether the contents were of the necessary quality. Within monastic communities and across networks of students and masters, patrons and clients, and friends and relations, such associative aids were essential for knowing what intellectual resources were available and how to access them. Monastic communities organized and directed intellectual resources. This gradually began to change from the end of the tenth century, when — as Claudio Leonardi observed — there was a significant increase in the production of autograph manuscripts.[78] Leonardi linked this to the rise of a more self-conscious, individual

---

76 Brian Stock, *The Implications of Literacy: Written Language and Models of Interpretation in the Eleventh and Twelfth Centuries* (Princeton: Princeton University Press, 1987), 90.

77 Rutger Kramer, *Rethinking Authority in the Carolingian Empire: Ideals and Expectations during the Reign of Louis the Pious,* Early Medieval North Atlantic (Amsterdam: Amsterdam University Press, 2019).

78 Claudio Leonardi, *Letteratura latina medievale (secoli VI–XV). Un manuale,* Millennio medievale 31 (Florence: SISMEL Edizioni del Galluzzo, 2002). See also Giorgia Vocino, "Migrant Masters and Their Books. Italian Scholars and Knowledge Transfer in Post-Carolingian Europe," in *Using and Not Using the Past After the Carolingian Empire, c. 900–c. 1050,* ed. Sarah Greer,

learning dissociated from the "imperial" schools and culture of the Carolingian world, and to the rise of new private libraries as well as a new curriculum. But before the late tenth century, the production and use of personal handbooks was centered in monasteries and so was, paradoxically, a communal affair.

The somewhat random set of manuscripts previously labeled as "vademecums" cannot be used to identify other vademecums, then, but it does reveal that "vademecums" were a much wider and more numerous category of early medieval manuscript than has previously been assumed. The variety of the vademecums discussed here suggests that almost any miscellany may have been used in a range of diverse ways. Interventions in handbooks by individuals — both famous masters and intellectuals, but also the obscure anonymous scribes known only through their hands, who form the vast majority — are especially valuable, not as traces of unique historical personalities but as evidence of how the balance between collaboration and authority was achieved and maintained. The social logic of personal handbooks therefore underpins the cultural and intellectual history of early medieval communities.

Alice Hicklin, and Stefan Esders (London: Routledge, 2020), 241–61. I am grateful to Giorgia for allowing me to read her paper before publication.

Bibliography

Manuscripts

Angers, Bibliothèque municipale, MS Rés. 91. https://commulysse.angers.fr/ark:/54380/a011504254863VZPMmB/e8cf7ecc9a.

Autun, Bibliothèque municipale, MS S 022 (020 A). https://bvmm.irht.cnrs.fr/mirador/index.php?manifest=https://bvmm.irht.cnrs.fr/iiif/21896/manifest.

Bern, Burgerbibliothek, MS 87. https://www.e-codices.unifr.ch/en/list/one/bbb/0087.

Bern, Burgerbibliothek, MS lat. 363.

Basel, Universitätsbibliothek, MS F II 23. https://www.e-codices.unifr.ch/en/list/one/ubb/F-II-0023.

Basel, Universitätsbibliothek, MS F III 15d. https://www.e-codices.unifr.ch/en/list/one/ubb/F-III-0015d.

Brussels, Bibliothèque royale de Belgique, MS 10127–10144. http://belgica.kbr.be/fr/coll/ms/ms10127_44_fr.html.

Cologne, Erzbischöfliche Diözesan- und Dombibliothek, MS 117: http://www.ceec.uni-koeln.de/ceec-cgi/kleioc/0010/exec/pagemed/%22kn28-0117_194.jpg%22/segment/%22body%22.

Fulda, Hochschul- und Landesbibliothek Fulda, MS 100 Bonifatianus 1. https://fuldig.hs-fulda.de/viewer/!thumbs/PPN325289808/1/.

Fulda, Hochschul- und Landesbibliothek Fulda, MS 100 Bonifatianus 2. https://fuldig.hs-fulda.de/viewer/!thumbs/PPN438486781/1/.

Fulda, Hochschul- und Landesbibliothek Fulda, MS 100 Bonifatianus 3. https://fuldig.hs-fulda.de/viewer/!thumbs/PPN325292043/1/.

Laon, Bibliothèque municipale Suzanne Martinet, MS 265. https://arca.irht.cnrs.fr/ark:/63955/md526969zc59.

Laon, Bibliothèque municipale Suzanne Martinet, MS 298.

Laon, Bibliothèque municipale Suzanne Martinet, MS 468. https://gallica.bnf.fr/ark:/12148/btv1b8492139c.

Leiden, Universiteitsbibliotheek, MS Voss. Lat. Oct. 15.

Munich, Bayerische Staatsbibliothek, MS Clm 6426. http://daten.digitale-sammlungen.de/~db/0000/bsb00003258/images/index.html?seite=00001&l=de.
Paris, Bibliothèque nationale de France, MS lat. 2109. https://archivesetmanuscrits.bnf.fr/ark:/12148/cc600027/cd0e56.
Paris, Bibliothèque nationale de France, MS lat. 7501. https://archivesetmanuscrits.bnf.fr/ark:/12148/cc12453z.
Paris, Bibliothèque nationale de France, MS lat. 9085. http://archivesetmanuscrits.bnf.fr/ark:/12148/cc772311.
Paris, Bibliothèque nationale de France, MS lat. 9433. http://archivesetmanuscrits.bnf.fr/ark:/12148/cc94653d.
Paris, Bibliothèque nationale de France, MS lat. 10439. http://archivesetmanuscrits.bnf.fr/ark:/12148/cc72160j.
Paris, Bibliothèque nationale de France, MS lat. 13246. http://archivesetmanuscrits.bnf.fr/ark:/12148/cc743249.
Paris, Bibliothèque nationale de France, MS lat. 15679. http://archivesetmanuscrits.bnf.fr/ark:/12148/cc76272z.
Salzburg, Archiv von St. Peter, MS A.I.0.
St. Gall, Stiftsbibliothek, Cod. Sang 217. https://www.e-codices.unifr.ch/en/list/one/csg/0217.
St. Gall, Stiftsbibliothek, Cod. Sang. 222. http://www.e-codices.unifr.ch/en/list/one/csg/0222.
St. Gall, Stiftsbibliothek, Cod. Sang. 397. http://www.e-codices.unifr.ch/en/list/one/csg/0397.
St. Gall, Stiftsbibliothek, Cod. Sang 761. https://www.e-codices.unifr.ch/en/list/one/csg/0761.
St. Gall, Stiftsbibliothek, Cod. Sang. 878. http://www.e-codices.unifr.ch/en/list/one/csg/0878.
Valenciennes, Bibliothèque municipale, MS 407 (389), 17bis. https://gallica.bnf.fr/ark:/12148/btv1b84516477/f37.item.
Vatican City, Biblioteca Apostolica Vaticana, MS Pal. lat. 161. https://digi.vatlib.it/view/MSS_Pal.lat.161.
Vatican City, Biblioteca Apostolica Vaticana, MS Pal. lat. 1341. https://bibliotheca-laureshamensis-digital.de/bav/bav_pal_lat_1341 and https://digi.vatlib.it/view/bav_pal_lat_1341.

Vatican City, Biblioteca Apostolica Vaticana, MS Reg. lat. 339 +
St. Gall, Kantonsbibliothek, Vadianische Sammlung, MS 317.
https://digi.vatlib.it/view/MSS_Reg.lat.339.

Vatican City, Biblioteca Apostolica Vaticana, MS Reg. lat. 1021.
https://digi.vatlib.it/view/MSS_Reg.lat.1021.

Vatican City, Biblioteca Apostolica Vaticana, MS Vat. lat. 3852.
http://digi.vatlib.it/view/bav_vat_lat_3852.

Würzburg, Universitätsbibliothek, MS M.p.th.f.61. http://
vb.uni-wuerzburg.de/ub/mpthf61/index.html.

Primary

Bischoff, Bernhard. *Katalog der festländischen Handschriften des neunten Jahrhunderts (mit Ausnahme der wisigotischen)*, Volume 1: *Aachen-Lambach*. Wiesbaden: Harrassowitz, 1998.

———. *Katalog der festländischen Handschriften des neunten Jahrhunderts*, Volume 2: *Laon-Paderborn*. Edited by Birgit Ebersperger. Wiesbaden: Harrassowitz, 2004.

———. *Katalog der festländischen Handschriften des neunten Jahrhunderts (mit Ausnahme der wisigotischen)*, Volume 3: *Padua-Zwickau*. Edited by Birgit Ebersperger. Wiesbaden: Harrassowitz, 2014.

Hartmann, Wilfried, ed. *Die Konzilien der karolingischen Teilreiche, 860–874*. Hanover: Hahnsche, 1998.

Regenos, Graydon W., trans. *The Letters of Lupus of Ferrieres*. The Hague: Martinus Nijhoff, 1966. DOI: 10.1007/978-94-011-9499-0.

Secondary

Andrist, Patrick, Paul Canart, and Marilena Maniaci. *La syntaxe du codex: essai de codicologie structurale*. Bibliologia 34. Turnhout: Brepols, 2013.

Auvray-Assayas, Clara. "Qui est Hadoard? Une réévaluation du manuscrit Reg. lat. 1762 de la Bibliothèque Vaticane." *Revue d'histoire des textes* 8 (2013): 307–38. DOI: 10.1484/J.RHT.5.101115.

Barlow, Claude W. "Codex Vaticanus Latinus 4929." *Memoirs of the American Academy Rome* 15 (1938): 87–124. DOI: 10.2307/4238603.

Beccaria, Augusto. *I codici di medicina del periodo presalernitano.* Rome: Ed. di Storia e Letteratura, 1956.

Beck, Hans-Georg. *Vademecum des byzantinischen Aristokraten. Das sogenannte Strategikon des Kekaumenos.* Byzantinische Geschichtsschreiber 5. Graz: Verlag Styria, 1964.

Bergmann, Rolf, and Stefanie Stricker. *Katalog der althochdeutschen und altsächsischen Glossenhandschriften,* Volume 4. Berlin: De Gruyter, 2005. DOI: 10.1515/9783110918250.

Billanovich, Giuseppe. "Dall'antica Ravenna alle biblioteche umanistiche." *Aevum* 30, no. 4 (1956): 319–62. http://www.jstor.org/stable/20858940.

Bischoff, Bernhard. "Bücher am Hofe Ludwigs des Deutschen und die Privatbibliothek des Kanzlers Grimalt." In Bernhard Bischoff, *Mittelalterliche Studien: Ausgewählte Aufsätze zur Schriftkunde und Literaturgeschichte,* Volume 3, 187–212. Stuttgart: Anton Hiersemann, 1981.

———. "Eine Osterpredigt Liudprands von Cremona (um 960)." In Bernhard Bischoff, *Anecdota novissima: Texte des vierten bis sechzehnten Jahrhunderts,* Quellen und Untersuchungen zur lateinischen Philologie des Mittelalters 7, 20–34. Stuttgart: Anton Hiersemann, 1984.

———. "Eine Sammelhandschrift Walahfrid Strabos (Cod. Sangall. 878)." In Bernard Bischoff, *Mittelalterliche Studien: Ausgewählte Aufsätze zur Schriftkunde und Literaturgeschichte,* Volume 2, 34–51. Stuttgart: Anton Hiersemann, 1967.

———. "Libraries and Schools in the Carolingian Revival of Learning." In *Manuscripts and Libraries in the Age of Charlemagne,* translated by Michael Gorman, 93–114. Cambridge: Cambridge University Press, 1994.

Bozzolo, Carla, and Ezio Ornato. *Pour une histoire du livre manuscrit au Moyen Âge: Trois essais de codicologie quantitative*. Equipe de recherche sur l'humanisme français, Textes et études 2. Paris: CNRS, 1980.

Carruthers, Mary. *The Book of Memory: A Study of Memory in Medieval Cultures*. Cambridge: Cambridge University Press, 2008. DOI: 10.1017/CBO9781107051126.

Chambert-Protat, Pierre. "Florus de Lyon, lecteur des Pères: documentation et travaux patristiques dans l'église de Lyon au IXe siècle." PhD Dissertation, École doctorale de l'école pratique des Hautes Études, 2016.

———. "Le manuscrit Montpellier 157 de Mannon de Saint-Oyen et la collection *De pascha* de Florus de Lyon." *Revue bénédictine* 128, no. 1 (2018): 95–141. DOI: 10.1484/J.RB.5.115656.

Cinato, Franck. "*Accessus ad Priscianum*. De Jean Scot Érigène a Létald de Micy." *Archivum Latinitatis Medii Aevi* 70 (2012): 27–90. DOI: 10.3406/alma.2012.1122.

Clemens, Raymond, and Timothy Graham. *Introduction to Manuscript Studies*. Ithaca: Cornell University Press, 2007.

Contreni, John J. Review of *Rhetoric and Reckoning in the Ninth Century: The Vademecum of Walahfrid Strabo,* by Wesley M. Stevens. *The Medieval Review,* June 18, 2020. https://scholarworks.iu.edu/journals/index.php/tmr/article/view/31090.

———. *The Cathedral School of Laon from 850 to 930: Its Manuscripts and Masters*. Münchener Beiträge zur Mediävistik und Renaissance-Forschung 29. Munich: Arbeo-Gesellschaft, 1978.

Da Rold, Orietta. "Codicology, Localization, and Oxford, Bodleian Library, MS Laud Misc. 108." In *Makers and Users of Medieval Books: Essays in Honour of A.S.G. Edwards,* edited by Carol M. Meale and Derek Pearsall, 48–59. Cambridge: Cambridge University Press, 2014.

Dorofeeva, Anna. "Miscellanies, Christian Reform and Early Medieval Encyclopaedism: A Reconsideration of the Pre-Bestiary Physiologus Manuscripts." *Historical Research* 90, no. 250 (2017): 665–82. DOI: 10.1111/1468-2281.12198.

———. "Reading Early Medieval Miscellanies." In *Scribes and the Presentation of Texts (From Antiquity to c. 1550): Proceedings of the 20th Colloquium of the Comité international de paléographie latine, Beinecke Rare Book & Manuscript Library, Yale University (New Haven, September 6-8, 2017)*, edited by Consuelo W. Dutschke, Barbara A. Shailor, Kristen Herdman, Carson Koepke, and Alexander Peña, 495–514. Bibliologia 65. Turnhout: Brepols, 2021. DOI: 10.1484/M.BIB-EB.5.124988.

Fischer, Bonifatius. "Bibeltext und Bibelreform unter Karl dem Großen." In *Karl der Große: Lebenswerk und Nachleben, II. Das geistige Leben*, edited by Bernhard Bischoff, 156–216. Düsseldorf: L. Schwann, 1965. Reprinted in Bonifatius Fischer. *Lateinische Bibelhandschriften im frühen Mittelalter*. Vetus Latina: Aus der Geschichte der lateinischen Bibel 11, 101–202. Freiburg: Herder, 1985.

Ganz, David. "Paris BN Latin 2718: Theological Texts in the Chapel and the Chancery of Louis the Pious." In *Scientia veritatis: Festschrift für Hubert Mordek zum 65. Geburtstag*, edited by Oliver Münsch and Thomas L. Zotz, 137–52. Ostfildern: Thorbecke, 2004.

Gorman, Michael. "Theodulf of Orléans and the Exegetical Miscellany in Paris Lat. 15679." *Revue bénédictine* 109, nos. 3–4 (1999): 278–323. DOI: 10.1484/J.RB.4.01384.

Grupp, Uwe. "Der Codex Sangallensis 397 — ein persönliches Handbuch Grimalds von St. Gallen?" *Deutsches Archiv für Erforschung des Mittelalters* 70 (2014): 453–63.

Gumbert, Johann P. "Codicological Units: Towards a Terminology for the Stratigraphy of the Non-Homogeneous Codex." In *Il Codice Miscellaneo: Tipologie e funzioni. Atti del Convegno internazionale, Cassinom 14-17 Maggio 2003*, edited by Edoardo Crisci and Oronzo Pecere, 17–42. Segno e Testo 2. Turnhout: Brepols, 2004.

———. "Zur Kodikologie und Katalographie der zusammengesetzten Handschrift." In *La descrizione dei manoscritti: esperienze a confronto*, edited by Edoardo Crisci, Marilena Maniaci, and Pasquale Orsini, 1–18. Studi e ricerche del Dipartimento di Filologia e Storia 1. Cassino: University of Cassino, 2010.

Hamesse, Jacqueline. "Les florilèges philosophiques, instruments de travail des intellectuels à la fin du moyen âge et à la Renaissance." In *Filosofia e teologia nel Trecento: Studi in ricordo di Eugenio Randi,* edited by Luca Bianchi, 479–508. Textes et Études du Moyen Âge 1. Turnhout: Brepols, 1994. DOI: 10.1484/M.TEMA-EB.4.00418.

Haseloff, Günther. "Der Einband des Ragyndrudis-Codex in Fulda — Codex Bonifatianus 2." In *Von der Klosterbibliothek zur Landesbibliothek: Beiträge zum zweihundertjährigen Bestehen der Hessischen Landesbibliothek Fulda,* edited by Artur Brall, 1–46. Bibliothek des Buchwesens 6. Stuttgart: Anton Hiersemann, 1978.

Hausmann, Regina. *Die theologischen Handschriften der Hessischen Landesbibliothek Fulda bis zum Jahr 1600. Codices Bonifatiani 1–3, Aa 1–145a.* Wiesbaden: Harrassowitz, 1992.

Hawk, Brandon W. *Preaching Apocrypha in Anglo-Saxon England.* Toronto Anglo-Saxon Series 30. Toronto: University of Toronto Press, 2018. DOI: 10.3138/9781487516970.

Hen, Yitzhak. "A Liturgical Handbook for the Use of a Rural Priest (Brussels BR 10127–10144)." In *Organizing the Written Word: Scripts, Manuscripts and Texts.* Edited by Marco Mostert. Proceedings of the First Utrecht Symposium on Medieval Literacy, Utrecht Studies in Medieval Literacy 30. Turnhout: Brepols, 2022.

———. "The Church in Sixth-Century Gaul." In *A Companion to Gregory of Tours,* edited by Alexander C. Murray, 232–55. Leiden: Brill, 2016. DOI: 10.1163/9789004307001_009.

Hobson, Geoffrey D. *English Binding Before 1500.* Cambridge: Cambridge University Press, 1927.

Jackson, Eleanor E. "To Hold Infinity in the Palm of Your Hand: The Insular Pocket Gospel Books Re-Evaluated." PhD Dissertation, University of York, 2017.

Jeauneau, Édouard. "Les ecoles de Laon et d'Auxerre au IXe siècle." In *La scuola nell'Occidente latino dell'alto medioevo,*

495–522. Settimane di Studio del Centro Italiano di Studi sull'alto Medioevo 19. Spoleto: Presso la sede del Centro, 1972.

Keefe, Susan A. *A Catalogue of Works Pertaining to the Explanation of the Creed in Carolingian Manuscripts.* Instrumenta Patristica et Mediaevalia 63. Turnhout: Brepols, 2012. DOI: 10.1484/M.IPM-EB.5.112164.

———. *Water and the Word: Baptism and the Education of the Clergy in the Carolingian Empire.* Volume 1. Publications in Medieval Studies. Notre Dame: University of Notre Dame, 2002.

Klein, Thomas. "Zu Herkunft, Sprache und Übersetzer des Vocabularius Sti. Galli." *Zeitschrift für deutsche Philologie* 1 (2012): 3–32. DOI: 10.37307/j.1868-7806.2012.01.03.

Kramer, Rutger. *Rethinking Authority in the Carolingian Empire: Ideals and Expectations during the Reign of Louis the Pious (813–828).* Early Medieval North Atlantic. Amsterdam: Amsterdam University Press, 2019. DOI: 10.5117/9789462982642.

Köpp, Peter. ed. *Vademecum eines frühmittelalterlichen Arztes. Die gefaltete lateinische Handschrift medizinischen Inhalts im Codex 217 und der Fragmentensammlung 1396 der Stiftsbibliothek in St. Gallen.* Veröffentlichungen der Schweizerischen Gesellschaft für Geschichte der Medizin und der Naturwissenschaften 34. Aarau: Sauerländer, 1980.

Lecouffe, Marie-Eugénie. "Les Nuits attiques d'Aulu-Gelle au Moyen Âge et à la Renaissance. Histoire de la transmission d'un texte." MA Thesis, École des Chartres, 2011.

Leonardi, Claudio. *Letteratura latina medievale (secoli VI–XV). Un manuale.* Millennio medievale 31. Florence: SISMEL Edizioni del Galluzzo, 2002.

Lewis, Charlton T., and Charles Short. *A Latin Dictionary: Founded on Andrews' Edition of Freund's Latin Dictionary.* Oxford: Clarendon Press, 1879.

Leyser, Karl. *Communications and Power in Medieval Europe: The Carolingian and Ottonian Centuries.* Edited by Timothy Reuter. London: Bloomsbury, 1994.

Lieftinck, Gerard I. "Le ms. d'Aulu-Gelle à Leeuwarden executé à Fulda en 836." *Bullettino dell'Archivio Paleografico Italiano*, nuova serie 1 (1955): 11–17.

Lifshitz, Felice. *Religious Women in Early Carolingian Francia: A Study of Manuscript Transmission and Monastic Culture*. Fordham Series in Medieval Studies. New York: Fordham University Press, 2014. DOI: 10.5422/fordham/9780823256877.001.0001.

Mainoldi, Ernesto S. "Una proposta di nuova attribuzione ad Almanno di Hautvillers." *Archives d'histoire doctrinale et littéraire du Moyen Âge* 76, no. 1 (2009): 7–28. DOI: 10.3917/ahdlm.076.0007.

Maniaci, Marilena. "Costruzione e gestione dello spazio scritto fra Oriente e Occidente: principi generali e soluzioni specifiche." In *Scrivere e leggere nell'alto Medioevo*, 473–512. Settimane di studio del Centro italiano di studi sull'alto Medioevo 59. Spoleto: Centro Italiano di Studi sull'Alto Medioevo, 2012.

McGurk, Patrick. "The Irish Pocket Gospel Book." *Sacris Erudiri* 8 (1956): 249–70.

Meagher, Luanne. "The Gellius Manuscript of Lupus of Ferrières." PhD Dissertation, University of Chicago, 1936.

Meehan, Bernard. "Irish Pocket Gospel Books." In *The St Cuthbert Gospel: Studies on the Insular Manuscript of the Gospel of John*, edited by Claire Breay and Bernard Meehan, 83–102. London: British Library, 2015.

Merlette, Bernhard. "Écoles et bibliothèques à Laon du déclin de l'Antiquité au développement de l'université." In *Actes du 95e Congrès national des sociétés savantes (Reims, 1970): Section de philologie et d'histoire jusqu'à 1610*, 21–54. Paris: Bibliothèque nationale, 1975.

Mordek, Hubert. *Bibliotheca capitularium regum Francorum manuscripta: Überlieferung und Traditionszusammenhang der fränkischen Herrschererlasse*. Munich: Monumenta Germaniae Historica, 1995.

Mütherich, Florentine. *Psalterium Sancti Ruperti: Handschrift a I O der Stiftsbibliothek St. Peter, Salzburg.* Graz: Akademische Druck- und Verlagsanstalt, 2007.

Ornato, Ezio. "The Application of Quantitative Methods to the History of the Book." In *The Oxford Handbook of Latin Palaeography,* edited by Frank T. Coulson and Robert G. Babcock, 650–68. Oxford: Oxford University Press, 2020. DOI: 10.1093/oxfordhb/9780195336948.013.34.

Patzold, Steffen. *Presbyter: Moral, Mobilität und die Kirchenorganisation im Karolingerreich.* Monographien zur Geschichte des Mittelalters 68. Stuttgart: Anton Hiersemann, 2020.

Patzold, Steffen, and Carine van Rhijn, eds. *Men in the Middle: Local Priests in Early Medieval Europe.* Boston and Berlin: de Gruyter, 2016. DOI: 10.1515/9783110444483.

Pezé, Warren. "Nouvelles approches sur le fait controversial au haut Moyen Âge." In *Les régimes de polémicité au Moyen Âge,* edited by Bénédicte Sère, 31–44. Rennes: Presses universitaires de Rennes, 2019.

———. "The Making of the *De Praedestinatione* of Ratramnus of Corbie (Including the Identification of a New Personal Manuscript)." In *The Annotated Book in the Early Middle Ages: Practices of Reading and Writing,* edited by Mariken Teeuwen and Irene van Renswoude, 125–55. Utrecht Studies in Medieval Literacy 38. Turnhout: Brepols, 2017. DOI: 10.1484/M.USML-EB.5.115019.

Rankin, Susan. "The Earliest Sources of Notker's Sequences: St. Gallen, Vadiana 317, and Paris, Bibliothèque nationale lat. 10587." *Early Music History* 10 (1991): 201–33. DOI: 10.1017/S0261127900001133.

Reimitz, Helmut. "The Social Logic of Historiographical Compendia in the Carolingian period." In *Herméneutique du texte d'histoire,* edited by Osamu Kano, 17–28. Nagoya: Graduate School of Letters, Nagoya University, 2012.

Rhijn, Carine van. *Leading the Way to Heaven: Pastoral Care and Salvation in the Carolingian Period.* The Medieval World. London: Routledge, 2022.

———. "The Local Church, Priests' Handbooks and Pastoral Care in the Carolingian Period." In *Chiesa localo e chiese regionali nell'alto medioevo*, 689–706. Settimane di studio del centro italiano di studi sull'alto medioevo 61. Spoleto: Fondazione CISAM, 2014.

Robinson, Pamela R. "'The "Booklet': A Self-Contained Unit in Composite Manuscripts." *Codicologica* 3 (1980): 46–69. Reprinted in *The History of the Book in the West: 400 AD–1455*, edited by Pamela R. Robinson and Jane Roberts, 159–82. The History of the Book in the West: A Library of Critical Essays 1. London: Routledge, 2016.

Ruf, Paul, Sigrid Krämer, and Christine Elisabeth Ineighen-Eder. *Mittelalterliche Bibliothekskataloge Deutschlands und der Schweiz*. Volume 1. Munich: Beck, 1918.

Skemer, Don C. *Binding Words: Textual Amulets in the Middle Ages*. University Park: Pennsylvania State University Press, 2006.

Spiegel, Gabrielle M. "History, Historicism, and the Social Logic of the Text in the Middle Ages." *Speculum* 65, no. 1 (1990): 59–86. DOI: 10.2307/2864472.

Stevens, Wesley M. *Rhetoric and Reckoning in the Ninth Century: The Vademecum of Walahfrid Strabo*. Studia Traditionis Theologiae, Explorations in Early and Medieval Theology 24. Turnhout: Brepols, 2018. DOI: 10.1484/M.STT-EB.5.112367.

Stock, Brian. *The Implications of Literacy: Written Language and Models of Interpretation in the Eleventh and Twelfth Centuries*. Princeton: Princeton University Press, 1983.

Stricker, Stefanie. "Vocabularius Sancti Galli." In *Althochdeutsche und altsächsische Literatur*, edited by Rolf Bergmann, 494–500. De Gruyter Lexikon. Berlin: De Gruyter, 2013.

Sullivan, Richard E. "The Context of Cultural Activity in the Carolingian Age." In *The Gentle Voices of Teachers: Aspects of Learning in the Carolingian Age*, edited by Richard E.

Sullivan, 51–105. Columbus: Ohio State University Press, 1995.

Tischler, Matthias M. *Einharts Vita Karoli. Studien zur Entstehung, Überlieferung und Rezeption.* Schriften der Monumenta Germaniae Historica 48. Volume 1. Hanover: Hahn, 2001.

Turcan-Verkerk, Anne-Marie. "Faut-il rendre à Tertullien l'*Ex libris Tertulliani de execrandis gentium diis* du manuscrit Vatican latin 3852?" *Revue des Études augustiniennes et patristiques* 46, no. 2 (2000): 205–34. DOI: 10.1484/J.REA.5.104823.

———. "Florus de Lyon et le ms. Roma. Bibl. Vallicelliana, E 26. Notes marginals." In *La tradition vive. Mélanges d'histoire des textes en l'honneur de Louis Holtz,* edited by Pierre Lardet, 307–16. Turnhout: Brepols, 2003. DOI: 10.1484/M.BIB-EB.3.1408.

Tuvill, Daniel. *Vade Mecum: A Manuall of Essayes Morrall, Theologicall. Inter-wouen with Moderne Obseruations, Historicall, Politicall.* London: Nicholas Okes, 1629.

Van de Vyver, André. "Hucbald de Saint-Amand, écolâtre, et l'invention du Nombre d'or." In *Mélanges Auguste Pelzer. Études d'histoire littéraire et doctrinale de la scolastique médiévale offertes à Monseigneur Auguste Pelzer,* 61–79. Louvain: Bibliothèque de l'Université Editions de l'Institut Supérieur de Philosophie, 1947.

Vocino, Giorgia. "A Peregrinus's Vade Mecum: MS Bern 363 and the 'Circle of Sedulius Scottus.'" In *The Annotated Book in the Early Middle Ages: Practices of Reading and Writing,* edited by Mariken Teeuwen and Irene van Renswoude, 87–123. Utrecht Studies in Medieval Literacy 38. Turnhout: Brepols, 2017. DOI: 10.1484/M.USML-EB.5.115018.

———. "Migrant Masters and Their Books: Italian Scholars and Knowledge Transfer in Post-Carolingian Europe." In *Using and Not Using the Past After the Carolingian Empire, c. 900–c. 1050,* edited by Sarah Greer, Alice Hicklin, and Stefan Esders, 241–61. London: Routledge, 2020.

Von Euw, Anton. *St. Galler Buchkunst vom 8. bis zum Ende des 11. Jahrhunderts,* Volume 1: *Textband.* Monasterium Sancti Galli 3. St. Gallen: Verlag am Klosterhof, 2008.

Von Padberg, Lutz, and Hans-Walter Stork, eds. *Der Ragyndrudis-Codex des Hl. Bonifatius.* Paderborn: Bonifatius Druck-Buch-Verlag, 1994.

Wilmart, André. *Codices Reginenses Latini. II: Codices 251–500.* Vatican City: Biblioteca apostolica vaticana, 1945.

AFTERWORD

Manuscripts as Layered and Entangled Objects: New Ways to Explore the Manuscript Book

Mariken Teeuwen

In two events in Dublin, in the Fall of 2018 and Spring of 2019, a group of scholars including myself explored an exciting new strategy to understand the medieval manuscript book by focusing on how these manuscripts are entangled in networks, on the invitation of Anna Dorofeeva and Michael J. Kelly. New Philology has already taught us that medieval books are much more than mere vessels of texts and that the individual objects containing the texts deserve the attention of scholars just as much as the texts per se. These objects can inform us about the historical and cultural context of texts, about readers, function, appropriation, etc. Textual variance, which traditional philology forced into the background (or to the bottom of the page, in an apparatus) and used primarily for stemma, was put center stage by New Philology, to deepen our understanding of how, why, when, where, and by whom texts were copied and read. In our two events, however, the desire to understand manuscripts better took us even further, beyond the appraisal of the variant to interrogating medieval manuscripts as dynamic objects that keep changing over time as they move from one possessor to the other. Our goal was not only to see the textual content of the manuscripts in context but also to see the agency of changing audiences and functions as reflected in the book. Spurred on by the increasing availability of photographic reproductions of manuscripts in online environments, our focus shifted from the main textual content to the material that is generally not visible in editions: the material added on flyleaves or in the margins, and the codicological and paleographical choices made by the makers, concerning, for example, size, layout, and representation. Stepping beyond the content, the manuscript books show themselves as layered objects, entangled in multiple networks of people who use them and adapt them to their personal needs, circumstances, or tastes. An analysis of these layers allows us to see the networks of makers, owners, and readers.

This new strategy to look for evidence of entanglement was exciting because it allowed us to understand the manuscript book as an object of agency, bringing out the people behind the book, their goals, intended audiences, intellectual practices, teaching methods, etc. It also forced us to reconsider terms and concepts that were driven by traditional philology and that started to feel unsuited to describe the reality of manuscript books: compendium or miscellany, commentary, summary, and extract. A general conclusion of the two events was that in the medieval manuscript texts are much more flexible than the concept "text" may allow. In our discussions, we adopted the term "floating-around-material" to refer to the material that is on flyleaves or in "empty" spaces and that tells the story of readers, users, and possessors of both the books and the texts in them in a new and revealing way. These texts on the limits of the book as an object could be called paratexts when they aid the reader in crossing the threshold to the text, but they are also to be understood as products of a community (or on occasion an individual owner) that manages their pool of knowledge in the way they see as fitting.

In the two events, it was clear that the theme struck a chord with a group of scholars interested in a wide variety of topics and coming from different disciplines: law, grammar, theology, exegesis, commentary traditions on the poets from antiquity, encyclopedic literature, letters, book lists, computus, and liturgy — all topics that featured in our papers and discussions. The concepts of compilation and entanglement really managed to get all of us to rethink our ways of understanding our own niches of medieval textual culture in which we specialized. Perhaps, however, this universal appeal was also due to the fact that in our first joint exploration the concepts were rather fuzzy: "compilation" and "entanglement" could be taken to describe the relation of one manuscript to another (or others); textual units in manuscripts and their relation to one another; one center producing manuscripts and its relation to other centers of production; networks of people producing or exchanging manuscripts and how they related to each other; even an exchange of techniques used to make a stack of parchment leaves into a book. All of these aspects of manuscripts could be studied and analyzed, and each aspect brought different forms of entanglement into focus. As such, entanglement not only picks up the trail of New Philology, but also creates alternative paths of exploration from endings. It follows up on the growing realization that the material book tells the story of writers and how they present their texts, and of readers and how they read their texts.

The chapters in this volume are each great examples of this approach: they study texts, but explicitly look at the stages of their production and use for socio-historical information. Texts are not fixed entities, but time-, place-, and people-specific snapshots of processes of change, and this is witnessed by their textual selections, arrangements, and visual representations. The next step, perhaps, would be to develop the central concept into different models of entanglement as visible in the material object and compliant with approaches from different angles: form, for example, or content, or the people involved.

Entanglement in the Glossed Book

The theme of entanglement is particularly useful, I would argue, when one considers a topic that has been my focus of research for many years now: glossed books.[1] In these books, layers of agency can be seen in full action, not only in the content of the annotations, but also in the practices of annotating, guiding the reader, and critical reading, and the process of dismissing, adding, or transforming texts. In fact, in the early modern age, making annotations in the margins was so much part and parcel of the practice of reading and learning that reading without making notes was considered a waste of time by some.[2] The practices

---

1 See, among others, Mariken Teeuwen, *Harmony and the Music of the Spheres. The 'ars musica' in Ninth-Century Commentaries on Martianus Capella*, Mittellateinische Studien und Texte 30 (Leiden: Brill, 2002); Mariken Teeuwen, "Writing between the Lines: Reflections of Scholarly Debate in a Carolingian Commentary Tradition," in Mariken Teeuwen and Sinéad O'Sullivan, eds., *Carolingian Scholarship and Martianus Capella: Ninth-Century Commentary Traditions on 'De nuptiis' in Context*, Cultural Encounters in Late Antiquity and the Middle Ages 12 (Turnhout: Brepols, 2011), 11–34; Mariken Teeuwen, "Marginal Scholarship: Rethinking the Function of Latin Glosses in Early Medieval Manuscripts," in Patrizia Lendinara, Loredana Lazzari, and Claudia Di Sciacca, eds., *Rethinking and Recontextualizing Glosses: New Perspectives in the Study of Late Anglo-Saxon Glossography*, Textes et Etudes du Moyen Âge 54 (Turnhout: Brepols, 2011), 19–37; Mariken Teeuwen, "Carolingian Scholarship on Classical Authors: Practices of Reading and Writing," in Erik Kwakkel, ed., *Manuscripts of the Latin Classics* (Leiden: Leiden University Press, 2015), 23–52; Mariken Teeuwen, "Writing in the Blank Space of Manuscripts: Evidence from the Ninth Century," in Barbara Crostini, Gunilla Iversen, and Brian M. Jensen, eds., *Ars Edendi Lecture Series* (Stockholm, 2016), 1–25; Mariken Teeuwen, "Voices from the Edge: Annotating Books in the Carolingian Period," in Mariken Teeuwen and Irene van Renswoude, eds., *The Annotated Book in the Early Middle Ages: Practices of Reading and Writing*, Utrecht Studies in Medieval Literacy (Turnhout: Brepols, 2017), 13–36; and Mariken Teeuwen, "Reading Boethius around 900: Manuscripts of Boethius's Texts and Their Annotations," in Warren Pezé, ed., *Knowledge and Culture in Times of Threat: The Fall of the Carolingian Empire (c. 900)* (Stuttgart: Hiersemann, 2020), 279–303.
2 Ann Blair, *Too Much to Know: Managing Scholarly Information before the Modern Age* (New Haven: Yale University Press, 2010), esp. chapter 2,

of making notes are not an invention of the early modern age, nor, for that matter, of the Middle Ages. They are a continuation of a set of older techniques, which were transformed and developed further to fit new purposes in the process. This can be easily illustrated with early medieval manuscripts, with their *nota* signs, cut-and-paste signs, marginal keywords and summaries, schemes, etc. These annotating practices are generally recognized as spontaneous or "on-the-spot" responses of readers, reflecting their process of reading. Books with sets of glosses or commentaries, on the other hand, are generally viewed as books in which multiple texts were copied: the main text and the commentary text.[3] But the division is rarely straightforward: annotated books are often the result of a process in which faithful copying and on-the-spot selecting, changing, and adding all took place. In each copy, a selection was made from previous authorities, from existing sets of glosses and from texts that were used to create new glosses. The rich dynamic that resulted has for a long time been ignored by scholarship, but the growing online visibility of medieval manuscripts has shifted the paradigm: texts in manuscripts are more often than not flexible and variable, which opens the potential of marginal annotations and other adaptations to read them as sources for intellectual history. How and why did readers use their books? Why did they collect certain texts and paratexts in a single volume? Gloss collections are layered and entangled materials, that have tentacles in communities and traditions.[4] And even when it is not easy to interpret the material evidence in such a way that the narratives of entanglement can be laid bare, the effort of trying opens our

---

"Note-Taking as Information Management," 62–116.

3 Rita Copeland, "Gloss and Commentary," in *The Oxford Handbook of Medieval Latin Literature,* ed. Ralph Hexter and David Townsend (Oxford: Oxford University Press, 2012), 171–91.

4 See, among others, Sinéad O'Sullivan's chapter in this volume, and James E.G. Zetzel, *Marginal Scholarship and Textual Deviance: The "Commentum Cornuti" and the Early Scholia on Persius,* Bulletin of the Institute of Classical Studies, Supplement 84 (Oxford: Oxford University Press, 2005).

eyes to medieval manuscripts in a new way. Let me illustrate this with a single example.

Leiden, Universiteitsbibliotheek, MS BPL 88

Leiden, Universiteitsbibliotheek, MS BPL 88 (BPL 88 from here on) is a manuscript containing a copy of Martianus Capella's fifth-century *De nuptiis Philologiae et Mercurii,* with a peculiar set of texts and paratexts: it contains, for Books 1–8 of Capella's encyclopedia on the seven liberal arts and the text of *De nuptiis,* glosses in the margin, which have been identified as the "oldest commentary tradition." This was a set of glosses accreted over time and settled into a more or less fixed shape by the second third of the ninth century, when we find it copied in approximately sixteen manuscripts.[5] It is unknown which author, or maybe authors, produced the commentary and equally unknown where and when precisely it was produced, but the manuscript evidence suggests a production around 830 or 840 in the intellectual heartland of the Carolingian empire: Corbie or Laon.[6]

In BPL 88, the glosses matching this commentary tradition are written in two hands using Caroline minuscule. The first hand, contemporary with the scribe of the main text body, copied a first layer of glosses in a tiny, very regular, neat Caroline

---

5   The manuscripts of the oldest commentary tradition have been studied by me in Teeuwen, *Harmony and the Music of the Spheres,* and more recently and thoroughly by Sinéad O'Sullivan, *Glossae aeui Carolini in libros I–II Martiani Capellae De nuptiis Philologiae et Mercurii,* Corpus Christianorum Continuatio Mediaevalis 237 (Turnhout: Brepols, 2010). We both made an effort to give a complete overview of the previous scholarship on these manuscripts. For BPL 88 specifically, see Teeuwen, *Harmony and the Music of the Spheres,* 117–26 and O'Sullivan, *Glossae,* LV–LXI. O'Sullivan has drawn a stemma of the sixteen manuscripts of the oldest commentary tradition on CXXX. The Leiden manuscript, BPL 88, is available online in the Digital Collections of Leiden University Library: http://hdl.handle.net/1887.1/item:2028417.
6   The earliest copies have been attributed to northeastern France: Corbie, Auxerre, and Reims.

minuscule only 1 mm (.04 in.) high. The scribe used both the margins and the space between the lines, and was precise in using reference signs to tie gloss and lemma together. The ink they used was light brown. The second hand, also contemporary, used a darker ink. They added glosses in a less careful fashion and can be found emending and filling in lacunae in the text. It seems that this hand may have been the hand of a senior scribe, checking and correcting both the copying of the text and the glosses, and adding, here and there, missed elements. These two Caroline glossing hands appear in the first twenty-one quires of the manuscript: the part of the manuscript that contains the first eight books of Martianus's *De nuptiis,* that is, the two introductory books with the frame story of Mercury on his search for a bride, the books of the trivium (3–5, Grammar, Rhetoric, and Dialectic), and three books of the quadrivium (6–8, Geometry, Arithmetic, and Astronomy).

In the ninth book of the encyclopedia, however, where there is an introduction to the last of the quadrivial arts, music, a new hand appears in the margin which adds material from the commentary attributed to John Scottus Eriugena. This hand, moreover, wrote in an Insular minuscule, and has been identified as the hand of I2 or Nisifortinus, the assistant of John Scottus.[7] His glosses occupy interlinear and marginal space. On the first page, the first and second Caroline hands are still also active, but after this page, only the second hand can still be spotted, and the first hand disappears. This constellation of text, paratext, and hands is witnessed in the whole of the book on music, which occupies the two last quires of the manuscript (fols. 168–181, quire 22 and 23, a regular eight-leaf quire and a composite quire of six leaves, with three different types of layout).

For understanding the peculiar mix of commentary traditions, it is important to note that the last two quires have been

---

7   Mariken Teeuwen, "I2's Interest in Music. Two Manuscripts that Witness his Knowledge and Scholarship," in *Litterarum dulces fructus: Studies in Early Medieval Latin Culture in Honour of Michael W. Herren for his 80th Birthday,* ed. Scott G. Bruce (Turnhout: Brepols, 2021), 435–60.

identified as a separate codicological unit, with an origin deviating from the first twenty-one quires. For the first part of the book, Auxerre or Corbie have been suggested, based on paleographical evidence, for the second part Reims.[8]

In addition to the set of texts and hands described above, there is evidence of new scribal activity in the manuscript's first pages: on fols. 1r–2v, material is found that ties the manuscript to the monastic community of St. Peter's Abbey in Ghent in the eleventh century. Hands that wrote in the peculiar style promoted by Wichard (abbot from 1034/1035 to 1058) added schemes exploring the topic of Dialectica, a figure representing the planets and the zodiac, an *accessus ad auctorem* about Martianus, the refrain from one of his poems *scande caeli templa* (with musical notation), and a Greek alphabet with numerical values that can occasionally also be seen on later pages of the book. The connection to St. Peter's is not only based on paleographical evidence. On fol. 2v, we also find an anathema, identifying the book as property of the church of St. Peter in Ghent.[9]

Now, if we apply the concept of entanglement to this manuscript, we could use the concept to analyze multiple aspects of it. We could analyze the constellation of texts present in the book and see how this delivers a network of manuscripts in which these textual units also appear in a manner that points at relations between this manuscript and others. For the text of Martianus Capella's *De nuptiis*, this has been done in the philological analysis preceding the work of editing the work, but in the most recent edition by James Willis, the manuscript is not included

---

8 Teeuwen, *Harmony and the Music of the Spheres*, 118–19; Jean Préaux, "Deux manuscrits gantois de Martianus Capella," *Scriptorium* 13 (1959): 15–21; Claudio Leonardi, "I codici di Marziano Capella I," *Aevum* 33, no. 4 (1959): 451–53, 457, 462–64; Claudio Leonardi, "I codici di Marziano Capella II," *Aevum* 34, no. 1 (1960): 62–63; and Jean Préaux, "Les manuscrits principaux du 'De nuptiis Philologiae et Mercurii' de Martianus Capella," in *Lettres latines du Moyen Âge et de la Renaissance*, ed. Guy Cambier, Carl Deroux, and Jean G. Préaux (Brussels: Latomus, 1978), 76–128, at 79, 101, 123.

9 BPL 88, fol. 2v: "Liber s. petri gandensis ecclesiae. Sevanti benedictio. Tollenti maledictio. Qui folium ex eo tulerit. vel curtaverit. anathema sit."

in the stemma. The manuscript is one of a group of manuscripts that contain a late-antique correction note by Securus Melior Felix at the end of Book I, dated to 534, and that also bears evidence of being copied from an exemplar in *scriptio continua,* with corrected and faulty word divisions. It was therefore considered one of the prime witnesses of the text.[10] The gloss tradition added to the first eight books are part of a commentary tradition with a relatively steady transmission: Sinéad O'Sullivan collected the evidence of sixteen manuscripts and created a stemma.[11] BPL 88 sits in one of the three groups (Group B) with five other manuscripts. Group A has six witnesses and Group C has three.

It is, however, more difficult to assess the relation of the glosses written by I2 in Book 9 to other witnesses of this text. Of John Scottus's commentary on *De nuptiis,* generally known as the *Annotationes in Marcianum* since Cora Lutz edited them under this title in 1939, only a few copies survive, and these are quite different from each other. Cora Lutz edited the *Annotationes* on the basis of a single manuscript: Paris, Bibliothèque nationale de France, MS lat. 12960, a late ninth-century manuscript written in Corbie, in which the commentary was copied separately in a continuous form, without the text of Martianus. The manuscript contains a multitude of texts, which were perhaps bound together because of their shared philosophical character: Aristotle's *On interpretation* (in Boethius's translation); three different commentary traditions on Martianus Capella; and part of John Scottus's *Periphyseon*. A second witness of John's commentary was found by Lotte Labowsky in the early 1940s: a late ninth- or early tenth-century manuscript Oxford, Bodleian Library, MS Auct. T.2.19, probably written in the monastery of St. Vincent

---

10 Préaux, "Les manuscripts principaux," and Danuta Shanzer, *A Philosophical and Literary Commentary on Martianus Capella's De nuptiis Philologiae et Mercurii Book I,* Classical Studies 32 (Berkeley: University of California Press, 1986), 8–13.
11 Sinéad O'Sullivan, *Glossae,* LV–LXI, stemma on CXXX.

in Metz.[12] The glosses on most books were similar enough to assume that this was a copy of the same commentary, but the glosses added to Book I of *De nuptiis* were so different that a debate about their authorship and authenticity developed. Several scholars suggested scenarios for the differences in the two versions: perhaps it was a deliberate reworking of material by John Scottus himself, because of criticism from fellow scholars with whom he crossed swords in the ninth-century debates; perhaps the glosses were the notes written down by students at different stages of John's teaching career.[13] The facts are that we have an edition of only one version of John Scottus's *Annotationes* and that it is clear that other witnesses are quite deviant. When I compared the glosses added to Book IX in BPL 88, I found a result that differed across the individual folia, but a rough analysis of the first three folia (fols. 168r–169r) resulted only in a match for approximately half the material. Nevertheless, if we were to draft a network of manuscripts based on these texts, then BPL 88 would, because of the presence of a version of the *Annotationes*, be connected to Paris, BnF, MS lat. 12960 and Oxford, Bodleian Library, MS Auct. T.2.19.

Considering the text transmission of *De nuptiis,* the manuscript is related to about twenty manuscripts that manifest a close tie to a no longer existing exemplar in *scriptio continua*, with a correction colophon by a sixth-century grammarian. And because of the text transmission of the oldest gloss tradition, as found in the first eight books, the manuscript is related to a group of five manuscripts, according to O'Sullivan's stemma

---

12 Lotte Labowsky, "A New Version of Scotus Eriugena's Commentary on Martianus Capella," *Medieval and Renaissance Studies* 1 (1941–1943), 187–93, and Édouard Jeauneau, "Le commentaire érigénien sur Martianus Capella (*De nuptiis,* Lib. I) d'après le manuscrit d'Oxford (Bodl. Libr. Auct. T.2.19, fol. 1–31)," in *Quatre thèmes érigéniens,* Conférence Albert le Grand, 1974 (Montréal: Institut d'études médiévales Albert-le-Grand, 1978), 91–166.

13 Teeuwen, *Harmony and the Music of the Spheres,* 43–47, and Teeuwen, "I2's Interest in Music," 443–44.

of the oldest gloss tradition.[14] It has a clear sister-manuscript: Vatican City, Biblioteca Apostolica Vaticana, MS Reg. lat. 1987. This manuscript reproduces not only the text of the glosses, but even the shape of their tie-marks and occasionally the layout of the glosses on the page, even when this layout does not match that of the main text.

If we look, however, at the presence of I2 in the last two quires of this manuscript, a different network of manuscripts can be drafted: that is, those that contain the hand of I2, or "Nisifortinus," as he was lovingly nicknamed by Édouard Jeauneau to underline his habit of softening the words of his controversial master, John Scottus Eriugena, with an introductory *nisi forte* (if not perhaps).[15] His hand has been studied in detail by Jeauneau and Dutton, who describe a set of eight manuscripts in which the hand of I2 is found, either in combination with the hand of John Scottus himself (one manuscript), or alone (seven manuscripts).[16]

---

14 O'Sullivan, *Glossae*, CXXX: BPL 88 is in a group with Leiden, Universiteitsbibliotheek, MS BPL 36; Paris, Bibliothèque nationale de France, MS lat. 8670; St. Petersburg, Rossiyskaya Natsional'naya Biblioteka, MS Class. lat. F.V. 10; and Vatican City, Biblioteca Apostolica Vaticana, MS Reg. lat. 1987.

15 Édouard Jeauneau, "'Nisifortinus': le disciple qui corrige le mâitre," in *Poetry and Philosophy in the Middle Ages. A Festschrift for Peter Dronke*, ed. John Marenbon, Mittellateinische Studien und Texte 29 (Leiden: Brill, 2001), 113–29.

16 The manuscript in which both the hand of John Scottus and that of Nisifortinus is found is in Reims, Bibliothèque Carnegie, MS 875—the famous manuscript of John Scottus's *Periphyseon* that contains his own rewritings. The seven manuscripts in which I2 is found are, in addition to BPL 88: Bamberg, Staatsbibliothek, MS Patr. 46; Bamberg, Staatsbibliothek, MS Philos. 2/1; Laon, Bibliothèque municipale Suzanne Martinet, MS 55; Paris, BnF, MS lat. 13908; Paris, Bibliothèque nationale de France, MS lat. 14088; and Paris, Bibliothèque Mazarine, MS 561. Édouard Jeauneau and Paul Dutton, *The Autograph of Eriugena*, Corpus Christianorum, Autographa Medii Aevi 3 (Turnhout: Brepols, 1996). See also Paul Dutton, "Eriugena's Workshop. The Making of the Peryphyseon in Rheims 875," in *History and Eschatology in John Scottus Eriugena and His Time,* ed. James McEvoy and Michael Dunne, Ancient and Medieval Philosophy, De Wulf-Mansion Centre, S. I, 30 (Leuven: Peeters, 2002), 141–67.

Furthermore, in BPL 88 we find additional texts added in the eleventh century and connected to the monastic community of St. Peter in Ghent. The largest part of the material gathered on the fly leaves is a set of schemes, playing with the basic principles of argumentation: squares of opposition and syllogisms. Research by Irene O'Daly revealed that they follow, in fact, the order of Boethius's first commentary on and translation of Aristotle's *De interpretatione (Peri hermeneias),* so that on these fly leaves we find, essentially, a summary in diagrams of this work.[17] With this element, BPL 88 thus connects to new series of manuscripts: those in which Boethius's commentary and translation are found, and those in which schematic visualizations of squares of opposition are found.

In addition to the dialectical schemes, we find an unfinished drawing of the zodiac, with its division into the planetary spheres and the sphere above with the zodiacal signs: the lines are drawn, but the labels are not filled in. We also find, on the page opposite of the start of Martianus Capella's *De nuptiis,* an *accessus ad auctorem,* two opening lines of a poem from Martianus's work, with music notation added above the words, and a scheme of the letters from the Greek alphabet with their names and numerical values. Each of these elements allow us to draw lines to other manuscripts: where the same *accessus* is found; where the same poem is provided with musical notation; or where the same scheme of numerical values for Greek letters is found. Finally, we find on this page the *anathema,* claiming the book as property of the church of St. Peter in Ghent. Thus, this page alone opens up a multitude of possible relations, to text collections, to textual units that are bound to different kinds of knowledge collections, to persons, and communities.

The concept of entanglement allows us to sketch different layers of this object that tie it to multiple constellations of other

---

17 Irene O'Daly, "Reasoning through Syllogisms," at online exhibition *The Art of Reasoning in Medieval Manuscripts,* curated by Irene O'Daly, Irene van Renswoude, and Mariken Teeuwen, https://art-of-reasoning.huygens.knaw.nl/syllogism.

objects and the people behind it, on the level of the texts that are found in it, the textual material found in it, the analysis of collation and layout schemes, hands, etc.

So, to sum up, in my single example I studied one manuscript book to tease out the networks to which it is bound. They were multiple, diverse across time and space, driven by different aspects of the book: the texts assembled in it, the hands working in it, the material added to it in its later life. These networks were certainly entangled, and it is the levels of entanglement that can lead to new insights as to where, when, by whom, how, and why books were read, enriched with new materials, appropriated, taken apart, and bound in new constellations.

In a paper for a conference in Leiden, Paul Dutton referred to annotated margins as "the choppy seas" in which our main texts float, dangerous and confusing terrain for philologists.[18] If we follow this metaphor, the main texts are the ships built to withstand the unruly waves: the main texts, are, in other words, shaped to be in harmony with the material around them as much as the material around them is shaped to respond to the main texts. Parts of books such as flyleaves, inserted slips, or material added in originally blank spaces can definitely also be considered as such; so can entire books, such as compilations, miscellanies, or florilegia. The treacherousness of the terrain, however, opens up possibilities to draw lines between texts, their presence in certain constellations, and their physical characteristics; and with these lines we can explore new paths into the social reality of the manuscript book. This is exactly the challenge that the contributors to the two events, organized by Anna Dorofeeva and Michael J. Kelly, set themselves, and the chapters assembled here, I argue, show the success of the new approach.

---

18 Paul Dutton, "Rules of Engagement for Those Venturing into Margins," lecture for the symposium *The Art of Reasoning in Medieval Manuscripts*, Leiden, November 2–3, 2017.

Bibliography

Manuscripts

Bamberg, Staatsbibliothek, MS Msc. Patr. 46. https://mdz-nbn-resolving.de/details:bsb00140804.
Bamberg, Staatsbibliothek, MS Msc. Ph. 2/1. https://mdz-nbn-resolving.de/details:bsb00140804.
Laon, Bibliothèque municipale Suzanne Martinet, MS 55.
Leiden, Universiteitsbibliotheek, MS BPL 36. http://hdl.handle.net/1887.1/item:3129007.
Leiden, Universiteitsbibliotheek, MS BPL 88. http://hdl.handle.net/1887.1/item:2028417.
Oxford, Bodleian Library, MS Auct.T.2.19.
Paris, Bibliothèque nationale de France, MS lat. 8670. https://gallica.bnf.fr/ark:/12148/btv1b9072627k.
Paris, Bibliothèque nationale de France, MS lat. 12960. https://gallica.bnf.fr/ark:/12148/btv1b9080778w.
Paris, Bibliothèque nationale de France, MS lat. 13908. https://gallica.bnf.fr/ark:/12148/btv1b10545846c.
Paris, Bibliothèque nationale de France, MS lat. 14088. https://gallica.bnf.fr/ark:/12148/btv1b9076764f.
Paris, Bibliothèque Mazarine, MS 561.
Reims, Bibliothèque Carnegie, MS 875. https://bvmm.irht.cnrs.fr/consult/consult.php?REPRODUCTION_ID=4738 (partial).
St. Petersburg, Rossiyskaya Natsional'naya Biblioteka, MS Class. lat. F.V.10.
Vatican City, Biblioteca Apostolica Vaticana, MS Reg. lat. 1987. https://digi.vatlib.it/view/MSS_Reg.lat.1987.

Secondary

Blair, Ann. *Too Much to Know: Managing Scholarly Information Before the Modern Age.* New Haven: Yale University Press, 2010.

Copeland, Rita. "Gloss and Commentary." In *The Oxford Handbook of Medieval Latin Literature,* edited by Ralph J. Hexter and David Townsend, 171–91. Oxford: Oxford University Press, 2012.

Dutton, Paul. "Eriugena's Workshop. The Making of the Peryphyseon in Rheims 875." In *History and Eschatology in John Scottus Eriugena and his Time. Proceedings of the 10th International Conference of the Society for the Promotion of Eriugenian Studies, Maynooth and Dublin, August 16–20, 2000,* edited by James McEvoy and Michael Dunne, 141–67. Ancient and Medieval Philosophy 130. Leuven: Leuven University Press, 2002.

Jeauneau, Édouard. "Le commentaire érigénien sur Martianus Capella (*De nuptiis,* Lib. I) d'après le manuscrit d'Oxford (Bodl. Libr. Auct.T.2.19, fol. 1–31)." In *Quatre thèmes érigéniens,* edited by Édouard Jeauneau, 91–166. Conférence Albert le Grand, 1974. Montréal: Institut d'études médiévales Albert-le-Grand, 1978.

———. "'Nisifortinus': le disciple qui corrige le mâitre." In *Poetry and Philosophy in the Middle Ages. A Festschrift for Peter Dronke,* edited by John Marenbon, 113–29. Mittellateinische Studien und Texte 29. Leiden: Brill, 2001.

Jeauneau, Édouard, and Paul Dutton. *The Autograph of Eriugena.* Corpus Christianorum Autographa Medii Aevi 3. Turnhout: Brepols, 1996.

Labowsky, Lotte. "A New Version of Scotus Eriugena's Commentary on Martianus Capella." *Medieval and Renaissance Studies* 1 (1941–1943): 187–93.

Leonardi, Claudio. "I codici di Marziano Capella I." *Aevum* 33, no. 4 (1959): 443–89. https://www.jstor.org/stable/20859258.

———. "I codici di Marziano Capella II." *Aevum* 34, no. 1 (1960): 1–99. https://www.jstor.org/stable/20859287.

O'Daly, Irene. "Reasoning through Syllogisms." At *The Art of Reasoning in Medieval Manuscripts,* online exhibition curated by Irene O'Daly, Irene van Renswoude, and Mariken Teeuwen. https://art-of-reasoning.huygens.knaw.nl/syllogism.

O'Sullivan, Sinéad, ed. *Glossae aeui Carolini in libros I-II Martiani Capellae De nuptiis Philologiae et Mercurii.* Corpus Christianorum Continuatio Mediaevalis 237. Turnhout: Brepols, 2010.

Préaux, Jean G. "Deux manuscrits gantois de Martianus Capella." *Scriptorium* 13, no. 1 (1959): 15-21. DOI: 10.3406/scrip.1959.2997.

———. "Les manuscrits principaux du 'De nuptiis Philologiae et Mercurii' de Martianus Capella." In *Lettres latines du Moyen Âge et de la Renaissance,* edited by Guy Cambier, Carl Deroux, and Jean G. Préaux, 76-128. Collection Latomus 158. Brussels: Latomus, 1978.

Shanzer, Danuta. *A Philosophical and Literary Commentary on Martianus Capella's De nuptiis Philologiae et Mercurii, Book I.* Classical Studies 32. Berkeley: University of California Press, 1986.

Teeuwen, Mariken. "Carolingian Scholarship on Classical Authors: Practices of Reading and Writing." In *Manuscripts of the Latin Classics,* edited by Erik Kwakkel, 23-52. Leiden: Leiden University Press, 2015.

———. *Harmony and the Music of the Spheres. The 'ars musica' in Ninth-Century Commentaries on Martianus Capella.* Mittellateinische Studien und Texte 30. Leiden: Brill, 2002.

———. "I2's Interest in Music. Two Manuscripts that Witness his Knowledge and Scholarship." In *Litterarum dulces fructus: Studies in Early Medieval Latin Culture in Honour of Michael W. Herren for his 80th Birthday,* edited by Scott G. Bruce, 435-60. Instrumenta Patristica et Mediaevalia 85. Turnhout: Brepols, 2021. DOI: 10.1484/M.IPM-EB.5.125571.

———. "Marginal Scholarship: Rethinking the Function of Latin Glosses in Early Medieval Manuscripts." In *Rethinking and Recontextualizing Glosses: New Perspectives in the Study of Late Anglo-Saxon Glossography,* edited by Patrizia Lendinara, Loredana Lazzari, and Claudia Di Sciacca, 19-37. Textes et Etudes du Moyen Âge 54. Turnhout: Brepols, 2011. DOI: 10.1484/M.TEMA-EB.4.00833.

———. "Reading Boethius Around 900: Manuscripts of Boethius's Texts and Their Annotations." In *Knowledge and Culture in Times of Threat: The Fall of the Carolingian Empire (c. 900),* edited by Warren Pezé, 279–303. Monographien zur Geschichte des Mittelalters 69. Stuttgart: Hiersemann, 2020.

———. "Voices From the Edge: Annotating Books in the Carolingian Period." In *The Annotated Book in the Early Middle Ages: Practices of Reading and Writing,* edited by Mariken Teeuwen and Irene van Renswoude, 13–36. Utrecht Studies in Medieval Literacy 38. Turnhout: Brepols, 2017. DOI: 10.1484/M.USML-EB.5.115016.

———. "Writing Between the Lines: Reflections of Scholarly Debate in a Carolingian Commentary Tradition." In *Carolingian Scholarship and Martianus Capella: Ninth-Century Commentary Traditions on 'De nuptiis' in Context,* edited by Mariken Teeuwen and Sinéad O'Sullivan, 11–34. Cultural Encounters in Late Antiquity and the Middle Ages 12. Turnhout: Brepols, 2011. DOI: 10.1484/M.CELAMA-EB.4.3002.

———. "Writing in the Blank Space of Manuscripts: Evidence From the Ninth Century." In *Ars Edendi Lecture Series,* edited by Barbara Crostini, Gunilla Iversen, and Brian M. Jensen, 1–25. Studia Latina Stockholmiensia 62. Stockholm: Stockholm University Press, 2016.

Zetzel, James E.G. *Marginal Scholarship and Textual Deviance: The "Commentum Cornuti" and the Early Scholia on Persius.* Bulletin of the Institute of Classical Studies Supplement 84. Oxford: Oxford University Press, 2005.

Contributors

Elizabeth P. Archibald is Teaching Associate Professor of History and Director of the Medieval and Renaissance Studies Program at the University of Pittsburgh. She is a specialist in the cultural and intellectual history of medieval Europe and the author of the book *Ask the Past: Pertinent and Impertinent Advice from Yesteryear* (Hachette Books, 2015).

Lucia Castaldi is Professor of Medieval and Renaissance Latin Literature at the University of Udine. She researches philology, manuscript transmission, and Pope Gregory the Great and his hagiographies (principally the one written by John the Deacon in the ninth century). She is director of the research project Mediaeval Latin Texts and Their Transmission (Te.Tra) and member of the scientific committee of the *Edizione Nazionale dei Testi Mediolatini d'Italia* (ENTMI).

Anna Dorofeeva is Lecturer in Digital Paleography at the University of Göttingen Institute for Digital Humanities. She has held research fellowships at the University of Frankfurt, University College Dublin, the University of Durham, and the Free University of Berlin. She is the author of *Reading Nature in the Early Middle Ages: Writing, Language, and Creation in the Latin Physiologus, ca. 700–1000* (Arc Humanities Press, 2023). Her research interests center on early medieval book history, especially digital paleography and codicology.

Michael Eber is a post-doctoral researcher at Universität zu Köln. His PhD dissertation, written at Freie Universität Berlin and published in 2023, analyzed the reception of the Three Chapters Controversy in Merovingian Gaul through the lens of canon law manuscripts. He has also worked on Late Antique definitions of heresy, Merovingian saints' lives, and Carolingian canonesses.

Thom Gobbitt is a medievalist whose research stands at the overlap of the history of the book, the history of early medieval law from the late sixth to early thirteenth centuries, medievalism, narratology, and ludology. He has been a postdoctoral researcher at the Austrian Academy of the Sciences, Vienna on various projects since 2012, and is currently the historian for the European Research Council's PresentDead project. His own research to date focuses on the production and use of law-books containing the Lombard laws and related collections of Frankish and Saxon capitularies, and he is currently preparing an edited volume focusing on the representation of the medieval past in tabletop games.

Cinzia Grifoni is a senior postdoctoral researcher at the Institute for Medieval Research of the Austrian Academy of Sciences in Vienna. She is currently leading the project "Margins at the Centre" in the framework of the Elise Richter Excellence Programme (FWF project number V811-G). Her research focuses on the study of the Trivium and the Bible, intellectual networks, and knowledge exchange and annotation practices in Carolingian Europe. A classical philologist by training, she specialized in medieval Latin for her doctoral thesis.

Michael J. Kelly is a historian and Fulbright scholar working at the intersection of the abstract and the real, past and history.

At Binghamton University (SUNY), he lectures on history, theology, and blockchain studies and runs a lab attempting to "math the past." Kelly is the co-editor of the Visigothic Symposia and Gracchi Books, and his publications include *Isidore of Seville and the "Liber Iudiciorum": The Struggle for the Past in the Visigothic Kingdom* (Brill, 2021) and the volume *Theories of History: History Read Across the Humanities* (Bloomsbury, 2018). He is currently writing a monograph on the concepts of "human nature" and "value" in Visigothic Hispania.

Sinéad O'Sullivan specializes in the reception of classical, biblical, and late antique texts in the early Middle Ages. Her main focus is on early medieval glosses and their reception. Currently she is investigating glosses for insight into crafting knowledge in the Carolingian age, focusing on annotations on Virgil and the Psalms.

Laura Pani is Professor of Latin Paleography at the University of Udine. Her research is focused on the history of Latin handwriting in the Middle Ages and on manuscript traditions, particularly involving Paul the Deacon's *Historia Langobardorum* but also Carolingian manuscripts and writing centers. She also works on late medieval cursive handwriting and the edition of documentary sources. She is editor-in-chief of *Scrineum Rivista*.

Mark Stansbury is lecturer emeritus at the University of Galway. His research focuses on paleography and he is the co-director of the Earlier Latin Manuscripts project (https://elmss.nuigalway.ie).

Evina Stein is an independent manuscript researcher based in Beirut, Lebanon. She is a trained Latin philologist and manuscript specialist working with early medieval manuscripts. She was a VENI postdoctoral researcher at the Huygens Institute for the History of the Netherlands, an institute of the Dutch Royal Academy of Arts and Sciences in Amsterdam, from 2018 to 2021. Her recent work includes a monograph on the use of annotation symbols in Late Antiquity and the early Middle Ages, a database of manuscripts of the *Etymologies* of Isidore of Seville, and a digital edition of glosses to this work.

Mariken Teeuwen is senior researcher at Huygens Institute for the History of the Netherlands, Royal Netherlands Academy of Arts and Sciences in Amsterdam. She specializes in manuscript studies and practices of learning in the Middle Ages, especially practices of annotating texts. She is also involved in several digital humanities projects, such as the appliance of AI to Latin paleography and the building of a virtual library for manuscripts in Dutch collections.

www.ingramcontent.com/pod-product-compliance
Lightning Source LLC
Chambersburg PA
CBHW061924220426
43662CB00012B/1798